D1191092

EMPIRE OF DESIRE

Empire of Desire

THE ABOLITION OF TIME

Thierry Hentsch

Translated by Fred A. Reed

Talonbooks

Talonbooks
P.O. Box 2076, Vancouver, British Columbia, Canada V6B 3S3
www.talonbooks.com

Typeset in Times and printed and bound in Canada.
Printed on 100% post-consumer recycled paper.

First Printing: October 2008

The publisher gratefully acknowledges the financial support of the Canada Council for the Arts; the Government of Canada through the Book Publishing Industry Development Program; and the Province of British Columbia through the British Columbia Arts Council for our publishing activities.

Le temps aboli. L'Occident et ses grands récits was published in the original French by Les Éditions Bréal (France) in 2005. Financial support for this translation provided by the Canada Council for the Arts and the Department of Canadian Heritage through the Book Publishing Industry Development Program.

NATIONAL LIBRARY OF CANADA CATALOGUING IN PUBLICATION

Hentsch, Thierry, 1944–2005
    Empire of desire : the abolition of time / Thierry Hentsch ; translated by Fred A. Reed.

Translation of: Le temps aboli.
Includes bibliographical references.
ISBN 978-0-88922-587-9

    1. Narration (Rhetoric). 2. Literature—History and criticism. 3. Time in literature.
4. Desire in literature. 5. Civilization, Western, in literature.
I. Reed, Fred A., 1939– II. Title.

PN3383.N35H46213 2008   809'.923   C2008-903038-9

TRANSLATOR'S ACKNOWLEDGMENTS

I would like to express my gratitude to Karl Siegler for his unfailing support and commitment to a publishing project of such extraordinary breadth and sweep. The translation you now hold in your hands—Thierry Hentsch's intellectual and spiritual legacy—has been nurtured by our long-running dialogue about the very nature of the text, and is all the richer and stronger for it. Thanks also to Gregory Gibson, who polished the manuscript to the sheen it now possesses.

And finally, I wish to pay tribute to Meryem Yildiz, my indefatigable and devoted research assistant, without whose skill, patience, and eagle-eyed attention this book would simply never have existed.

TABLE OF CONTENTS

TRANSLATOR'S PREFACE

ON DECEMBER 9, 2004, Thierry Hentsch and I traveled by car to Toronto to attend a promotional event for *Truth or Death*, the English version of *Raconter et mourir*, the first volume of his magisterial investigation into the Western narrative tradition.

The early winter weather had been clear and bright, the hours of travel enlivened by music—from the felicitous precision of Bach to the boldness of Handel—and conversation. It was, above all, a journey of renewal of a friendship that had begun twelve years earlier, when I translated his seminal *L'Orient imaginaire (Imagining the Middle East)*. It was also to be our final meeting. For it was then that he revealed to me the existence of the inoperable cancer that would end his life on July 9, 2005 at age sixty-one. On our return from Toronto the following day, the pale December sunlight had given way to freezing rain, then snow.

In mid-June 2005 we had one last conversation. I called to tell him I had just contracted to translate the second volume of his masterwork, *Le temps aboli*, which you now hold in your hands, dear reader, as *Empire of Desire: The Abolition of Time*. Both of us were pleased, but death was already in his voice then. The end came quietly three weeks later.

Thierry Hentsch was born in Switzerland, and emigrated to Canada in 1975 to begin an academic career at l'Université du Québec à Montréal (UQAM), where he went on to become head of the Political Science Department and a leader of the University Professors' Union. Beyond his adopted personae of academic and trade unionist, Thierry Hentsch was one of those rarest of individuals: an independent public intellectual, known and respected beyond the walls of his university for his analytical brilliance and fierce defense of the principles of justice. These qualities, his sharply critical view of Western involvement in the Middle East, and his respect for and knowledge of Muslim-Arab culture made him an eloquent opponent of such violent adventures as the First Gulf War (1991) and its bastard offspring, the

Global War on Terror. His death deprived the global anti-war movement of one of its most articulate voices. Never shrill, in the image of his writing, that voice mercilessly laid bare the mythical constructs that underlie the West's self-image as bearer of a civilizational will to power that, having assumed the mantle of Truth, has become all the deadlier for it.

Empire of Desire, the second volume of Thierry Hentsch's centuries-spanning anti-canonical survey, turns aside—or more properly deflects itself—from what I would identify as the core argument of its first volume. *Truth or Death* argues, in the penetrating investigation of the Gospel that constitutes its nodal point, for the primacy in Western civilization shaped by Christianity, of the notion of the Truth of salvation as solely available to those who accept the Resurrection of Christ and the concomitant killing of God necessary for its attainment. The red thread that winds through the text of Hentsch's second volume, sometimes visible on the surface, sometimes concealed though ever present, traces the mutation of the salvation imperative, a process he illustrates through close analysis of the seminal texts of the Western narrative tradition.

As religious transcendence gradually fell into eclipse in the West, the Truth that had been derived from it migrated into the secular sphere, where it would emerge as the unspoken yet omnipresent justification for our civilization's quest—substituting itself for the God in whom it had ceased to believe—to remake the world in its image. What had once been Christian Truth, intimately linked to personal salvation, thus became a prescription held out to all those who did not or do not possess it: either to accept Our Truth, or to face your death. To decline or to refuse, as European colonialism and latterly, the United States as the "armed man" of the Western tradition have both demonstrated, was not an option—that both, in their most virulent phases, trace their lineage back to the Enlightenment did not escape Hentsch's keen eye and he does not allow it to escape ours.

Though by no means turning its back on the cultural critique that distinguished its previous volume, *Empire of Desire* embodies a subtle shift in the author's sensibilities and concerns. Its purview is multifaceted: at once an eclectic, penetrating, and wide-ranging survey of the last four centuries of the Western narrative tradition that casts aside any pretensions to the canonical; a deft evocation, in half-tints and suggestive touches, of the emergence of Desire rooted in the Platonic notion of Eros as the centerpiece of the West's unavowed (and unavowable) self-image; a reaffirmation of the primacy of the past and of memory through the act of literary creation; and above all, in its ultimate essay on Proust's *Remembrance of Things Past*, a valedictory message—an intellectual testament and last farewell.

Looking back, it is difficult not to see premonition shimmering in his choice of title—*Raconter et mourir*—for the French original of *Truth or Death*, which could be translated as "to tell the tale, and to die." The well-springs of the narrative impulse, which Hentsch traces back to the origins of the pre-Christian literary tradition the West has appropriated for its own, can be located in humanity's encounter with the reality that death is the inescapable conclusion of all life. "Death" he writes, "is man's great obsession. It reveals all that has gone before; it is the ultimate moment of truth, the final reckoning whose ineluctable advent illuminates our lives."[1]

The final chapters of *Empire of Desire*—those dedicated to James Joyce's *Ulysses* and Marcel Proust's *Remembrance of Things Past* can best be seen as precisely such a moment of final reckoning. Never any less impassioned by the texts he reads, Thierry Hentsch in these chapters adopts a bold, new strategy: he writes about *Ulysses* in the style of Joyce, about *Remembrance* in the style of Proust.

Earlier, the essay on Georg Hegel's the *Phenomenology of Mind* grapples like a mind-wrestler with a work Hentsch candidly admits to being "beyond [his] powers." Written to the accompaniment of thundering guns as the "soul of the world," alias Napoleon Bonaparte, arrives with his armies before the gates of the philosopher's native Jena where the battle of Reason against Prussian feudalism would be joined, the *Phenomenology* for Thierry Hentsch remains "radically resistant to telling." Yet, for all its radical resistance—or because of it—he sets himself the task.

The tale, told like a military campaign in a series of bold sallies and head-long retreats, reveals perhaps more about Hentsch than it does about Hegel. The search for textual intelligibility in a work that arguably possesses none points to an almost gleefully assumed humility: "At the risk of admitting my own intellectual weakness, I affirm without hesitation that this text, the *Phenomenology of Mind*, is partially, if not fundamentally, delirious." Strong judgment indeed of a work written at a moment that its author considered "the end of history"; but ultimately an accurate judgment of a work that must be read, given the distance and the events that separate us from the intellectual intoxication of Jena, as the tale of a failure of the spirit.

Ulysses is a completely different matter. Veering from Stephen Dedalus's high-falutin' disquisitions to Leopold Bloom's sulking and skulking through

1. Thierry Hentsch, *Truth or Death: The Quest for Immortality in the Western Narrative Tradition*, trans. Fred A. Reed (Vancouver: Talonbooks, 2004).

the nightstreets of Dublin, Hentsch takes the measure of Joyce's obtuse masterwork with the verve of delight. In its quality as a farce of monumental proportions, where death returns again and again "like a pathetic, petty refrain" we recognize in retrospect a figure that foreshadows the emotional palette of his ultimate chapter.

Far from killing the modern novel, he argues, *Ulysses* "has opened boundless space before it"—a judgment that knowingly ignores *Finnegan's Wake*, which, some might argue, seeks not only to kill the modern novel, but also all language. But such a crime, he asserts, lies beyond the power of any single author to perpetrate. Had such been Joyce's intention, he failed. Our liberty as readers, Hentsch concludes, has no other goal than itself. Here perhaps lies, he suggests with a wink, the only identifiable "truth" of *Ulysses*.

The table is now set for *Remembrance of Things Past*.

Along byways of prose as elegiac and sinuous as the ways of Swann and the Guermantes, Thierry Hentsch now calls forth the narrator's emotional memory of the house at Combray and his chance encounter with the madeleine dipped in the linden tea his aunt would prepare for him: "only on contact with the textured fragrance that had kept alive within it the vividness neither time nor habit could tarnish, do the rest of the house and the surrounding countryside spring back into life."

Death's "pathetic, petty refrain" re-emerges here as the society composer Vinteuil's "little phrase" evoked by Proust's narrator, an intimate musical thread that winds its way through the entire work (much as a sonata by Mozart or a Bach partita was never missing from the piano in Hentsch's home). And as the "little phrase" frames the narrative of Swann's love and "betrays the capricious, unpredictable, arbitrary character of the signs that point to its ephemeral presence," so too a series of similar moments remind us that the characters of *Remembrance* exist in "a kind of eternal present, in a state of indeterminate and near-suspended time."

While traveling by coach through the countryside near Combray, the narrative *I* encounters three trees lining the road to Hudimesnil. It will encounter them only this once and never again; the sense of irrevocable loss is overpowering. Where the *I* had experienced the bliss of immortality at the taste of the madeleine, it now perishes at the sense of loss. Death is short-lived of course, but it "foreshadows that definitive death from whom none will return."

Impossible not to detect in this "little phrase" the foreshadowing of the definitive death that Thierry Hentsch would by then have intuited. Swann, years later, has returned to the whirl and effervescence of Parisian high society as an invited guest at the Guermantes mansion, where he encounters the faces of the past distorted almost beyond recognition by the cruelty inflicted by time upon the flesh. Yet at the same moment, he feels himself "spiritually abstracted from time's tyrannical and destructive order. Only death can henceforth prevent him from carrying out the task that the moments of immortality he has just experienced" have imposed upon him.

Only death: life's great unknown, prefigured here by the "little patch of yellow wall" in Vermeer's *View of Delft* that Bergotte, the author of whom the narrator had been so enamored when he was living with Albertine, carries away with him when he dies, by stroke, in front of the canvas of the same name (underlining the importance for Thierry Hentsch of this micro-episode, Vermeer's painting is reproduced on the cover of the French original). Death, in fact, has imprinted its ineluctable advent on the "masks" that hobnob in the Guermantes salon, heightening the sense of urgency that sweeps over the narrator. And, as if in defiance of death, the face of a girl whose entire life lies before her and who brings together, in his eyes, all that time has accumulated, commingled, and condensed in her, represents the master key to the recapture of memory:

> Was she not—are not, indeed, the majority of human beings?—like one of those star-shaped cross-roads in a forest where roads converge that have come, in the forest as in our lives, from the most diverse quarters?[2]

In her thus meet the two faces of childhood: hers and the narrator's recognized in the "lost years" and the faint image of his youth from which surges once more the unrequited love that recalls—with powerful resonance—the opening scene of the motherly kiss denied. Love unrequited, argues Thierry Hentsch, in Proust fertilizes thought: "By the most tortuous and tormented pathways, Proust's thought dovetails with that of Plato and Spinoza."

The sudden appearance of the name of Hentsch's beloved antinomian philosopher of Amsterdam is here invoked to elevate erotic knowledge to a level contemporaneous with, though more painful than, that of the *Symposium*: such knowledge has validity only for men and women who are convinced "that *true life*, the life *we are at greatest risk of dying without ever having known, is life reflected upon.*"

2. Marcel Proust, *Remembrance of Things Past*, trans. C. K. Scott-Moncrieff, Terence Kilmartin, and Andreas Mayor (New York: Random House, 1981), p. 1084.

For such a life, once understood, "gives us the strength to die in awareness of having lived, happy at having transformed dross into gold, at having transformed suffering into intelligence."

Thierry Hentsch was one of the master alchemists of our day. His life and work embodied, with a peculiar combination of modesty and brilliance, the transformation of a narrative of narratives from an ordering of cultural icons into an impassioned critique of his (and our) own civilization; the transfiguration of his suffering and untimely death, through a life intensely reflected upon, into luminous intelligence.

Fred A. Reed
Outremont, Québec
August 2008

FOREWORD

THE INTRODUCTION TO *Truth or Death* can be fully applied to the entire journey that continues with this volume. But a sequel can never follow what it purports to carry forward with all the docility expected of it. What lends the two volumes their continuity is, above all, the possibility of reading both at random. Had I been thoroughly consistent in my thoughts, I would have written no preamble to the essays that comprise this, the second volume; I would have imposed no organization, made no attempt to connect one to another except by what they say, arranged them arbitrarily, as I had read the texts. Which is to say that there is nothing necessary about the "order" I suggest in these pages; it reflects no preconceptions. Nor does it mirror a problem set that suddenly thrust itself upon me in the course of writing, as happened with the first volume, when it became clear that the Gospel story had to be, rightly or wrongly, the pivotal point of my readings. The short "reader's guide" that opens *Truth or Death* remains apposite to this volume as well: each chapter can be read as a distinct text, at the reader's whim.

Though the spirit in which I have read has not changed, the span of time covered by the narratives I examine is here much shorter: a bit less than three centuries, from 1665 to 1922, as opposed to three millennia for its predecessor. *Truth or Death* embraced a period that stretched—the pure folly of it!—from Sumerian antiquity to the threshold of the European classical age. *Empire of Desire* begins with Molière's *Don Juan*, written a mere thirty years after the *Discourse on Method*, and concludes with Proust, who died in 1922, the year when Joyce's *Ulysses* was published. The final volume of *Remembrance of Things Past* was published in 1927. But to take 1922 as a vintage year, bringing together as it did the two authors who exerted a determinant influence on twentieth century Western literature, seemed to me emblematically seductive.

For at that historical moment something had come to an end just as something else had begun: a certain kind of literature had run its course, another was emerging. Yet that "turning point" may conceal more continuity than meets the eye. Since its inception literature has always spoken in multiple voices, its paths intersecting, diverging, reaching backward and forward in time, sometimes across centuries, even millennia. Uniting it is a common factor, whose enduring quality Proust reveals more effectively than anyone before him: its relationship with time. If it is true, as I wrote in the previous volume, that to tell stories and to leave tracks is both to cheat death and to accept our mortal condition, then literature, and art in general, could be seen as an effort constantly repeated, constantly failing, and constantly beginning anew, to abolish time. Hence the subtitle of this book, which comes not from reading Proust, but from delving deep into Herman Melville's *Moby Dick*, the whaling epic that brought me back in so many ways to the venerable Homer. So much then for our end point, which should more properly be called a pregnant pause, a point of suspension.

Our starting point, or more properly, the point where we resume our narrative—perhaps it can even be seen as a suture?—seemed almost self-explanatory. *Truth or Death* ended with the Cartesian attempt to re-establish truth on the ruins of Elsinore Castle. In *Hamlet*, the curtain falls on the specter of God, while Descartes attempts to breathe new life into the *I* of consciousness through his own efforts, alone. His attempt was magnificent but doomed, as *Don Juan* testifies. Hamlet stretches out his hand to Don Juan. But where the former laments the loss of the divine, the latter insolently rejoices in it and carries on with his conquests. The flames that will devour the libertine are assuredly not those that blaze forth from the mouths of the pious. If hell exists, it is more likely to be Sade's or Faust's. It is to be found on earth. Hell may well be, in many ways, the modern form of love: Eros, in the sadness of absence; Plato's desire for oblivion, stigmatized by centuries of Christianity. Modern man desires. He desires to desire, moving without respite from one object to another, in a state of self-imposed oblivion.

Such is the unceasing quest that underlies modern-day Western literature. The impossibility of attaining the object of its search nourishes it at every turn, even when it holds itself up to mockery. In the search for desire, each character, each author helps to sketch out the most striking traits of the modern West's self-image. Don Juan falls endlessly short of it. For fear of losing it, the Princess of Clèves keeps desire alight beneath the ashes, exactly where her contemporary, Phedra, perishes of it. Desire is, in a sense, that which both Gulliver and Candide, each in his own way, eventually turn their back on, while Jacques the Fatalist tracks it with a jaundiced and sometimes worried eye. Sade squanders it, while Rousseau interminably plies his wounded self with it. Faust seeks to recapitalize it in a form of humanism as conquering as it is unbound. Hegel lifts it up to the unattainable heights of the spirit. Melville's hero expends himself as he harpoons it to death, but the desire to kill desire drags Captain Ahab to a watery grave. Bouvard and Pécuchet, those impenitent waverers, will never know a thing about it: desire constantly eludes them; the best they can do is copy. The Brothers Karamazov drag it through the muck or exalt it in its holiness, but they cannot escape the stench of the world. And all the while, Zarathustra husbands its secret in spite of himself. In Freud and Joyce, desire is laid bare beneath the scalpel of analysis and excess. Proust, in his minute and detailed vivisection, keeps it alive: in his hands desire becomes the artist's instrument of choice and brings us back to the upsurge of the erotic in Plato.

From the living soil of all these desires, a soil that is constantly being turned over, ceaselessly being fertilized with hope and suffering, spring the finest of flowers. I have chosen but a few. Some cannot be ignored; others reflect personal choices I make no attempt to justify. The only possible justification for the choice of a particular text, as I wrote in the first volume, is the way we choose to read it. Nor have I forgotten the conflicted coexistence of fiction and philosophy, which I drew attention to in the opening pages of *Truth or Death*, a troubling fusion that reaches its peak in the *Phenomenology of Mind*. Hegel fashions from it a rich, powerful, obtuse yet resonant alloy. Though its reading presents the gravest practicable obstacles, I could not afford to ignore it, nor them. If there is a turning point to be sought, it must be sought here, in this dizzying intellectual achievement, to which the existential vertigo of Zarathustra *responds*.

Finally, if I have suspended my readings with Proust it is, rather obviously, because he stands at the inception of this enterprise, and even before, as my inseparable companion. He is the one in whose company despair can find no toehold, the one with whom I have learned with every passing day that literature is nothing more than life reflected upon, recaptured; that it is the breathtaking expression of those simple instants that poets have sought since time out of mind, and whose fleeting pleasures give us, for a spark of eternity, the conviction that we have abolished time itself.

1

DON JUAN:
THE LOVES OF A SCOUNDREL

MOLIÈRE'S DON JUAN, whom his manservant Sganarelle—who functions as both his double and his negative—introduces as "the greatest scoundrel ever walked the earth," as "a madman, a dog, a devil, a Turk ... a heretic who believes neither Heaven nor saint, nor God nor the bogeyman. He lives the life of an absolute beast. He is an Epicurean hog," (I, i, 13)[3] says of himself:

> Beauty delights me wherever I find it, and I fall a willing slave to the sweet force with which it seeks to bind me. However my heart may be engaged, the love I have for one woman has no power to make me unfair to the rest. My eyes see the merits of each, and pay homage and tribute wherever it is due. If I see an attractive woman, my heart is hers; and, had I ten thousand hearts, I would give them all to a face that was worthy of them. After all, the growth of a passion has infinite charm; and the true pleasure of love is its variety. How deliciously sweet to lay siege to a young heart; to watch one's progress day by day; to overcome by means of vows, tears, and groans, the delicate modesty of a soul which sighs in surrender; to break down little by little the weakening resistance, the maidenly scruples that her honor dictates, and bring her at last where we would have her be. But once we have had our way with her, there is no more to wish for. The best is behind us. And so we slumber on, lulled by our love, until a new object appears to reawaken our desire, and lure us on with the charms of new conquest. There is nothing so sweet as to overcome the resistance of a beautiful

3. Molière, *Don Juan and Other Plays*, trans. George Graveley and Ian Maclean (Oxford: Oxford University Press, 1989). References in parentheses are to act, scene, page.

woman; and where they are concerned, I have the ambition of a conqueror, who goes from triumph to triumph, and never be satisfied. Nothing shall stand in the way of my desire. My heart is big enough to love the whole world; and I could wish, like Alexander, that there were more worlds still, so that I might carry yet further my prowess in love. (I, ii, 37–38)

It is all too apparent! Don Juan is incapable of loving; he does not even seek love. He is happy enough to flit from one mirror to another. Once he has stepped away, the image vanishes. Once conquered, the coveted face tires him. All attraction lies in the preliminaries. Were the conquest impossible, beauty's inaccessibility would perhaps make him think twice. But each quarry, almost without exception, eventually succumbs. His power of seduction ensures, before the fact, the success of his undertakings, which continue endlessly. No sooner has one resistance been overcome than he must find another to vanquish. This incessant process of renewal, or so it seems, makes it possible for the seducer to make light of all questions, of all suffering, with sovereign indifference to the wrongs he may commit against the women he seduces. For him to experience suffering, his conquest must not suffice, it must be impossible; its object must be irreplaceable. Yet Juan lingers no longer in regret than in love. Should one opportunity elude him he will seize the next. No long-term desire for possession drives him. That there exists a fair maiden to triumph over is more than enough. It is not at all certain, in fact, that he wishes, or is even able, to possess her—suggesting that his personality symbolizes, as is often argued, a double impotency, both amorous and sexual.

But were Don Juan little more than an impotent seducer his character would have none of the power of fascination it has so clearly enjoyed in Europe, from Tirso de Molina (1625) to Mozart (1787) and beyond. Were seduction his only, or even his principal *raison d'être*, he would resemble all the skirt-chasers of history and literature: his charisma and his desire would eventually fade away, or be caught in the nets of passion, or break down in the face of insurmountable resistance. But the machinery of seduction never breaks down. In him we encounter not the slightest sign of weariness at an unchanging routine, nor at the amorous bookkeeping that Mozart and Da Ponte's Leporello so scrupulously keep up to date. Only death brings it to an end. An "edifying" death that bears out Sganarelle's remonstrance: the flames of a hell that he has obstinately refused to believe in are already licking at the godless one's legs. But the *diabolus ex machina* fools no one. It is a way of eluding the censors. Or the symbol of a netherworld that the punishment promised by the Church illustrates yet at the same time conceals. It is simply another terror, which the hero affects not to notice, and which his alter ego of a manservant cannot comprehend.

Don Juan's insouciance is suspect; it is too ostentatious to be true. His amorous conquests are too repetitive, too mechanical, and too predictable to satisfy. Not that the attraction of beauty, in the case of Juan, is feigned—here, in fact, lies the hero's most appealing side—but it is an attraction that leads him from one delusion to another in an interminable race at the end of which nothing remains. In Juan's case, his powerful wits lead nowhere. His fine words? Nothing but hot air! Liberty's harvest? A fistful of straw. The manservant's arguments against his master's godlessness may be weak, but the latter has very little to offer to support his unbelief. Challenged by Sganarelle to spell out exactly what he does believe, Don Juan replies, startled: "I believe that two and two make four, Sganarelle, and that four and four make eight." To which the servant has a fine time replying:

> That's a fine thing to believe! What fine articles of faith! Your religion then is nothing but arithmetic. Some people do have queer ideas in their heads, and those that have been educated are often the silliest. I never studied like you, thank God, and no one can boast he taught me anything. But, to my poor way of thinking, my eyes are better than books. I know very well that this world we see around us is not a mushroom grown up in a single night....
>
> My argument is that there is something wonderful in Man, which none of your clever scientists can explain. (III, i, 61–62)

Each of the protagonists upholds, in a manner of speaking, an aspect of the Cartesian credo, much simplified of course. But Sganarelle's is the richer of the two. Where the master caricatures the spirit of geometry, whose power to speak truth Descartes subordinates, as we know, to the existence of God, his servant evokes that "something wonderful" that awakens men to the idea of truth, that 'wonderfulness' that Don Juan himself finds in the faces of the beautiful women whom he pursues in all the vanity of his ardor, never able to fathom a deeper meaning. In his simplicity—more than once too simple by half—the seducer's double understands more fully than does his master the love of beauty that impels him to seduce it. The master's loss is far weightier than the servant's ignorance. The latter's social status leaves him very little leeway for action. He cannot speak his mind, while the lord's outspokenness, up to and including the open expression of his "hypocrisy," knows no limit. Precisely because it presumes to disport itself without limitation, his liberty creates in us a sense of vertigo. In Mozart's *Don Giovanni*, the feeling of vertigo feeds upon the effervescence of the music. Liberty takes on a troubling, almost blinding glare to which we will return.

The central theme of *Don Juan*, in Molière's version at least, is not love, nor even seduction. The play contains, strictly speaking, but a single seduction scene (II, ii), followed a bit further on by an attempt at deception by the two "prey" of the day, Catherine and Mathurine. The only other female character, Dona Elvira, the woman betrayed, makes her first appearance solely to obtain an explanation, to remonstrate and, toward the end, to offer her assistance, all the while protesting that she has given up on him. This is, in fact, the one and only love scene in the play. "Save yourself, Don Juan, I beseech you," Dona Elvira implores, "if not for your own sake then for the love of me," (IV, vi, 81). So tender is her tone that even the hero cannot fail to be moved. "Her simplicity of dress, her sorrow and her tears have reawakened some few sparks of a fire I had thought quite burnt out," he confides to Sganarelle (IV, vii, 81). Cynicism or not, his confession suggests that something may well have happened between them. The salvation she seeks for him, and for herself, may not be quite as religious as she would have liked. But, whatever the circumstances, Don Juan is incapable of love. Once more, love is not what he seeks. Liberty is his only desire: the liberty to live, to flit butterfly-like from flower to flower even if, by doing so, he must pay back a debt of hypocrisy to the world around him. His is the liberty to lie, which he hastens to grant himself when he attempts to mislead Dona Elvira about the reasons for his flight, and which he later employs to seduce Charlotte.

But duplicity and hypocrisy are by no means of the same order. As in war, the former is part of the tactics of evasion and conquest, one of the weapons in the arsenal of freedom of action. But if you wish to pursue your monkey business in peace, society requires the latter. When, at the beginning of Act 5, he adopts the pose of sanctimonious repentance, Don Juan not only compounds villainy with abjectness, he abdicates his freedom of speech, and censures the manifestation of his free will and his independence. Put differently, he discharges the public exercise of his philosophy and, along with it, the desire for truth, the pride, and the love of beauty that so powerfully contribute to his attraction. "I liked you better as you were before," exclaims his confidant, the only person who, henceforth, will know his true nature. Pathetically, Don Juan has come to imitate the poltroonery of the world, which, only a short time before, he used to justify his scorn of religious prohibitions. The turnabout is a curious one indeed: the rebel, as a mere matter of convenience, appears to have lost all self-respect. Hard to believe.

As long as he does not join in the prevailing hypocrisy, Don Juan indeed stands as a new hero of truth. The "novelty" of his heroism is this: the truth for which he struggles is in essence hedonistic, egotistical. The one cannot live without the other: the emancipation of desire appears, necessarily, to depend upon the satisfaction of the ego. The ego allows itself to take its pleasure openly, if need be against accepted custom and the rules toward which the social order requires a semblance of respect. His egotism takes the form of a rather gentle seduction, though there had been an aborted plan for abduction. But this is a secondary consideration. Once his ego has been given primacy over the social order, there can be no limit to his goals and his means. This is something Mozart and Da Ponte well understand when they lend a criminal tone to the murder of the Commendatore, who is slain when he stands in the way of the man who has attempted to rape his daughter (Molière does not elaborate on the circumstances). The truth that the hero incarnates has nothing to do with the transcendence that haunts the literature of Christianity and that bestows order on Cartesian metaphysics. In fact, it stands full against them. No longer is some higher order a point of reference, nor love of one's neighbor—only his exploitation: "Love thyself, at thy neighbor's expense." Already, Sade can be seen, lurking in the shadows. "Nature" has legitimized the ego's subordination of everything to the pleasures to which it incites us. For Juan, in this hypocrisy-ridden society, the only truth is that of desire, of conquest at all costs, and of the alignment of forces that either facilitates or hinders its full deployment.

That it proves the optimum vector for seduction should come as no surprise: here lie our most ancient, most primitive, most repressed impulses—not to mention the murderous potential of an exacerbated desire for possession. But the categorical imperative of the ego can well extend into all other facets of life. This is precisely what society, beneath its orderly exterior, holds up before us: codify them as we will, the alignment of forces and the egotism that underlies their alignment are no less real. The social hierarchy, its origin-based inequalities, its rules and taboos, its religion and its "good behavior"—all work to consolidate and to justify the complex edifice of injustice. In his struggle against the established order, and against the hypocrisy that hides it from view, Don Juan operates on two potentially contradictory levels: the imperialism of the ego (in all its universality) and the structure of domination within which his birth has given him license to exercise the liberty he professes—in marked contrast with the submissive spirit of his servile double.

Thanks to his social rank, Don Juan feels no need to resolve the contradiction. His conquering mentality draws no distinction between the pretty girls that he encounters along his way, be they noblewomen or common wenches. The prestige that goes with his title facilitates matters for him. The gentlemanly liberty he demands flows from the inequality of social relations inherent in the system, and harks back, faintly, to the *jus primae noctis* claimed by the feudal lords. The hero's playful insolence is part of the order of things; finding as it does its expression in affairs of the heart, it should entail no political consequences. But consequences there are: they cannot be escaped. By abusing his position in society to exercise a liberty that so openly contradicts the sacraments of the Church, Juan threatens the established order on two fronts: with all the arrogance of his nobility he displays the abuses permitted by the order, while denouncing its ideology as false. The transcendental truth is in fact a class truth—or, as Marxist criticism was later to put it, a "bourgeois truth."

In other words, the liberty the seducer enjoys on the field of love, particularly insofar as it is openly proclaimed, puts all established truths at risk, up to and including the entire society these very truths bind together. Echoing Molière, this liberty is affirmed, in Mozart, to an overwhelming degree. It is expressed, in fact, in a turnabout of sacrilegious audacity. Toward the end of Act 1 (Scene 5), Don Giovanni invites to a ball he has organized to seduce Zerlina the maskers who are pursuing him (Donna Anna, daughter of the Commendatore whom the seducer has murdered, her fiancé Don Ottavio, and Donna Elvira, the abandoned spouse). Generously, Don Giovanni throws open the doors to the festivities in the name of liberty. On his tongue, it is the liberty to seduce and to lead astray by all possible means. But such is the brio of his cry, "*Viva la libertà!*" that, quickly losing its sarcastic edge, it sweeps away all the guests, the maskers included, into a flight of irresistible enthusiasm. *Viva la libertà!* is then taken up in a *tutti* whose beauty and power overwhelms any notion of mockery. There can be no doubt that Mozart's music invests this contagious musical moment with a depth that far exceeds its donjuanish intrigue. Amorous seduction is suddenly propelled to the heights of a universal truth. Repeated by the chorus, *Viva la libertà!* rises up, swelling, resounding like a hymn to victory that embodies one of the deepest of all human aspirations. We sense that nothing can stand in the way of the onrushing, impassioned throng. Music has transmuted fraudulent license into a soul-stirring hymn, in which it is difficult not to detect resonances of the Revolution that would break out two years later in France. The sudden transition from libertinage to liberty stands forth with a nearly unimaginable corrosive power that cannot but open fissures in the social order.

Society can tolerate moral infractions, on the condition that they remain hidden, or at least discreet. But it cannot tolerate the affirmation of the primacy of desire—whatever its qualities might be. Whether Don Juan likes it or not, the affirmation of such primacy is a political matter. And it is precisely because Molière is so well aware of this fact that he ultimately guides his character back onto the pathway of hypocritical conformism. But no one is taken in by his volte-face: he may well have made his hero of amorous liberty out to be an odious individual, but the inferior quality of his "conversion" can only reflect upon the society he pretends to return to. This turn of events, far from soiling liberty itself, degrades only its herald and, to an even greater degree, the order that he sides with in the end. But the act of taking sides is caricature, as Don Juan explains with ill-concealed cynicism:

> The mask of a good man is the best mask to wear. At no time could the profession of a hypocrite be carried on more advantageously than today. That sort of imposture is always respected; and, even if it is found out, no one dare say anything against it. All other vices come under censure, and everyone is free to rail against them; but hypocrisy is privileged and enjoys special immunity. (V, ii, 86)

To admit to hypocrisy is to drive home the point in yet another way: Molière uses the degeneracy into which he has thrown his character to place in his mouth, in one of the most audacious tirades of his entire theatrical output, what he would never have had a gentleman of good family utter.

That a consummate scoundrel interprets critical truth is not merely a theatrical ploy to avoid the foreseeable reactions of the censors. True enough, his "profession of faith," occurs in a particular set of circumstances: the cabal that "men of good will" are setting up against his *Tartuffe*—and Molière does not miss the opportunity to lay into them. But above and beyond the short-term conflict the tirade conveys, on a deeper level, an ideological impasse: the truth that the dramatist places in the mouth of his fallen hero is a purely negative one. Don Juan's vision is right enough, he speaks the truth, but has no "wisdom" to offer other than that by which one "adjusts one's behavior to fit in with the vices of one's age" (5, 2, 219). Which leads in turn to his death shortly thereafter by exemplary punishment, as if in answer to the sign he had sought from above to consider changing his ways: now the cup is full, and his insolence receives from Heaven its just desserts.

But we hardly notice that, in the new state of mind he feigns adopting, the protagonist can play his new role to the hilt, and avoid supreme punishment by mimicking repentance. In the penultimate scene, the specter of a veiled woman, who reminds us of Dona Elvira, gives him one last, fleeting chance to make amends—in *Don Giovanni*, the statue of the Commendatore offers him the final opportunity. In Mozart as in Molière, the hero refuses, and in doing so, becomes once more a hero. No longer must he simply bow before the vices of society. The gentleman's honor is at stake: "No, it shall never be said that I was capable of repenting, happen what may" (V, v, 90). At this juncture, repentance is no longer a simple social accommodation, but an act of irreparable cowardice. Or a derisive evasion: if God exists, he cannot be fooled. Faced with death, the self-respecting man ceases his playacting. What at first glance seems to be the punishment long awaited by the law-abiding becomes, on reflection, the occasion for a spectacular redemption. At the instant of truth Don Juan does not yield; the scoundrel and seducer dies as a free-thinking hero: he sacrifices his person, and along with it, all the anticipated pleasures of his conquests, as a bearer of witness to truth.

But his truth does not become "positive" for all that. It remains negative (after all, it has cost him his life), but negation, however miserable it might have been in its social conformism, now appears as tragic in its spirit of resistance. Egoism, whose truth the seducer had hoped to experience in full, leads him to its fatal outcome. If this is the case, it is because the truth he seeks is, in both senses of the word, mortal: it concerns both the way in which one leads one's life, with no concern for, and not the remotest hope of, a life to come. Worse still, it exposes him to death. The expression is not too strong: the social order pitilessly eliminates those who dare to live their lives in opposition to it. Elimination may be physical, civic, social, or economic, for the social order is simply defending itself against an attitude and a posture that strike to its very foundations.

The nature of the attack is fundamental, as can be seen from the reactions touched off by the celebrated scene of the beggar, which Molière's troupe was forced to suppress from the second performance on, and which would long be struck from the various published versions of the text.[4] In it, a poor man points out to Don Juan, who is lost, the road that leads to the city:

MAN
If you could spare me a little something, Sir ...

---

4. The first edition, of 1682, was hardbound: the printer was required to remove contentious pages, among which appeared the scene of the pauper. An Amsterdam bookseller published the entire text in 1683. This text was twice reprinted (in 1694 and 1699), only to be later forgotten. It was not until 1813 that an edition that included the pauper scene reappeared (see the note to George Couton's edition, op. cit., pp. 145–146).

DON JUAN

Oho! So your advice was prompted merely by self-interest!

MAN

I am a poor man, Sir, and I've lived alone in this wood for ten years. I will pray Heaven to give you every happiness.

DON JUAN

Pray Heaven to give you a new coat. That will do you more good than bothering about other people.

SGANARELLE

You don't know this gentleman, my good fellow. He doesn't believe in anything but two and two make four, and four and four make eight.

DON JUAN

How do you pass your time here among all these trees?

MAN

I pray all day for the prosperity of the people who give me alms.

DON JUAN

You are quite comfortably off then, I suppose?

MAN

Alas, no, Sir! I am in the greatest penury.

DON JUAN

What? A man who prays all day can't fail to be well off.

MAN

I assure you, Sir, I often haven't even a crust to put in my mouth.

DON JUAN

That's strange. You're not very well rewarded for your trouble. See here. I'll give you a gold Louis, if you'll utter a blasphemy.

MAN

Oh, Sir, would you have me commit such a terrible sin?

DON JUAN

The question is, do you want this gold piece or not? I'll give it to you if you blaspheme. Come now.

MAN

Sir ...

DON JUAN
You shan't have it unless you do.

SGANARELLE
Come along! Just one little blasphemy. There's no harm in it.

DON JUAN
Here you are, take it! Take it, I say! Blaspheme!

MAN
No, Sir. I would rather die of starvation.

DON JUAN
Oh, very well then. I give it to you for the love of ... humanity.
(III, 63–64)

The gesture is sweeping—and sacrilegious. It points simultaneously to the importance the dramatist attaches to his lead character's nobility, and the lofty station he assigns to the love of humanity, which, by implicit contrast with the standard formula, surpasses the "love of God." Don Juan thus testifies to his love for humanity by his respect for the beggar's resolute and authentic religious fervor. The former subsumes the latter. As for liberty, it is a matter for the entire human race, believers and unbelievers, rich and poor alike.

This scene occupies a central position. Located at almost precisely the midpoint of the drama, it follows—and tempers—the libertine's "arithmetical" profession of faith. Seen in retrospect, it also functions as preparation, foreshadowing the final scene. The beggar and the gentleman have one thing in common: their inability to prostitute themselves. Where the former refuses to trade his believer's dignity for a gold coin, the latter disdains to save his life at the price of his liberty. Both hold fast to the truth, from which they draw their self-respect. But neither their truths, nor what is at stake for each of them, carry the same weight. One refuses to jeopardize his eternal life for a *Louis d'or* (Pascal's wager); the other refuses to abjure his mortal verity for the hope of an eternal life he does not believe in. One renounces naught for all; the other, all for naught. Or, put differently, for his idea of himself. It may be supreme arrogance, or perhaps a desperate attempt to grasp something ephemeral that is fated to vanish along with the very sacrifice he has accepted: life, against a fleeting self-image. For a sensualist, it is a bizarre trade-off.

The scene of the *Louis d'or* brings out, with utmost conciseness and intensity, the eponymous hero's contradictory impulses. In the space of a breath Don Juan moves from the most abject blackmail to the loftiest sublimity, just as, one and one-half centuries later, in Mozart's hands, the clarion call to licentiousness seamlessly assumes the full force of a hymn to liberty. Moreover, what makes Don Juan's gesture so compelling is that it springs directly from the abjectness that has gone before. Coming from a well-intentioned man, it would have been little more than a banal homily. But from a faithless, lawless individual, following the cruel byplay that we have witnessed, the gift and the words that accompany it ring out like a challenge, and glimmer like an instant of hope. So unexpectedly does love of humanity surge forth that the phrase brings tears to the eyes. All the while, we can understand why a stage director might wish to give it a tone of perfect cynicism and mockery. Sudden fraternity, or ultimate sarcasm: both interpretations are possible.

I resolutely opt for the upsurge of fraternity, for it underlines the protagonist's deep-seated ambivalence. If the scene itself caused so much commotion that it could not be performed again, it is precisely because of what it briefly reveals as being admirable in this unscrupulous sensualist. A Don Juan painted entirely in tones of black would not provoke the slightest sympathy, and would be of scant interest. His erratic behavior, on the other hand, thrusts directly before us the ambiguity of our own feelings and, over and above them, those of humankind at large. But the very humanity that Don Juan invokes with such magnificent insolence is itself problematic. Nothing in the piece can sustain the expectations that his pronouncement for an instant touch off—excepting the code of honor that governs, imperatively, relations between gentlemen. As for the rest, the humanity of Don Juan, to be understood as positive, is nowhere to be found. Paradoxically, it surfaces only in poor Dona Elvira, that is, in withdrawal from the world. Abandoning her humanity, the lady betrayed returns to the convent-like isolation of divine love.

Suddenly we find ourselves thrown back upon the negative core of the libertine credo. In the distorted image of his conquests the rake stands before us as a purely destructive force. Or, to use a fashionable formula, Don Juan can do no more than "deconstruct." How can we not wonder about the meaning of a cast of characters that confers this critical task upon a man—rare outbursts of generosity notwithstanding—with so little to recommend him? It is difficult to see only the comic impulse. *Don Juan*, taken as a whole, has precious little comic tone, no more than Mozart's *Don Giovanni*, even though the master-servant relationship provides a strong element of humor (in both senses of the term). Fear of the censors is also a factor. The least that we can say, in this regard, is that the ruse by which a scoundrel and avowed hypocrite becomes the vector of social criticism simply does not work. First the scabrous scene of the beggar, then the entire piece, for all its success, was withdrawn outright, probably on the advice of well-meaning individuals.

Real or not, fear of censorship often forces the inventive spirit to surpass itself. This is precisely what Molière has achieved: *the style of the scoundrel allows truth to stand forth in a way that it would not have in the speech and manners of a gentleman of breeding.* Expressing love of humanity through the insolence of an immoralist superbly underscores its fragility, for such love must ultimately and entirely depend upon the capriciousness of he who formulates and dispenses it. Behind his princely concession (symbolized by the *Louis d'or*—which may well also indicate that the king would be well advised to awaken to the reality over which he rules!), lurks something quite apart from the brute arbitrariness of one particular gentleman well accustomed to lording it over his fellow men: *the insoluble difficulty faced by human beings in general once they have no one but themselves as a point of reference.* Don Juan dies not for pride alone, but also because his profession of disbelief leads nowhere; because the humanity he claims is no more substantial than his conquests. "Human" for Don Juan means all that lends itself to the untrammeled exercise of his passions, which confirms his own concept of honor. The concept is unilateral, exclusive, and utterly unmindful of reciprocity. Such a notion applies only among select individuals, a restriction in turn that makes it literally impossible for Don Juan to grasp the full power of his social criticism. Even if we suppose, for an instant, that he has intuited its scope and thus accepted the implied formal, judicial equalization that would extend the principle of reciprocity to all men and women, without distinction of origin or class, such universal reciprocity remains elusive.

Kant, who, in his *Critique of Practical Reason*, was to carry the categorical imperative to its most rigorous extreme ("act so that the maxim of thy will can always at the same time hold as a principle of universal legislation"),[5] admitted that the principle remains operative only upon condition that men agree upon the existence of God, that is, upon the primacy of a transcendental law to which each individual can refer. In the absence of such a law, Kant's imperative no longer holds true: the thief will insist that everyone may become a thief, the killer that all may kill, and so on and so forth, until, as each individual becomes the arbiter of what he considers to be admissible on the pretext that he is prepared to accept the consequences, society finally collapses. Only brute force remains, to be wielded without any possible mediation. Such is the threatening horizon toward which the demand of the libertine leads us.

5. Immanuel Kant, *Critique of Practical Reason*, trans. Thomas Kingsmill Abbott (Courier Dover Publications, n.d.), p. 31.

Like *Hamlet, Don Juan* places God's absence at center stage, but with one vital distinction. For Hamlet, that absence resembles a melancholy acknowledgment, the result of an actual loss (the son has not consciously wished the death of the Father) in the face of which the hero, perplexed and unable to bring himself to act, is carried along to his death in the hope that it will prove no more nightmarish than life. It is clear that for Don Juan, who in front of the Commander's mausoleum expresses his astonishment "that a man, who in his lifetime was content with quite a simple home, should want to build such a grand one for when he no longer has any use for it" (III, v, 70), there is no afterlife. He is impervious to both fear and loss. In this man of the world lurks neither doubt, nor nostalgia for transcendence. God is not simply "absent," in the elliptical sense that the fleeting appearances of the specter in *Hamlet* may suggest. There is no enigma in Juan's mind: Heaven is a chimera that men have devised to suit themselves. Even when the statue of the Commander begins to move, the hero refuses to see in it a sign from on high. Succinctly, not only is the elimination of the Father taken for granted; it is to be wished: "Every dog should have his day. No father ought to go on living after his son is of age" (IV, v, 78), he exclaims suggestively after the death of his father, Don Louis (once again, the king's name), who has come back to return him to his senses. The fact that the figure of the Commander (another father image) remains in the shadows may well indicate the symbolic nature of the initial murder we know nothing about. For one to behave as he does, and to exist in a state of fully-fledged disbelief, should one not first have done with God?

Should we take the text at face value, there can be no doubt that the statue, when it exacts revenge, is carrying out divine will. Revenge is not simply *ex machina*, as we noted earlier: it may well symbolize the abyss that awaits the hothead. But Molière lends the entire episode of the Commander a preposterous air that makes it hard for us to take it seriously (there were a thousand other ways to exact expiation from the libertine). This is not to say that the scene is lacking in rich dramatic possibilities, as Mozart's verve testifies. In his version, the statue's arrival and Don Giovanni's consumption by flames constitute a musical moment of the highest intensity. But between the gruesome and the infernal, Molière, faithful to the character he has created, remains ambiguous until the end. Meaning that the double-edged question of God and free will remains unanswered, whole.

It would not be wrong to read *Don Juan* as a denunciation of hypocrisy and a condemnation of impiety, but to restrict ourselves to a first reading would be to emulate Sganarelle, who imagines that his master's death has made everyone happy except himself, and who, *comédie oblige*, brings the play to an end as he shouts despairingly: "Oh, my wages, my wages!"

The loss is laughable when seen against what liberty's hungry breath lays bare as it shatters the hypocrisy that binds society: humanity's inability to live with itself. Don Juan is solitude's hero *maudit*. And we are all, to a greater or lesser extent, so many Sganarelles deaf to our own desires, who, crushing what remains of our dreams of humanity, rush forward breathless to claim our wages.

2

THE PRINCESS OF CLÈVES:
LOVE AS ANNIHILATION

A NAME above all: Clèves. Like a solemn kiss, there is something tender and affirmative about it, a symbol in perpetuity of the first woman, the living Eve. Clèves as "feminine," as key, as nub of a split, as cleft. The heroine is cleft, incised by love, like her womb by the wound of her sex—which, of course, is never mentioned. And yet the secret door at which love must necessarily come knocking, and through which it will never enter, is ever present. The man who knocks is Nemours: love and its negation, inter-woven in the name of he whose exemplary behavior—he is not a duke for nothing—falls short. Confounded by virtue? No, virtue is but a balm, a reward for having turned back in fear: fear of love's power; fear of a suppurating scar; fear of a yawning void that nothing can fill. At the very instant when all becomes possible, when nothing stands in the way of onrushing love, the heroine desists. Or resists, as you will. In any event, she refuses, even when no obstacle remains. Love's key cannot open the lock.

The puzzle remains full-blown. What exactly does Madame de Clèves so fear that love cannot overcome, except love itself? What is the wound that the consummation of love, cannot heal but only aggravate? In presenting us with this puzzle, *La princesse de Clèves* (1678) makes love itself the principle of love's impossibility. The only obstacle to love is love itself. The novel may well owe its power and its novelty to this tight loop.

For Orpheus and Eurydice, for Dido and Aeneas, in *Tristan and Iseult*, in *Romeo and Juliette*, in *Phedra* (1677), outside causes frustrate love; external obstacles thwart the desires of those who suffer its pangs. The gods, reasons of state, family, taboo, incest, and death stand in the way. Seen at even greater proximity, it is to these very external obstacles that such loves owe their imperishable beauty. Romeo and Juliette's love owes its intensity to its impossibility; for it to remain intact the lovers must die. Had Aeneas been able to set up house with Dido, he would have eventually tired of her, as did Ulysses of Calypso. Had Hippolyte not been her husband's son, Phedra would not burn for him with the same ardor. Had Tristan and Iseult been happily married, their story would never have been told. Orpheus is perhaps alone in that he destroys the object of love with love, incapable of resisting for a moment longer the fatal desire to look back upon she who, a few steps later, would be his forever. Instead he loses her forever, knowing full well that it is too soon, knowing that his glance will be fatal, yet driven by an insurmountable force that, quite literally, turns his head. But what with Orpheus is irrational, a leap of the unconscious seems all too deliberate with Madame de Clèves. Her renunciation has been fully considered.

To understand her choice, we must pay close attention to the storyline. Its main thrust is simple enough, but its details are complex and perhaps even a bit forced. The action takes place in the middle of the sixteenth century, at the court of the king of France, during the last years of the reign of Henri II, son of François I. But the manners and the psychology of the characters seem much more in keeping with those of the court of Louis XIV.

Everything seems to turn to the advantage of the two principal protagonists, the Duke of Nemours and Mademoiselle de Chartres (the future princess of Clèves). By their rank, their beauty, their high-spiritedness, and by the esteem they command, they surpass all the other individuals of their sex, in a social setting that is itself exceptionally rich in talent and elegance.[6] Though they are made for one another, they do not meet. Or rather they meet too late.

Shortly after her arrival at court, where she is an unknown newcomer, Mademoiselle de Chartres, unbeknownst to her, attracts the sustained attention of the Prince of Clèves, who is immediately smitten by her and attempts to discover her identity. Several unfortunate attempts at marriage, arranged by her mother, Madame de Chartres, follow. These episodes take place while the Duke of Nemours, who is occupied with the possibility of a marriage to Elizabeth of England, is absent from Paris. Mademoiselle de Chartres, with her mother's encouragement, agrees to marry the prince, a man of good breeding, prudent, pleasing in appearance, estimable. But she consents without love, and in ignorance of love. "Monsieur de Clèves saw only too well

---

6. The novel begins: "There never was in France so brilliant a display of magnificence and gallantry as during the last years of the reign of Henri II" (3). Superlatives follow: "At no court had there ever been gathered together so many lovely women and handsome men ... " (3). Marie-Madeleine de Lafayette, *The Princess of Clèves*, edited and with a revised translation by John D. Lyons (New York: W. W. Norton, 1994).

how far removed she was from feeling for him as he should have liked, when he saw that she had no idea of what that feeling was" (15). The realization should have lead the prince to reconsider, particularly when, during his early advances, he cautions Mademoiselle de Chartres not to marry him out of a sense of duty. Nor does the young bride's lack of ardor escape the attention of her mother, who undertakes "great pains to attach her to her future husband, and to impress upon her what she owed ... for the proof he had given her of his love in choosing her at a time when no one else ventured to think of her" (16). An extraordinary woman whom no one has ventured to think about: Clèves has all but consciously chosen the impossible.

Nemours, who has just returned from a journey, meets Madame de Clèves at a ball given by the king. The dance ends precisely at the instant when the king, noticing that the princess is seeking another consort just as the duke is entering the hall, "called out to her to take the gentleman who has just arrived" (17). All begins with a royal injunction, cast as an imperative that neither can avoid. The two obey, are struck by one another, and Nemours promptly falls in love. So deeply that he forgets all else: the Queen of England, his love of seduction, and all other women. Without revealing his emotions, he thinks of her alone. All can see that he is a changed man, but no one knows why. The powerful inclination the heroine rapidly comes to feel toward Nemours leads her, through a succession of circumstances to which we will return, to understand that she is the source of his transformation. So it is that the two lovers come to recognize one another in their shared passion, without ever touching, without ever speaking. Recognition of the fact eventually impinges upon the awareness of the husband, who rapidly dies of sorrow. The road to fulfillment is free at last. But to Nemours's despair, Madame de Clèves refuses to take it. Not love but the absence of love will ultimately have united the lovers.

Profoundly united they will remain, their mutual passion standing apart from their social surroundings, which conspire simultaneously to exacerbate and to obstruct it. Among the French aristocracy of the sixteenth and seventeenth centuries, love and marriage rarely—if ever—coincided. The particular coincidence of their love is the exception that confirms the rule. Seen in this light, the marriage of Mademoiselle de Chartres with the Prince of Clèves is manifest in its ambiguity: it hews to the rule insofar as she does not love him, but contradicts it in that he loves her. That dissymmetry drives the plot forward. It creates in the heroine an emotional vulnerability that she has never known before, while forbidding he who has awakened each of them to declare the same emotions. If the Prince of Clèves did not love her, Nemours could present himself, even proclaim himself as a lover. But Clèves loves her, and in a manner that forces his wife's respect. The road to any other amorous attachment is blocked.

Yet the emotion of love must insinuate itself into this closed system; it must insinuate itself, stifled and magnified by adversity, into the protagonists' awareness. The twists and turns of the plot lead implacably in this direction. The unspoken, the misspoken, and the misunderstood become love's darkly efficient guides. Two persons, outside the couple, have discovered the secret: the Chevalier de Guise, whose insight is due to the hopeless love he feels for the heroine, is a dangerous onlooker whose premature death opportunely eliminates him; and Madame de Chartres, the mother who, suddenly struck down with a fatal illness, on her death bed warns her daughter against the precipice over which she fears she will tumble (28). Aside from these two individuals, only the two principle protagonists know. Rather, they suppose it to be so. And at times, in the throes of jealousy, they even come to doubt it themselves.

The approach of a ball to be given by the Marshal of Saint-André, which Nemours, outside Paris on a royal mission, cannot attend, touches off the dance of intimations. On a visit to the heiress apparent, Madame de Clèves learns from the Prince of Condé that he has just come from a meeting in which Nemours has declared, against all common sense, that "a ball is most distressing for lovers" (24); that the greatest possible suffering is to know that his mistress will be in attendance without his being present, and that there can be only one occasion at which he could allow her to be present, that is, when he himself should give her permission (25).

> As soon as the Prince of Condé had begun to speak of what Monsieur de Nemours thought of the ball, Madame de Clèves was very anxious not to go to that of the Marshal of Saint-André. She readily agreed that it was not fitting for a woman to go to the house of a man who was in love with her, and she was glad to have so good a reason for doing a kindness to Monsieur de Nemours....
>
> Madame de Chartres argued for some time against her daughter's decision, which she thought singular, but at last yielded, and told her she must pretend to be ill, in order to have a good excuse for not going, because her real reasons would not be approved and should not be suspected. (24–25)

Nemours, who has had to absent himself from court without knowing that his mistress will not attend the ball, and who has had to return without suspecting the secret feelings that dissuaded her from going (he is unaware that she has heard his words from Condé's mouth), decodes the meaning of her absence from the gentle taunting of Madame de Clèves by the crown princess in his presence the following day:

> "You look so well," said the crown princess, "that I can scarcely believe you have been ill. I fancy that the Prince of Condé, when he told you what Monsieur de Nemours thought about the ball, convinced you that you would do a kindness to the Marshal of Saint-André by going to his ball, and that that was the reason you stayed away."
>
> Madame de Clèves blushed at the dauphiness's accurate guess, which she thus expressed before Monsieur de Nemours.
>
> Madame de Chartres saw at once why her daughter did not go to the ball, and in order to throw Monsieur de Nemours off the track, she at once addressed the dauphiness with an air of sincerity. "I assure you, Madame," she said, "that your Majesty pays an honor to my daughter which she does not deserve. She was really ill, but I am sure that if I had not forbidden it, she would have accompanied you, unfit as she was, to have the pleasure of seeing the wonderful entertainment last evening."
>
> The dauphiness believed what Madame de Chartres said, and Monsieur de Nemours was vexed to see how probable her story was; nevertheless the confusion of Madame de Clèves made him suspect that the dauphiness's conjecture was not without some foundation in fact. At first, Madame de Clèves had been annoyed because Monsieur de Nemours had reason to suppose that it was he who had kept her from going to the ball, and then she felt regret that her mother had entirely removed the grounds for this suspicion. (25–26)

"Kept her from" are the key words of the first episode, in the course of which the lovers reveal their mutual inclination *as if* in spite of themselves. Each desires to be indirectly recognized by the other without appearing to have wished it. "Keeping from" first reveals, then conceals the amorous impulse. Kept from attending the ball—it was on the occasion of just such a ball, let us remember, that the protagonists met for the first time—Nemours informs all who might care to listen that he is troubled before the fact by the thought that his mistress might attend in his absence, while taking care not to reveal the slightest detail of her identity. By keeping herself from attending in turn, Madame de Clèves provides her lover with an invisible surety, then becomes frightened that the true motives for her decision may reveal her intentions, and finally regrets that her mother has prevented the surety from assuming its full significance. In front of our eyes unfolds a hesitation waltz between the irrepressible need to show all and the absolute necessity to show nothing. Such is the insoluble contradiction through which amorous passion carves out and, from that moment on, sweeps along in its own path.

Each of the subsequent episodes can be read as repetition, each time amplified, of the initial imbroglio, through which both the impossibility of speaking one's heart and the inability to remain silent move forward in tandem, intermingling with and nurturing one another.

The death of Madame de Chartres brings the progression to a momentary halt; it allows the princess to take her distances from the people around her and to still her throbbing heart. But mourning also bodes well, in an initial tête-à-tête with Nemours, for the possibility of a first avowal. Breaking the silence that has locked the two lovers in their mutual predicament, Nemours offers his condolences. Altogether too happy to speak of her mourning, Madame de Clèves describes in fine detail its effect upon her. Nemours skillfully exploits the change the princess claims to have undergone to speak of himself, and from there, to slide from affliction to love. The most difficult thing of all, he says, is not to display one's feelings, but to hide them from the public by rejecting the pleasures of the court in such a way that she—who is its object—understands the strength of the attachment expressed by his removal.

> Madame de Clèves readily understood the reference to her in these words. It seemed to her that she ought to answer them and express her disapproval; it also seemed to her that she ought not to listen to them or show that she took his remarks to herself: she believed that she ought to speak, and also that she ought to say nothing. The remarks of Monsieur de Nemours pleased and offended her equally; she saw in them a confirmation of what the crown princess had made her think,—she found them full of gallantry and respect, but also bold and only too clear. Her interest in the prince caused an agitation which she could not control. The vaguest words of a man one likes produce more emotion than the open declarations of a man one does not like. Hence she sat without saying a word, and Monsieur de Nemours noticed her silence, which would have seemed to him a happy omen, if the arrival of Monsieur de Clèves had not put an end to the talk and to his visit. (39)

The same agitation overwhelms the princess when she sees the duke removing from the table to which his back is turned what she intuits to be a locket containing her portrait, a suspicion later confirmed by the object's disappearance. Or when she decides to confess everything to her husband, then abandons the idea as folly. Fully aware of the nature of her feelings for Nemours—which she now knows are those that Monsieur de Clèves "had so sought from her"—and obliged to abandon the "hope of not loving him," she is "determined to give him no further sign of it" (40). But she can only partially master her resolve. When the duke falls from his horse in front of her, the concern and the pity written on her face as she bends toward him speak more eloquently than words.

The diversion of a letter that has the potential to destroy Nemours will knot love's ties in a manner even less anticipated and yet more perfidious. Hard upon the heels of the ambiguity of speech and the betrayal of the eyes, come the depredations of the written word. It may well be that this very episode provided Edgar Allan Poe with the inspiration for his famous short story, "The Purloined Letter." Jacques Lacan, in a seminar devoted to a close analysis of Poe's tale, pointed out that it should be described as "having been detoured" to correspond with the original English *purloined*.[7] For in both cases, we are dealing with a *detour* that accelerates the tempo of desire. Some believe that Nemours has lost the letter; others know that it has found its way into the pocket of the Vidame of Chartres. But ultimately it has been passed on to the crown princess who, unable for a moment to read it, hands it over to Madame de Clèves, as it is addressed to the duke. It is a fortuitous detour (the dauphiness knows nothing of the secret links between the duke and her confidante) by which the princess, believing Nemours to be enamored of another and loved by her in return, feels jealousy's brutal pangs. But the letter has put into play nothing less than the most intimate, most secret relations between the vidame and the queen, who would take as an unpardonable affront the revelation that her lover is entertaining other amorous passions.

The rumor spreads like wildfire at court. No sooner has the vidame realized that he has lost the letter, than the queen already knows it is in circulation. The vidame pleads with Nemours to claim it as his own. But he is only able to overcome his friend's resistance by providing him with written proof that he can produce in his mistress's presence to clear himself. What the vidame, like everyone else, does not know is that the mistress in question is none other than his niece (Madame de Clèves) and that Nemours cannot

7. Jacques Lacan, *Écrits, The First Complete Edition in English,* trans. Bruce Fink, Heloise Fink, and Russell Grigg (New York: W.W. Norton, 2005), p. 21.

rehabilitate himself except by going directly to her on the pretext of rescuing his uncle from the queen's wrath. Madame de Clèves refuses to see him, finally agreeing only when her husband constrains her to do so, and then with extreme coldness. This proof of her anger causes the lover even greater rejoicing; he now realizes he can clear his name, which he does with relative ease. The letter, once a source of jealousy, now leads to quiet complicity. To save the vidame, Nemours and the princess together draft a false letter, but there is no fooling the queen: the vidame will be irremediably diminished in her eyes. Though the false letter cannot save the vidame from the effects of the real one, together the two letters tighten the ties that bind the lovers.

The awareness of their rapprochement causes the princess to shrink back violently. Dismayed at the signs of jealousy and passion she has involuntarily conveyed to Nemours, she feels compromised in her own eyes; she sees herself as betrayer of her husband, while at the same time "ashamed to appear so unworthy of esteem in the eyes of her lover" (63). Unwittingly, she herself will rehabilitate her image in the eyes of the latter, who is far too happy at the signs of love he has received to even consider deploring them. Through circumstances we need not expand upon, Nemours fortuitously and secretly witnesses the poignant encounter in which the princess brings herself to admit to her husband, who is disturbed by her insistence at shutting herself off from the world, her feelings for another man whose identity she absolutely refuses to reveal, but in whom Nemours quickly recognizes himself. Goaded by her spouse's insistent questioning Madame de Clèves, in spite of herself, delivers incontrovertible proof: the other man is the one who, in front of her very eyes and before she could react, removed her portrait.

> He [Nemours] first gave himself up to that joy; but it was not of long duration, for he reflected that the same thing which showed him that he had touched the heart of Madame de Clèves, ought to convince him that he would never receive any token of it, and that it was impossible to gain any influence over a woman who resorted to so strange a remedy. (354)

The princess's only possible motive for making the terrible confession that threatens to forfeit her husband's esteem can be located precisely in the hope that her confession is the surest, most honorable way of preventing her from acting upon the feelings she is experiencing, and of saving her marriage. Such, at first, is the impact of her confession in the mind of Monsieur de Clèves, for all the suspicion that torments him for a moment with regard to the manner in which the portrait may have fallen into the lover's hands. But

Madame de Clèves' admirable behavior is of no avail in the face of the insatiable curiosity that makes it impossible for her husband to go on living without knowing the identity of his rival. The confession, contrary to its intent, touches off an unstoppable process by which all is undermined, and of which Nemours will rashly make himself the accessory.

In his distress the duke confidentially relates to the vidame, as though it were someone else's tale, the story of all that has befallen him. This is enough for the story to make the rounds at court as being that of Nemours, until finally it reaches the ears of Madame de Clèves via the crown princess's mouth; she utilizes the arrival of the duke to call upon him as witness. Momentarily at a loss, Nemours becomes indignant at the vidame's betrayal of his confidence, and indirectly, of his friend's. Though he may successfully mislead the crown princess, he well knows that he cannot fool Madame de Clèves. Fully aware that she cannot imagine that she is the original source of the indiscretion, he perfidiously attributes it to the incaution in which jealousy can entangle a husband.

In fact, the spouses accuse one other of revealing a tale that no one could have invented. Nemours's heedlessness has transformed the confession into a poison that eventually taints him. Since it is impossible to ascertain how the secret of their meeting has been divulged, and for all the bitterness that their mutual suspicions have occasioned, the spouses have maintained sufficient esteem for one another to keep the peace, and agree that the only way to put an end to the rumors (for, after all, the only name to have made the rounds is that of Nemours) would consist of the princess making it clear to Nemours that she has had nothing to do with the tall tale that, by his fault, has been propagated. But so mortified is the duke by his own indiscretion and by its consequences, that only one way is left for him to express his love: to flee, on his own initiative, from her whom his fault has caused so much suffering, and to hope to regain her esteem.

For all that, Clèves now knows a good deal more than the name of his rival (which he, by subterfuge, has indirectly extracted from his wife): he knows that Nemours knows himself to be loved by her whom he loves. And this knowledge rapidly becomes the instrument of his destruction. Everything, in the eyes of the husband, is transformed into a subject of suspicion. The princess refuses to allow Nemours into her apartments? It can only be a sign of the particular relationship she entertains with him. She withdraws to the country? Nemours's movements immediately become suspect. Clèves has him followed. And as the lover cannot stop himself from prowling about her isolated dwelling place, the prince draws mistaken conclusions from his spy's report, refusing to hear him out: infidelity, he incorrectly believes, has been consummated. Stricken by the news, he never recovers. In a state of intense despond at his wife's betrayal, the prince declares, when confronted with the sincerity of the princess's protests, that he is happy to die before, finally, he admits she may be innocent. But it is too late, the illness has progressed and the prince succumbs, leaving the princess "almost crazed by the intensity of her grief." She is carried away to a convent, and finally brought back to Paris "before she was able to realize her afflictions."

> When she began to be strong enough to think about it, and saw what a husband she had lost, and reflected that she was the cause of his death by means of her love for another man, the horror she felt at herself and at Monsieur de Nemours cannot be described. (96)

The prince's death should have, by rights, legitimized a theretofore-impossible liaison. In reality it looms before her as an even more insurmountable obstacle. Her fidelity to the deceased becomes more radical than her fidelity to her husband.

The idea that loyalty to a deceased person is stronger than that due a living being draws on the fact that a dead person can no longer, by either word or behavior, discharge us of the obligation he has bequeathed to us. In the princess's mind, the burden of his legacy only magnifies the burden of her guilt. The proscription appears inviolable; the narrative might well have come to an end against such an absolute barrier. It does nothing of the kind. It carries us on, as we shall soon see, to another impossibility, an internal one, that has loomed implicitly since the beginning. The princess's debt to her husband's memory does not, after all, have the absoluteness it appeared to have had during the shock of mourning. For even this most exemplary of husbands, perhaps more than anyone else, could also claim his share of faults.

The first and most grievous, the fault that takes precedence over all the others: to have married for love a woman whom he knows full well does not reciprocate his passion. We must not forget that we are in a world in which marriage is first and foremost a business matter, a quasi-political alliance; in such a world, marriage for love is the exception. An exception, not to say an extravagance, of that kind can only be justified, if it can be justified at all, by reciprocity. At minimum, the passion must be mutual. It is precisely because it occurs so rarely, because it is almost impossible, that at court business, alliance and love are one—and that the flames of passion, for the most part, flare outside of marriage. The heart is faithful to the mistress and to the lover. Conjugal fidelity can exist, but it is of another order, and is exercised on another plane. Rarely are the two fidelities united. As Monsieur de Clèves so tellingly puts it when he learns that his wife loves another man: "I have all the jealousy of a husband and of a lover" (67). Such words have no meaning unless the two functions are normally distinct. Merging the two would have had dangerous implications for a young woman who, in her utter ignorance of love, could not have committed herself simply to being his spouse. Had the marriage been one of convenience, the princess would surely have felt freer to become Nemours's mistress. Let us bear in mind, however, that the prince of Clèves had taken advantage of the failure of Madame de Chartres's marital projects for her daughter to conclude, thanks to the death of her father, an alliance that the deceased had not approved. The prince had not acted unfittingly, nor was his advantage dishonorably gained, but he had demonstrated a serious lack of forethought: in the hope that the lady he demands in marriage will accept out of love, he concludes the match in spite of everything, knowing full well that the condition he himself has formulated has not been, and that it is at risk of never being, satisfied.

By recounting the double-dealing of the "virtuous" Madame de Tournon, the Prince of Clèves suggests that he is prepared to assume that risk, when he relates to his wife the advice that he has given to the friend who has been hurt by such a display of ambiguity. He wisely cautions her about letting herself be carried away.

> "'I give you the advice,' I said to him, 'which I should take myself; for I am so touched by sincerity that I believe that if my mistress, or my wife, were to confess that anyone pleased her, I should be distressed without being angered, and should lay aside the character of lover or husband to advise and sympathize with her.'"
>
> At these words Madame de Clèves blushed, finding a certain likeness in her own condition, which surprised her and distressed her for some time. (32)

Most likely, the memory of these words of advice will not be without effect on the princess's eventual confession to her husband. But it is he, above all, who encounters the greatest difficulty in abandoning his role as lover and husband. Far from responding, by his acts, to the extraordinary confidence that the princess has placed in him, and to the firmness she has exhibited, the husband continues, consciously and unconsciously, to behave in such a way as to torment the lover that he is as well, and to subvert his wife's resolutions to distance herself from Nemours. To the bitter end, the princess is irre-proachable, all except in her feelings. These feelings are independent of her will; her husband's attitude can do nothing to overcome them. Monsieur de Clèves, in the final analysis, must accept ultimately responsibility for his jealousy and for the death it will entail. The princess's guilt has no reason to last beyond the mourning period she owes to a respectable husband with whom she was never in love and who, in adversity, ultimately revealed him-self to be beneath his own lofty idea of himself.

If we look at it again, the prince's death is hardly the insurmountable obstacle it first appeared. What resentment the princess may have felt toward Nemours gradually recedes, as does he: out of respect for his mistress's pain, and to expiate his unfortunate indiscretion, the duke behaves in the most exemplary fashion: he refrains from inflicting the burden of his presence upon the princess. And when, one month later, fortune, aided by the curiosity of Madame de Clèves, once more joins the two lovers, all necessary condi-tions are now in place. They may, without the slightest shame in the eyes of the world, consummate their love and marry. Of course the princess seeks to invoke a higher duty, explaining to Nemours that her refusal is motivated not by the outside world, but by herself. "For I know," she says, "it was from you he got his death, and on account of me." But the ultimate reason for her refusal lies elsewhere: "That which I believe I owe to the memory of Monsieur de Clèves would be frail indeed, were it not sustained by my need for tranquility, and the reasons for my tranquility must be sustained by those of my duty." Once again, the amorous impulse stands as the only true obsta-cle for the princess to conquer, and yet she cannot. "Her reasons for not marrying Monsieur de Nemours seemed strong so far as her duty, and irrefutable so far as her tranquility, was concerned" (107). The fearsome power that threatens her tranquility can be none other than passion. The moment when, during the lovers' first and last true conversation, the mistress reveals both her love and its impossibility to her lover, this magnificent and magnificently painful moment, is the high point of the book. The princess speaks as she had never before spoken to a soul; as she will never again speak to a soul:

> "I think it but a slight reward for your affection that I should
> hide from you none of my feelings, but should let you see them
> exactly as they are. This probably will be the only time in my life
> that I shall take the liberty of letting you see them; nevertheless, I
> cannot confess to you without deep shame that the certainty of not
> being loved by you as I am, seems to me a horrible misfortune; that

if there were not already insurmountable claims of duty, I doubt if I could make up my mind to risk this unhappiness. I know that you are free, as I am, and that the situation is such that society would probably blame neither of us if we should marry, but do men keep their love in these permanent unions? Ought I to expect a miracle in my case, and can I run the risk of seeing his passion, which would be my only happiness, fade away? Monsieur de Clèves was perhaps the only man in the world capable of keeping his love after marriage. My fate forbade my enjoying this blessing. Perhaps, too, his love only survived because he found none in me. But I should not have the same way of preserving yours; I believe that the obstacles you have met have made you constant;…"

[Then, after Nemours has protested:]

"I confess," she said, "that I may be moved by my emotions, but they cannot blind me; nothing can prevent my seeing that you are born with every disposition for gallantry, and with all the qualities proper to secure speedy success. You have already been in love several times,—you would be again very often. I should not make you happy; I should see you interested in another as you have been in me: this would inflict on me a mortal blow, and I should never feel sure that I should not be jealous." (103–104)

[Further on, after Nemours's claim that she is enforcing upon herself a law that neither reason nor virtue imposes, these final words:]

"It's true," she replied, "that I make a great sacrifice to duty which exists only in my imagination. Wait to see what time will do. Monsieur de Clèves has just died, and that fatal event is too recent for me to judge clearly. Meanwhile you have the pleasure of having won the love of a woman who would never have loved had she not seen you; be sure that my feelings for you will never change and will always survive, whatever I do." (105)

Ironically "time," slipped enigmatically into the princess's declaration of farewell as the sole, frail straw of hope Nemours can aspire to grasp, "time" that instead of weakening his ardor strengthens his resolve, "time" combined with the absence of the beloved object, will ultimately overcome his love. Time, however, vindicates no one. The only certainty is that the mistress did not wish to risk seeing, through her tears, time insidiously at work against her love. That very love to which, the better to preserve intact, she refuses to lend the slightest opportunity.

The Princess of Clèves is the novel of absolute love. For the first time, so forthrightly, love towers tyrant-like over the heart of the very subject it afflicts. So totally does it hold sway that there remains no place for Eros. By banishing Eros once and for all, the princess refuses to open herself to that which, ever since Plato's *Symposium*, manifests itself as absence in the West's version of amorous love. She may well have the most virtuous of reasons for remaining faithful to her husband's memory, and the reasons behind her denial intertwine with one another in a tight and complex knot. Still, she has behaved irreproachably, and the blame that Nemours has incurred for a brief moment is more than compensated by this secret heroism, which regains for him the fullest respect and love of his mistress. His love, the solitary hurt that Nemours conceals from all eyes, and that she catches by surprise, without him knowing it, deep in a public garden, reaches its pinnacle at the very instant when nothing any longer stands in the way of its consummation. The husband's death may well (in spite of itself) release the young woman from the insidious trap in which he had ensnared her. Even before, the duty of sincerity was in the end the only fidelity he could ask of her; the only one, in any event, he had ever truly enjoined her to observe (though he hoped never to have to certify it), as he preferred, at the risk of losing his status as lover and husband, to know rather than not to know the future passions of his spouse.

Under the code that governs amorous relations at court, which the king is first to exemplify, the princess could well have openly and almost legitimately taken Nemours as a lover even while her husband was alive. By declining to do so, she obeys not the unwritten laws of marriage, but the knowledge that her husband is madly in love with her, possessed in a manner of speaking by an emotional state that she will only understand when it is too late. The tragedy lies, rather, in the imbalance to which she has so ingenuously given her consent—if indeed the unconscious renunciation of love can be described as tragic at all. For, in the final analysis, in accepting the hand of Clèves, but without being able to gauge all that she has committed herself to, Mademoiselle de Chartres has turned her back on love, as well as on the passion she carries unknowingly within her, the passion that Nemours will set alight. It is as though, in the fatherless heroine's subconscious, love has lain forever as an impossibility, like an impulse that cannot assume an earthly shape except in the imagery she has created within herself. The fact that Clèves' passion cannot be reciprocated perfectly matches the hidden world of the woman he has wed. In this world the princess cannot but apportion herself as a gratuitous gift, leaving her body to her husband while preserving only her thoughts for her lover. Thus she experiences the most refined form of the only love she is capable of: a love divided and disincarnate. So deep is the split that she is unable to achieve with someone else what she can experience for herself alone. The only way for her to leave her body to her deceased husband, and to preserve the passion of her living lover, is to remain single. Duty and tranquility are thus reconciled—ostensibly.

If *The Princess of Clèves* looms so large as a monument of French classicism (and beyond, for French was at the time emerging as the favored language of European nobility), it is because it stands as the most condensed, the most narcissistic example of the *roman d'amour*. The novel represents the archetype of absolute love, impossible love, of the simple fact that the heroine can only be loved as though in a novel. Madame de Clèves is not interested in whether or not she is actually able to love Nemours, in all his troubling masculinity, in all his inadequacies and his defects. She would rather hold fast to the image of herself as reflected by him. Clearly enough, the classic mirror effect typifies all passionate love, but *The Princess of Clèves* succeeds in demonstrating it with an intensity and an intelligibility far above the commonplace. For the heroine, true love is a novel, that it can be *nothing other than a novel*: here lie its power, and the inner coherence of its structure.[8] It is a novel in which the other, the object of love, must absolutely remain imaginary and unattainable.

Unattainable is precisely and deliberately what Madame de Clèves *makes* Monsieur de Nemours in prolonging that which he had previously been despite herself, by force of circumstances. In doing so, she is acting quite unlike Racine's heroine Phedra, who precedes her by one year on the French stage. Like her's, Phedra's passion collides with an immovable object: Hippolyte, the object of her amorous furor, is the son of her husband Theseus. But the misleading announcement of the latter's death appears to remove this final obstacle, and her confidante, her evil genius Œnone, does not fail to remind her, whispering:

> Live.
> You have no longer reason to reproach
> Yourself; your love becomes a usual love;
> Theseus in dying cuts the sacred knots
> Which made the crime and horror of your passion.
> > (*Phedra*, 1, 5, 189)[9]

8. I owe this conclusion to the perspicacity of Isabelle Moatti, who formulated it during a lively discussion of *La princesse de Clèves*. This does not mean, however, that she shares my entire reading of the text.
9. Jean Racine, *Five Plays*, trans. Kenneth Muir (New York: Hill and Wang, 1960). References are to act, scene, and page).

Here, the news of death invalidates the proscription, but transforms Phedra's love into a *common* affair, with all the disenchantment the terrible term implies. In the short term, however, it releases a passion that has preserved its incestuous, sulfurous quality, and which Theseus's surprise return transforms once more into full-blown guilt. Ultimately, it is to her faltering heart, in a strange kind of Freudian slip, that Phedra declares before Hippolyte the blazing love she believed she could conceal, and which decency would have enjoined her to postpone until after the funeral of the deceased. But Phedra has run up against another, major unknown factor: she does not know Hippolyte's feelings. In the event, he does not love her, and flees the flames that are consuming his stepmother. But the damage has been done, and the fire spreads. Theseus believes his son to be caught up in incest and condemns him to death; Phedra kills herself, not merely because she knows she is guilty, but because she has learned that Hippolyte loves another woman.

In his preface to *Phedra*, Racine craves our pardon for displaying passion, invoking the reasonable and miserable moral of renunciation that the spectacle the devastation it wreaks should inspire. Not for an instant do I believe him. Not for an instant do I believe that Racine has insulted either Eros or Aphrodite. In this, the most powerful, most violent, most concentrated of all his dramas, he causes the explosive admixture of beauty and terror to explode with far too much violence. Beauty and terror are fused in love's crucible. It is difficult to know to what extent Racine conveys the spirit of the day—the spirit, might we venture, of a certain aristocracy still possessed of the remnants of heroism that here find their expression in the nobility of amorous rapture. From this perspective, our era seems light-years removed from Racine's century, unless of course Racine himself was already far removed from his contemporaries. How is it possible to experience such overwhelming power, and not regret living in the age that is ours? Passion certainly transcends time, but the spirit of the age, in our times, hardly lends itself to such feelings, and can hardly transmit them. I fear that there is something anorexic about the literature of our era. By way of contrast, in terms of excess, *Phedra* and *The Princess of Clèves* complement one another admirably, not because the princess flees the darts of passion, though she dreads them, but because she dreads the slow dwindling of passion even more. She nurtures within herself and for herself the very destructive force that keeps her secretly alive, and that with Phedra bursts upon the stage, until it immolates her. With her, the murderous charge explodes; with the princess, the charge remains dormant, like a precious asset untouched and unspent.

In this light, Madame de Lafayette's novel possesses the emblematic quality of metaphor. As it tracks the autistic trajectory of amorous passion, it expresses in more general terms the way in which Western civilization has begun to view the other, and to invest its object: as inconceivable, even undesirable as a subject endowed with its own existence, autonomous of the thought that has conceived it. The other seen as that object, which because of its manifest difference, cannot assume its rightful place and be granted its full meaning, cannot be loved—or detested—except through the prism of our representation of the world. It is not our task here to decide whether this propensity to integrate the other into our dreams is unique to Western civilization—it may well be that it is, *mutatis mutandis*, the identifying mark of all civilizations. It is simply to note that this integrating power has no need of the other to be effective in deploying its effects, just as, in order to love, Madame de Clèves has no need of Nemours, and prefers even to do without him. What else to conclude but that our civilization is the first to make the attempt to love, and to so integrate, to appropriate the other on such a monumental scale? In this regard, European classicism has probably bequeathed to us the most enduring insignia of its absolutism: we may well have inherited from it the thirst for a way of understanding the world that spares no other culture. Could this "understanding," in its imaginary and prophylactic dimensions, not conceal an unspoken fear: the fear of contact with the other, of living the kind of experience that is truly disturbing, the fear of experience that, on another level, is so like the princess's refusal to risk disenchantment and turmoil by living with her lover?

3

GULLIVER:
THE UPSIDE-DOWN MAN

A S EVERYONE KNOWS, Swift plays with the size of things. His Gulliver is a giant among the Lilliputians, and a Lilliputian among the giants. His upsizing and downsizing has so struck readers that most can recall only the first two of his four voyages, to Lilliput and to Brobdingnag. As the second does not fall lightly to the tongue, only the name of Lilliput has endured. In fact, Lilliput and its inhabitants have become such celebrities than *Lilliputian* has become a synonym for tiny.

But on his last two journeys Gulliver travels through worlds where things have reverted to their normal proportions; there he encounters people his own size. Strangeness expresses itself in a different way. In Laputa, the overlords inhabit an island hovering above the earth. From it, they can easily suppress the merest hint of rebellion anywhere on that portion of the surface that lies beneath them under their control. The metaphor speaks for itself; its strangeness owes less to the improbability of their situation than to the unexpected character of the island's masters. Obsessed neither by power nor wealth, they are ingenuous dreamers who practice worthless scientific pursuits and remain insensitive to the poverty of those whom they lord it over, and who are forced to obey them.

The land of the Houyhnhnms, where his fourth and last journey takes him, lays before us the spectacle of a society in which roles have been reversed: the wise men, the Houyhnhnms, have horses' bodies, while the fanged, clawed, shaggy animals that serve them, the Yahoos, have human bodies—hair and claws aside. At first glance, they are men worse than men, for they are by nature deprived of reason. But in conversation with his Houyhnhnm host and friend, Gulliver concludes that men are worse than the

Yahoos, for they enjoy the gift of reason and yet make such ill use of it, in contrast to how admirably these marvelous horses wield it. So impressed is Gulliver that, unlike Ulysses, he has no desire to return home. The other, the stranger, the Houyhnhnm, emerges as the being with whom the narrator would like most to identify, and not the one he wishes to leave, as in his earlier journeys. Yet leave he must, against his will, to find himself, horrified, in the midst of a society in which he will never again feel completely at home.

First impressions notwithstanding, the thread that links his four journeys is not disproportion, but inversion. Inversion of size in the first two; inversion of values in the last two. Inversion takes on particular force in the fourth journey, where it transforms Gulliver's return into a nearly insurmountable ordeal, or, if nothing else, into a profoundly painful experience. It is as though the narrator, in the course of his successive peregrinations, has wished to familiarize himself with the most extreme of all things implausible, the Lilliputians, the giants, the hovering island, only to arrive at the least apparent but most striking and most powerful strangeness, to which only speech — the exchange of words — can grant him access. The least apparent inversion becomes the most significant, the most fraught with meaning.

Swift's readers have long argued whether, in the writer's eyes, the narrator's admiration for the Houyhnhnms and the wisdom of the Houyhnhnms themselves are truly admirable, or parodies. Swift's intentions continue to elude us, and the insoluble controversy throws no light upon the meaning of the work. Here, as throughout this book, I have focused on the text, seeking out what it tells us today.

*   *   *

Gulliver's Travels certainly bears the seal of its age: it draws a satirical portrait of the era, indirectly singling out real situations and existing political figures; Chapters 5 through 7 of the fourth volume deal at length with the wars between the princes of Europe, the state of England under Queen Anne, and the English Constitution. It is particularly significant that these issues are raised during Gulliver's discussions with his Houyhnhnm hosts. Via the specific case of England, the eternal question of human nature is posed, the question that pervades the entire work.

What, in fact, is man? An excrescence amongst the Lilliputians; a toy, a thinking doll in Brobdingnag, the midpoint between all and nothing, to use

Pascal's formula. That is to say: reduced to himself, with no measure for comparison, he is a kind of nullity, a non-entity. Man does not exist, only Gulliver the individual exists: such is the theory that the narrator involuntarily puts to the test in the course of his tribulations.

What anyone might make of his size weighs upon him even as it exposes him to the most painful slights. It awakens the distrust and the jealousy of the small, who, like the Lilliputians who tie Gulliver down, will go to any lengths to restrict him. But it is also because the narrator finds himself so disproportionately huge, in the literal sense, that the others appear so tiny, setting off among them jealous hatred of his size. Gulliver may proclaim his good intentions to his Lilliputian hosts as much as he wants, he may use his prodigious power in positive ways, he may capture the enemy fleet and put it at his mercy, he may even extinguish the blaze that threatens to destroy the imperial palace with his urine. No matter: his self-image becomes an insurmountable obstacle to relations with those around him. The best of intentions are of no avail when one feels oneself to be superior; Gulliver finds himself in a situation in which his obvious physical disproportion prevents him from thinking otherwise. The latent power of his first travel lies in that it makes clear that no matter how good the greatest of men may be, no matter how generous, his greatness necessarily binds and betrays him. Everything, without fail, turns against him, beginning with his immense appetite, which is ruinous for his hosts. Ultimately, Gulliver will be accused of treason. He is forced to flee a land where he believes he has done nothing but good, if he wishes to escape mutilation or death by poison.

His clear conscience shines forth in all its ambivalence in the fire episode. A blaze has broken out in the empress's apartments, and spreads so quickly that the Lilliputians cannot contain it with the equipment at hand. In these extreme circumstances, the narrator concludes that he has no choice but to urinate upon the heart of the blaze, and saves the rest of the palace. He is well aware of the gravity of the measures employed:

> It was now Daylight, and I returned to my House, without waiting to congratulate the Emperor; because, although I had done a very eminent piece of Service, yet I could not tell how his Majesty might resent the manner in which I had performed it: For, by the fundamental Laws of the Realm, it is Capital, in any Person, of what Quality soever, to make water within the precincts of the Palace. But I was a little comforted by a Message from his Majesty, that he would give Orders to the Grand Judiciary for passing my Pardon in form; which however, I could not obtain. And I was

> privately assured, that the Empress conceiving the greatest abhor-
> rence for what I had done, removed to the most distant side of the
> Court, firmly resolved that those Buildings should never be
> repaired for her use; and, in the presence of her chief Confidants,
> could not forbear vowing Revenge. (54)[10]

The service rendered is praiseworthy, but it is the praiseworthiness of his person that places the narrator in double jeopardy. First, in a positive sense, due to the formidable capacities with which his size has endowed him, which the law cannot have foreseen, then, negatively, due to what his particular powers oblige him, as it were, to violate. The prohibition against urination in and around the palace, valid for normal people, nobles and commoners alike, cannot apply to Gulliver's circumstances and exceptional situation. But at the same time, his extreme measures have inflicted a double humiliation on his "beneficiaries": they underline their impotence, in the most literal sense, and irremediably soil the loftiest of their dwellings. No matter what he does, the giant cannot survive in the land of the dwarves.

But a dwarf can survive perfectly well in the land of the giants. He can even look forward to high honors, for no one will fear him, nor envy him. But the narrator is immeasurably smaller than even a midget: his "nurse" (the daughter of the farmer who discovers him, and who will continue to protect him) calls him *Grildrig*; "the word imports what the Latins call *Nanunculus*, the Italians *Homunceletino*, and the English *Mannikin*" (90), the narrator relates. The infinitely tiny Gulliver faces dangers entirely different from those of Lilliput. The danger of being literally invisible, of being inadver-tently crushed by even the fall of an apple (an ironic allusion to Newton?), the danger of falling prey to normally inoffensive animals such as monkeys, rats, dogs, cats, and wasps, against which he can always draw his sword. But the danger against which he has no defense is that of becoming an object of increasing curiosity, a circus act, and a source of ever-greater profit for the impressario who exploits him. Forced into a succession of representations that attain a frenzied pace, Gulliver would have soon died of exhaustion had his arrival in the capital not attracted the benevolent attention of the queen. From that moment on, Gulliver approaches the throne with ease and captures the king's attention, succeeding in gaining royal accreditation, despite the warnings of the court wise men, as a being fully possessed of reason and thus qualified to advise on most matters.

10. Jonathan Swift, *Gulliver's Travels* (London: Penguin Classics, 2001).

Despite his best efforts to convince the most responsive members of his entourage that he comes from a world where all men are of his height, and in which all other beings are accordingly proportioned, he remains a prodigious miniature, a collector's item, a zoo in and of himself. The repugnance of the majority of normal people to consider him to be a man stems as well from the fact that the very sight of his minuteness makes normal human dimensions "contemptible," for they can "be mimicked by such diminutive insects" as he (100). All the while, sensitized by his disproportion to details that cannot normally be observed, he sees everything as through the lens of a powerful microscope. As an involuntary witness to the undressing of the maids of honor, whom his nurse occasionally takes him to visit, Gulliver crudely notes, when confronted with their nudity:

> For, they would strip themselves to the Skin, and put on their Smocks in my Presence, while I was placed on their Toilet directly before their naked Bodies, which, I am sure, to me was very far from being a tempting Sight, or from giving me any other emotions than those of Horror and Disgust. Their Skins appeared so coarse and uneven, so variously coloured when I saw them near, with a Mole here and there as broad as a Trencher and Hairs hanging from it thicker than Packthreads; to say nothing concerning the rest of their Persons.... The handsomest of these Maids of Honour, a pleasant frolicsome girl of sixteen, would sometimes set me astride upon one of her Nipples; with many other Tricks, wherein the Reader will excuse me for not being over particular. But I was so much displeased, that I entreated *Glumdalclitch* to contrive some excuse for not seeing that young Lady any more. (110–111)

The way the scene is described is by no means entirely free of ambiguity. The young lady is pretty, pleasant, frolicsome, and her erotic games appear to contradict the idea that she behaves in his company as though he were "a Creature who had no sort of Consequence" (110). In fact, she toys with him, as she would play with a miniature sex object, and we can easily imagine, among those things about which he remains silent, that an eventual erection provokes the amused and tender delight of the "mommy" who manipulates him. The narrator's horror and disgust express, semi-consciously, the sense of the forbidden that an infant may feel in the real or imaginary sexual games it plays with its mother. Be that as it may, Gulliver, in this episode more than any other, involuntarily regresses toward early infancy. In the broadest sense, nothing he says or does can be taken seriously by the adult world around him. Gulliver is more alone than any other child in the world, without any possible partner, not even the queen's dwarf, who is all too pleased and proud to find someone even more trifling than himself. The king, who seems to be the only one to converse with Gulliver as an equal (a sign perhaps of the true vantage point that his title and function grant him), does not miss an occasion to make fun of the naïveté—which is quite infantile, in fact—with which the narrator boasts of the institutions and exploits of his native England. Taking him into his hands and "stroking [him] gently," the king congratulates his "little Friend Grildrig" on his "admirable Panegyric" about his country, ending amiably: "I cannot but conclude the Bulk of your Natives to be the most pernicious Race of little odious Vermin that Nature ever suffered to crawl upon the Surface of the Earth" (123). What we have is a device by which Swift can attribute this peremptory judgment of England to the distance from which, in contrast to the narrator's microscopic acuity, giants look down upon the world. Seen from high above and far away, there is little to admire about man's hanky-panky and skullduggery.

The harshness of the royal verdict on England does not discourage Gulliver's hopes to return to his native land. His cage may well be a gilded one, but his life in Brobdingnag is a prison from which he despairs of ever escaping. Only heaven's miraculous intervention can deliver him this time. Thanks to the inattention of a page assigned to guard him, an eagle carries his traveling box up into the clouds where, attacked in full flight by another of its species, the bird abandons his capture upon the high seas. Gulliver is rescued by an English ship and returned safe and sound to his native land. His second experience has reinforced the first: everything is a matter of size and proportion, and man can judge himself only in relation to his environment, by gazing at his image reflected in the world's great mirror. Having spent three years in a society of giants, during which time he avoided looking at his reflection for fear of having "too poor an idea" of himself, Gulliver finds himself once more among people his own size, but with a giant's outlook that reminds him of Lilliput.

Because he had for so long "winked at [his] own Littleness as People do at their own Faults," some time will pass before the narrator ceases to consider those like him as "the most little contemptible creatures" that he has ever beheld (117). His rehabilitation seems extraordinarily long: nine months of travel with his boon companions, in a setting where people have regained their normal proportions, hardly suffice. Upon his return, Gulliver behaves as though he has just left Brobdingnag, taking the people around him for Pygmies. He utters a slip of the tongue, admitting that he bends over when going into his house "for fear of striking his Head." But his reflex action better matches the habits acquired where everything is too small, rather than where it is all too large, the idea being that we have unexpectedly returned to the Lilliputian world.[11] Embarrassed by his exaggerations, the narrator stresses that he mentions these details "as an Instance of the Great Power of Habit and Prejudice" (231). His real design is revealed: its aim is moral edification.

The tale's moral intentions are confirmed and underlined in Gulliver's third journey, which casts him ashore in a *politically* and *mentally* different world. On both levels, as we have seen, the two preceding worlds resemble, *mutatis mutandis*, that of our own Europe in the eighteenth century, except that they appear technologically less advanced. The inversion of size has been used only to illustrate how much the other resembles us, yet how different he remains, or, more simply put, to direct our attention to the strangeness of our own manners and customs. The journey to Laputa, unlike its predecessors, propels the narrator into a technically more advanced world (in certain ways at least) that is subject to a visibly abusive and totally hare-brained political regime.

A perfectly round midair island resting atop a diamond 150 toises thick, four and one-half miles in diameter and equipped with a powerful magnet, physically and politically dominates that portion of the globe that corresponds to its field of attraction. On the king's orders, his engineers can cause its altitude to vary, up to a maximal elevation of four miles, and, by lateral maneuvers, cause it to move sideways above that portion of the earth's mantle containing the mineral layer that drives its magnet. The island is called Laputa, and the dependence (or dominion) that it lords over, Balnibarbi, an onomatopoetic name that evokes barbarity.

Swift adores word-play, not only in his own language, but in other European tongues as well, French in particular. The narrator's own linguistic hypotheses for Laputa seem barely convincing, and ill-conceal that we find ourselves, with that name, dealing with a certain whorishness. There is a salty slant to the narrator's efforts to correct this received etymology, which, in old Laputian, suggests height and dominance. His interpretation, drawn from the analysis of two syllables from modern Laputian, *Lap outed*, evokes in English something resembling a ventral expulsion that might well be more like a fart, perhaps even excrement.[12] Gulliver's scatological conjecture may well be the hidden, prosaic face of the narrator's poetic interpretation of the

---

11. It should be noted that no readjustment will be necessary after the return to Lilliput, despite the fact that he spent two years there (one year less than in Brobdingnag).
12. Swift's scatological inclinations are well documented.

Laputian: "*Lap* signifying properly the dancing of the sun Beams in the Sea, and *outed*, a Wing" (346).

If we mix all these possible meanings together, Laputa may well be at once a whore and a floating turd that takes itself, in a flight of superiority, for a wing scintillating with sunshine. What follows indicates that this combination of etymological elements is anything but far-fetched. The inhabitants of the island certainly do not take themselves for shit, and display nothing but indifference for the world far beneath them. That world need only stay where it is to "benefit," in a manner of speaking, from the scientific genius so assiduously cultivated on the lofty heights. But the Laputians, whose heads incline either to the right or to the left, one eye focused upward to the zenith while the other is "turned inward," these Laputians have the greatest difficulty in concentrating on concrete matters and in attending to what is going on around them. Their minds are "so taken up with intense Speculations" that those who are able to afford it are accompanied by servants whose task it is to tap them gently on the eyes and ears with a blown bladder "fastened like a Flail to the end of a short stick" to alert them to what they should be seeing and hearing (148).

Mathematics and music are the only two sciences they respect, and in which they excel. So all-consuming is their passion that the narrator is served "a Shoulder of Mutton cut into an equilateral Triangle" and "two Ducks, trussed up into the form of Fiddles" (150). He attends the performance of a piece of music that lasts three hours without interruption, and from which he emerges "quite stunned," lacking an ear "adapted to the Music of the spheres" so beloved of the Laputians (151). But their love for geometry remains purely theoretical, to such an extent that their clothing is ill-fitting and their houses rickety. Their disdain for practical matters and their fascination with mathematics are accompanied by an altogether startling interest in politics, and by an unstinting concern for public affairs. For all that, the king has not the least curiosity to learn about the manners and customs of the countries where his guest had been, but only about the state of mathematics there (155).

Politics and mathematics clearly do not have "the least analogy" (152), and the aberrations to which their combination can lead give Swift an opportunity to ridicule certain European mathematicians (including Newton) who use their scientific renown to meddle in the affairs of the state—a criticism that has lost none of its pertinence. These few cutting remarks aside, Laputa is presented as a humorous, ever-so-slightly facile caricature of the kingdom of the philosophers. The insistence on music and mathematics refers us back to the pedagogical primacy, which, in Plato's *Republic*, Socrates accords to music and gymnastics, not to mention the motto that graced the entry to the Academy: "No one who is not a geometrician may enter into our house."[13] Is the narrator criticizing Plato, or his simplistic interpreters? I have no idea. One thing is certain, the spectacle of Laputa and its government of dreamers and wise men has forever disgusted our narrator. Their malfeasance is confirmed by the economic and social devastation that their theories, imported to the continent, have brought upon the land and the inhabitants of Balnibarbi. From a human standpoint, their promises of a better world and their scientific innovations have brought about nothing but regression, calamity and desolation.

Here, at the dawning of the Age of Enlightenment, is a striking criticism of the very idea of scientific progress, at least as the driving force of economic and social progress. This is not to say that technical innovations themselves are totally inefficacious; we need only take due note of the prodigious potentialities of the floating diamond and its magnet, whose function the narrator describes in minute and admiring detail. But this technical marvel, quite precisely intended to give the Laputian ruling class an exceptional overview of the needs and interests of its subjects, threatens them in the end with annihilation, and maintains them in a state of servility inimical to their growth and prosperity. In Balnibarbi the narrator sees only sterile efforts and catastrophic inventions. He notes only one instance of agricultural success, and it can be attributed to the very traditional methods that public opinion, against all evidence, does everything in its power to condemn. Production itself can look forward to no good from technical innovation. We are dealing with much more than a mere critique of England's repressive policies toward Ireland: an expression of the general idea that scientific progress has no positive effect on manners and customs, nor upon the economy. Those thinkers who rely on the former to ameliorate the latter are fooling themselves. Quite against the temper of the times, the narrator displays an anti-modern ferocity.

Absurdity reaches its peak at the Academy of Speculative Sciences, where an engineer has devised a machine to manufacture text—machine writing before the fact—with which he intends to "Give the World a complete Body of all Arts and Sciences" (171). Another school toils mightily to compress language, going so far as to suggest that all words be suppressed, to be replaced with the objects they represent. The plan has "only one inconvenience attending it," that it would oblige anyone with extensive business

13. Ibn Khaldun, www.muslimphilosophy.com.ik/Muqaddimah/Chapter6/Ch_6_20.htm.

dealings to carry "a greater Bundle of Things upon his back" (172). But it is at the School of Political Projectors that Gulliver encounters the most mind-boggling professors:

> These unhappy people were proposing schemes for persuading Monarchs to choose favourites upon the Score of their Wisdom, Capacity and Virtue; of teaching Ministers to consult the Public Good....
>
> But, however I shall so far do Justice to this Part of the Academy, as to acknowledge that all of them were not so visionary.... This illustrious Person had very usefully employed his Studies in finding out effectual Remedies for all Diseases and Corruptions, to which the several kinds of public Administration are subject by the Vices or Infirmities of those who govern, as well as by the Licentiousness of those who are to obey. [He goes on to mention, inter alia, the "Vertigoes and Deliriums," the "Scrofulous Tumours" and the "sour frothy Ructations" suffered by the representatives.] This Doctor therefore proposed, that upon the meeting of a Senate, certain Physicians should attend at the three first Days of their sitting, and at the Close of each day's Debate, feel the Pulses of every Senator, after having maturely considered, and consulted upon the Nature of the several Maladies, and the methods of Cure, they should on the fourth day return to the Senate House, attended by their Apothecaries stored with proper Medicines, and before the Members sat, administer to each of them Lenitives, Aperitives, Abstersives, Corrosives, Restringents, Palliatives, Laxatives, Cephalalgicks, Ictericks, Apophlegmataicks, Acousticks, as their several cases required, and according as these Medicines should operate, repeat, alter, or omit them at the next meeting. (175–176)

Even more audaciously, the same Doctor purports to resolve bitter partisan rivalries by simultaneous surgery upon the half-brains of the leaders of each party. The anti-modern who has just finished railing against the political uses of mathematics shows a sudden enthusiasm for the improvements that experimental science promises to bring to politics. The social body, like the individuals who represent it, is ill; the best treatment for it is medical care, or surgery—perhaps because this art, we should not forget, is also that of the narrator who is not, in the final analysis, irrevocably closed to the idea of progress.

The final stages of Gulliver's third travel are hardly calculated to reassure the narrator about the evolution of the human species. A short trip by way of Glubbdubdrib, the island of sorcerers and magicians, presents him with the opportunity, thanks to the consideration of the governor, to evoke and to question directly the great figures from the past, who no longer have any reason to lie. To hear these great historical personalities, from Alexander and Hannibal to Caesar and Brutus, most of what is said about them is false. Aristotle, reduced to a pathetic state, recognizes his errors and strikes down the innovations of modern philosophers; only that great fabulist, the magnificent Homer, preserves his stature, and his penetrating gaze. But the most distressing aspect of this upstream excursion into history comes when he realizes how mediocre are the historical protagonists of recent centuries. "I was chiefly disgusted with modern History" (185) and "it gave me melancholy Reflections to observe how much the Race of human kind was degenerate upon us, within these three hundred Years past" (186).

Nor do Gulliver's experiences in Luggnagg bring him any respite. He witnesses a royal ceremony that is perfectly abject and degrading. Each person granted an audience must literally lick the ground covering the distance between him and the throne; the king makes known his favor or disfavor by the degree of cleanliness or filth in which he orders the floor to be strewn, when he does not simply have it dusted with a deadly poison. Those who have fallen into disgrace reach the king's feet with their mouths so crammed that they cannot utter a single word "because it is Capital for those who receive an audience to spit or wipe their Mouths in his Majesty's Presence" (190). Luggnagg has another particularity: among its inhabitants, who are "polite and generous People" (312) one finds a privileged few known as *Struldbrugs*, who are born with a red circular spot above the left eyebrow, an infallible indication that they will never die. Asked what he would do were he immortal, Gulliver dreams of the immensity of the knowledge and riches he would be able to accumulate, and of all the ideas he would put into practice, naïvely assuming that he would remain forever in the prime of life. Shown immediately afterward, the reality of the *Struldbrugs*, the narrator observes, is that they continue to age, and that their eternity is gradually transformed into a state of ever-advancing deterioration, turning them into impotent, jealous creatures that have become unbearable to society as a whole. Without a regret, Gulliver takes ship for Japan and from there returns safe and sound to his own country.

His uneventful journey's end contrasts sharply with the painful return from the fourth and last. Until then, Gulliver had been discovering the weirdness of the world, which is surprising only because it is unfamiliar. For all its visible, and visibly deceptive, differences, humanity is everywhere the same. Each people expresses, in its own way and commensurate with its particular makeup, the same madness, the same incapacity for wisdom. The Laputians, for all their gifts of and propensity for contemplation, contrive to torment themselves with the prospect of the imminent catastrophes proclaimed by their reading of the stars. From his encounters with the other, Gulliver returns, a bit wiser certainly, but not in the slightest transformed. The realization that everything is everywhere the same does not cure him of the desire to set out once more. A case of fidgety feet, the reason for which he cannot understand, drives him from his home and off to sea. He cannot sit still, cannot live peaceably with his fellows. Only when he reaches the land of the Houyhnhnms will he find out why. Only upon contact with these marvelous horses will the narrator understand what being human means, and bring himself to confront his latent misanthropy.

The discovery is anything but painless. Gulliver begins by dissociating himself from the Yahoos, those beasts with human bodies. He attempts to convince his Houyhnhnm hosts that, appearances notwithstanding, human beings have nothing in common with the Yahoos. But the more he attempts to show how humans are different from this race of hairy, sharp-clawed savages, the more he realizes that the differences he describes hardly compliment the human species. "But when a Creature pretending to Reason, could be capable of such Enormities," notes his Houyhnhnm host, responding to the narrator's account of those who look like him, he "dreaded lest the Corruption of that Faculty might be worse than Brutality itself" (228). Like any creature mired in "Brutality," the Yahoo is not endowed with reason; self-examination is foreign to him. Such a possibility exists for man alone, but, as the three previous travels have demonstrated, man makes nothing of it.

Like the narrator, man is capable of self-scrutiny, yet everywhere he flees himself. Man could appeal to reason to gain self-knowledge; instead, he uses it at every turn to justify his flight. Instead of acquiring wisdom through reason, man uses reason to justify his madness. Reason turns against wisdom, and ultimately supplants it. Exposed to the serenity of the Houyhnhnms, Gulliver realizes what he has been fleeing in all his travels: the horror that is man. This time, the knowledge he has gained from his companionship with the Houyhnhnms transforms him, and relieves him of the slightest desire to return. Gulliver has finally found a home; he no longer wishes to budge.

Admittedly, the Houyhnhnms are far from perfect. Conscious of their superiority to the inferior beings around them, the Yahoos in particular, they cannot imagine that anyone other than themselves—Gulliver in the event—might make positive use of reason. So powerful are their negative prejudices and their racism toward the Yahoos that they cannot spare someone who, though he resembles them physically, is utterly unlike them in terms of intelligence, speech and morality. Rather like the English, the Houyhnhnms consider themselves inimitable, and have no desire to transmit anything to anyone.

Their closed-mindedness abruptly reminds our narrator of his own humanity. His rejection appears to have been a necessity after all. No moral improvement can help Gulliver: he cannot cease to be human. Just as the philosopher who steps out of his cave and contemplates the sunlight must return to the cave and convince his fellow prisoners that such light exists, Gulliver must return to his own and there testify to what he has seen: the workings of wisdom among horses who are infinitely better and infinitely happier than humans. Without knowing it, the Houyhnhnms also comply with the natural order. Their perfection is too good to be true, and the narrator must eventually wake up from his dream. There is something more unreal about these perfect beings than all the other creatures Gulliver has encountered in his travels. Their unreality is embodied, in my view, in the fact that their name is unpronounceable. Almost all the names of the peoples he encounters are difficult to articulate and, worse yet, to remember, but that of the Houyhnhnms is the only one which, like YHWH, cannot be uttered. Any attempt to do so is a waste of breath.

For all that, contact with the unutterable (the narrator speaks of the "his barbarous English" [226], unable to convey the subtlety of the language of the Houyhnhnms) has a powerful impact. Gulliver cannot escape unscathed from his encounter with them, from his dream. No, he will carry the wounds inflicted upon him for the rest of his days. In the homeward journey that follows his expulsion from the land of the Houyhnhnms, Gulliver, as he flees by canoe from an inhospitable island where he had been sheltering, receives an improbable arrow wound on the inside of his knee. As Jeannette Winterson[14] has judiciously observed, it is common in the horseracing world to disable a rival with an imperceptible incision that makes it impossible for him to win, but not to run. Gulliver may well be able to run (or, in the event, to row), but he cannot win. "I shall carry the Mark to my Grave," (261) the narrator notes in passing. The parentheses (the sentence is in parentheses in the text) says all that need be said. The narrator identifies with the horses of his dreams, with the marvelous Houyhnhnms, and means to remain faithful

14. See her introduction to Jonathan Swift, *Gulliver's Travels* (Oxford: Oxford University Press, 1999), pp. v–xiii.

to them until his death. Yet these are the very Houyhnhnms who, by forcing him to leave, have laid him open to the imperceptible and indelible wound that he will carry to his death. In the *Odyssey*, the old wet-nurse recognizes her Ulysses when she touches the childhood scar on his ankle. It is a sign of recognition by which the old woman can welcome her beloved child with secret joy. In Gulliver's case, no one can recognize the invisible sign, which he receives in the prime of life, on his painful journey of return. The best his friends and family can do is to encourage him to pick up his normal life where he had left it. But for him, normality no longer exists. Gulliver has returned from his dream with an intimate wound that no one can either see or understand. None of his family can grasp why Gulliver no longer feels at home. He alone understands that his last travel, which is the adventure of the soul, and a spiritual experience, has stripped him of any possibility of domesticity. Such is the price he who dares to stray too far from mankind must pay; he who, though it be only in a dream, has beheld beauty.

At the end of the last tale, *Gulliver's Travels* takes an unexpected turn, which colors all the facetiousness that has, until the critical instant of the wounded return, characterized the narrative. All of a sudden the narrator is no longer playing. All that had appeared to be supercilious and light-hearted becomes unbearable; Gulliver's progress now becomes almost imperceptibly tragic. Modern man, the man who has not followed Gulliver's path to its conclusion, stands before a tragedy he cannot fathom, before a fate he cannot even perceive as tragic.

4

CANDIDE:
THE UTOPIA OF EVIL

B ENEATH ITS APPARENT SIMPLICITY Voltaire's *Candide* poses, in
particularly brutal terms, the question of how it is to be read. How easy
it would be to glide over the text on the wings of an alert, direct, and precise
pen that, at first glance, leaves nothing in the shadows. The world is
presented as though it were a series of portraits of family life, or like a classic
comic book[15] (*Tintin*, for instance) whose theme and unifying principle is the
meticulous, flawless depiction of human abomination. We can laugh, and just
as quickly forget. We can tire of it, and close the book in irritation. We can
attempt to surmise what Voltaire intended to *say* (always a risky matter) or
study how his tale was received in its time (as literary history strives to do).
Finally, we can speculate about the impact of *Candide* today, forgetting to
take into consideration that today's reality is totally distinct from the reality
of Voltaire's day. Simple enough then: we need only enter into the text. But
when we do so, the difficulties we encounter will be more than anticipated, a
result of the particular impermeability that arises from the two-dimensional
representation I have just sketched out. In these circumstances, I can think of
no better way of engaging it than via the library of one of the characters
whom Candide encounters on his journey, the only one into which he will
venture in the entire book, the richly appointed and opulent collection of the
Venetian nobleman Pococurante.

How, indeed, would Voltaire's most celebrated work fit into the library,
let alone the carefree spirit of Signor Pococurante, who shows the peripatetic
Candide around his palace in Chapter 25? None of the great classics, starting

15. This allusion to comic books, and in a broader sense, my reading pleasure, I owe to the edition of
Candide published in "La Petite Bibliothèque Philosophique de Joann Sfar," by Bréal, Paris, 2003. In it, the
drawings and comments of "court clerk Sfar" add a marvelous new dimension of pleasure and intelligence.

with Homer, finds favor with our redoubtable reader. To the great surprise of Candide, "who had been taught never to judge anything for himself," the Venetian lashes out at the indiscriminate use made of authors of renown: "Fools admire everything in a celebrated author. I only read to please myself, and I only like what suits me" (174).[16] Martin the skeptic approves. It may well be that this wise man, whom life has sorely tried (and whom Candide befriended in Surinam) is perhaps, here more than anywhere else, the narrator's spokesman.

But it may also be that he, our narrator, identifies more (or as much) with that other scholar and "man of taste" who, at the Parisian dinner party in Chapter 22, explains what distinguishes a good tragedy or a good novel:

> The man of taste explained very clearly how a play might have some interest and hardly any merit; in a few words he proved that it was not sufficient to bring in one or two of the situations which are found in all novels and which always attract the spectators; but that a writer of tragedies must be original without being bizarre, often sublime and always natural, must know the human heart and be able to give it speech, must be a great poet but not let any character in his play appear to be a poet, must know his language perfectly, speak it with purity, with continual harmony and never allow the sense to be spoilt for the sake of the rhyme....
>
> Candide listened attentively to these remarks and thought highly of the speaker; and, as the marchioness had been careful to place her beside him, he leaned over to her ear and took the liberty of asking her who was the man who talked so well. "He is a man of letters," said the lady, "who does not play cards and is sometimes brought here to supper by the abbé; he has a perfect knowledge of tragedies and books and he has written a tragedy which was hissed and a book of which only one copy has ever been seen outside his bookseller's shop and that was one he gave me." "The great man!" said Candide. "He is another Pangloss." (162–163)

Could the narrator be making sport of himself? Possibly. Whatever the case, Candide confuses, in the same outburst of complacent admiration, the tasteful Parisian gentleman and the paltry German philosopher who had once served as his mentor at Thunder-Ten-Tronckh Castle, a magnificently pitiful character whose name, Pangloss, suggests that he is capable of expounding on anything and everything. The narrator misses not an opportunity to taunt

---

16. Voltaire [François-Marie Arouet], *Candide and other writings* (New York: Modern Library, 1984).

him and, with him, the philosophical optimism that he professes, come hell or high water: all is for the best, in this best of all possible worlds.

To open *Candide* in the library of one of the most cultivated, most fulfilled individuals, the rare, the "infrequently encountered" Pococurante, or to place it in the hands of a cultivated Parisian gentleman, is to raise within the narrative (and thus outside of time) the question of its scope and destination. If ever there were a text that would seem difficult to read out of context, without taking into account its author—assuredly his century's nearest thing to an emblematic figure—this is surely, more than any of his other novels, the one. Not only because it was the best known and most widely read in its day as it is today, but also because it is the most radical. Only by taking the text at face value, paying no attention the ideas Voltaire propagates in an *oeuvre* as vast as it is prolific, that teems with subjects, tones, and humors of virtually every kind (especially given the immense space taken up by his correspondence) can its full *extremity* be experienced.

So, let us venture into *Candide* while attempting to forget its author. We cannot fool ourselves of course: to overlook such a detail is next to impossible—for no other reason than the quality of the style (reading the *text* elicits an effort that the ease with which it was written incites us constantly to abandon, in a cleverly channeled fluidity that flows off the reader like water off a duck's back). Yet the dissociation between the narrator and Voltaire is far from arbitrary. In fact, it is essential, considering that the author introduces himself as a simple translator:

CANDIDE
OR
OPTIMISM

Translated from the German
By Doctor Ralph
With the additions discovered in the pocket of the doctor upon
his death in Minden, in the year of our Lord 1759.

And what, pray, does said Doctor Ralph so trippingly relate? A cock-and-bull story. A tale of misery, a sordid, unbelievable yarn chock full of the plausible and the historically factual. A condensed version of the woes of the world, a litany of misfortune, injustice, and absurdity, a compendium of the atrocities men inflict upon one another. Sade minus the sexual gymnastics. Sade minus the discharge of voluptuous pleasure, assuming that such a thing can be found in Sade. Candide, his tribulations and his encounters are the thread that strings together the elements in this theory of calamity; they lead him from Westphalia to Turkey, by way of Portugal, Paraguay, Eldorado, Surinam, France, and Venice. Expelled from the wondrous château where he had been adopted by his presumed uncle, the Baron of Thunder-Ten-Tronckh, who banishes him for having kissed his daughter Cunegonde with her enthusiastic consent, Candide the bastard wanders the earth driven onward by the hope of rediscovering his beloved, whose death he hears of early on, whom he unexpectedly finds alive, and whom he loses once more to a lubricious governor, only to find her once again much later for a second, and conclusive time, bloated, grown ugly and bitter by her state of servitude, no longer good for anything but pastry making, whom in spite of everything he marries, and settles down to live a modest life with her and a handful of companions met along his way, on a tiny estate that barely provides for their needs.

It is not necessary to keep in mind the fine details of the story and its multiple ramifications. First and foremost, the tale is a canvas on which the narration inscribes motifs in the form of situations, scenes, characters, words—which are then held up to be reflected upon. They are all connected to a single fundamental question, and interconnected by a single leitmotif. The question: is life worth living? Is it possible to be an optimist in this world? We already know that Pangloss, the know-it-all, answers in the affirmative, against all evidence. As for the leitmotif, it is Candide's love for the beautiful Cunegonde—the ridiculousness of whose name presages the final decline of the unfortunate woman it burdens.

Love is the power that carries Candide through misfortune, the force that guides him beyond passion and to accept quotidian reality. Nurtured by absence and by the beauty of the memory that accompanies it, the amorous impulse flickers and dies ignominiously in the ugliness of her presence. Everything that Candide has endured in the name of love is revealed in the end to have served another goal that is summed up in the famous injunction to cultivate one's garden. Call it wisdom or call it resignation, the reader must ultimately decide. Whatever the case may be, Candide's endurance is shown to have been well and truly nourished by a chimera, and the reality that replaces it provides slender recompense indeed for his long and painful wanderings. Were they worth it all? True, the hero (if we can call him that) has not chosen them. Except, perhaps, when he decides, for the love of Cunegonde, to leave Eldorado.

Candide and Cacambo's[17] sojourn in the inaccessible and marvelous Eldorado introduces a midpoint break in the tale.[18] The protagonists have arrived there in error, following an exceptionally perilous river journey:

> The river continually became wider; finally it disappeared under an arch of frightful rocks which towered up to the very sky. The two travelers were bold enough to trust themselves to the current under this arch. The stream, narrowed between walls, carried them with horrible rapidity and noise. After twenty-four hours they saw daylight again; but their canoe was wrecked on reefs; they had to crawl from rock to rock for a whole league and at last they discovered an immense horizon, bordered by inaccessible mountains. The country was cultivated for pleasure as well as for necessity; everywhere the useful was agreeable. (144–145)

The experience has all the trappings of a second birth: a gut-wrenching descent into the womb, then emergence from it and a miraculous ascent into paradise. The new Eden they have discovered echoes the "earthly paradise" (112) from which Candide was expelled at the beginning of the story, paying for his amorous passion for his cousin[19] by eviction from "the best of castles" (111). The same love impels him to depart, of his own "free will," from the utopia where he could have remained. But this "free will" of his, on reflection, is as fictitious as the land he is leaving. How can one reside in a place that does not exist? As if on cue Cunegonde arrives with a subjective justification of why Candide must break with the fantasy-charged ideal of his place of residence, far from the cruel world which he had momentarily departed to dwell in the dream of its diametrical opposite: the best of all possible worlds.

Having been momentarily interrupted, the narrative may resume. From the imaginable Candide falls back into the possible, with its lot of calamity. The difference being that he emerges wealthier—enormously so, to the point of caricature—from his passage through a dream, even if that artificial wealth, so abundant in Eldorado that its inhabitants spurn it, rapidly disintegrates under the hammer blows of misfortune and human rapacity. In the end he contrives to conserve only the modest sum that will provide him a garden plot to cultivate. Material wealth stands as an ironic metaphor for the wisdom that constitutes the true treasure of this imaginary land. The expedition to

---

17. The suggestive name of the valiant manservant who has accompanied Candide ever since his departure from Cadiz for the Americas.

18. Narrated in Chapters 17 and 18 (of the work's thirty chapters), the episode begins six pages after the middle of the story and occupies seven pages.

19. Candide nonetheless avoids falling victim to the Bulgarian men-at-arms who ravish the castle and its inhabitants, into whose ranks he will be press-ganged, and from whom he will contrive to escape.

Eldorado has left him only a tiny measure of worldly goods and wisdom, but it gives him the strength to meet new calamities with equanimity and to find solace in the meager teaching he has gleaned from the repeated experience of misfortune.

Candide is a modern, laughable version of Gilgamesh and of Ulysses. Like Ulysses, he is not the master of his fate. But they differ in that he has no home of his own to return to, no realm to reconquer, no suitors to vanquish; the woman he is reunited with has, unlike Penelope, lost all attraction. Like Gilgamesh, his epic leads him to the simple life. But that life, and its setting, are not those from which he has been expelled. The quest for love leaves him suspended far longer in his illusions than does the Sumerian hero's quest for immortality. Gilgamesh is king, he returns home after a series of exploits as a king, fully cognizant of his duties, fully capable of taking the measure of his kingdom and the care it demands of him. Driven from pillar to post by circumstances, Candide has, strictly speaking, achieved nothing. But his tribulations lead him modestly to construct his own realm. Where Gilgamesh embodies the collective, the city, Candide represents only himself: the innocent individual forced to carve out a minuscule enclave where he can work and live in peace in a world—a universal city—that is rolling full speed toward the abyss. There is no guarantee that his garden will not, like the fine château of his infancy, be destroyed by another band of Bulgarians, or be engulfed by an earthquake. The story does not say. It leaves him hanging, in fact, peacefully enjoying his worldly goods, as if the awareness that it is his to cultivate henceforth has spared him all the world's horrors and absurdities. In the final analysis, Candide's garden, the "ego" he so assiduously cultivates, looks strikingly like the Eldorado he had for an instant dreamed of, now shrunken and withered.

But Voltaire's "novel" is only a tale. It is neither psychological nor realistic, though it contains elements of both. It is a tale pieced together from fragments of reality assembled in an order so implausible as to be a caricature. Its lively tone sweeps us away down a fast-flowing river whose banks we cannot see for the innumerable rapids. Its onrushing rhythm may well be, unconsciously, a device for accelerating the speed of the tale. Yet it is a story in which nothing changes, in which abominations and follies recur *ad nauseam*. It has been said that Sartre was the Voltaire of his age, and the novel that assured his fame, *Nausea*, has certain affinities with *Candide*. The difference is that Sartre's hero, Roquentin, mired in his tiny provincial town, *knows* he is nauseated, and hopes for nothing, neither from the people around him, nor from himself. He is a trapped man; trapped like a rat, who spends his days studying his cage. Roquentin stinks of old cheese.

Candide, as his name indicates, is a virgin. When he sets out on his journey, he knows nothing but the teachings of Pangloss. Nurtured by these teachings, Candide is possessed of a natural optimism, optimism more moderate than his master's, but insufficiently thought out. Events are registered upon it as upon a blank page. Are they even registered at all, one wonders? They happen. Ever the diligent student, Candide takes due note, reporting them mechanically as unfortunate but necessary detours on the road to the best of all possible worlds so dear to his master. Every cloud has a silver lining, as the saying goes. And what then? The cloud is thick, almost opaque: forced to commit acts that revolt him—for our guileless hero will be induced to kill, and not always in self-defense—doubts enter his mind. There are even moments when he wonders if Pangloss's hopelessly wide-eyed optimism can resist experience.

The meeting, and the decision to hire Martin as a traveling companion (while he himself believes his first master to be long dead), embody Candide's still-faltering awareness of this skepticism. Quite unlike Pangloss, Martin perceives the world as being plunged deep into darkness, irrevocably delivered over to the forces of evil. Worse, old Martin does not have, as does Candide, the advantage of hoping to lay eyes on Cunegonde once more. For it is this very hope that keeps the younger man's preference for the Panglossian system intact.

On the deck of the ship that carries them from Surinam to Europe the two boon companions regale one another with their respective philosophies. What does he think of "moral and physical evil?" Candide asks his fellow traveler.

> "Sir," replied Martin, "my priests accused me of being a Socinian; but the truth is I am Manichean." "You are poking fun at me," said Candide, "there are no Manicheans left in the world." "I am one," said Martin. "I don't know what to do about it, but I am unable to think in any other fashion." "You must be possessed of the Devil," said Candide. "He takes so great a share in the affairs of this world," said Martin, "that he might well be in me, as he is everywhere else; but I confess that when I consider this globe, or rather this globule, I thank that God has abandoned it to some evil creature—always excepting Eldorado.
>
> "I have never seen a town which did not desire the ruin of the next town, never a family which did not wish to exterminate some other family. Everywhere the weak loathe the powerful before

whom they cower and the powerful treat them like flocks of sheep whose wool and flesh are to be sold. A million drilled assassins go from one end of Europe to the other murdering and robbing with discipline in order to earn their bread, because there is no more honest occupation; and in the towns which seem to enjoy peace and where the arts flourish, men are devoured by more envy, troubles and worries than the afflictions of a besieged town. Secret griefs are even more cruel than public miseries. In a word, I have seen so much and endured so much that I have become a Manichean." "Yet there is some good," replied Candide. "There may be," replied Martin, "but I do not know it." In the midst of this dispute, they heard the sound of cannon. The noise increased every moment. Every one took his telescope. About three miles away they saw two ships engaged in battle; and the wind brought them so near the French ship that they had the pleasure of seeing the fight at their ease. At last one of the two ships fired a broadside so accurately and so low down that the other ship began to sink. Candide and Martin distinctly saw a hundred men on the main deck of the sinking ship; they raised their hands to Heaven and uttered frightful shrieks; in a moment they were engulfed.

[We learn the ship that has just been sunk belongs to the Dutch sea captain who stole almost all of Candide's wealth, and that a red sheep has miraculously escaped from the vessel.]

"You see," said Candide to Martin, "that crime is sometimes punished; this scoundrel of a Dutch captain has met the fate he deserved." "Yes," said Martin, "but was it necessary that the other passengers on his ship should perish too? God punished the thief, and the devil punished the others...."

They argued for a fortnight and at the end of the fortnight they had got no further than at the beginning. But after all, they talked, they exchanged ideas, they consoled each other. Candide stroked his sheep. "Since I have found you again," said he, "I may very likely find Cunegonde." (155–157)

The episode is vintage Voltaire. Philosophy is doing what it does best: arguing. The world, with roaring canon, interrupts Candide's peroration. It is not long before mutual slaughter turns into spectacle. Horror, in all its complacency, comes close enough to be contemplated at leisure, in its minutest details. Our philosophers have the best seats in the house, opera glasses at their fingertips. When the cries of distress have finally been swallowed up by the waves, philosophy reasserts itself. In the end, the event confirms each man's position. Martin rails against mankind, and Candide is overjoyed to have rediscovered his sheep. Nothing has changed; only the pleasure of conversation remains.

Like the battle scene, the entire tale is an attack on philosophy, on its vanity and its impotence. And yet, the tale itself cannot avoid the subject of philosophy, touching and retouching as it goes, in the assorted tableaux that the work lays before us for contemplation. The narrative, a rambling succession of episodes as plausible as they are absurd, is little more than a pretext for a practical philosophy, an approach that, by setting systems back to back, sets out to condemn prejudice, stupidity, small-mindedness, and injustice. The preceding episode sweeps any notion of providence overboard. Later, we encounter another, equally efficacious example: Candide's celebrated response to a Black slave whose hand has been cut off because he lost a finger in a sugar-crusher, his leg amputated for attempting to flee the plantation: "This is the price paid for the sugar you eat in Europe" (152). These are shocking words indeed, among the most appalling in the book. In one cutting phrase they encapsulate black slavery, white brutality, exploitation, colonialism, inequality, and, precociously, all the cruelty inherent in globalized trade. Everything is said in twelve words, with crystal clarity. No high-minded theory can add an iota of truth to a stunning accusation that resonates with us just as clearly as if it were describing our own age. And yet it is only a claim, one that tersely sums up an injustice whose roots and explanation Candide makes no attempt to determine. We eat sugar at the expense of the Blacks: a sinister commonplace that seems no more than the inevitable outcome of the very history that condemns the weak to toil for the mighty.

So, here we have a narrator who grants himself full license to relate the sound and the fury of the world in a series of breathtaking short cuts through which he flits with all the agility of a goatherd gamboling along precipitous paths to the sound of his pipe. In the age-old battle between philosophy and fable, Voltaire (whom I am obliged to reintroduce here) has chosen sides. The author of *The Philosophical Dictionary* turns the accusation on its head: fiction now points the finger of accusation at the discourse of truth; turning the Platonic warning on its head, fable lashes out at philosophy's illusions and duplicity. Voltaire is clearly not interested in *proving* that the world is going badly. Not only does he need no proof, others before him have made it, though perhaps with less verve. No, his verve is pointed less at the world, less against the progress to which he means to contribute by his thought, but aimed instead at philosophy that, in presenting our world as the best of all possible worlds, effectively discourages any attempt to change it. Nothing in the tale, however, rallies us to fight against demoralization, nothing points in a particular direction, no matter how approximate, that would allow us to so much as contemplate overcoming it. The invitation to cultivate our garden offers one, narrow perspective: withdrawal to the inner reaches of a world that remains irremediably and inexplicably evil.

Turning fiction against philosophy may seem to be inconsequential, superficial, or insubstantial. It is none of the above. It is, in fact, thought's deep-seated revolt against itself, expressed with a malicious delight whose destructive power may well have partially escaped its author. This destructive power it draws from the fact that thought's revolt against itself creates no thought. The most destructive aspect of the human desolation through which Candide wanders is not the state of the world in and of itself, which is depicted in a form so exaggerated, so caricatured that it has lost its sting; it is the inability to conceive of another world—with the exception of Eldorado. The inability to postulate anything but the unattainable brings us face to face with a here-and-now that is unthinkable. The episode of the naval battle leaves the discussion, and the philosophy, precisely where they were before being interrupted by the roar of the cannon. Just as, at the very end, in an echo of this very immobility, Pangloss and Martin find themselves symbolically reunited in the garden they cultivate along with Candide, philosophical pessimism and optimism rub shoulders and neutralize one another as they do so. We wonder, worried, whether the task to which Candide has devoted himself is not, ultimately, an invitation to think no more about the world; an invitation to be content with the unexamined present.

It is impossible to overlook the fact that a philosopher, or at least a thinker, has taken as his subject the inanity of philosophy. In the tale, that inanity finds its fullest expression among those who practice the philosopher's trade and provides, in fact, the substance of the "Conclusion" (the title of the thirtieth and last chapter). For Martin, "firmly convinced that people are equally uncomfortable everywhere," such a conclusion is self-evident; there is nothing new about the resolve to accept "things patiently" (185). But for Dr. Pangloss, the confession that he had "always suffered horribly" should have lead him to re-examine his incorrigible optimism; "but having once maintained that everything was for the best, he had continued to maintain it without believing it" (186). In the final analysis, Pangloss is not lacking lucidity; quite simply, he lacks an alternative.

Ensnared in a philosophical impasse of their own making, Candide, Martin, and Pangloss make one last attempt:

> In the neighborhood there lived a very famous Dervish, who was supposed to be the best philosopher in Turkey; they went to consult him; Pangloss was the spokesman and said: "Master, we have come to beg you to tell us why so strange an animal as man was ever created." "What has it to do with you?" said the Dervish. "Is it your business?" "But, reverend father," said Candide, "there is a horrible amount of evil in the world." "What does it matter," said the Dervish, "whether there is evil or good? When his highness sends a ship to Egypt, does he worry about the comfort or discomfort of the rats in the ship?" "Then what should we do?" said Pangloss. "Hold your tongue," said the Dervish. (187)

Pangloss wishes to continue the discussion, but the Dervish slams the door in their faces. Meanwhile, the news has been bruited about in Constantinople: two viziers and the mufti have been strangled, and several of their friends impaled. Our boon companions attempt to learn their names from a friendly old man "taking the air under a bower of orange trees at his door" (187):

> "I do not know," replied the old man. "I have never known the name of any mufti or of any vizier. I am entirely ignorant of the occurrence you mention; I presume that in general those who meddle with public affairs sometimes perish miserably, and that they deserve it; but I never inquire what is going on in Constantinople; I content myself with sending there for sale the produce of the garden I cultivate. Having spoken thus he took the strangers into his house."
> [They are served sherbets, candied fruit, and other delicacies.]
> "You must have a vast and magnificent estate?" said Candide to the Turk. "I have only twenty acres," replied the Turk. "I cultivate them with my children; and work keeps at bay three great evils: boredom, vice and need." (187–188)

After philosophy's ultimate insult, wisdom stands revealed. The two episodes follow one another in rapid succession, blending into one another as if to suggest two complementary "lessons." The first is that philosophy has nothing more to say, ultimately, but "shut up." The second is that to involve oneself in matters of state is to expose oneself to the gravest danger, and often warrants well-deserved punishment. Let us live discreetly, far from the eyes of the powerful, and work only as much as we need in order to provide for our needs. "'Let us work without theorizing,' said Martin; ''tis the only way to make life endurable'" (188). His "without theorizing" dismisses Pangloss's exegetic effort, an attempt to justify by paraphrasing Genesis: "man was not born for idleness." Man's vocation for labor, which Pangloss suddenly attempts to ground in the Bible, has already been answered earlier on: worse than all the evils of the world is boredom. Work, for Martin, provides an answer to the two monsters, which like Scylla and Charybdis threaten humanity: "the convulsions of distress" or "the lethargy of boredom" (186).

Such are the outlines of the "philosophy" with which, for all the Dervish's insolence, and thanks to the kindly old man's example, our adventurers bring their tribulations to a close, as they resolve to live peaceably from the fruits of their garden plot. All of which enables Pangloss to point out (ironically?) to Candide that:

> "All events are linked up in this best of all possible worlds;
> for, if you had not been expelled from the noble castle, [a short list
> of his misfortunes follows here] you would not be eating candied
> citrons and pistachios here." "That's well said," said Candide, "but
> we must cultivate our garden." (189)

So ends the tale, with the self-assured repetition of an injunction that has since become a proverb.

While Pangloss indeed speaks with all the sincerity of a German philosopher, upholding *in extremis* his (putatively) Leibnizian optimism, his seriousness rings hollow with irony under the narrator's mocking pen. What remains to be seen is whether the same irony can also be applied to the kitchen garden that Candide and his companions seem so self-satisfied to cultivate. The reader must make up his mind. In taking leave of him at the entrance to his own garden, the narrator enjoins him, in one manner or another, to meditate, and, as a first step, to reflect on the nature of the row he has been invited to hoe.

Each of us is free to give the answer that suits him best. But whatever that answer, we can agree that Voltaire's garden is not a political one. Whether we take it literally or (cumulatively) as a metaphor for the ego, for the inner world, the family, for a circle of friends, the immediate neighborhood (village, locality, municipality), for his enterprise, the garden, in all cases, stands as the antithesis of the public good, involvement with which can, as we have seen, put our lives quite frankly at risk. Nor are "public affairs" from which, if we are to take the kindly old man's advice, it would be wise to abstain precisely equivalent to the public good. "Affairs" refers instead to their negation. To be involved in affairs, in politics, is not exactly to demonstrate concern for the public good. Before us lies the entire distinction, so fundamental in Plato, between partisan politics and the politics conceived as pursuit of the common good. While it is impossible to tell if Voltaire is making the same distinction (with or without the help of the Platonic dialogues), he is clearly urging us to mistrust power, those who wield it, or believe they wield it. Indeed, all of *Candide*, from the first line to the last, unfolds in a world bereft of any concern for the common good. The very notion that such a thing might exist is resoundingly conspicuous by its absence. In this world—politically speaking—only power exists: power that manifests itself, at all times and in all circumstances, by its abuse.

Except in Eldorado. An admission is in order: politics as devotion to the common good, whose radical absence I have just underlined, is wholly incarnate in that ideal land. But we know that this land is even more illusory, more chimerical than Candide's love for Cunegonde. Eldorado is nothing but the invert caricature of the world, setting itself up in parenthetic removal from it, as something inaccessible. By virtue of the simple fact that everything there is for the best, that everything proceeds smoothly, the question of politics simply does not arise. Had we had any lingering doubts, it is surely enough to refer back to the words of an old man from Eldorado, spoken in the course of a short summary of his country's religion: "here we are all of the same opinion" (148). In this utopian portrait, which must rank among the most insignificant ever presented in European literature, that kind of comment should send a chill down our spine, alongside the following, which may be derived from it. Candide is speaking to his manservant Cacambo.

> "If we remain here, we shall only be like everyone else; but if we return to our own world with only twelve sheep laden with Eldorado pebbles, we shall be richer than all the kings put together; we shall have no more Inquisitors to fear and we can easily regain Mademoiselle Cunegonde." (150)

It is not enough to conclude, along with the narrator, that "these two happy men resolved to be so no longer" (150). Eldorado is, after all, an anti-world that is nowhere to be found, a world—we cannot repeat it often enough—our adventurers can attain and where they can reside in their dreams alone. What we do have is the expression of an irrepressible attraction—in addition to Candide's love for Cunegonde—for wealth, its display, and the inequality it legitimizes; the craving to amass private goods to mind-boggling heights (higher than that of all kings), in total disregard for the common good. The dream of Eldorado does not give Candide, obsessed by his desire to *regain* Cunegonde, the slightest nostalgia for as much as the merest possibility of a common good. At the heart of a country that so harmoniously expresses the common good, the only goods that interest him (Cunegonde included) are private. In other words, the common good is pure illusion. It would be no overstatement to conclude that Candide shares, however guilelessly, in the very human rapacity against which Eldorado has so miraculously protected itself. So much so, in fact, that cultivation of his garden might well be interpreted (I insist on *might well*) as fulfilling, on a small scale, the aspiration to private possession. Minus the accumulation. The distinction is by no means a small one.

By cultivating his garden, Candide not only turns his back on his dreams of luxury and grandeur, he turns over the soil, meager though it may be, of a tiny parcel of this world, his own, whose immense bleakness he has had ample occasion to measure. In a world abundantly depicted as unjust, the total absence of the politics of the common good has reduced it to that. Injustice is such—omnipresent, redundant, and repetitive—that it conceals all other worlds than its own. The world is a surface eroded by oppression, by human iniquity and imbecility. Politics cannot survive the forces of erosion; neither Candide nor anyone else even bothers to think politically. No more so in Eldorado than anywhere else. His journey to this tiny, never-to-be-found world thus assumes another, broader significance: *Eldorado, in its perfect unreality, is the sign of the equal unreality of the wholly evil world of which it is the negative image.* That is to say, this entirely evil world has no greater reality than the entirely good one. In the final analysis, *Candide* does not paint a picture of the world; it carries us away to the utopia of evil: precisely the utopia in which Candide resolves to cultivate his garden.

That changes everything. To cultivate one's garden can no longer have any philosophical consequences in a fictitious world, that is to say, in a world given over to perfect randomness. As an activity it has forfeited all value, all wisdom. And yet, in the fiction of this entirely evil world, no other attitude is possible. Whether the world be fictitious or unlivable, or even should it be both at once, it cannot be lived in; the only solution is to seek refuge in oneself. The narrator has yanked away the ladder, and abandoned us, scratching our heads, in the garden of his tale, which in turn has all the appearance of impossibility.

5

JACQUES THE FATALIST:
FICTITIOUS FREEDOM

HOW ABRUPTLY IT BEGINS:

How had they met? By chance, like everybody else. What were
their names? What's it to you? Where were they coming from?
From the nearest place. Where were they going? Does anyone really know where they're going? What were they saying? The *Master*
wasn't saying anything, and *Jacques* was saying that his Captain
used to say that everything that happens to us here below, for good
and for ill, was written up there, on high.

Master: That's saying a lot.

Jacques: My Captain also used to say that every bullet shot out of
the barrel of a rifle had its billet.

Master: And he was quite right.

After a brief pause Jacques exclaimed: "The innkeeper and his inn
can go to hell!"

Master: Why would you want to see a fellow man consigned to
Hell? It's not Christian.

Jacques: Because while I'm getting drunk on his rotgut wine, I
forget to water the horses. My father notices. He gets angry. I shrug
my shoulders at him. He picks up a stick and lays it across my
shoulders a touch hard. A regiment was passing on its way to camp
at Fontenoy. I enlist out of pique. We reach our destination and
battle commences ...

Master: ... and you stop the bullet that's got your name on it.

Jacques: You guessed. Got it in the knee, and God knows what adventures, happy and unhappy, followed that shot. They all hang together exactly like the links in a chain, no more and no less. For instance, if it hadn't been for that shot, I don't think I'd ever have fallen in love, or walked with a limp.

Master: So you've been in love?

Jacques: Have I been in love!

Master: And all on account of a shot from a rifle?

Jacques: All on account of a shot from a rifle.

Master: You never mentioned it before.

Jacques: No, I don't think I did.

Master: Why was that?

Jacques: Because it could not have been said before nor after this moment.

Master: And that moment has now come and you can speak of being in love?

Jacques: Who can tell?

Master: Take a chance. Make a start.

Jacques began to tell the story of his loves. It was after lunch. The weather was sultry. His Master nodded off. Night came upon them in the middle of nowhere: they were lost. The Master fell into a terrible rage and freely set about his servant with a whip and the poor devil said at every thwack: "That one was apparently written up there too … "

You see, Reader, I'm into my stride and I have it entirely in my power to make you wait a year, two years, three years, to hear the story of Jacques's love affairs, by separating him from his Master, and making the both of them undergo all the perils I please. What's to prevent me marrying off the Master, and telling you how his wife deceived him? or making Jacques take ship for the Indies? and sending his Master there? or bringing both of them back to France on the same vessel? How easy it is to make up stories! But I'll let them off lightly with an uncomfortable night, and you with this delay. (3–4)[20]

In two brief pages the characters are established: the Master, Jacques, the captain, the horses, the father, the Devil, God, the narrator and the reader.

20. Denis Diderot, *Jacques the Fatalist and His Master*, translated and with an introduction and notes by David Coward (Oxford: Oxford University Press, 1999).

And with them, the principal elements of existence: chance, necessity, narrative, wine, oblivion, religion, wandering, subordination and domination, war, wounds, love. With one blow—struck by a bullet, then by lightning—our hero is first crippled, and then falls in love. The opening sets the tone and establishes the style: seamlessly, without transition, the story shifts from one narrator to another, changing place, time, and register at will. The reader has been warned: everything has been decided beforehand, nothing will take place according to expectations; the narrator will do exactly as he pleases.

At first glance, *Jacques the Fatalist and His Master* is a cock-and-bull story. The effect of surprise springs from its disjointed, syncopated composition, of course; but it can also be traced to the erasure, by habit and sloth, of the strangeness that permeates the novels that inspired it. Since we no longer read Rabelais and Cervantes with the freshness they deserve, Diderot's tale—because it is less well known—is more disorienting, more disconcerting than its models. Unlike Panurge and Sancho Panza, Jacques the Fatalist has not been worn down by fame. The public knows little of Jacques, for the excellent reason that he is merely a Jacques, a peasant without a patronymic dignified by anything more than a valet's stature, who serves a master so commonplace that the narrator cannot be bothered to name him. Despite a handful of bravura passages, valet and master, taken together with the same anonymity, are as un-heroic as possible, taking after Sterne's[21] characters in *Tristram Shandy*, from which Diderot has in part borrowed both the intrigue and the apparent disorganization.

Jacques the Fatalist startles us not only by its structure, which is not quite as new as it seems at first glance (*Tristram Shandy* caused a sensation, and spawned numerous imitations), but, even more surprisingly, by its place in the literary canon. Or rather, the lack of same! What is truly striking is that an attempted destabilization of such magnitude—Sterne's like Diderot's—has had so little impact on the evolution of Western literature, that it did not simply kill off the modern novel. Where Cervantes declares war on the knightly romance, Diderot seems intent on undermining the very idea of the novel.

No only is the narrator not writing a novel, he insists; no, he rails against the discretionary power that the novelist he refuses to be continues to wield. For if the story of his travels keeps veering off into the ditch, it can only be

---

21. *The Life and Opinions of Tristram Shandy, Gentleman*, by Laurence Stern (born in 1713, the same year as Diderot, but dead well before him, in 1768), was published from 1759 to 1767 in nine successive books. *Jacques le fataliste et son maître* was probably written between 1773 and 1775, and circulated during Diderot's lifetime in serial form to subscribers of the *Correspondance littéraire*. It appeared in book form for the first time in French (a German translation was published in 1793) only in 1796. The plot borrowed from Sterne appears in Book VIII of *Tristram Shandy*.

because the narrator has decided that it will do so. "No!" interjects Jacques; the book has been "written higher up"; the narrator can do nothing about it. As for the journey, the tale is a catalog of the unexpected. On principle, our two happy wanderers have no idea where they are going, nor do they proceed as they wish. It is not the tale of their adventures that is being told, but that of Jacques's loves. Those he is all too happy to relate to a listener who is equally happy to listen, but who is being constantly interrupted by his misplaced curiosity and the contingencies of the road. The narrative, in fact, threatens to end before the valet can finish telling his story. Yet these inter-ruptions, observes Jacques as he catalogs the multitude of diversions that have lead him into his own amorous adventures, "all hang together exactly like the links in a chain" (3). They provide the raw material for all adven-tures, for all lives, the content of the "great scroll" where, on high, "every-thing was written at the same time" and "unrolls a bit at a time" (7).[22] The narrator is not quite the creator he pretends to be; he merely unravels the threads woven by fatality from time immemorial. So, when he first interrupts Jacques's narrative and informs us that it is up to him whether he dispatches the protagonists to the Caribbean and puts Jacques's love life on indefinite hold, the narrator is deceiving either himself or us. He boasts of a power that is not his.

Those would surely be his hero's feelings. The fatalist is Jacques, after all; we know nothing whatsoever of the narrator's philosophy. On several occasions he insists that he has contradicted his character's determinism. Yet the narrator has no scruples about sitting in for fate, or about sight-reading its score, all the while insisting how easy it is to do so, how easy to make such a reading. So great is his clairvoyance that it reaches into the reader's soul: "I also think I sense that you're not too happy with this, Buger. I can't think why. It was the real name of my wheelwright's family. Their records of baptism, death certificates, and marriage lines are all made out in the name of Buger. Buger's descendants, who still occupy his premises today, are called Buger." (175) So saying, he flies off into an ironic tirade on the suit-ability or unsuitability of a proper name, based on the quality—illustrious or obscure—of the person who bears it. The power of a name like Caesar or Pompey is, in the final analysis, as ridiculous as the "dogs called Pompey" the "streets are full of" (175–176). Everything is a matter of perspective, a question of codes, and, like the great names, the narrator's omniscience,

---

22. Barbara K. Toumarkine writes in the introduction to the French edition: "The progression of Jacques the Fatalist takes place according to a systematic preference for sharp breaks. We can enumerate one hundred eighty of them for twenty-one distinct tales" (*Jacques le fataliste*, op. cit., p. 23). She also refers to: Erich Köhler, "L'unité structurale de *Jacques le fataliste*," *Philólogica Pragensia*, no. 13, 1970, pp. 186–202.

pressed into the service of fiction, stands revealed as futile, for "there's nothing easier than turning out a novel" (199). But we will never know with any certainty whether the creative intelligence that manipulates his characters like so many marionettes considers itself manipulated in turn by a hand high above his. He avoids saying so. The "power" he puts on display may well also be the illustration, if not the caricature, of the system so dear to his valet. One thing remains certain: the self-styled Master is master of nothing; he who pretends to be guided by fatality intends to become the master.

In fact, *Jacques the Fatalist* propounds a master-servant dialectic that may have inspired Hegel. The continuously interrupted narrative detailing the sequels of the bullet wound suffered by Jacques in the celebrated battle of Fontenoy ultimately reveals the object of his affections: a certain Denise (the feminine form of Diderot's first name), daughter of a certain Jeanne whom Jacques has rescued and who in turn rescues him, sending him to have his knee cared for by her daughter at the château where she is employed, which just happens to be the residence of an old friend of Jacques, Monsieur Desglands, Seigneur of Miremont, where the master had once been a guest, encountering there none other than Denise, a girl of remarkable beauty, coveted by all. "I and most of the men who ever stayed with Desglands all tried our damnedest to get her into bed but we never succeeded" (139). A bitter confession: the valet has succeeded where he had failed, and the master must accept the fact:

> *Master*: Anyway, Jacques, so there you are under Desglands's roof, Denise is within reach, and Denise has been authorized by her mother to come to your room at least four times a day. The trollop! To think she would go for someone like Jacques!
>
> *Jacques*: Someone like Jacques? I'll have you know, sir, that a Jacques is much a man as the rest.
>
> *Master*: You're wrong, Jacques. A Jacques isn't as much a man as the rest.
>
> *Jacques*: Sometimes he's better than the rest.
>
> *Master*: Jacques, you're getting above yourself. Just get on with the story of your love-life, and remember that you are not and never will be anything but a Jacques.
>
> *Jacques*: When we were at the inn where we encountered the bandits, if Jacques hadn't been a bit more of a man than his Master …
>
> *Master*: Jacques, don't be impertinent. You're taking advantage of my good nature. If I was fool enough to promote you above your

station, I can easily demote you again. Now, pick up your bottle and your tea-kettle, Jacques, and betake yourself off below stairs.

Jacques: You can say what you please, sir, but I'm very happy here. I'm not going anywhere.

Master: You will go below stairs, I tell you.

Jacques: I'm sure you don't really mean this, sir. What! After accustoming me these past ten years to living with you as your companion on an equal footing ...

Master: I've decided to put a stop to all that.

Jacques: After putting up with all my cheek ...

Master: I won't put up with it any more.

Jacques: After seating me next to you at table and calling me your friend ...

Master: You don't understand the meaning of the word friend when it is used by a superior to his inferior.

Jacques: When everybody knows that your orders are like wind in a chimney until they've been confirmed by Jacques, when your name has been so closely linked with mine that the one is inseparable from the other and everybody always says "Jacques and his Master," after all that, you suddenly want to uncouple them! No, sir, it can't be done. It is written on high that so long as Jacques shall live, so long as his Master shall live, and even after they're both dead, people will go on saying "Jacques and his Master."

Master: And I'm telling you, Jacques, you will go downstairs and you will go now, because I'm ordering you to.

Jacques: If you want me to obey you, sir, order me to do something else.

At this point, Jacques's Master got to his feet, grabbed Jacques by the lapels, and said grimly: "Go!"

Jacques answered coolly:

"I'm not going."

His Master shook him hard and said:

"Shift your bones you insolent dog! Do what I tell you!"

Jacques, more coolly still, replied:

"Call me an insolent dog if you like, but this is one insolent dog who isn't going anywhere. Listen, sir, my legs, as they say, don't always do what my head tells them to. You're getting all worked up for nothing. Jacques will stay where he is and won't go down the stairs."

Then Jacques and his Master, having remained relatively calm up to this point, both fly off the handle at the same time and start yelling:

"Get downstairs!"

"I won't!"

"You shall!"

"Shan't!"

Hearing the hullabaloo, the landlady came up and asked whatever was the matter. (141–143)

The argument turns nasty in the presence of the landlady who, with the agreement of the two disputants, contrives to set herself up as arbiter. In one stroke she abolishes the equality that had grown up between master and servant, only to re-establish it immediately. Jacques goes downstairs, then comes right back up. No sooner has Jacques, escorted by the landlady, crossed the threshold, than his master rushes to embrace him—and restrain him. The valet seizes the opportunity and imposes a treaty confirming the nature of their relationship. Its two clauses are: (1) considering that the master cannot manage without his valet, the latter shall abuse his advantage "each and every time the opportunity arises"; (2) considering the reality of the balance of power and the futility of opposing "the rule of necessity," the Master shall enjoy the title, and the valet, the thing itself.

Master: So by your reckoning, your lot is preferable to mine?

Jacques: Who's arguing?

Master: But by your reckoning, I should take your place and put you in mine.

Jacques: If you did, do you know what would happen? You'd lose the name and you wouldn't get the thing. So let's stay as we are—we're both pretty well off the way things stand—and let's spend the rest of our lives creating a new proverb.

Master: What proverb's that?

Jacques: "Jacques leads his Master." We shall be the first it's said about, though it will thereafter be said of many others who are better men than we are.

Master: That seems very hard to me, very hard.

> *Jacques*: Sir, my dear Master, knock your head against a brick wall for long enough and it will fall on you. SO, that's what's been agreed between us.
>
> *Master*: But does a law that is necessary require our consent?
>
> *Jacques*: Of course. Don't you think it would be helpful to know once and for all, to be sure and certain exactly where we stand? (146)

There is something manifestly absurd, as the Master quite correctly points out, in wishing to draw up a hierarchy in the mastery of events, given that their course totally escapes our control. Man, after all, is not free: he is not free to act other than as if he were! Believing himself free to act, for man, is an integral part of that which determines who he is. If man did not entertain such beliefs, he would be something else; he would not be man. Absent such a belief, there would be no responsibility, no science, no social order, no hierarchy, no conflict, no battle of Fontenoy, no wound, and no love. And, maybe even no narrative.

What fascinates us most about the novel (especially the adventure novel) is that we do not know how it will end. At the very least, we do not know what will happen to the protagonists even though we already know or intuit the end; we believe that its characters can react in different ways, and make choices. If there were only a single avenue open, no one would go on reading. What keeps the reader turning the pages of *Jacques the Fatalist*, narrative twists and turns aside, is the desire to know whether Jacques will attain his goal, whether he will see his story through to the end, and, most of all, whether he will conquer his heart's desire. All of these things do happen, we know. But we don't know if we will find out how they happen, just as Jacques has no idea, at the time, just where the innkeeper's rotgut wine, or the caprice that made him enlist will lead him. Jacques himself may well, following along in the trajectory of the bullet that wounded him at Fontenoy, transform into some kind of *ex post facto* necessity the course that leads him zigzagging into the arms of the lovely Denise: for he knows how the story has turned out thus far. Unsurprisingly, the narrative transforms all that constitutes it into necessity. But when the bullet strikes him, Jacques knows nothing of the "billet"[23] that comes with it. The happenings of daily life are experienced discretely, part of the invisible and unforeseeable succession of events that produces them; only after the fact are they incorporated into the narrative

---

23. Let us recall that at the beginning of the narrative Jacques repeats a celebrated sentence from *Tristram Shandy*: "My Captain also used to say that every bullet shot out of the barrel of a rifle had its billet."

chain. The narrative itself is revealed as the creative force; determinism can exist only in the past; only through narrative does it become necessity.

The conclusion is unavoidable: the true and only master is the narrator. Jacques is no more the master of his tale than of his fate. Even though he mouths nothing but nonsense, only the narrator can expose him for the liar he is. Thus, the *thing* that Jacques claims—whose title he leaves to his master—is, in the light of his own philosophy, nothing but an empty shell. By his own admission, Jacques no more possesses the thing than he does the title. The titled master and the "effective" master are both, on the same level, playthings of fate. In spite of that, if the valet acts as though he were free, and the master of his acts, it is only because, in the heat of action, he does not know how everything will turn out. In him, the will to act becomes one, semiconsciously, with the will to know. Jacques lives his life in the same way that we read his adventures: to learn how they take place—rather than to find out how they reach their ineluctable conclusion. For, even though we might not wish to know anything about it, we all know the ultimate end that gives our lives meaning. The one thousand and one twists and turns of existence all converge upon the same point. But from this very fatality emerges something resembling another kind of freedom. Death's ineluctability, which is the same for all, lends life's ups and downs a remarkable gratuitousness.

Here lies the narrator's liberty. We need no longer know whether or not the teller of the tale espouses or opposes the philosophy of his creature, Jacques, nor should we be surprised that he feels no need to make up his mind. We know only that the end is the same for all, as the bullet whose trajectory begins the narrative indirectly but unequivocally confirms. The bullet that hits Jacques strikes him in only the knee. One day the *billet*, in whatever form, will take his life. Meanwhile, we are perfectly free to improvise. The narrator's power is the power of invention.

And yet the narrator inflicts upon his reader a noteworthy paradox: he employs his total freedom to narrate fatality. The fatal bullet, and the wound that it causes, resonates with the ball that strikes Gulliver in the knee at the end of his last voyage, leading to the equally fatal wound of love. Fatality, wounds, and love seem inextricably linked. All for the best, or so it would appear: Jacques finally marries Denise and fathers her children. Yet their happiness is fragile; he cannot help wondering, like Panurge, if one fine day his wife may not cuckold him with his master or with the appropriately-named Desglands, for neither has given up the idea of seducing her. But he throws himself at the feet of chance: "If it is written on high that she will be unfaithful, then whatever you do to prevent it, Jacques, unfaithful she will be.

If on the other hand it is written on high that she will not be unfaithful, then whatever they do to make it happen, unfaithful she will not be. Go to sleep, friend" (240), and he nods off.

But this happy ending is only one of the three versions provided by the publisher, based on certain memoirs that the narrator has "good reason to believe are highly suspect" (237). The narrator, meanwhile, turns his attention to his master's deplorable murder of a "friend" who had earlier and egregiously misled him in his amorous affairs, and whom he unexpectedly encounters at journey's end. His master having taken flight, Jacques is left to the tender mercies of the law, which dispatches him to prison. "And there I shall call it a day," concludes the narrator, "because I've told you everything I know about my two characters. 'But what about Jacques's love life?' Look, Jacques said over and over that it was written on high that he'd never finish the tale, and I now see that he was right" (236). At which point he invites the reader, angered by this latest interruption, to continue the story as the spirit moves him, or to carry out an investigation to find Jacques in the tedium of his cell, and ask him the questions that he will be only too happy to answer.

The narrator is thus urging us to continue, to invent, to become creative intelligence in our own right, to decide Jacques's fate. At the same time he is asking us whether, at the end of the day (and at the end of the tale), the bullet that struck him at Fontenoy has found a good or a bad billet. As if to say that each man's fate remains indecipherable until his dying breath, and the question of free will shall remain forever suspended. The narrator makes every effort to avoid drawing conclusions; no longer the creative spirit/demiurge that he claimed to be throughout the story, he now attempts to pass himself off as a mere purveyor of information. Scrupulous reporter that he is, suddenly he refuses to do anything more than convey what he knows, virtuously refusing to extrapolate beyond what Jacques himself relates. But in handing narrative responsibility over to the reader, he also yields to him his power: a gift that is in itself a creative act. For the narrator ultimately decides to have Jacques imprisoned, and to leave his unfinished narrative in our hands.

Up until the very end, the narrator continues to contradict himself, allowing a fundamental ambiguity about the nature of his role to arise: is he servant or master of the narrative? Either the narrator is the supreme manipulator of his characters, all of whom are subordinated to his free will, absurd in their pretension to be the masters of anything whatsoever, to seek to protect or to alter their social standing; or the narrator is himself the accurate and exacting historian, at the service of his creation Jacques, led along by him like his master, that is to say, as suggested by the philosophy of his eponymous protagonist who is subject, like everyone else, to the fatality that governs his narration. His demiurgic pretensions are little more than empty boasts, in the image of the character fate has bestowed upon him: despite his claims, he could tell no other tale. Once more, the boundaries of the alternative remain blurred, for though it is possible that the universe is fundamentally predetermined, it is also certain that it remains perfectly unpredictable.

Whether our lives are predetermined or not ultimately matters little. More importantly, the nature of the question itself opens up infinite spaces to our powers of imagination. It is far easier, after all, to change the course of a work of fiction than to give direction to our lives and shape the course of events. Behind the idea of the inevitable, and through the narration of the contingent, the narrative stands forth as the only eventual locus—let us call it the least improbable locus—of human liberty. With a subtlety that makes our heads spin, Diderot probes deeply into the very thing that makes it possible for us to stay alive: the freedom to tell the tale. Even if this freedom were perfectly illusory, we would still find in narrative a capacity for invention that would most surely join forces with whatever of our free will remains. What appears at first glance to be the death of the novel opens it instead to infinite possibility. Imagination is inexhaustible. The narrative tradition has proclaimed it for centuries; *Jacques the Fatalist* reaffirms it in the most exhilarating, most striking, most joyous way.

Such liberty can be carried to extremes, much further than in life itself, which it knows so little of. The baseness, the sordidness, the sleaziness that we would not dare admit to in our own lives flourish in the novel, and the reader—who has just been delighted by the daringly explicit scene in which Jacques has his way with someone else's lady-friend—would be ill-advised to criticize its narrator for his salacious anecdotes. In fact, he forgives him; more than that, in the classics, in Horace, in Juvenal, or La Fontaine he delights in them without reservation, for the best authors enchant their readers with all that they touch. As for the bad writers, no one will read them and they will do no harm. So, even though "Jacques is a tasteless mishmash of things that happen, some of them true, others made up, written without style and served up like a dog's breakfast" (185), the reader has nothing to complain about:

> I rather enjoy—pausing to change the names—writing down
> the stupid things you do. Your follies make me laugh, but what I
> write offends you. To be perfectly frank, Reader, I'd say that of the

two of us the more unkind is not me. I'd be only too happy if it were as easy for me to defend myself against aspersions as it is for you to defend yourself against being bored or imperiled by my book. Just leave me alone, you miserable hypocrites. Carry on fucking like rabbits, but you've got to let me say fuck: I grant you the action and you let me have the word. (185)

The narrator is not as innocent as he claims, and it is not at all inconsequential that the word and the thing itself trade accusations—object and word in the strictest sense. Above and beyond the power that it bodies forth in the work of fiction, liberty, whatever its metaphysical status, which remains by definition indefinable, cannot but infect the desire to act and to think. "To speak is to do," Lacan would later declare. The invention of liberty leads to action, and, even more, to the thought of action. It is political. To think is to act, to refuse to submit. I believe I can discern at work here a kind of mirthful answer to the resignation that ends in Candide's perpetual gloom, the moroseness that pervades Gulliver's final return. Not without good reason, nor without nostalgia does the narrator refer his reader to Rabelais's Holy Bottle and "those truly inspired by the gourd" of centuries past (187). The fatality of misfortune does not govern the world, for misfortune in the form of the famous bullet—ultimately the effect of rotgut wine—leads to a happy outcome, even though happiness remains fragile, transitory, and, at tale's end, in the most literal sense, inexpressible. Unspoken at least, as the narrator has set aside his narration, relating instead the ending as a battery of hypotheses, contriving to say, in one final pirouette, what he does not tell!

The choice of the knee is no less a political one. The reference to Gulliver seems crystal clear. Inescapably the wound, which is hidden and mortal in the case of Gulliver, becomes open and life-giving in the case of Jacques: a subtle and malicious rejoinder to Swiftian pessimism. We must remember that Gulliver returns home against his will, having been driven from the land of his dreams, and bearing an invisible incision of the kind that is inflicted on horses to eliminate them discreetly from the running: a spiritual flaw that makes it impossible for him to return in full to human society. With Jacques, his master and his narrator, there is no spiritual nostalgia, no broken dream; we never leave dry land. The horses are real, as opposed to Gulliver's fabulous Houyhnhnms. They are horses that, in spite of themselves, act as mounts, as facilitators, as warners. One of them is even entrusted with a false message.

One of the adventures of *Jacques and His Master* hangs on a case of horse theft that leads to the purchase of a rather worrisome replacement, a steed bizarrely determined to lead its rider, Jacques, to the foot of a gibbet. The scene is repeated several times creating an altogether sinister premonitory effect (true enough, through no fault of his own, Jacques will go to prison but not to the gallows). Finally, in an aside, we learn that that particular horse until recently belonged to a hangman who, being a good loser, will ultimately recover it. The ominous presage is revealed for what it is: a habit. And so, things return to the order of the comprehensible. Horses are not exceptional beings, and all forms of magic have their explanation. To ignore our fate is one thing, to believe that it may be governed by sinister, incomprehensible forces is another. Once again, liberty must be learned: all that is incomprehensible and strange, like all that is miraculous, derives from our ignorance alone. Our unwarranted fear of the supernatural must not keep us from acting. Though ignorance may guide it, all action, as its consequences evolve, becomes thinkable.

Decidedly *Jacques the Fatalist* provides a paradoxical lesson in liberty. Because we do not know what will become of us, because the supernatural no longer determines the process of becoming, we are free to act. Free, but without knowing the effect of our liberty: such is our fate. Fatality only acts in our stead, only ultimately exercises its tyranny if we abandon to it the entire field of our imagination. To paraphrase the celebrated maxim attributed to William of Orange, it can be said that there is no need to know the result of our acts in order to begin an undertaking, nor need we confirm their rightness in order to persevere. Is this the morality of irresponsibility? No, true irresponsibility would be to refuse the consequences of our acts without reflecting on them, to ignore the ignorance that governs them. But everything in Jacques's attitude tends toward acceptance of that ignorance and leads him to reflect upon its implications. Only such acceptance makes it possible to act freely, or, to put it more precisely, *gratuitously*, for the pleasure of experiencing the unexpected. Formulated in slightly anachronistic terms, the liberty to which the narrator summons us would be the liberty to yield to the movement of our subconscious without fear of the perils of the world, as both our subconscious and the world contrive to divert us from what we believe to be our path. *Jacques the Fatalist* sketches out the idea of a kind of liberty that has already distanced itself from that of the classic Kantian subject. The subject does not possess the freedom to dispose of his acts as granted by the law; he benefits, in Derrida's words, from a "certain space" left by the indeterminate nature of "the one who or which comes."[24] Such a weak, contingent conception of the subject is sharply at odds with the

24. Jacques Derrida, *For What Tomorrow: a dialogue / Jacques Derrida and Elisabeth Roudinesco*, trans. Jeff Fort (Stanford: Stanford University Press, 2004).

one that, in Diderot's day, dominated Enlightenment philosophy: that of a subject in full control of itself, called upon to master nature; quite the opposite, it foreshadows what today we would call deconstruction.

Consigning our wanderings, our illusions and our delights to narrative has become the most satisfying, the most joyful way for us to possess, after the fact, whatever has struck us, escaped us, astonished us. We are only free in relation to the past, but thus liberated we can confront the unforeseen, and experience the present moment more fully.

6

SADE:
ABSOLUTE LICENCE

THE THINKING SUBJECT OF THE CARTESIAN NARRATIVE, whose moral unity Kant struggles to preserve amid the ruins of metaphysics, begins to crack beneath the hammer blows of the licentious libertine. The Marquis de Sade posits nature as a vital force, which no one can resist with impunity, without either damaging or diminishing himself. His thought is widely said to be abyssal. We shall soon see that the abyss in question is, strictly speaking, bottomless.

The character of Don Juan has given us a magisterial introductory lesson in amorous liberty. A lover of life as much as of women, he practices seduction while never taking sensual pleasure in its object. As against Don Juan's preening and strutting, Sade's debauchery has a dismal, ominous aspect: sensual pleasure he may well experience, but he is incapable of seduction. Underneath his aristocratic veneer, he stands as the total, egotistical, bourgeois appropriation of the other in its most naked, most brutal form: a factory of individual licentiousness in its purest state. He is, beneath the gleam and glitter of the Ancien Régime of his style, fornication writ large, the subconscious will to banish absence, once and for all.

Philosophy in the Bedroom brings together two professionals in debauchery, Dolmance and Madame de Saint-Ange, who will be joined later by the latter's brother, the Chevalier de Mirvel. Their objective in meeting is to initiate a young girl of fifteen, Eugenie, into the facts of life. Outstanding in their pedagogical skills, Dolmance and Saint-Ange deliver an intensive course of instruction in which practice continually reinforces and illustrates theory. Their exceptionally gifted pupil rapidly passes through the paper-thin barrier of propriety, and gives free reign to nature with a vigor that fills her preceptors with admiration and delight. For they are merely revealing to Eugenie her own natural dispositions, releasing her from the prejudices that bind or hinder their complete and legitimate fulfillment. The course of study, advancing by stages, surpasses her initiators' expectations: not only does their pupil give herself gluttonously over to the lubricious exercises that Dolmance so masterfully orchestrates, but she is quick to spice them with her own fantasies. Surpassing the lessons of her instructors, she insists, as recompense for the ardor of her application, on their active complicity in inflicting mortal punishment upon her prim and prudish mother. Cruelty is as good as its word; practice will rise to the heady heights of theory. Having done everything she can to save her daughter from debauchery, Madame de Mistival undergoes, before the entire company, the unbending rigor of its law: raped front and rear by a valet whose virile member is infected by a virulent case of syphilis, her two orifices are then stitched up in such a way as to ensure that the poison within her "will more promptly cinder her bones" (363).[25] In vain the chevalier, who would advocate a less cruel form of libertinage, attempts to temper the impact of Dolmance's rhetoric upon Eugenie: the young girl is too well-born not to hear in all its vitality the voice of nature, which the implacable philosophy of "the most corrupt, the most dangerous man" (*Philosophy*, 191) causes so effortlessly to prevail.

Little matter where the narrator's personal feelings may lie, nor what his imagination might owe to his lengthy imprisonment. All that matters is the inexorable logic that sweeps the initiate's convictions away and crowns her education. At first glance the logic is that of nature, the narrative's principal actress; Dolmance is but its spokesman and punctilious servant. But, clamor the objectors, we must reverse the terms. Is it not the libertine who bends nature to serve his ends? Can philosophy be anything more than a nasty varnish applied to the complacent display of all possible sexual deregulation? Let us presume nothing: only in the reading can the philosophical compass of this tale of sordid lubricity be established. Let us begin by taking Sade at his word, without flinching at the unbearable display of lust and of violence. For if we do not, there can be no asking why this philosophy lesson takes place in the bedroom.

Or, more properly, in the brothel. For it is there, in the sexual act in all its forms, that nature stands best revealed; it is there that, in orgiastic excess, it most powerfully discloses itself to its creatures. Not as reproductive power, the appendage of its destructive power; but as the capacity for sensual pleasure, of which reason can do no better than persuade us to use without limits.

25. The Marquis de Sade, *Justine, Philosophy in the Bedroom and other writings*, trans. Richard Seaver and Austryn Wainhouse (New York: Grove Press, n.d.), herein referred to as *Philosophy*.

The lesson of reason is that nature asks nothing of us; that we can, to the best of our abilities, ask everything of it. In its indifference to good and evil nature is an inexhaustible source of inspiration, of suffering and of gratification. We are free to choose. No other work invests nature with such ferocious neutrality as Sade's.

Classical European thought approaches nature in two ways: either as a more or less readable order to be decoded and respected—an order that underlies the concepts of science and natural law, that implies the existence of a form of transcendence whose concrete expression is nature, as in Descartes, and as a way of naming God, as in Spinoza; or as disorder (with or without a Creator, willed or non-willed by Him) upon which man must, if only for his own survival, place limits: the Hobbesian option. In either case nature has a sign, a positive or a negative. In Sade, nature has no sign, even though it nods toward man, enjoining him to seek sensual gratification. This injunction seems to attribute to nature a particular truth, but it is a truth offered neither as value, nor as knowledge to be attained, nor as harmony to be understood, and even less as a curse to be fought and resisted. Nature, in all its manifestations, is its own truth: its only intention is to be. Nature, reality and truth are one. Far from lamenting it, the Sadian hero, the libertine, the debauchee, takes full advantage of its indifference (in the fullest sense of the term) to act as he sees fit. In contradiction to Plato's teachings, wisdom consists of allowing one's inner nature to speak, whatever the consequences for oneself or for others; for passions and penchants can surge up from nowhere else but nature: all are legitimate. Dolmance's entire argument is predicated upon the idea that the only laws are those of a nature without finality, without conscience.

Unless we are to posit, in nature or outside of it, a general intention, the argument seems beyond challenge. But its infallibility rests on an altogether presumptuous postulate: that Dolmance knows the nature in whose name he speaks. Who could doubt that he knows his own, that he speaks of it all the more eloquently as he gives it free reign? But claim though he will that nature whispers in his ear and to all his senses, it will never be what he believes it to be, or what he wishes it to be, that is to say, his own nature. To others, nature may well "speak" in different ways. Dolmance implicitly admits as much: if, to use his own words, "we fuck because we are born to fuck" (*Philosophy*, 226), and if fucking is not necessarily directed to reproduction, then instead of fearing to violate them we should not hesitate "to contradict what fools call the laws of Nature" (*Philosophy*, 229). Once we have established that its laws can be foolishly interpreted, it should come as no surprise that Nature has, if not several voices, at least several ears. Dolmance will never be anything more than an interpreter; but an interpreter who believes himself qualified to speak in its name, which the narrator unhesitatingly invests with all his talent. If we wish to read Sade in all his power we must admit that, of all the characters of *Philosophy in the Bedroom*, Dolmance is his most articulate, most audacious spokesman.

What could be more logical, in fact, than to attempt to reap all life's possible pleasures? In the name of what must we repress in ourselves the propensity for sensual pleasure? Should not our sole duty be, contrariwise, to elevate by all possible means such pleasure to the highest degree of refinement and intensity with the greatest possible frequency, particularly in the area where it is most at home? That the pleasure *par excellence* be that of sex is easy enough to explain: it not only represents the register in which nature has concentrated its greatest power and demonstrated its greatest ingenuity; of all human activity, sexuality is the domain where pain is most likely pleasure's gain. To the dizzying confluence of sensual gratification and suffering is added the additional excitation of the awareness that one is breaking the strictest taboos: sodomy thus augments sexual intercourse, rape magnifies sodomy, incest amplifies rape; by this token there could be no loftier pleasure for an unscrupulous father than to abuse his child by ripping its anus.

Here lurks a paradox: the libertine draws greater pleasure still from what fools call evil, while he, the debauchee, rejects the very idea. Such an idea, which he judges to be useless, has nonetheless a powerful effect on him, if only by virtue of the fact that it is socially prevalent. The sensual gratification the libertine so assiduously cultivates is derived not only from Nature but also from everything that in society, and in its manners and customs, frustrates it. It is all the more piquant to observe Nature's laws in the knowledge that they contradict human morality and legislation—the well-known attraction of the forbidden fruit. But if the lubricious imagination is stimulated by contact with society, it can only flourish in the isolation of the bedroom or, as in *Justine*, as in *The 120 Days of Sodom*, in any other hermetically closed space, hideaway, château, or convent, from which nothing filters through to the outside, and where nothing can penetrate without the assent of the debauchees who govern it—as though the unspeakable, even when told as a tale, must be kept in a state of total secrecy, like the most dangerous criminals. The enjoyment of lust is therefore inconceivable in the state of nature, in that which Sade's century would call the wild world.

For all its claims to wildness, licentiousness cannot do without the civilization in whose midst it must conceal itself. Precisely because wildness lies within us, muzzled by education, the libertine finds such pleasure—or such rage—in releasing it. It is as if the search for pleasure knew instinctually how much it needed, in one form or another, the explosive charge of evil, the tamping—the repression—that multiplies its power; as if sexual liberty (like all liberty) could dream of itself in full-blown fury only when sequestered under lock and key. On the same order of ideas, negation and the enjoyment of evil are both inseparably essential to Sadian delinquency. He who negates crime delights in what he himself calls his scoundrel's nature. Far from being abolished, wickedness is a necessity; cruelty "a virtue and not a vice." But whatever Dolmance may claim, the cruelty of which he speaks, "simply the energy in a man civilization has not yet altogether corrupted" (130), cannot be virtuous from the standpoint of nature, but only by opposition to the social order that represses it.

Nature, the otherness of civilization and its codes, constructs itself in opposition to them, taking them as its fulcrum the better to take its distance from them. Nature is a purely theoretical concept, in the most literal sense: it speaks truth about the civilization it distinguishes itself from. It calls into radical question the arbitrariness of manners, customs, and laws. Though it may be impossible to agree upon a positive definition of nature as *reality* opposed to civilization, we must admit, along with Sade, that crime, cruelty, and licentiousness exist only for the latter. Whether or not nature exists, "crime against nature" is rigorously impossible. Either nature well and truly exists, in which case Sade is right in claiming that it's absurd to "imagine Nature having allowed the possibility of committing a crime that would outrage her" (*Philosophy*, 326); or Nature is a fictitious state, in which case the crimes that offend it are as inconsistent as it is. In both cases, "outrage against nature" is an invention of civilization, which, whatever else it may do, cannot return to a state it has no knowledge of, and which the existence of social relations, however minimal they might be, utterly contradict. In Sade, the heart of the matter is that social connections stand apart from the concept of nature as civilization's other. That exclusion robs them of all legitimacy, of all potentiality. In the Sadian concept of nature, there exists no ethic other than individual pleasure; the very foundations of political engagement vanish.

In theory the libertine, reason's hero, can play the entire field. That is his dream. Were it not for society and its rules, he would "really" be free to do so, that is to say, within the limits of the balance of brute force in which his acts take place. As it is true that, in a state of civilization, social constraint is often effective, he is justified in seeking to evade constraint to the greatest possible extent (another reason for the secrecy that surrounds places of torture and debauchery): he hardly cares that his dream may be a nightmare for his neighbor, as long as he can revel in it with impunity; cruelty is ample justification for the voluptuousness that it provides he who exerts it, "regardless of whether [his] proceedings please or displease the object" that serves him (*Philosophy*, 252). In any event, the exercise of reason is enough to convince him of his full moral liberty. Reason is the Sadian hero's decisive weapon.

Reason, whose torch Sade raises high, is that of his day and age, that of the Enlightenment, that of Kant (as Lacan clearly understood). We could define it as the faculty of properly guiding one's judgment, as prefigured earlier by Descartes. But there is a vital difference: Descartes locates its source in God. The possibility of such guidance depends on its first premises, beginning with methodical doubt, infallibly arriving at the conviction that truth (or God) exists. Enlightenment Reason introduces a critical break: forgoing the relationship with God, it affirms that science must be postulated outside this relationship. Kant, by demonstrating that metaphysical questions remain beyond the purview of reason, by affirming our inability to grasp the world as it is, in and of itself, by demonstrating that we can pretend to study and understand it only in terms of how it appears to us, that is to say, as an ensemble of phenomena (in opposition to things in and of themselves), removes truth from the field of scientific knowledge.

Sade goes one step further: he removes truth from the field of morality. His atheism is profoundly consistent, rigorous, and inflexible. If neither God nor truth exists, there remains only the will to power in the service of the quest for private pleasure. With reason's finely honed blade the Sadian hero eliminates all that restrains his impulses, all that limits the expression of his desires, up to and including the least admissible of them, the better to experience his own truth, *at whatever cost*. Heroism, in the event, is the audacity that allows the libertine, above and against all social conventions, to go to every extreme in gratifying his passions. In the face of extremity, Sade never flinches. He moves resolutely forward, to the abyss.

Should you have the impression that *Philosophy in the Bedroom* hangs back from the edge of the abyss, that it is too restrained, open *The 120 Days of Sodom*: one of the few narratives that can actually provoke nausea. One wonders, in fact, how a man, even a man locked away as Sade was, could possibly have *written* it. First published retroactively in 1904, the book shakes Western literature with a tremor[26] comparable that of the impact of the

---

26. The expression is that of Annie Le Brun, in *Soudain un bloc d'abîme* (Paris: Jean-Jacques Pauvert, 1986), in which we find probably the most daring analysis of *The 120 Days of Sodom*.

Shoah upon history. It is as impossible to put down as it is impossible to read from beginning to end. So cunningly orchestrated are the gradations of atrocity that they leave no room for the lassitude that arises elsewhere in Sade's work from the repetition of lubricious combinations and the suffering that accompanies them. Things are far too sordid for boredom to set in. Far better to speak of revulsion—even though I cannot help thinking that, contrary to what happens when we read *Philosophy in the Bedroom*, *The 120 Days of Sodom* attempts to transport us, assuming such a thing to be possible, beyond disgust. I am attempting to suggest that in this catalog, Sade causes nature to speak. But the nature to which he gives voice is no longer neutral; it is composed of purest atrocity. In reality, nature has simply vanished: the castle of Silling set in the depths of the Black Forest, where the executioners lock themselves away with their victims, is so isolated, so inaccessible that it is simultaneously beyond society and beyond nature. The surrounding nature, in the form of an impenetrable forest, is little more than a ring of silence that separates lubricity from the world.

The absolute isolation provides their untrammeled sexual abandon with such security, such artificial plenitude, that one of the protagonists presumes to complain:

> Mealtime arrived. The Duc wished to advance the thesis that if happiness consisted in the entire satisfaction of all the senses, it were difficult to be happier than were they.
>
> "The remark is not a libertine's" said Durcet. "How can you be happy if you are able constantly to satisfy yourself? It is not in desire's consummation happiness consists, but in the desire itself, in hurdling obstacles placed before what one wishes. Well, that is the perspective there. One needs but wish and one has. I swear to you," he continued, "that since my arrival here my fuck has not once flowed because of the objects I find about me in this castle. Every time I have discharged over what is not here, what is absent from this place, and so it is," the financier declared, "that, according to my belief, there is one essential thing lacking to our happiness. It is the pleasure of comparison, a pleasure which can only be born of the sight of wretched persons, and here one sees none at all. It is from the sight of he who does not in the least enjoy what I enjoy, and who suffers, that comes the charm of being able to say to oneself: 'I am therefore happier than he.' Wherever men may be found equal, and where these differences do not exist, happiness

shall never exist either; it is the story of the man who knows full well what health is worth after he has been ill." (361–362)[27]

Durcet, he in whom the impotence and the scarcity of discharge—"rare and uneasy" (*120 Days*, 210) as he puts it—exacerbate his lust, and the fury with which he pursues sexual gratification, may well complain of satiety but he finds temporary relief in the rule the four debauchees adopt. This rule stipulates that the young female and male virgins brought to the castle cannot be deflowered before, respectively, the second and third month of orgy. We are onlookers, in a general sense, to a minutely calculated gradation of torment inflicted upon the victims in parallel to the gradation of the narratives of the four "storytellers," brothel keepers, and whores hired to share the treasures of their experience. Their successive narrations, which range from merely degrading first-degree passions to murderous ones of the fourth degree, gradually fire the imagination to incandescence. It is a progression calculated to introduce into the midst of abundance a sense of artificial restraint that does not stop our accomplices from discharging until they can fuck no more, the necessity of which is confirmed in the first storyteller's lucid observation: "I have already had the honor to remark in your Lordships' presence, that it is most difficult to fathom all the tortures man invents for himself in order to find, in the degradation they produce, or the agonies, those sparks of pleasure which age or satiety have made to grow faint in him" (*120 Days*, 512).

Her observation is a slap in the face of the four libertines. All of them are over fifty, with the exception of the bishop, whose forty-four years of age do not prevent him from being far less vigorous, and thus far more economical with his seed than his elder brother, the Duc de Blangis, he whose potency and excesses are almost limitless. But even when the body remains strong, imagination falters. In one manner or another, all four are so corroded by debauchery that they must immerse themselves ever deeper in the extremes of behavior provided by the implausible setting of the castle of Silling to stimulate their lubricity. Quite literally, that lubricity of theirs is immersed in shit.

In essence, the first part, and the only portion to warrant a detailed narrative, accounting for three quarters of the entire work (293 out of 388 pages)—the other three parts being little more than schematic summaries to be developed—is devoted to the anal stage. The protagonists never stop shitting, ingesting, and regurgitating it from all their orifices; thickly they spread it, licking up the prodigious gold of earliest infancy. But the marvelous is

27. The Marquis de Sade, *The 120 Days of Sodom and Other Writings*. Compiled and translated by Richard Seaver and Austryn Wainhouse (New York: Grove Press, 1987), herein referred to as *120 Days*.

missing: childhood gold is nothing but adult excrement; coprophagia flourishes at the most tender and pinkest of assholes as it does at the most gaping, most repugnant of holes. Sexual pleasure floats through *120 Days* like a turd through the sewers. Even though coprophilia, especially in the company of the loved object, need not necessarily warrant scorn or disgust, the Sadian narrative never stops underlining its morbidity. In the majority of cases, it is well and truly filth that excites the coprophile to ejaculation. Love, even in the most physical meaning of the term, is absent from the castle of Silling. The narration is lubricious, obscene, pornographic, but never erotic. It contains nothing of the unease we feel on reading, for instance, Pauline Réage's *Histoire d'O*. Preliminaries, foreplay, sensuality, caresses, mystery, and refinement have no place in the world of the Sillingian libertines: all are one-dimensional cardboard figures. Their aristocratic veneer conceals neither feelings nor imagination; they are consistent, so to speak, only in their furious dedication to sexual release. And yet this very sexual release, excesses included, is mind-numbing in its platitude.

Worse still, it is *encyclopedic*: no single practice can be forgotten, no detail neglected. Each "passion" is related in precisely the right place, according to the prescribed gradation. Should the tale of the putative "story-teller" stimulate her listeners beyond the bounds of the permissible, those excesses, for which the narrator begs to be excused, are passed over in provisional silence. The reader is requested to wait until they appear on the agenda. In fact, it would be no exaggeration to say that the catalog of *120 Days* is clinical, and utterly non-inciting. Though the storytellers may contrive to excite the masters of the orgy—a drug that is essential, as we have seen, to exacerbate their wilting desires—, they hardly enflame the reader. Worse, the impact of their narrative on the behavior of the masters is treated in a purely matter-of-fact, expeditious manner that is far inferior to the verve of the storytellers. It is as if the imitation can do no better than send back the faint echo of the model. Not because the acts are lessened in themselves, but because the combination of mimesis, repetition and brevity devalues them. With all its precision, its mechanized operations, and its transmission belts, the heavy machinery kills the reader's desire more certainly than it does the victims' bodies. The more days go by, the more the verve we had observed at the outset, even among the storytellers, is gradually worn away, to be snuffed out almost entirely beneath the spine-chilling, nauseating, mortal enumerations—figurative as well as literal—of an increasingly skeleton-like scenario. It is hard to believe that the progressive desiccation of the narration, which is reduced to a table of contents, and ends in a simple subtraction (as Annie Le

Brun rightly notes), does not deliberately keep pace with the increasing horror of the list of crimes and deaths.

Sade, held prisoner in the Bastille, finished copying the scroll upon which he composed *120 Days* in the final days of November 1785. He then hid it away in one of the walls of his chamber, from which he was suddenly removed on the night of July 3–4, 1789, to be transferred to the mental hospital at Charenton. The prisoner was never to recover the precious scroll, which fell into other hands. He would later describe the loss as irreparable. But we will never know what he intended to do with his manuscript. We only know that he spent more than three years reworking it, apparently without result. Was it a failure of will, a failure of ability? We will never know. What we do have is a narrative in the raw, neither finished nor unfinished: everything is there, but in a form that grows progressively more terse and succinct. The author's intentions are indecipherable. All that we have to go on is the text, and the atmosphere it creates.

That atmosphere suffocates and chills. It is glacially indifferent to our passions, to our suffering, to our very sense of being in the world, at farthest remove from the quotidian concerns of fiction. If it is true that Western literature tends to take as its themes the exploits, the hurts, the joys, and the dreams that make its heroes so singular, then *120 Days* casts a cold and merciless light upon the futility of such concerns: the human being is nothing but the raw material of sexual pleasure, in the manner of soldiers described as canon fodder. Whatever singularity he or she might possess is strictly anecdotal; it dissolves in the classification of passions whose object it provisionally becomes. The human being is eminently expendable, disposable. The masters themselves, the chevalier, the bishop, the president, and the financier are vulgar types: pawns of their impulses, no less laughable than their victims, and in the final analysis, no less "victims" than them. They possess only enough wits to convince themselves that their servitude is liberty—at far remove from Molière's Don Juan, a man of honor in whom the libertine's egotism has not entirely killed off the image of the ego, nor the love of the gratuitous act.

The protagonists of *The 120 Days of Sodom* cannot be described as antiheroes (such as are to be found in Rabelais, Cervantes, or Shakespeare); they are pure specimens, automatons reduced to unstinting obedience to the cyclical and constantly increasing tyranny of their obsessions. It would be hard to imagine a more radical murder of *joie de vivre*; equally hard, surprisingly, to sink into the abyss. The banality with which the tale is laid out before us ends up stripping it of any power to turn our heads. Sade depicts horror with the dedication and the clarity of a painter of traditional family scenes: his yawning chasm has no depth. I have argued that he seeks to lead us beyond disgust; but the destination remains, when all is said and done, as invisible as it is unattainable. Let us hazard one, geometric image: *120 Days* describes, taking defecation as the y-axis and gradation of torments as the x-axis, the asymptote of the absence of sensual gratification or of abjectness, depending upon whether we prefer sensual gratification or abjection. Do we find here anything resembling the function of nature?

With this question uppermost in mind I would like to return to *Philosophy in the Bedroom*, to examine one last, curious excrescence: the political pamphlet that Sade feels obliged to embed in it. The insertion is as strange as it is meaningful. Eugenie, exhausted by a double penetration that has brought her to the peak of voluptuousness, calls for a bit of theory, asking, "whether manners are truly necessary in a governed society." Dolmance answers by pulling from his pocket a pamphlet purchased that very morning at the Palace of Equality:

> MADAME DE SAINT-ANGE
> Let me see it. (*she reads*) "Yet another Effort, Frenchmen, If You Would Become Republicans." Upon my word, 'tis an unusual title: 'Tis promising; Chevalier, you possess a fine organ, read it to us.
>
> DOLMANCE
> Unless I am mistaken, this should perfectly reply to Eugenie's queries.
>
> EUGENIE
> Assuredly!
>
> MADAME DE SAINT-ANGE
> Out with you, Augustin: this is not for you; but don't go too far; we'll ring when we want you back.
>
> LE CHEVALIER
> Well, I'll begin. (*Philosophy*, 295)

Eugenie has already gotten the message; but the people must not hear it. An aristocrat's reflex? Irony? It is hard to say. As a political program, its position and status are fraught with ambiguity. Sade writes, on December 5, 1791, to his steward in Provence: "What, at present, am I? Aristocrat or democrat? Tell me please, as for my part, I do not know." After being set free the previous year by the Assembly, he participated in the deliberations of his section of the Convention in 1793, before being incarcerated that same year for "modérantisme" (perhaps because of the content of *Aline et Valcourt*, the philosophical novel written the previous year, and that was being printed even as he was arrested in December 1793). Thanks to the fall of Robespierre he eluded the guillotine, and was released in October 1794, one year before the publication, in London, of *Philosophy in the Bedroom*, meaning that *Français, encore un effort si vous voulez devenir républicains* was probably written sometime between 1794 and 1795. Today, the irony of the title leaps off the page. Madame Saint-Ange finds it singular, promising. The tone of the text is urgent, serious:

> I am about to put forward some major ideas; they will be heard and pondered. If not all of them please, surely a few will; in some sort, then, I shall have contributed to the progress of our age, and shall be content. We near our goal, but haltingly: I confess that I am disturbed by the presentiment that we are on the eve of failing once again to arrive there. Is it thought that goal will be attained when at last we have been given laws? Abandon the notion; for what should we, who have no religion, do with laws? We must have a creed, a creed befitting the republican character, something far removed from ever being able to resume the worship of Rome....[28]
>
> Frenchmen, an end to your waverings: all of Europe, one hand raised halfway to the blindfold over her eyes, expects that effort by which you must snatch it from her head. Make haste: *holy Rome* strains every nerve to repress your vigor; hurry, lest you give Rome time to secure her grip upon the few proselytes remaining to her. Unsparingly and recklessly smite off her proud and trembling head; and before two months the tree of liberty, overshadowing the wreckage of Peter's Chair, will soar victoriously above all the contemptible Christian vestiges and idols raised with such effrontery over the ashes of Cato and Brutus.
>
> Since we believe a cult necessary, let us imitate the Romans: actions, passions, heroes—those were the objects of their respect. Idols of this sort elevated the soul, electrified it, and more: they communicated to the spirit the virtues of the respected being. Minerva's devotee coveted wisdom. Courage found its abode in his heart who worshipped Mars....
>
> Let us give over thinking religion can be useful to man; once good laws are decreed unto us, we will be able to dispense with religion. But they assure us, the people stand in need of one; it

28. The Rome referred to is that of Catholicism, not ancient Rome, to whose cult the narrator will later suggest eventually returning.

amuses them, they are soothed by it. Fine! Then, if that be the case, give us a religion proper to free men; give us the gods of paganism. We shall willingly worship Jupiter, Hercules, Pallas; but we have no use for a dimensionless god who nevertheless fills everything with his immensity, with an omnipotent god who never achieves what he wills, a supremely good being who creates malcontents only, a friend of order in whose government everything is in turmoil. No, we want no more of a god who is at loggerheads with nature, who is the father of confusion, who moves man at the moment man abandons himself to horrors; such a god makes us quiver with indignation, and we consign him forever to the oblivion whence the infamous Robespierre wishes to call him forth. (*Philosophy*, 296–301)

The above should be more than enough to convince us that Sade is not jesting. Even the idea of eventually resuscitating the gods of the Roman pantheon seems untinged by irony: no one, in any event, is likely to take these divinities seriously. Their value as distraction would in the end help to reinforce paganism and atheism. For what ultimately matters is civic education. By replacing "deific stupidities" with "excellent social principles" children would be instructed in "their duties toward society." They would be taught that their happiness as individuals "consists in rendering others as fortunate as we desire to be ourselves"; thus would they become "sufficient for individual happiness" (*Philosophy*, 303). Deep in the secret temple of unbridled lubricity, what we see is the return in force of a quasi-Lockean morality, or perhaps of a paler version of the Kantian imperative; concern for the civic virtues reappears precisely where the imperative of sexual licence encounters not the slightest obstacle, nor concerns itself even remotely with reciprocity. Having read it through, Dolmance opines that he can only partially subscribe to the pamphlet's premises; its style and content create, with respect to the principles previously enunciated, "the appearance of a repetition"—a correlation that Eugenie, interrupting, claims not to have noticed (*Philosophy*, 339). Between Dolmance's hardline libertine rhetoric—whose practical application *120 Days* lays before us in its most extreme coherence—to the exhortations of *Yet Another Effort, Frenchmen* lies a clear-cut disparity, as significant as it is deliberate.

Simply enough, this disparity stems from the reintroduction of social concerns into a rhetorical system, which had up to that time completely excluded them. In principle, as we have seen, the Sadian theory of sexual licence, which posits the other as the raw material of sexual pleasure, eradicates the very notion of society. To allow nature to speak is to silence civilization. But civilization, for all Sade's claims, is itself a product of nature seen in its totality: nothing that is of the world can exist outside of it. Just as the state of nature, for the man who styles himself as civilized, is nothing but a construction of the mind, so the contradiction between nature and society is, as we know, imaginary. In short, human "nature" has, by all evidence, impelled human beings to join forces and to establish institutions, symbolic structures whose necessity Sade appears to accept. Practically speaking, the Sadian theory of sexual licence cannot be generalized, and Sade himself is clever enough to know it. What then is he attempting to do? The specific function of *Yet Another Effort, Frenchmen* is to reveal his intentions: to eradicate, irrevocably, the merest idea of transcendence.

Society's laws and rules are pure convention; they owe nothing to any superior principle whatsoever—an excellent reason for decreeing the fewest possible principles. Turning to the duties that bind man to his fellows, the pamphlet declares:

> The point is not at all to love one's brethren as oneself, since that is in defiance of all the laws of Nature, and since hers is the sole voice which must direct all the actions in our life; it is only a question of loving others as brothers, as friends given to us by Nature, and with whom we should be able to live much better in a republican state, wherein the disappearance of distances must necessarily tighten the bonds.
>
> May humanity, fraternity, benevolence prescribe our reciprocal obligations, and let us individually fulfill them with the simple degree of energy Nature has given us to this end; let us do so without blaming, and above all, without punishing, those who, of chillier temper or more acrimonious humor, do not notice in these yet very touching social ties all the sweetness and gentleness others discover therein; for, it will be agreed, to seek to impose universal laws would be a palpable absurdity: such a proceeding would be as ridiculous as that of the general who would have all his soldiers dressed in a uniform of the same size; it is a terrible injustice to require that men of unlike character all be ruled by the same law; what is good for one is not at all good for another.
>
> That we cannot devise as many laws as there are men must be admitted; but the laws can be lenient, and so few in number, that all men, of whatever character, can easily observe them....
>
> From these first principles there follows, one feels the necessity to make flexible, mild laws and especially to get rid forever of

the atrocity of capital punishment, because the law which attempts a man's life is impractical, unjust, inadmissible. Not, and it will be clarified in the sequel, that we lack an infinite number of cases were, without offense to Nature (and this I shall demonstrate), men have freely taken one another's lives, simply exercising a prerogative received from their common mother; but it is impossible for the law to obtain the same privileges, since the law, cold and impersonal, is a total stranger to the passions which are able to justify in man the cruel act of murder. Man receives his impressions from Nature, who is able to forgive him this act; the law, on the contrary, always opposed as it is to Nature and receiving nothing from her, cannot be authorized to permit itself the same extravagances: not having the same motives, the law cannot have the same rights. (*Philosophy*, 309–310)

In what might be considered a negation (partial at least) of free will, Sade lays before us a striking dialectic of sexual licence and the law (or, if you prefer, of impulse and prohibition). Nature, in varying proportions according to the individual, has granted us both egotism and fraternity. Law thus finds itself—virtually—in nature; nature must have its place in law. Life lived on common terms is an unavoidable fact of human existence. But the rules that govern it, being necessarily universal, are necessarily unjust when measured against the diversity of temperaments and characters. Because it can never be more than a stopgap measure, because it emanates from no superior principle, the law must be minimal. The same holds true for its sanctions, since there can be no moral basis for punishment. In other words, only the broadest possible latitude that it accords to sexual licence—the aristocratic licence of those best qualified and most intent on exercising it—can justify the law. Seen against the background of our modern-day legislative constructions, Sade's imperative may seem at first glance naïve. Yet the introduction of the principle of sensual pleasure into the social contract is perhaps the most revolutionary, the most vigorous product of Enlightenment political thought: the same principle is today resurgent in Western societies, to the detriment of the principle of solidarity.

By virtue of the contradiction it brings to light, the Sadian dialectic of sensual pleasure and law shatters the Kantian categorical imperative. While recognizing such an imperative as necessary, Sade argues that it can be constructed only upon the liberty of sensual pleasure—not to mention that libertinage, in addition to what it provides the individual, well serves the interests of the republican state as well, for it powerfully nurtures the insurrectional thrust indispensable to a regime feared and hated by other powers (*Philosophy*, 215–216). Indeed, as such licence disturbs the philosopher of Königsberg, he hastens to reinvest practical reason and action with the very transcendence that he has driven from pure reason, and from science. In driving God out of all authority, whether metaphysical, physical, or moral, Sade stands revealed as a *consistent* Kantian. But *consistency* is precisely what the philosophy of modernity rejects, what it does not wish to see; precisely what transforms Sade into a thinker as diabolical as he is damned, extracted from the hell of libraries in the hope of confining him to the delightful garden of literary torments. Wasted effort! Sade is fuckingly political. Maybe even more than he would have ever cared to admit.

Sadian radicalism derives its specificity not only from the determination to have done with God and with all ideas of transcendence, but, even more so, from his avowed anti-humanism. In examining the question of murder, the author of *Yet Another Effort, Frenchmen* speculates to what extent such an act could be criminal, under the laws of nature:

> It is probable that we are going to humiliate man's pride by lowering him again to the rank of all of Nature's other creatures, but the philosopher does not flatter small human vanities; ever in burning pursuit of truth, he discerns it behind stupid notions of pride, lays it bare, elaborates upon it, and intrepidly shows it to the astonished world.
>
> What is man? And what difference is there between him and other plants, between him and all the other animals of the world? None, obviously. Fortuitously placed, like them, upon this globe, he is born like them; like them he reproduces, rises, and falls; like them he arrives at old age and sinks like them into nothingness at the close of his life span. Nature assigns each species of animal, in accordance with its organic construction. (*Philosophy*, 329–330)

The disappearance of an individual, or even of an entire species, does not cause nature to flinch. To kill, Dolmance teaches Eugenie, is not a crime, "destruction being one of the chief laws of Nature." Destruction, in fact, is more imaginary than real, for life is a state of perpetual transformation. In killing, the murderer "does but alter forms" and brings the natural cycle to completion (*Philosophy*, 237–238).

So depreciating man seems incompatible with the political program of *Yet Another Effort, Frenchmen*. Is the man thus depreciated not the very man who Sade, at one with Kant on this point, wishes to make "major"? But his version of majority is a diluted one. To become major, man must gaze without complacency upon where he stands in relation to the world. Man is either with God or without god. If he is mature enough to get by without the Father, he must assume his solitude and his insignificance to the bitter end. His duties to his fellow men are purely practical and egotistical; their observance, little more than a function of each individual's aptitudes and leanings.

In Sade's political program the decriminalization of the violation of another's integrity is far-reaching: murder does not exist as a crime, neither in the eyes of Nature, nor in those of society, which cares no more than Nature about the loss, no matter how widespread, of its members. Here, the pamphlet Dolmance has pulled from his pocket corresponds perfectly with his philosophy. But legitimizing impulses, including the most murderous ones, can only weaken the pact that binds society. So all-pervasive is sensual pleasure that it risks canceling the effects of the law—a fact Sade conveniently ignores. But, as if to make sure that we understand how seriously he takes the preeminence of sensual pleasure, up to and including its "criminal" side, he brings *Philosophy in the Bedroom* to a close, in a manner of speaking, with the infection and closing of Madame de Mistival's organs (stitching up her lips is a way of bringing the prude down a peg or two), to remind her that her daughter "is old enough to do what she pleases; that she likes to fuck, loves to fuck, that she was born to fuck" (*Philosophy*, 366).

In returning to the extremism and violence of untrammeled sexual licence in Sade, it becomes clear that we must call his work into question at its most painful point of convergence. Sade would be little different from the libertines, or the political philosophy of the day, were it not for his unflinching focus upon the destructive force of sexual licence. Ecstasy is indivisible, subsuming darkness and light, death and life. Kant sets out to safeguard the pleasant, innocent, agreeable aspects of the Enlightenment. But truth is neither necessarily pretty to behold, nor pleasant to hear. Sade shines the light of reason on all that is most meaningless and terrifying about man's "majority": total liberty; to seek pleasure and the excitation of the senses by all possible means in a world without values, a world that expects nothing of us and promises us nothing. By pretending to demonstrate "into what an abyss of folly one is hurled when, in reasoning, one abandons the aid of reason's torch" (*Philosophy*, 326), Sade shows us the precipice reason leads to, when reason becomes nothing more than a sequence of logical operations starting from the pleasure principle while Nature looks on indifferently.

Something is missing from the sinkhole of intermingled pleasure and pain to which Sade beckons us. That something is reality. If we are to return to the primacy of unrestricted sensual pleasure, he implies, then we must also re-examine what we have defined as its banality: the banality of a descriptive narration that reduces sensual pleasure to the monotonous, exacerbated repetition of fucking. Sade's libertine hero is totally programmed for a single, brief instant of eruption. Should he rest or take nourishment, he does so the better to begin again; should he hold back and delay ejaculation, he does so the better to exacerbate it. Everything converges on facilitating discharge. The Sadian libertine is to love what the general who knows only how to load a cannon is to military strategy. The nature he ceaselessly invokes is like a battlefield on which the only release that counts is that of shooting. Which may well be true, in a strict sense, of what is pompously called the theater of war as probable locus of a succession of barely-concealed erotic discharges. But even if we were to limit ourselves to the war metaphor, no conflict can be reduced to mere target practice. War, nature, and man are all far more complex.

But something very real indeed lurks in the Sadian abyss, despite the reality deficit that makes it hard to believe; something that, since the century of the Enlightenment, has never been far from the theater of our imagination: the liberty of sensual pleasure *in all its forms*. The power of the Sadian narrative, and its deadliest venom, is the implacable light it brings to bear on a fundamental contradiction of the political discourse of modernity. As the law arbitrarily restricts desire; as it becomes a last resort, a regrettable necessity, an affront to the irreducible diversity of individuals and the passions that drive them, it cannot but be unjust. Confronted with the idea of the common good, the imperative of individual "happiness" dissolves. It is so reduced, in fact, that it can hardly be given Hobbes's already minimal prescription: to ensure the life and physical integrity of individuals. If the law is at the service of sensual pleasure alone, assuming that we take the insubordination seriously, then no law is possible. And, *a fortiori*, no social project. Even if we accept that the collectivity pass such laws as to prevent the excessive infringement of individual pleasures upon one another; if we accept that it may wish to impose limitations upon the jungle of pleasures in conflict (by prohibition of murder or torture for sexual satisfaction), it would only be giving another locus to the power struggle: the domination of knowledge, of money, of intelligence, or of any other symbolic form would replace physical domination.

Truth to tell, the conditional is unnecessary: the dominant powers of our world are constantly summoning us to the high mass of consumption. *Enjoy yourself*[29] is the one-size-fits-all slogan for our times. Whether we have intuited it or not, Sade is the precursor of our age, an age in which the liberty of sensual pleasure commingled with financial accumulation[30] knows no more bounds. "The economy" has dethroned "nature" in dictatorial power. The former henceforth dictates the latter's "laws" so pervasively that it passes itself off as the ultimate expression of the "natural" order.

The radical reduction of life to sexual (or, in a broader sense, sensorial) gratification, like the atheistic negation that justifies it, draws its water from the well of the very absolutism it claims to reject. In many ways atheism, the fanatical denial of God, is but the obverse of the fanatical version of monotheism and of the cult of Reason that had been set up in its place. Sade, by stripping it of its reasonable, Kantian appearance, lays bare the negative countenance of Enlightenment Reason. Sade is Kant in all his nudity. A nudity that kills even desire, about which Durcet, that frustrated pleasure-seeker, and prisoner of his insurmountable and insatiable needs in the inner-most reaches of Silling Castle, expresses dark regrets. The obsessive pursuit of sensual pleasure, of fucking, of ejaculation leaves no room whatsoever for absence.

By abandoning the spheres of transcendence, by allowing us to see it wallowing in the muck, truth, for Sade as for us, has relinquished none of its absolute power. Now that there is nothing chimerical about it, or so we believe, its tyranny becomes all the more real. Beneath the multiple facets of diversity, the One still looms dominant. Like God, money is invisible and omnipresent. It circulates freely, dispensing pain and pleasure, punishing impiety, rewarding piety, amusing itself by bringing low its most faithful servants as if to put—like Job—their faith to the test. Sade is less cruel, but his quest for sensual pleasure is more utopian. The baleful glare of his glacial, rationalist vision sweeps like a searchlight beam across Enlightenment polit-ical philosophy and proclaims, clad in its most lubricious finery, what may well become our nightmare.

29. In English in the original.
30. A "confusion" that is quite explicit in the opening pages of *The 120 Days of Sodom*, in which the four libertines are presented as being among the "leeches" who had become enormously wealthy at the expense of the State and the people during the ruinous wars that marked the glorious reign of Louis XIV.

7

ROUSSEAU:
THE SICKNESS OF THE EGO

T HE WORKS OF SADE, which proclaim a sexual licence that overwhelms
them, can be read as the autobiography of a phantasm. His incessant
invocation of Nature ultimately takes as its subject man, and all that is
unmentionable in him. Man as lubricity, and nothing more: such is the
configuration that, in the Sadian imagination, governs the interpretation of a
nature to which no one can lay exclusive claim, let alone define. In contrast
to that frigid, externalized, imperative representation of nature stands
Rousseau's intimate version, which in its own distinct way also takes as its
subject man, and the truth of man left to his own devices. Like Sade, but in a
manner diametrically opposed, Rousseau lays bare the political project of the
Enlightenment, with the help of the revelatory mechanism that, in his eyes,
constitutes the original sense of self. His certainty is quasi-Cartesian,
grounded less in reasoned intuition than in the experience of existence in its
pure state. The *Confessions* relate the genesis of this experience, and the
conflicts to which it exposes the narrator in his relations with his fellow men
and with society.

No other narrator has proclaimed himself the misunderstood hero of his
own truth quite like Jean-Jacques Rousseau. *In him*, narrative, heroism and
truth find their ultimate fusion. In him, that is to say, in his person, in his life,
as in his writings. So intertwined are Rousseau's life and work that the latter
can be seen as a running commentary on the former, while the former
becomes, in the end, the consequence of the latter. The *Confessions* can
perfectly well be read in, of, and for themselves. But the tale they tell, in their
concern for justification, is so powerfully connected with the struggle
between Jean-Jacques and society that we can fully grasp their true intentions

only in the light of Rousseau's political and pedagogical views, and in that of his other autobiographical writings. Straying slightly from my customary approach, I propose to examine several texts that shed light on one another, all the while keeping the *Confessions* as my focus. I do not intend to write about Rousseau, nor to study his thought in all its aspects (which are numerous indeed), but to read, through his major autobiographical writings, the difficulties and even the suffering experienced by the modern *ego* at large in a society that it cannot shape; a society that all too frequently turns against it, against the very *ego* that attempts to conceive of it and to change it.

A short narrative embedded in the second letter to Monsieur de Malesherbes, which Rousseau in his *Confessions* asserts he is unable to reproduce, having already unburdened himself of it in the letter, makes it possible for us to date the crucial moment of his life when, on the road to Vincennes, private and public merge with a force that makes their encounter just short of indestructible:

> After having passed forty years of my life this way, dissatisfied with myself and with others, I fruitlessly sought to break the bonds that were keeping me attached to that society which I esteemed so little, and which chained me to occupations that were least to my taste through needs that I considered to be those of nature, and which were only those of opinion. Suddenly, a fortunate change happened to enlighten me about what I had to do for myself, and to think about my fellows about whom my heart was ceaselessly in contradiction with my mind, and whom I still felt myself brought to love along with so many reasons to hate them. Sir, I would like to be able to depict that singularly epoch-making moment in my life and one that will always be present to me if I live eternally.
>
> I was going to see Diderot, at that time a prisoner in Vincennes; I had in my pocket a Mercury of France which I began to leaf through along the way. I fell across the question of the Academy of Dijon, which gave rise to my first writing. If anything ever resembled a sudden inspiration, it is the motion that was caused in me by that reading; suddenly I felt my mind dazzled by a thousand lights; crowds of lively ideas presented themselves at the same time with a strength and a confusion that threw me into an inexpressible perturbation; I feel my head seized by a dizziness similar to drunkenness. A violent palpitation oppresses me, makes me sick to my stomach; not being able to breathe anymore while walking, I let myself fall under one of the trees of the avenue, and I pass a half-

hour there in such an agitation that when I got up again I noticed the whole front of my coat soaked with my tears without having felt that I shed them. Oh Sir, if I had ever been able to write a quarter of what I saw and felt under that tree, how clearly I would have made all the contradictions of the social system seen, with what strength I would have exposed all the abuses of our institutions, with what simplicity I would have demonstrated that man is naturally good and that it is from these institutions alone that men become wicked. Everything that I was able to retain of these crowds of great truths which illuminated me under that tree in a quarter of an hour has been weakly scattered about in my three principal writings, namely that first discourse, the one on inequality, and the treatise on education, which three works are inseparable and together for the same whole (Letters [Malesherbes, Pl., I, 1133–1136], 575).[31]

"The moment I read this I beheld another universe and became another man" (Book VIII, 327): the *Confessions* confirm the extraordinary significance of the revelation through which the narrator simultaneously experiences and grasps the truth that, for all society's stifling pressure, has never ceased to throb in his breast. Intelligence fuses with feelings whose glow illuminates a contradiction that he had heretofore only indistinctly realized: "the secret opposition between the constitution of man and that of society."[32] "Man" is none other than Jean-Jacques himself; the man who Rousseau, in an unprecedented enterprise, as he proclaims at the beginning of his *Confessions*, wishes to display to his fellows as being "in every way true to nature" (Book I, 17). This is the selfsame man who, in *Rousseau, Judge of Jean-Jacques*, purports to recognize in his own writings the man whom he has discovered in himself. At the end point of his circular progression, the narrator pronounces his earliest texts on the arts and sciences, on inequality, on the social contract, and on education as having been autobiographical from the start. Everything he has ever uttered of importance, every truth, flows from that deep wellspring continuously bubbling up within him, which he calls the *truth of nature*—the truth, at least, of his nature, that of Jean-Jacques himself.

So deeply does a sense of inner certainty pervade his political and pedagogical writings that their audacity, the scandal they touched off in his day, would cast the writer that Rousseau was to become almost in spite of himself,

31. Jean-Jacques Rousseau, *The* Confessions *and Correspondence, Including the Letters to Malesherbes*, vol. 5 of *The Collected Writings of Rousseau*, ed. Christopher Kelly, Roger D. Masters, and Peter G. Stillman, trans. Christopher Kelly (Hanover: Published for Dartmouth College by University Press of New England, 1995). References in parentheses are to works included in this anthology.
32. Jean-Jacques Rousseau, *Rousseau, Judge of Jean-Jacques*, trans. Judith R. Bush, Roger D. Masters, and Christopher Kelly (Published for Dartmouth College by the University Press of New England, 1990) pp. 129–130.

into a wrenching controversy that would ultimately strike to the very heart of his personal integrity, going so far as to momentarily imperil his sense of self. The strictly autobiographical work that he would later write emanates from the overpowering need to mend the break, to bind the wound, if only in his own eyes. For the enterprise to succeed, for him to convince himself of his truth, he vows to tell all, to hide nothing; he undertakes to speak the unspeakable, wagering that his courage will protect him from the opprobrium and ridicule truth has exposed him to.

Confessions, literally: only the admission of his failings and weaknesses can absolve him, can restore to him, if not in the eyes of the public, the original purity that will permit him to stand, book in hand, before his sovereign judge, and to proclaim aloud to posterity:

> I have displayed myself as I was, as vile and despicable when my behavior was such, as good, generous and noble when I was so. I have bared my secret soul as Thou thyself has seen it, Eternal Being! So let the numberless legions of my fellow men gather round me, and hear my confessions. Let them groan at my depravities, and blush for my misdeeds. But let each of them reveal his heart at the foot of Thy throne with equal sincerity, and may any man who dares, say "I was a better man than he." (Book I, 17)

This is navel-gazing of the highest order, a fair match for the wound *he* has never recovered from. It is, above all, an incredible attempt at redemption. Above and beyond his person and his life, what must be saved, what justifies the narrator's immoderation is the witness it bears to the first truth of man: his fundamental goodness. Jean-Jacques is unshakably convinced that he possesses such goodness, having experienced it early on at the innermost depths of his being. In Rousseau's sociopolitical writings the state of nature is never anything but the metaphorical extension of this primordial feeling. In his *Discourse on the Origins of Inequality*, he argues that this state "never existed among men" as an historical reality. It is impossible for us to retrieve, and extremely hard to see. Yet this simple conjecture is essential "to judge our present state correctly."[33] The state of nature is thus hypothetical; natural law cannot be found; the philosophical disputation surrounding them futile. Having reached this conclusion, Rousseau addresses the human race:

---

33. Jean-Jacques Rousseau, *A Discourse on the Origins of Inequality (second discourse), Polemics, and Political Economy*, ed. Roger D. Masters and Christopher Kelly, trans. Judith R. Bush, Christopher Kelly, and Roger D. Masters (Published for Dartmouth College by University Press of New England, 1990), p. 131.

> O man, whatever country you may belong to, whatever your
> opinions may be, attend to my words; you shall hear your history
> such as I think I have read it, not in books composed by those like
> you, for they are liars, but in the book of nature which never lies.
> All that I shall repeat after her, must be true, without any inter-
> mixture of falsehood, but where I may happen, without intending
> it, to introduce my own conceits.[34]

Rousseau cannot resist the desire to return to the first state, which he has just recognized as inaccessible, by invoking the very authority he has just rebuffed. Such is the increased inconsistency of an argument that ingenuously locates the risk of error exactly at the point where Rousseau has derived his strongest intuitions. By warning against subjectivity, he designates as a source of falsehood the very instance in which he would later uncover the foundation stone of his thought. The restriction seems trivial, but it embodies the major contradiction of his social theory, and of his life.

In the pastoral paradise of Bossey, the village in which part of his child-hood was steeped, and in the blissful later experiences that would reawaken its memory, Rousseau, by way of an ill-considered turnabout he would slow-ly come to identify, found critical leverage against the society that weighed so heavily upon him. But this same society, having failed to appreciate the inestimable gift he has bestowed upon it, would turn against him. The deter-mining moment of his childhood occurs. In it, Jean-Jacques will think back to the instant when his innocence came to an end: the famous matter of Mademoiselle Lambercier's comb. Her spankings, soon to end, would touch off his first erotic awakening. Unjustly, she accuses him of breaking one of her combs. There come exhortations, threats, and punishments: all to no avail. The little boy resists the incriminating circumstantial evidence — but he cannot prove his innocence. He emerges from the ordeal "shattered but triumphant" (Book I, 29). The breach of confidence, at childhood's incipient end, is irreparable. His primordial Eden has come to a close; now he must enter the iniquitous order of society:

> I feel my pulse beat faster once more as I write. I shall always
> remember that time if I live to be a thousand. That first meeting
> with violence and injustice has remained so deeply engraved on
> my heart that any thought which recalls it summons back this first
> emotion. The feeling was only a personal one in its origins, but it
> has since assumed such a consistency and has become so divorced

34. Jean-Jacques Rousseau, *A Discourse Upon the Origin and the Foundation of the Inequality Among Mankind* (Sioux Falls: NuVision, 2005), p. 10.

from personal interests that my blood boils at the sight or the tale of any injustice, whoever may be the sufferer and wherever it may have taken place, in just the same way as if I were myself its victim. When I read of the cruelties of a fierce tyrant, of the subtle machinations of a rascally priest, I would gladly go and stab the wretch myself even if it were to cost me my life a hundred times over.... This is perhaps an innate characteristic in me. Indeed, I think it is. But the memory of the first injustice I suffered was so painful, so persistent, and so intricately bound up with it that, however strong my initial bent in that direction, this youthful experience must certainly have powerfully reinforced it.

There ended the serenity of my childish life. From that moment I never again enjoyed pure happiness, and even today I am conscious that memory of childhood's delights stops short at this point. We stayed some months longer at Bossey. We lived as we are told the first man lived in the earthly paradise. (Book I, 30)

Jean-Jacques would be removed from the Lamberciers', billeted in the municipal clerk's office, and then apprenticed to a tyrannical master who spared no effort to make his work unbearable. Confidence, innocence, happiness, justice, and nature: everything dear to the narrator's memory has, in the space of a few months, collapsed. Nature, in Rousseau, means the idyllic countryside he was unjustly torn from, the state of original goodness from whose breast judicial error had wrenched him. Thirty years later, as he thinks back to that day, Jean-Jacques relives in his own way the tragedy of Genesis: expulsion from primordial enchantment leading to a painful awareness of fault (even though incomplete), work, and the social imperative. But, unconsciously, he also re-enacts the terrifying trajectory of birth that saw him torn, in the primal sense, from his mother who would die in delivery. The narrator attempts to distinguish, in himself, between the respective effects of his nature and of the event itself: he can only demonstrate, all too eloquently, that it is impossible to dissociate them; that his individual experience has shaped his political thought. The same painful experience recurs at other times in his life. The growing hostility of Parisian society, and of the literary world while he was writing his *Confessions* remind him of that far-distant loss, of that original incomprehension. Rousseau's feelings for nature, as does the incident that separates him from it, can point to a specific moment of genesis in his memory.

Instead, then, of being the hypothetical abstraction laid before us in the *Discourse on Inequality*, nature, in the *Confessions*, takes the form of a caring mother who nurtured and comforted Jean-Jacques's childhood, supplanting the real mother who died while giving birth to him. Inconsolable, his father attempted to compensate for the loss by transferring his love to the resemblance of he who was its cause. In his own way, in the incident of the comb, the child experiences his father's interminable period of mourning, his persistence in spoiling his son. "Guilty" from the moment of birth, Jean-Jacques begins by forgetting his guilt in nature, at Bossey—until his tutors, nominally just and compassionate people, brutally remind him of his original fault. The narrator does not return to the initial stain, the fatal birth; it disappears from the narrative along with the loving figure of the father. The original sin is crystallized in the comb, which he is unjustly accused of breaking. In his eyes it exists not as a fault but as a pure inevitability that reveals the malice of the world, which would sooner or later have raised its head.

Other paradises would line the narrator's path. *One* other, at the very least, in the person of Madame de Warens, his protector, mother, friend, sister, and mistress; followed, a few years after this decisive encounter, by the bucolic enchantment of Charmettes, where he was to live with her for one brief summer:

> Here begins the short period of my life's happiness; here I come to those peaceful but transient moments that have given me the right to say I have lived. Precious and ever-regretted moments, begin to run your charming course again for me! Flow one after another through my memory, more slowly, if you can, than you did in your fugitive reality! Indeed if it all consisted of facts, deeds, and words, I could describe it and in a sense convey its meaning. But how can I tell what was neither said, nor done, nor even thought, but only relished and felt, when I cannot adduce any other cause for my happiness but just this feeling? I rose with the sun, and I was happy; I saw Mamma, and I was happy; I left her and I was happy; I strolled through the woods and over the hills, I wandered in the valleys, I read, I lazed, I worked in the garden, I picked the fruit, I helped in the household, and happiness followed me everywhere; it lay in no definable object, it was entirely within me; it would not leave me for a single moment. (Book VI, 215)

Much later in life Rousseau was to rediscover, at Île de Saint-Pierre on the banks of Lac de Bienne, the pure joy of being he describes in the fifth and most celebrated of his solitary walks while, as he lies stretched out on the bottom of a rowboat, he lets himself drift with the current:

What is the source of happiness in such a state? Nothing external to us, nothing apart from ourselves and our own existence; as long as this state lasts and we are self-sufficient like God. The feeling of existence unmixed with any other emotion is in itself a precious feeling of peace and contentment which would be enough to make this mode of being loved and cherished by anyone who could guard against all the earthly and sensual influences that are constantly distracting us from it in this life and troubling the joy it could give us. But most men being continually stirred by passion know little of this condition, and having only enjoyed it fleetingly and incompletely they retain no more than a dim and confused notion of it and are unaware of its true charm. Nor would it be desirable in our present state of affairs that the avid desire for these sweet ecstasies should give people a distaste for the active life which their constantly recurring needs impose upon them. But an unfortunate man who has been excluded from human society and can do nothing more in this world to serve or benefit himself or others, may be allowed to seek in this state a compensation for human joys, a compensation which neither fortune nor mankind can take away from him.[35]

Rousseau, narrator *par excellence* of the sensibility of the *I*, forgets the wounds inflicted upon him by human society, and finds oblivion in a far more encompassing emotion. Better still, his rejection at the hands of society (which he cannot resist reminding us of in passing) becomes the very condition of his self-abandonment. Rousseau's individualism, for all its conquering swagger, is tainted by sadness, by absence, by defeat. Jean-Jacques's assault against the fortress called society has been repulsed; he can recover lost happiness only in the solitude and silence through which he floats, rocked by the wavelets of the lake, in his primordial cradle. If, *like God*, he is self-sufficient, it is because all beginnings, endings, and interruptions (starting with that of birth) are henceforth abolished. For all its "romantic" overtones, the narrator's *I* partakes of no overwrought romanticism. Nor does it function as an extension of the Cartesian *ego*; it aspires, instead, to dissolve it. Far from being "modern," Rousseau's *I* has already been wounded by modernity, from which it flees. Far from seeking self-realization in the uplift toward transcendence, it abandons all ambition the better to dissolve itself in immanence.

---

35. Jean-Jacques Rousseau, *Reveries of the Solitary Walker,* trans. Peter France (London: Penguin Classics, 1979), p. 89.

Rousseau's sociopolitical reflections take place between two moments: that of his idyllic childhood, which ends only with the separation from "Mamma" Warens, and that of the relief of the solitary walker, exhausted by his vain efforts. Between the two, over the three decades that separate Charmettes (1736) from Île de Saint-Pierre (1765), Rousseau throws himself into the quest for social success, and exhausts himself in the process. Crowned by early success, with the publication of the first two *Discourses*, insult and injury soon come to dog his path. His suffering is not simply the result of the personal disappointments of a country bumpkin faced with the jealousy and the self-importance of Parisian high society. It also bears tragic witness to the failure of a system of political thought that fully intended to save, in and by democracy, the intimate conviction that Jean-Jacques believes he has found in nature. To preserve the unity, the originality of the ego, even in the midst of the sovereign mass of the people, behold the curious proposal that lies at the heart of the *Social Contract*:

> "How to find a form of association which will defend the person and goods of each member with the collective force of all, and under which each individual, while uniting itself with the others, obeys no one but himself, and remains as free as before." This is the fundamental problem to which the social contract holds the solution.[36]

Not every edition of Rousseau casts his proposal in the form of a question, least of all in translation. But the interrogative would perhaps best express its singularity. Our author's proposed "solution" is theoretical, of course, but also *theoretically necessary*: individual consent can by no means be subordinated to the general will, even though in practice each citizen agrees to alienate a portion of his liberty with "the total alienation ... of all his rights"; acceptable as a condition provided it is "the same for all" and thus, "in no one's interest to make the conditions onerous for others."[37]

. But in Rousseau's formula lurks a contradiction, that of democracy itself: even in the rare and ideal situation that would allow all the citizens to congregate physically in the same place, it would be impossible for the people so assembled to decide on everything on a consensual basis, unless of course it were grounded in ancestral tradition that itself claimed consensus. But such a permanent deliberative body would be incompatible with the

---

36. Jean-Jacques Rousseau, *The Social Contract*, trans. Maurice Cranston (London: Penguin Classics, 1968), p. 60.
37. Ibid., p. 60.

diversity of economic activity, with urban life. Once such diversity has appeared, power, whether of the minority or the majority, raises its head. In the best of times, the social contract, in Rousseau's democratic definition, can only be that of the majority. For the equality it presupposes or advocates to protect the individual from collective tyranny, legality alone is not enough. Yet effective equality, if it is to mean anything at all, can only be established to the detriment of the civil liberty that every individual acquires by virtue of the social contract.[38]

Let us be quite frank: Rousseau himself does not believe that a social contract can bring about an effective democracy: "In the strict sense of the term, there has never been a true democracy, and there will never be."[39] Nonetheless, from a strictly theoretical viewpoint, the idea of a social contract is the sole possibility—unless one is to enlist divine authority. Its form and its implementation depend on circumstances, making it a regimented and codified transposition of the struggle for power. What our Jean-Jacques suffers from is quite precisely this struggle, in all its muffled brutality and duplicity. He has been wounded by contact with his fellow human beings; it is the wound that must be healed. The fusion of his individual's ego with collective consensus can be seen as another attempt, a social and political one this time, to regain the paradise he has lost. Because, he presumes, the memory of paradise exists in all others as it does in him—Rousseau—the common interest, which points toward unity, can claim the place nature has made for it in each man's heart. Nature here can be taken as that sense of peaceful belonging we (re)discover when we encounter it. For Rousseau recognizes no fewer than two natures: one, vegetable and bucolic, where each can enjoy the marvel of plants, animals, and landscapes; the other human and hostile, emerging from the unequal and conflicted relations that men set up spontaneously if there is no contract to govern them.

The *Social Contract* remained unfinished. Rousseau vowed to publish it, notifying his readers that he would not be completing the longer work on *Political Institutions* that the present writing would have been a part of, "which I undertook many years ago without thinking of the limitations of my powers, and have long since abandoned."[40] Limitations of his powers, indeed! For, as his childhood dreams have found no social outlet, they have run aground on the reefs of society. While preparing for publication the *Social Contract*, which he had hoped would articulate his incomplete political thought, Rousseau brings full circle the pedagogical considerations

38. *See* Ibid., p. 65.
39. Ibid., p. 112.
40. Ibid., p. 47.

developed in *Émile*. Now he presents it to the public, all the while denying he has written a treatise on education. If the social dream fails, if it is impossible to reform the adult collectivity, perhaps we can dream of educating children in another way. Their education in life would begin by awakening in them an awareness of their existence; they would learn to lend an ear to nature, to feel its impact, and yet they would not be left defenseless against society.

In the school of nature, with its hard knocks and its suffering, the child would be tempered by the test of freedom that would in turn help him to face the trials of social life with greater equanimity. Soon enough will come the servitude of institutions. In the meantime, the best policy is to encourage the child to seek within himself, to fortify himself in the free experience of life. Nature for Rousseau, far from being milquetoast, is an inspiration and a severe mistress all in one. Only for someone like Jean-Jacques who, wounded by his contemporaries, has turned his back on society, is she a place of refuge, a font of nostalgia. Émile is the child Rousseau would have wanted to be; Émile's education is the one he regrets having never received. Thus it comes as no surprise that for Jean-Jacques, nature—both in its delight and in its privation, both in its goodness and its didactic severity—remains tinged, always, with regret.

The irreducible contradiction that invalidates the social contract lies in the incompatibility between the collectivity's demands and the individual's conception of his uniqueness. In attempting to extend to the "we" of the political entity the "I" of individual consciousness, the political philosopher of the Enlightenment has taken on an impossible task. Rousseau, in fact, underscores its radical impossibility better than anybody else. Individual liberty and the inalienable rights of man are in fundamental, irremediable opposition with the common good—a thoroughly modern contradiction, unknown to the ancients. For them the individual and the liberty he enjoyed could exist only by virtue of his quality as a citizen, by his active belonging to the City, as Benjamin Constant so admirably demonstrated in his celebrated address on the liberty of ancients and of moderns.

But, in Rousseau, the "external" contradiction inherent in every society corresponds to the essential impossibility of an "internal" order. In him, the *I* that safeguards nature's first stirrings has, from and by the beginning, been shattered. Now we must return to the beginning, to look back afresh upon the distance traveled. Of his conception, when his father had returned to his wife after a long absence in Istanbul, Jean-Jacques writes: "I was the unhappy fruit of his return." Soon after, "I was almost born dead" (Book I, 19). Education would exacerbate his newborn's fragility. Recalling his first experience of reading in the company of his father at age six, where he locates uninterrupted awareness of himself, Rousseau deplores his father's "dangerous method," which he also condemns in *Émile*: his readings give life a novelistic image that neither experience nor thought could cure. Through the novel, literature and history (particularly Plutarch), culture, civilization, and society leave their mark on him. But the emotional climate in which the novelistic transmission takes place—the father's painful love for his deceased wife, which he transfers with burning tears to his son—colors the primordial awareness of existence with a deeply-rooted melancholy. Suffering, from the beginning, suffuses existence in the "pure" state, as it suffuses original innocence. Neither owes anything to nature, which Jean-Jacques first experiences only through the readings that forge his earliest consciousness.

On second reading, his sense of nature seems to originate less in Bossey than in an ego whose original infirmity, sustained by the sadness of an inconsolable father, seeks only to be made whole again. The two paradisal years spent in his discovery of the countryside would not be enough to bring about the reconciliation, would not slake his thirst for love and strengthen his character, especially since they were soon to be brought to a brutal end.

> My strongest desire was to be loved by everyone who came near me. I was gentle, so was my cousin, and so were our guardians. For a whole two years I was neither the witness nor the victim of any violence. Everything seemed to strengthen the natural disposition of my heart. (Book I, 25)

Jean-Jacques could only heal the wound of birth in a world where all would love him infinitely. The gentleness of the Geneva countryside—nature itself, in all its loveliness—is above all that of his benevolent tutors, until his confidence is broken, at the same time as Mademoiselle Lambercier's comb, turning his universe suddenly topsy-turvy. He is possessed by nostalgia, by an insatiable desire to be loved by everyone and everything.

Ultimately, this sense of nature finds its true refuge in the sickness of the ego. Jean-Jacques's infirmity is the particular—and particularly acute—expression of the state of vulnerability into which birth flings us. For all the failing and the straying he delights in exaggerating, the better to exaggerate the heroism of his confessions and protest his desire for innocence, the ego that Rousseau protects is cloven from the start, fated to the misfortune of having been born. The ego's connection with nature is largely circumstantial, and the idyllic sense of nature is a solitary one (in the *Fifth Walk*) only of necessity, in a being that has always thirsted for the loving company and the approbation of others. He experiences the bucolic paradise of Bossey with his cousin, under the benevolent authority of the Lamberciers; the idyll of Charmettes with "Mamma." Had it been up to him, Jean-Jacques would never have left her: "Ah! If only I had satisfied her heart as she had satisfied mine!" he exclaims in the *Tenth Walk*.[41] Much as the solitary walker may attempt to convince himself of his happiness at being removed from, and dispensed of human society, the taste for solitude that he ever so slightly overstates is almost everywhere shadowed with bitterness. Rousseau can never truly find consolation in the misunderstanding of his contemporaries, particularly those nearest to him, who are essential to his primordial Eden; people like Mademoiselle Lambercier, like Madame Warens whom Jean-Jacques would forever venerate. Then, later on, those who were to be a part of the all-too-brief society of his friends, individuals like Diderot who, in turning away from him, inflicted upon Jean-Jacques what must have been the cruelest "betrayal" of his Parisian life.

In rereading Rousseau's progress in this light, we can now understand where the *Confessions* fail. Their failure is magnificent, enchanting, written in a language of seductive beauty, which succeeds admirably in causing us to forget that his enterprise—to tell his story—may mislead us. The failure is not only Rousseau's, but extends much further: to the subject of modernity itself, snaring both Kant and Hegel. The *Confessions* derive their ambiguous power from the way the narrator tells his story. Not simply an account of the extraordinarily acute difficulties faced by his ego, they echo and amplify those of a modern ego so imbued with itself that it cannot grasp the enormity of its pretension: namely that the ego can generate, in and of itself, the meaning of life. The weight of its burlesque and tragic presence is already with us in the character of Don Quixote.[42] But Don Quixote remains a man misunderstood, isolated in his singular folly; he asks nothing of anyone. Jean-Jacques, however, is continually buttonholing those around him, proclaiming loudly, insistently, the misunderstanding and the isolation of which he feels himself a victim, even at the risk of giving offense. Paradoxically, his need for self-justification, and his desire for transparency blind him to himself.

Rousseau reflects only superficially the life he relates; he shines upon it the bright light of his good faith, convinced that he has left nothing in the shadows: certainly nothing essential, at any rate. He may be mistaken; he

---

41. *Reveries*, p. 153.
42. See *Truth or Death*, Chapter 14.

admits perfectly well he may forget, or even embellish, like a lens whose tiny defects of manufacture neither impede the flow of light nor substantially modify the truth of the ego he has set out to scrutinize. Then, too, in his *Fragments*, a fundamental doubt raises its head: "even among those who pride themselves the most for knowing men, each hardly knows anyone but himself" (*Fragments*, 585). Fraught with meaning, this sentence echoes the *Confessions'* oft-repeated avowal that the narrator is acting against his will, against his desires, against what reason requires of him. But these are the kind of confessions that ultimately help us accept his good faith. They confirm that, for all his claims, Jean-Jacques does not so much relate what he was as that which he would like to have been, that which he would have liked others to see him as, through the prism of his intentions, which were never anything other than praiseworthy. In a word, all that they would have seen had they only been able to read his "secret feelings" (Ibid., 585). Well enough, the narrator does not know himself; but he knows his heart and that is knowledge enough. It absolves him in his own eyes, and in the eyes of his readers, who are transfixed with empathy for his enterprise of truth. In Rousseau, and in the tale into which he transforms his life, self-ignorance remains secondary, episodic, repressed by the imperious need for self-justification, by the imperative to shatter the hostile and deforming mirror the world holds up to him. The desire for transparency abolishes the shadows. The wish to be transparent is, in a manner of speaking, to step through oneself without seeing oneself, without colliding with the opacity of our being, and with the shadowy figures that throng it.

Despite "this imperfect knowledge that one has of oneself," Rousseau deplores that it usually remains "the only means one uses for knowing others" (Ibid., 585). In fact, Rousseau is determined to write his life story to relieve readers of this illusion, the result of the self-esteem that would have us judge others as we judge ourselves, in order to instruct us to know our own hearts by "reading in someone else's"—meaning, in this case, in the heart of Jean-Jacques himself. For such a reading to be possible, Rousseau's undertaking must be unique, utterly unlike any other. Though he does not know "any other man up to now who has dared to do what I am proposing," it is because he pretends to read himself as though his heart were an open book (Ibid., 585). The exercise is unprecedented; one which autobiographers would do well to avoid. For they would then be faced with an irreconcilable contradiction:

> No one can write the life of a man except himself. His internal
> manners of being, his genuine life is known only to him; but he

disguises it when he writes it; under the name of his life he makes his apology; he shows himself as he wants to be seen, but not at all as he is. At most, the most sincere are truthful in what they say; but they live by their reticence; and what they keep silence about changes what they pretend to admit so much, that by saying only a part of the truth they do not say anything. (Ibid., 586)

The quality of sincerity, of total veracity extracts Rousseau from the contradiction inherent in all autobiography before him. If he has been true to his word, it is this quality that gives the narrative he is undertaking both its novelty and its unity. Rousseau offers nothing less, and nothing more, as a new point of departure in the history of self-narrative. The darkness all previous autobiographies have toiled so mightily to conceal, and that he, Jean-Jacques, will not hesitate to shine light upon, is due to amour-propre, which he takes considerable pains to distinguish from the love of self.[43] His is an Enlightenment psychology that, while nicely applicable to the subject of modernity's self-view, admits of no other internal darkness than that of bad faith. Or, at minimum, the residual ignorance of self that Rousseau appears to accept in each and every individual being has no untoward consequences. The governing truth of all autobiography lies in the good faith of he who lays it before us.

Rousseau thus appears, unbeknownst to himself, as an anti-Œdipus of sorts. The harsh truth that Sophocles' hero pursues matters little to him; nothing can undermine his confidence in the transparent integrity of his ego. To the bitter end, Jean-Jacques remains the man he takes himself to be: a person of good faith who has been unable to make himself understood. Until his dying breath, he remains certain he knows who he is, certain as well that he has never been mistaken about the nature of his feelings and his desires, which, he notes guardedly, have always remained deeply unsatisfied:

My passions have made me live, and my passions have killed me. What passions, it may be asked. Trifles, the most childish things in the world. Yet they affected me as much as if the possession of

43. See "First Dialogue" in *Rousseau, Judge of Jean-Jacques: Dialogues*, vol. 1 of *The Collected Writings of Rousseau*, ed. Roger D. Masters and Christopher Kelly, trans. Judith R. Bush, Christopher Kelly, and Roger D. Masters (Hanover: Published for Dartmouth College by University Press of New England, 1990): "The primitive passions, which all tend directly toward our happiness, focus us only on objects that relate to it, and having only the love of self as a principle, are all loving and gentle in their essence. But when they are deflected from their object by obstacles, they are focused on removing the obstacle rather than reaching the object; then they change nature and become irascible and hateful. And that is how the love of self, which is a good and absolute feeling, becomes amour-propre, which is to say a relative feeling by which one makes comparisons; the latter feeling demands preferences, whose enjoyment is purely negative, and it no longer seeks satisfaction in our own benefit but solely in the harm of another" (9).

Helen, or of the throne of the Universe, had been at stake. In the first place, women. When I possessed one my senses were quiet, but my heart never. At the height of my pleasure the need for love devoured me. I had a tender mother, a dear friend; but I needed a mistress. In my imagination I put one in Mamma's place, endowing her with a thousand shapes in order to deceive myself. If I had thought I was holding Mamma in my arms when I embraced her, my embrace would have been just as tender, but all my desires would have died. I should have sobbed with affection but I should have had no physical pleasure. Physical pleasure! Is it the lot of man to enjoy it? Ah, if ever in all my life I had once tasted the delights of love to the full, I do not think that my frail existence could have endured them; I should have died on the spot. (Book V, 209–210)

Rousseau knows he is in the grip of absence, but its source lies outside him. The quest for the object will suffice. It also typifies the relationship that modern thought has established, particularly in science, between subject and object. Rousseau's failure to encounter the object that would have meant his fulfillment has exhausted him. He would never have survived the encounter! But even at the cost of his life, he would have attained the fulfillment to which he would succumb. All this by way of underlining how ready he was to accept such an outcome—and there is nothing truly startling about hoping for such a fine death. In Rousseau, the impossible encounter with amorous plenitude finally joins hands with the impossibility of social recognition. Other people—life itself—are constantly passing him by; he is never the one who passes life by, who passes other people by. Never speaking of himself. For, in the final analysis, Rousseau would create a special place for the *self*, which he places at the far extremity of amour-propre, which, like most of us, he fails to encounter—that very *self* whose strangeness he can neither demonstrate, nor envision, and whose abyssal depths he cannot conceive of.[44]

There is a remarkable intensity about the infirmity he lays before us seemingly by inadvertence: its singular quality is nothing more than principial infirmity, the modern subject's blind spot that Freud would later reveal as internal fracture, as black hole. If the *Confessions* remain so compelling, it is because they convey masterfully the wound of childbirth that we would all be sorely tempted to return to and lick whenever the insupportable sovereignty of our ego stumbles and falls. In Rousseau, the inadequacy of the ego finds its expression, *a contrario*, in an existential lament that knows nothing of its roots, and that exonerates it from the painful duty of turning inward

44. These considerations on the impasse of the self in Rousseau are drawn from a cordial exchange with Anne Fortin, whose insights have been precious.

upon itself—a necessity laid down by Spinoza, a century earlier. It is the unconscious exposure of Rousseau's inadequacy that charms us, misleads and exasperates us. His tragedy is that of modern man who, in wishing to open his heart, to justify himself to the world, seals himself off instead. He is a suffering Narcissus, whose image only the malevolent breath of his fellow man can disturb.

There is much more to Rousseau than infirmity, of course; he is not merely the misunderstood hero of his truth. If that were all, he would be of little interest. For through the agency of his wound he speaks truth about the modern world. Rousseau, halfway between Augustine and Proust, can be seen as the symptom of the sickness of modern man, of the man who believes in himself and attempts to convince others of as much. Augustine develops his relationship with God, Proust his relationship with self-obliviousness. Rousseau can conceive only of his certainty about himself. We are fascinated, in the end, by his posture of weakness. Jean-Jacques is modern man, power-less against his image, who blames society for his impotence. Disconcertingly, he is modern and anti-modern all at once: his *I* partakes of modernity in both positive and negative senses. Positively, by playing back as emotion the illusion of the sovereignty of the subject. Negatively, by align-ing itself in the same breath against the triumph of modernity, with an intensity altogether proportional to the excess he inveighs against. A portion of Rousseau's excess is due to his own heroic resistance to the perverse impact of civilization. Rather like Hamlet, Rousseau's hero thrives on the very atmosphere he would love to disentangle himself from. Except that Shakespearian pessimism is irremediable: Hamlet cannot imagine what could possibly tear man from his essential distress; Jean-Jacques, meanwhile, rages against the civilizing arrogance that holds man far from the primordial state that society has not completely stifled in him, and that is ours to discover or rediscover.

By means of writing and in spite of it, the *Fifth Walk* prodigiously succeeds in describing this animal sensibility, this primitive anima. All the vain turmoil of the world, all its misfortune, are dissolved in the pure sensa-tion of existence the walker experiences as he drifts along in his rowboat. Even though the unfortunate Jean-Jacques cannot resist the temptation to define himself once more as "cut off from human society," he nonetheless contrives to forget his tribulations in the meandering current of an inexpress-ible felicity. Forgetfulness and abandon have replaced avowal: the idea behind the *Confessions*, the desire for self-justification, the desire to show oneself in the full truth of one's person, has ceased to apply. Instead, in this passage of a rare serenity, Rousseau reveals the full vanity of his autobio-graphical endeavor. In a moment of grace that pervades his writing, his grievances and resentments are diluted in the immediacy the solitary walker has recreated. The writing gives voice to the very thing that makes it obsolete. A spark of truth is released; it promptly destroys all that his writing has attempted so far to achieve as its task of rehabilitation. Rehabilitation and work are necessary no longer. The writing of the *Fifth Walk*, by opening the door to silence, casts a much gentler light upon the *Confessions*. They are to be valued not so much because of their narrator's concern for truth and trans-parency, but for what they bring together above and beyond his intentions: to give life to the moments of truth that surpass and submerge the incurable, narcissistic wound of he who speaks.

8

FAUST:
THE MASTERY OF THE WORLD

To PENETRATE INTO THE FAUSTIAN UNIVERSE is no small matter. Missteps, slips, and falls threaten at every turn. Just around each corner lurks the unexpected. Reading *Faust* is a kind of madness, like attempting to explore the Minotaur's labyrinth, the ruins of Troy, the Old Testament, the Way of the Cross, the Forest of Broceliand, Dante's journeys and the twists and turns of German romanticism all at once. Drawing little distinction between these worlds, the narrator scatters truths as well as diversions, falsities (I am sorely tempted to write "faustities") about him as he goes; the gentleman of good breeding he invests with a measure of blindness; the villain, with a measure of lucidity. Hardly surprising then that the reader's mind, caught up in the vortex, is intoxicated by the incessant play of light and shadow, of good and evil, of happiness and despair. Like Faust himself he slips from ecstasy to frustration, from irritation to serenity, always seeking, never satisfied, in perpetual quest for unknown worlds to conquer, for new tasks to accomplish; who finds peace only in that world beyond death where we, the living, cannot follow him.

The narrator does not simply blur the issue; he goes to such great length to conceal his own tracks that we no longer know who is telling the tale: Faust, or Mephistopheles? The characters they encounter? Goethe? Goethe, of course. *Faust* is, literally, his life's work. He began it at age twenty-four and continued to work on it until his death. There can be no doubt that the poet identifies with his hero. But Faust eludes him. Faust had existed before him, and would never entirely be his. A certain Georg Johann Faust (Goethe was to name his hero Heinrich), an alchemist, necromancer, physician, and charlatan, actually lived in Germany, from 1480 to 1540. His life and career nurtured a legend that was to inspire several authors before and after Goethe, including Marlowe. But that literary outburst cannot alone explain why the character himself, even in Goethe's text, has remained so elusive. The poet has clearly encountered a character that will not release him—for life. He may master—ah, what mastery!—the language in which he will wage his combat, but his double is constantly surpassing him. *Faust* is not told; it is lived. Life lived as incessant superabundance, which only death (the poet's and his hero's) can bring to an end; lived as no more and no less than the question of life itself, that of the meaning of our passage across this earth. In the battle of titans he wages against and with Faust, Goethe single-handedly takes on the human condition. *Faust* is the epic and lyric poem of the human condition as Goethe wished it to be, believed it to be, and experienced it.

Will, belief, action. We cannot always work our will, as Augustine knew all too well; what we can do we have not always willed; we often believe we have willed while dark powers sweep us along. *Faust* is the illustration, made act by its very writing, of those rifts, of that irony, of that so oft misguided, desire-charged wandering of his, through good and through evil. There is no narration to speak of, nor is there a narrator, nor even any possible stage setting for a tragedy that beggars description. As in Dante, who clearly inspires Goethe, we have the poet's vivid, tragic, and yet game-like experience as he struggles against himself through the ambiguous, riveting figure of his protagonist. His poetry, in its untranslatable beauty, is the breath that blows open all the doors onto the mad and chaotic world we call our own.

A lone character, then: Faust, this multiple-headed hydra. Yet the poem teems with characters, so many that we cannot keep track of them all. And even if we were to consider all those whom we encounter in this squirming catch as walk-ons, we would still be left with Mephistopheles, with Wagner, the Homunculus, the emperor, and others too numerous to mention ... not to forget the women, Margareta (or Gretchen), and Helen of Troy. But let us for the moment set the ladies aside, and focus our attention on the male of the species: on Faust, the pivotal axis. All the major male characters, including Mephistopheles, are doubles of the hero and of the poet who tells the tale. Like the latter, they are at once inseparable and separate.

What distinguishes Mephistopheles from Faust is made clear both at the beginning and at the end of the drama. At the end, the Devil proves incapable of snaring his protégé's soul; at the beginning, in his complicity with the Lord (*der Herr*). The Lord himself intervenes only once: outside the poem proper, in a prologue that does not seem entirely necessary, but that takes on its full meaning when seen against the entire work. In it, the principal elements of the Faustian drama are already present. Faust is trapped in a contradiction he cannot grasp, and whose solution escapes him. On hearing the three archangels praise divine good works, how easily Mephistopheles waxes ironic—he who denies that he possesses the art of words!—how easily he reminds the Lord that far beneath the celestial beauty of the spheres lies suffering humanity:

> The little god of earth remains the same queer sprite
> As on the first day, or in primal light.
> His life would be less difficult, poor thing,
> Without the gift of heavenly glimmering;
> He calls it reason, using light celestial
> Just to outdo the beasts in being bestial.
>
> (I, 40)[45]

Man is such a sad case that the idea of tormenting him provokes only disgust. As with Job in the Old Testament, the Lord refutes Mephistopheles by invoking his servant Faust. A strange servant indeed, responds the Devil, is that man who only half-realizes his folly, who finds nothing in the most beautiful stars, or in the greatest earthly joys, to assuage his insatiable desire. True enough, the Lord concedes:

> Though now he serves me in bewildered ways,
> My light shall lead him soon from his despairing,
> Does not the grower see in leafy days
> His sapling's years of blossom and of bearing?
>
> (I, 41)

At which point Mephistopheles lays down his famous challenge. He wagers that he will lose Faust and asks that he may guide him in his fashion along his journey. And the Lord, magnanimously:

> You shall have leave to do as you prefer,
> So long as earth remains his mortal dwelling;
> For man must strive, and striving he must err.
>
> (I, 41)

45. Johann Wolfgang von Goethe, *Faust, Part One*, trans. Philip Wayne (London: Penguin Books, 1969). Because citations from *Faust, Part Two* appear later in this chapter, references in parentheses include "I" or "II" to distinguish between the two parts.

These few exchanges succinctly lay down the limits of human action, and at virtually the same time, the outcome of Faust's wager, and his fate. From the start, the Lord serenely establishes the supremacy of his position in restricting the Devil's function to his victim's lifetime. And within those limits he views Mephistopheles' endeavor as a necessary evil. Among denying spirits, he prefers the diabolical:

> Man's efforts sink beneath his proper level,
> And since he seeks for unconditioned ease,
> I send this fellow, who must goad and tease
> And toil to serve creation, though a devil.[46]

(I, 42)

Mephistopheles has perfectly internalized his role, we soon realize, and subordinated it almost unconsciously to the divine order, in introducing himself, in his first meeting with Faust, as: "*Ein Teil von jener Kraft, / Die stets das Böse will und stets das Gute schaft*" ("Part of a power that would / Alone work evil, but engenders good" [I, 74].) The attentive reader is put on notice that Mephistopheles' wager, that he can win Faust's soul, is more than likely to fail. He knows too that the hero will continue to wander, to err, to stumble — for error, and wandering too, are inherent in the ardor of the human quest, and that unrelenting aspiration, *Streben*, stands for all that in man most pleases the Lord. Nature has no love of idleness, and the diabolical force that, year in year out, drives the most enterprising among us represents, here below, all that is best about our humanity. Even before the drama has begun, we can be all but certain that Faust will stray *and* that he will be saved.

At the same time, evil no longer looms as a simply external calamity. In fact, it is the hidden motor embedded in the human heart. Mephistopheles does little more than make it visible, manifest. Beyond the coldness of his cynicism and the compass of his sleight of hand, he ends up appearing all too human. All too like a human, he must acknowledge the limits of his power and his knowledge, not to mention the frustrations caused by his protégé's erratic behavior. Mephistopheles is by no means omnipotent, especially when he must respond to the exorbitant demands of him in whose service he feigns to be engaged, and whom he would prefer to lead. Unlike the relationship between Jacques and his master, it is difficult to know exactly who gives the orders, and who obeys. In the final analysis, both are the unconscious servants of a fate that eludes them. Only the Lord, himself absent from the

---

46. *Der reizt und wirkt und muss als Teufel schaffen*, literally: he who stimulates, acts and must create in his capacity as Devil.

stage throughout the drama proper, including the final apotheosis, may hold the invisible key.

Faust is a Don Juan who ends well, who escapes damnation: a happy outcome that appears to subvert the tragic nature of the drama. Yet the author has taken care to identify it as a tragedy: *Faust. Eine Tragödie*. The tragic aspect of the Faustian condition surely stems from the fact that the hero is not the master of his fate, but this alone cannot satisfactorily define it; the same condition, after all, can be found in comedy as well. In *Jacques the Fatalist*, Jacques is constantly aware that he is not the master of his life, which is not enough to transform him into a tragic hero. The precondition of the tragic is absolute evil, such as the *até* that strikes Œdipus, Antigone, and Phedra, the evil from which no one can recover.[47] Not only does Faust rebound after each of his misfortunes, but he ultimately—his soul, at least—rises up toward the absolute he has always dreamed of. We can hardly imagine a happier ending: Christian eschatology has been accomplished. For all the religious symbols strewn alongside it, there is nothing particularly Christian about the path that leads him there. Faust lives as a pagan, much of the ideal he pursues he will seek out in the ancient, pre-Christian world. Yet something about Faust's escape from misfortune remains obscure, something that the character himself cannot grasp. Though his death may have become an assumption, it has brutally cut short a life that is far from fulfilled. The soul's salvation removes none of the tribulations of the world that will live on after him. Perhaps the tragedy of his earthly adventure lies here, barely concealed from prying eyes, in the world he has left behind, where his best efforts have remained unfinished.

To grasp the tragic extent of his adventure we must first be able to relate it. Yet among the aspects of Faust's life is its resistance, quite like the play itself, to any attempt at narration: it stands before us as literally un-narratable. The fragmentation of the narrative in *Faust* is manifestly willed, quite as deliberately as in *Tristram Shandy* or *Jacques the Fatalist*. Except that for Goethe, disorganization, far from being a game, is cast as necessity that arises neither solely nor even principally from the drama's supernatural episodes, for some of them (such as the spaniel's transformation into Mephistopheles) can be easily staged. No, it derives from a far deeper, poetic choice that requires the abolition of time and space. Places and historical periods are condensed in such a way that the characters come and go in a single, borderless space-time continuum. Episodes accumulate pell-mell, as prefigured in the

47. Not in the play, in any event. Although we could claim that in Sophocles Œdipus finally recovers in *Œdipus at Colonus*, that is another work; in *Œdipus Tyrannos*, tragedy of tragedies, all comes to a bad end.

three pieces that precede the drama proper (Dedication, Prelude on the State, Prologue in Heaven).

Judging by the first scenes, the play appears to take place in a German university town between the Middle Ages and the Renaissance. But it quickly becomes apparent that this is precisely the time-space nexus that Faust is determined to escape, having devoted far too long to teaching and study, the results of which seem to him arid and denatured. He who has reached his prime, he who has devoted the best years of his life to knowledge, has achieved nothing.

The long nocturnal monologue that, as the curtain rises, begins with his sad litany sketches out in lapidary detail the unfortunate doctor's wild mood swings as though Faust were reliving, in the space of one hour, the high and the low points of an entire lifetime. His lamentations on the vanity, the sorrow, and moral and material poverty that science has bequeathed to him gives way to hope in magic: through it alone can he hope to apprehend the world in its essential truth, to deliver it from "huckstering with words" (I, 44). Moonlight affords his dream the enchanted path that beckons him toward the ethereal spheres; but its glow, expiring as it gleams dimly through the painted glass of his cell, illuminates only the dusty bric-a-brac of the books and objects that encumber it.

> And shall I wonder why my heart
> Is lamed and frightened in my breast,
> Why all the springs of life that start
> Are strangely smothered and oppressed?
> Instead of all that life can hold
> Of nature's free, god-given breath,
> I take to me the smoke and mould
> Of skeletons and dust and death.
> Up and away! A distant land
> Awaits me in this secret book
> From Nostradamus' very hand,
> Nor for a better guide I look.
>
> (I, 45)

Here lies a paradox: Faust believes for a brief instant that he can escape his bookish universe by opening a book! As he gazes at the sign of the macrocosm, his blood boils with renewed youth; the world stands before him in all the celestial energy of its creation, shot through with the divine. But the fabulous spectacle is, alas, only a spectacle. Abjuring the cosmos, a dejected

Faust falls back upon a lesser sign, that of the spirit of the earth, which he calls forth with all his powers, even though he must pay with his life. The Spirit reveals itself, and Faust finds himself unable to look upon it—*Weh! Ich ertrag dich nicht!* (I, 48) Though Faust claims to be its equal, the Spirit reminds him of the terror that made him crawl at His feet like a worm:

> SPIRIT
> You match the spirit that you comprehend,
> Not me! (*He vanishes*)
>
> FAUST (*filled with dismay*)
> Not you!
> Whom then?
> I, made in God's own image,
> And not with you compare! (*a knock*)
> Damnation, that will be my Servitor!
> My richest hope is in confusion hurled;
> He spoils my vision of the spirit world,
> This lickspittle of learning at my door.
>
> (*WAGNER in dressing gown and night-cap, carrying a lamp. FAUST turns reluctantly*)
>
> WAGNER
> Beg pardon, but I heard you, Sir, declaiming—
> Some tragedy, I'll warrant, from the Greek?—
> That's just some learned art at which I'm aiming,
> For people are impressed when scholars speak.
>
> (I, 49)

The sudden arrival of the master's famulus reveals his bad faith; he blames his valet for the decline precipitated by his failed encounter with the Spirit. Sinister and comic all at once, the shift in register reminds us that Faust's ambitions have now become the butt of derision. In the brief exchange of ideas between the master and his assistant, the latter peppers his speech with commonplaces and concludes ingratiatingly: "I cannot rest until my knowledge is complete." Wagner's stupid pretentiousness is enough to plunge Faust into his own feelings of impotence, of pettiness. From atop a bookshelf a familiar vial beckons, and assuages his melancholy. The lethal elixir remains the ultimate escape from mediocrity, the ascending, ethereal path toward "spheres of pure activity" (I, 54). That he would risk his life is more than an empty boast:

> The hour is come, as master of my fate
> To prove in man the stature of a god,
> Nor blench before the cavern black and fell,
> Imagination's torment evermore,
> But dare the narrow flaming path of hell
> And stride in strength towards the dreaded door.
> This risk I take in cheerful resolution,
> Risk more than death, yea, dare my dissolution.

(I, 54)

The cup touches his lips as the canticles of Easter sunrise, sounding from afar, bring to mind not his absent faith, but the rocking of his infant's cradle, and the kiss of heavenly love that were his that day: "Tears dim my eyes: earth's child I am again" (I, 66).

Unable to reach the Spirit, Faust will fall back upon lesser company, someone his own size, against whom he can measure himself, and who will agree in turn to operate at his own level: his double, Mephistopheles. If Wagner here stands for the scholarly, academic, humdrum reasonableness Faust hopes to jettison, Mephistopheles embodies the demon that has never ceased to lurk inside him. For all his cynicism, the demon in question is not only, or even essentially malevolent. It is also, in the Socratic sense, Faust's *daemon*: that long-repressed inner voice to which disgust at his long years of study now force him to lend an ear. Mephistopheles is life,[48] appetite in its crudest form, purged of all sentimentality; it is the brutality (except on one critical occasion, at the very end of the drama) that makes him insensible to love—and lucid about the secret wellsprings of Eros. Mephistopheles stands for a subconscious that is aware of itself, but that Faust is blind to. And, in the manner of the subconscious, he suggests breathtaking short cuts that his protégé follows without understanding why. Faust has not entirely turned his back on Eros. He is "too old to be content with play, / Too young to be untroubled by desire" (I, 84). Here lies his strength, his weakness, and the deeper meaning of his ambiguous pact with the Devil.

The terms of the pact are far from clear; the flaw, the inarticulateness embedded in its heart form a narrow and precious space within which the two parties can *play*, here understood both as game and as mechanical function. Faust does not invert Pascal's wager; he does not bet pleasure and earthly omnipotence against eternal damnation: that is not what the Devil, who knows

---

48. Mephistopheles invites Faust to break the chains that bind him and to taste life: *Damit du, loshebunden, frei / Erfahrest was Leben sei* (84): "With freedom such as gods may give, / Discover what it means to live!"

whom he is dealing with, is suggesting. Mephistopheles simply offers his assistance, but is cautious when it comes to discussing its price. We will see in due time: "If when we meet upon the other side / You undertake to do the same for me" (I, 86). Faust is in no rush to spell out the terms of the contract because he refuses to take seriously what the afterlife may hold in store; above all, he desires to taste the delights of this earth to the fullest, even at the cost of his own destruction.[49] We will return to the destructive side of Faustian desire, which pops up like a Freudian slip. The important thing, at this stage of the intrigue, is that Faust's impetuousness is not all that it seems. Mephistopheles concludes from his protégé's devil-may-care attitude that it will be enough to enslave him to his desires, but in reality it derives from Faust's awareness that his demon hasn't the faintest idea of what he is attempting to experience:

MEPHISTOPHELES
I'll show you arts and joys, I'll give you more
Than any mortal has seen before.

FAUST
And what, poor devil, pray, have you to give?
When was a mortal soul in high endeavor
Grasped by your kind, as your correlative
Yours is the bread that satisfieth never,
Red gold you have, dissolving without rest,
Like quicksilver, to mock the gatherer's labor;
The girl you give will nestle on my breast
Only to ogle and invite my neighbor....

FAUST
If I be quieted with a bed of ease,
Then let that moment be the end of me!
If ever flattering lies of yours can please
And soothe my soul to self-sufficiency,
And make me one of pleasure's devotees,
Then take my soul, for I desire to die;
And that's a wager!

MEPHISTOPHELES
Done!

---

49. *Das Drüben kann mich wenig kümmern; / Schlägst du erst diese Welt su Trümmern, / Die andre mag danach entstehen. / Aus dieser Erde guellen meine Freuden* ... ; "The other side weighs little on my mind / Lay first this world in ruins, shattered, blind; / That done, the new may rise its place to fill. / From springs of earth my joys and pleasures start ... " (I, 86).

FAUST
If to the fleeting hour I say
"Remain, so fair thou art, remain!"
Then bind me with your fatal chain.
For I will perish in that day.

(I, 86–87)

Faust has just upped the ante. But the misunderstanding persists. Mephistopheles believes he has caught him in the trap of concupiscence, of carnal desire, while his protégé, though vulnerable to the temptations of the flesh, seeks nothing less than love. Mephistopheles knows it; he is nobody's fool. His own diabolical function is to bring about, to incarnate the final schism, to turn the soul against itself, to take up residence at the nexus of amorous attraction and carnal impulse—those two draft horses of the soul, of which Socrates speaks in *Phedra*. By exploiting the division, Mephistopheles will undermine the nascent amorous passion between Faust and Margareta. But by destroying it he will inadvertently rescue the two lovers from hell. Henceforth passion, to claim its just desserts, demands Faust's rejuvenation. This he accomplishes by taking a potion Mephistopheles cannot concoct, but which he must procure from a witch trained by the Devil. Faust, even before taking a sip, perceives in a mirror the sublime yet terrifying image of the ideal woman of his heart's desire. But when, having drunk the beverage, Faust returns for a final glance in the mirror, his tutor scolds him:

Nay, nay, that paragon of womanhood
Shall reward your gazing in the flesh.
(*aside*) A dose like that without your guts, my boy,
and every other wench is Helen of Troy.

(I, 120)

The surreptitious naming of Helen in an aside, even before Margareta makes her appearance, will assume its full significance in the second part of the tragedy. For the moment, we must turn our attention to Margareta.

Their first meeting is a frivolous one. The seducer seems still under the influence of the drinking bout orchestrated by Mephistopheles in a Leipzig tavern before their visit to the witch's lair. Faust's first gesture could be straight out of *Don Juan*: he addresses the passer-by as "fair lady" and, without further ado, takes her arm, forcing her to tear herself away. He then summons Mephistopheles to play the pimp: "The girl, go win her sir, for me!" (*Hör, du musst mir die Dirne schaffen!*) (I, 120)—*Dirne*: girl in the vulgar sense; slattern. The gallant addresses the Lady; the debauchee, his devilish side, wants only to fuck her. But shortly thereafter, alone in Margareta's chambers among the objects that evoke her presence, the pleasure-seeker no longer recognizes himself. He melts with love, convinced that should he surprise her in her bed, he, the personification of Don Juan, or rather, "the upstart lout" (*Der grosse Hans*), would grovel at her feet (I, 125). In a rapid succession of scenes, even before the relationship gets underway, and in the absence of its object, Faust makes his way through all the strata of love, from the lightest and rawest to the most passionately infantile, the most abjectly servile.

Their budding liaison will follow the same curve. Loftiness of soul, passion, childishness, consummation, and dizziness follow one another in rapid succession until the final separation. Burned by the Faustian flame, the prudish Margareta herself oscillates between seduction and conquest on the one hand, and the double temptation of self-indulgence and the flesh, and of repentance and saintliness, on the other. Still, her original innocence remains intact; she is repelled by contact with the Devil's part that pops up like a malicious shadow beside her lover, whom she ultimately confounds, to her horror, with Mephistopheles. Faust, by now having become her brother's murderer, after having possessed then momentarily abandoned her in the wild night of Walpurgis, ends up joining in his prison cell the woman whose fate Mephistopheles had concealed from him. Incredulous, Margareta, amorous and liberated, welcomes him as a savior. All too quickly Faust's lips become a breath of ice (I, 195), her lover's hand, still dripping with the blood of her brother, reminds her of her own crimes, the murder of her child, the pain of death inflicted upon her mother. Nothing can relieve her guilt. The presence of Faust, who offers to stay with her, weighs heavily upon her:

MARGARETA
I will not yield to force! Let me alone!
Nay, come not near me with your murderous reach,
When all my love I gave you as your own.

FAUST
Dear heart, dear heart, now breaks the day.

MARGARETA
Day, yes, the day; the last dread day breaks in.
My wedding day it should have been....

We two shall meet again,
But never again in the dance....

On the scaffold I stand alone,
The crowd gazes up on high,
Each feeling the keen edge nigh,
As if my throat were his own!

FAUST
Would I have never been born!

MEPHISTOPHELES (*appearing without*)
Lost are you both if you stay.
Can you not see it is morn?
Away!
You hover and chatter yet
While my horses tremble and sweat.
Wherefore delay?
The dawn grows bright.

MARGARETA
What evil thing has risen from the ground?
He, ah, not he!—Forbid him from my sight!
On holy ground he has no right,
He wants my soul, to torture and confound,
He wants my death!

FAUST
Nay, you shall live!

MARGARETA
Into God's hand my trembling soul I give.

MEPHISTOPHELES (*to FAUST*)
Come, or I let you share her wretched end.

MARGARETA
Lord, I am thine, oh, save me and defend!
Father, let angels now have charge of me,
Encamped around in heavenly company.
Heinrich, I have a dread of thee.

MEPHISTOPHELES
She is condemned to die!

A VOICE (*from above*)
Is redeemed on high.

MEPHISTOPHELES (*to FAUST*)
Higher, to me! (*He vanishes, with FAUST*)

VOICE (*from within, dying away*)
Heinrich! Heinrich!

(I, 196–197)

Were the Faustian epic to end with this tragic denouement, Mephistopheles would emerge as the victor, having won his wager with Faust. But the best he can do is carry away Faust's body. The waning call of the inner voice (Margareta's) conveys what the lover, judged but saved, had earlier told her beloved: it will not be at the ball, but they will see one another again. Mephistopheles has, at best, won the first round. And what this round reveals to us about Faust is no less troubling. He stands before us like the plaything of disjointed, divided time (in a literally diabolical sense) in a way that once more echoes *Hamlet*. His disjointedness robs his acts—and his desires—of all coherence, of all continuity. In its dizzying spin the famous night of Walpurgis erases all memory. At most, his lascivious dance with a female demon brings Margareta's image alive for a split second. If we wish to find out, reading between the lines, what has become of her, we must await the gray light of the pre-dawn hour to understand how that wild night has simultaneously abolished and sped up time: as the prison scene indicates, the lover had time enough to bear a child, and to cause it (or leave it?) to die, assuming that both the newborn and its death are not the result of his delirium.

Like balm on the painful nightmare that ends the first part, the second opens with a scene of bucolic enchantment ... and obscenity. With the help of a troupe of elves, Ariel, the amicable and caring character borrowed from Shakespeare's *Tempest*, soothes the torments of the "saint or sinner" whose unhappiness he bewails. Are we dreaming? Faust, restored to the light of the world, made new, engorged with new desires, blinded for an instant by the ambivalent gleam of the rising sun that reminds him of the fires of hell, turns his back on the morning star. Once more he is prepared to throw himself into the "mirrored glitter" of life, which that very star holds out to him in its shimmering beauty.

It is not long before Faust's rebirth takes on, under the aegis of Mephistopheles, all the appearances of a carnival; it takes a political turn as well. We now find ourselves at the emperor's court where ministers and counselors are struggling to distract him from the merrymaking and bring him back to cold reality. Evil has corrupted the State: injustice flourishes, crimes go unpunished, ill-paid soldiers prey upon the populace, bankruptcy looms, the wine supply is depleted. General collapse looms. As if to confirm that debacle threatens the realm, a new king's fool, more impudent even than his predecessor, has taken up a position at the foot of the throne he bids fair to save from ruin. Brushing aside the suspicion that greets his ascension, Mephistopheles promises to bring about whatever the prince might wish, and more! The earth, he whispers seductively, is a buried treasure waiting to be dug up and turned to account. Is the emperor not already wealthy from all that lies unexploited below the ground? He need only issue a promissory note against the inexhaustible resources under his authority, and calculate in bank notes the full virtual value of the world he rules, which labor will fructify. On the strength of this promise, everyone can abandon himself to folly, and the carnival can begin. Surrounded by a multitude of figures from Greek mythology, Plutus takes the lead:

> The time is come to set the treasure free,
> To smite the looks I take the Herald's rod.
> They spring apart! From brazen cauldrons, see
> The flow comes welling up like golden blood,
> The wealth of crowns and rings and chains comes pouring
> In molten blaze that threatens their devouring.
>
> (II, 59)[50]

To illustrate how fire devours gold, Plutus orchestrates the lighting (or is it a mock version?) of a fire that threatens to raze everything in its path: the palace, the country, the emperor himself. But he commands the clouds and the rain to extinguish it in time. Whether it is an ephemeral flare-up or a magician's trick, it reminds us that riches are mere illusion. Yet illusion, by acting upon the imagination, by fanning the flames of desire, has the power to enrich. Be it metal or paper, money is nothing but appearance, yet we need only believe in it for appearance to become reality, and to reinvigorate the economy.

That is not enough for the emperor, though. Enrichment is for him a bagatelle. He is looking to amuse himself, and demands more enchanting magic: for "the loveliest type of woman and of man," Helen and Paris, to appear before him (II, 75). The task that Faust undertakes is of mind-

---

50. Johann Wolfgang von Goethe, *Faust, Part Two*, trans. Philip Wayne (London: Penguin Books, 1969).

boggling proportions, one that involves a perilous journey amongst the
pagans, a world that is of no interest to Mephistopheles, one that "occupies
its own peculiar hell" (II, 76). There is one way, he realizes, for him to
achieve his ends, but it will force him, against his will, to reveal the inner-
most secrets.

MEPHISTOPHELES
Goddesses dwell, in solitude, sublime,
Enthroned beyond the world of place or time;
Even to speak of them dismays the bold.
They are the Mothers.

FAUST
Mothers?

MEPHISTOPHELES
Stand you damned?

FAUST
The Mothers! Mothers—sound with wonder haunted.

MEPHISTOPHELES
True, goddess unknown to mortal mind,
And named indeed with dream among our kind
To reach them, delve below earth's deepest floors;
And that we need them, all the blame is yours.

FAUST
Were lies the way?

MEPHISTOPHELES
There is none. Way to the Unreachable,
Never for treading, to those Unbeseechable
Never besought! Is your soul then ready?

(II, 76–77)

In this enigmatic passage, possibly the most troubling of the whole
Faustian epic, Mephistopheles sends his protégé back to the unfathomable
primeval matrix, as if to punish him for having inconsiderately promised the
emperor the woman that Faust desires for himself. The quest for the feminine
ideal, personified by Helen, must begin with a return to the wellsprings of
life, to the undiscoverable locus of birth. Were the hero to be sent back to his
mother, we would still be within the human purview and there would be nothing strange about the reference, even though the matrix through which we

have emerged into the world, that "origin of the world" laid bare by Courbet, represents for each one of us the darkest, the most mysterious passage we have ever undertaken. The plural form, the Mothers, *die Mütter*, deepens the mystery, evoking as it does a kind of infinite cosmogony, single and at the same time multiple, wherein lies the principle of the universe. This primordial crucible clearly stands outside of time and place; no one can ever hope to attain it. Faust's quest is that of a madman, condemned to failure even before it begins; he can only return empty-handed, if he returns at all. The threat is sublime, mind-bending: these terrifying Mothers summon forth childhood fears, the horror of being swallowed up, sucked in, drawn back toward death by the very sphincter that propelled us into life.

But the threat is, ultimately, an infantile one, which the Devil seems secretly to mock. He arms Faust with a miraculous key that closely resembles the magic wands of fairytales, and feigns doubt about his companion's return, knowing full well that his doubt is a mere formality: as the court grows impatient to see Helen appear, Mephistopheles need only exclaim: "Mothers, O Mothers! Speed Faust on his way!" (II, 82), for him to reappear like a flower, mission accomplished! Instead of placing his life in danger, Faust has simply plunged deeper still into illusion. The two splendid figures that he brings back with him are pure virtuality. Seduced by a beauty that is far from extraordinary in the onlookers' eyes, the stage director is carried away by the phantoms that haunt his own theater. He dispatches Paris with a wave of his magic key, and makes ready to carry Helen away in his place. Then and there the vision collapses, bringing Faust down with it; it is left to Mephistopheles to carry his inert body away. The scene is pure Grand Guignol!

The farcical aspect is further accentuated in the next scene: Mephistopheles finds himself in the study that had been his protégé's at the beginning of the drama. Wagner, his erstwhile assistant, a man who is celebrated and respected, but who has remained humble and inconsolable at the inexplicable disappearance of his master, now rules in his stead, assisted in turn by a dreary famulus. Irony of ironies, the industrious thinker is on the verge of achieving the great work that Faust himself could not. Before Mephistopheles' eyes and perhaps thanks to his presence, Homunculus, a miniature, luminescent human being, comes into being in Wagner's phial. No sooner has he greeted his "little father" than the homunculus salutes the presence of his cousin Mephistopheles as a providential sign of the travail that awaits him. Seeing Faust lying there inanimate the tiny man escapes with his phial from the hands of his creator. Hovering luminous over the doctor's body, he reads his dreams. Where Mephistopheles cannot see, he can. He sees, amidst ravishing young girls, the beautiful Leda being seduced by the princely swan of legend. Homunculus, Mephistopheles' incandescent double, sends Wagner back to his pots and pans; he will now take Faust under his wing, and guide him into the timeless spheres where Mephistopheles appears to have lost his bearings, and his power. A second Walpurgis Night follows, a "classic" version this time around, an antique replica of the romantic night of the first part, during which, among myriad events, each one more wild and wooly than the one preceding it, Mephistopheles discovers that there are creatures quite capable of terrifying the Devil himself. These fearsome beings have assumed the appearance of the Phorkyades, the malevolent sisters of the Fates, who form a monstrous trinity beneath whose mask he will be able to function once more in a world that remains, in principle, closed to him.

Elevated to the second level of the mythological order, the narrative may now, in the third act of *Faust II*, either repeat, or carry on the tragedy of Helen. Admired, disparaged, "faithful" and, above all, desirous to forget her Trojan interlude, Menelaus's wife returns to her palace. There the Phorkyade, alias Mephistopheles, warns her against fate in the form of the mortal revenge of her deceived husband, and advises her that there is only one way to escape it. She must seek out in his castle the northern "barbarian," the lordly knight who alone can save her, alias Faust. In terms of barbarity, his castle is far more substantial, majestic, and well constructed than the grotesque palace of Menelaus. The signs of civilization have been inverted. There is no reason for the European Middle Ages to be jealous of Greek antiquity; they are demonstrably superior to it, in fact. That Faust himself is far more worthy of Helen than her sad husband goes without saying; he is also a far better abductor and protector than Paris. Now that Helen is held captive, and soon to be possessed by the guard imprisoned by her charms, love can at last contrive to flourish.

Love, or more precisely, the magic spell of love. Of it is born a miraculous infant, Euphorion, son of antiquity, of the Middle Ages, and of modernity. As his name indicates, the infant prodigy abounds in vitality; before long, driven by his ungovernable impulses, he escapes his progenitors. Imperious in love, Euphorion seeks to "force" a young girl whose rebel breasts he presses against himself; she, having predicted the death of her abductor, bursts into flame and escapes, ardent, from his embrace (II, 205). Leaping from rocky crags to mountain peaks, aspiring to mount ever higher, bedecked with wings, Euphorion, burning with the fire of his own desire, ends up like Icarus, plunging to earth. Euphoria consumes itself more quickly than even fire a heap of straw. The miracle of love stands forth for what it is: pure mirage. Cruelly torn, Helen takes her leave of Faust; he in turn keeps only her veil to remember her by. That length of gauze, that fabric seemingly woven from mist, is all that remains of Faust's fusion with the specter of his wild and willful love. But, as the Mephistophelian Phorkyade comments ironically, enough of Helen and Euphorion's rags and tatters are left for "poet's consecration, to stir up envy in their guilds devout" (II, 210). Once again, the poet holds up both his epic and his hero to magnificent mockery. Now he need only bring him back to earth.

Helen's love clearly matches the love of Margareta. The difference being that Margareta is real, as is her death, while Helen is imaginary, as is her disappearance. Reason enough perhaps to conceal the trysts of the former, and to expose, however briefly, those of the latter. No matter how perverted, Margareta remains chaste. Helen, the legendary harlot, has nothing to preserve, and shamelessly sells her wares. Exactly as the mock-tragic chorus that comments upon the scene:

> Not for majesty to deny
> Joys that are sweet,
> Yet in willfulness broadcast,
> Plain before the eyes of the people.

> (II, 191)

There is yet another negative symmetry: Margareta's unnamed child dies in concealment, probably from its mother's criminal intent or negligence, like a failed abortion. Meanwhile the aptly named Euphorion gives every appearance of sinking his teeth avidly into life, until he dies early of his excesses. Unless, like his mother before him, the fleeting apparition of his phantasmagorical figure has only vanished in the smoke of the Faustian dream that conjured him up the first place. Faust experiences the passion and the loss of Margareta like a trauma that only forgetting can cure—which the idyllic setting of the first scene of *Faust II* ensures. By contrast, Helen's passion and loss have all the appearances, the final break notwithstanding, of the cure itself, and of the indispensable experience of catharsis. Not for nothing is Act 3 cast in the form of a Greek tragedy, which frees Faust of his phantasms of fusion. He will have ultimately experienced love, in a brief instant of fulfillment and loss in the same breath, along with the love object, of the merest illusion of absolute love. At the beginning of the following act his loss deliberately takes on theatrical overtones: a cardboard cloud comes to rest on a rocky platform that Mephistopheles, within seconds, will recognize as the primordial fulcrum of hell. The cloud creaks open, Faust emerges, the cloud closes, elongates and, as it floats away, assumes the shape of a goddess worthy of Juno, Leda, or Helen, undulating magnificently in the firmament. The ethereal image quickly comes to rest in the Orient, like a distant glacier, then, rising up once again, incarnates (if we may say so) the beauty of the soul: "... all that's best within my soul," exclaims Faust, "it bears away" (II, 216).

Faust can now return, purged of the evil of love, to the affairs of the world. Mistaking his ambitions, Mephistopheles offers him pleasure, voluptuousness, glory—in vain.

FAUST
So realm and rule to me will fall;
The glory's naught, the deed is all.

MEPHISTOPHELES
Yet unborn poets will proclaim
To all posterity your fame,
More fools with folly to inflame.

FAUST
Shut out from life, you have no part
In things that stir the human heart
Your bitter mind where envy breeds
What can it know of human needs?

(II, 220)

He goes on to inform Mephistopheles, now resigned, that he seeks nothing less than to turn back the waves. Now, it just so happens that the emperor is experiencing military difficulties for having believed that he could "govern and indulge his appetite" at the same time. What a woeful error! For "he who has to hold Command of men must have a leader's mind" (II, 223). In exchange for the duo's assistance in reconquering his empire and regaining power, Faust will be awarded the ocean shore as his fiefdom.

Without fear of anachronism, we can affirm that from that moment on, Faust's sexual impulse takes a new tack, and is channeled toward activity in the world. The Faustian ambition stands revealed, and can henceforth burst forth in its pioneering, civilizing dimension. His goal is no longer to possess the woman, but to conquer the earth. Such a conquest involves a kind of repression of the feminine, seen as the price for mastering nature. There is little doubt that Spengler is referring to this entrepreneurial thirst when, in his celebrated *Decline of the West*, he describes Western civilization as "Faustian." But that insatiable thirst dissatisfies Faust.

His dissatisfaction takes the form of a peculiar irritation he feels as he attains the pinnacle of success, at the sound of a bell, which echoes the Easter service of the first part, a cruel reminder of the lost paradise of childhood. As a messenger brings him news of the arrival of his last vessels, laden with the rich booty that Mephistopheles and his henchmen have pirated for him; as he is proclaiming his good fortune (*Dich grüsst das Glück zur Höchsten Zeit*: "fortune's crown for you is wrought"), the sound of a bell echoes across the dunes (*Das Glöckchen läutet auf die Düne*). The chapel whence comes the chiming of the bells belongs to a peaceable couple with the mythical names of Philemon and Baucis. Symbolizing the ripe, shared love that Faust has never attained, they live peacefully on a delightful little estate bordering the Faustian empire. The elderly couple's bell (*Glocke*) rings in ironic response to Faust's good fortune (*Glück*). The assonance is not fortuitous: chiming repeatedly, accompanied by the scent of sweet linden, it introduces a crack into the Faustian empire. Excessively interpreting his irritation, Mephistopheles and his stooges, who have been assigned the task of uprooting and resettling Philemon and Baucis far from their master's ears, contrive "by mistake" to burn down chapel, house, and garden along with their inhabitants. Faust curses their mindless violence without dwelling overlong on his own responsibility—"command too rash, too soon obeyed" (II, 262), he concludes. It seems not to occur to him that the violence, the predatory fury, are part and parcel of the logic of his insatiable enterprise of domination and accumulation, inseparable from what Mephistopheles calls the "invisible trinity" of war, trade, and piracy (II, 256).

The signs of his imminent end come calling. Four hags dressed in gray rise up before him in the depth of night: Want, Guilt, Care, and Need,[51] prefiguring their sister, Death. Only the figure of Care (*Sorge*) remains with him, for she is the most difficult to dismiss. She subsumes in herself all four, and insinuates herself into every situation, even those where her sisters dare not tread. Safe from want and from need, Faust may feel no guilt but he is defenseless against the poison of Care. Her insidious presence at the twilight of his life drives him to a curious kind of summing up, which is in the same breath a confession:

CARE
Is, then, black Care unknown to you?

FAUST
My way has been to scour the whole world through.

---

51. Respectively: *Mangel, Schuld, Sorge, Not.* The first and last are almost interchangeable, both meaning absence, necessity, need, and deprivation.

Where was delight, I seized it by the hair!
If it fell short, I simply left it there,
If it escaped me, I just let it go.
I stormed through life, through joys in endless train,
Desire, fulfillment, then desire again;
Lordly at first I fared, in power and speed,
But now I walk with wisdom's deeper heed....

CARE
He finds, once within my power,
His world is useless, from that hour,...

Always on the future waiting,
Nothing ever consummating.

FAUST
No more! You get no hold on me,
I spurn the folly that you say.
Get hence! Your wretched litany
Might lead the shrewdest man astray.

(II, 264–265)

[Care continues her description of the torments of he who falls under her spell.]

FAUST
'Tis hard, I know, of daemons to be rid,
The spirit-bond is difficult to sever;
But you, O Care, in stealing action hid,
Creep with power I will acknowledge never!

CARE
That power more potent you may find,
As with a curse I go my ways;
For mortal men through all their life are blind,
Which you, my Faust, shall be to end your days.
(*She breathes upon him*)

FAUST (*blinded*)
Deep falls the night, in gloom precipitate;
What then? Clear light within my mind shines still;
Only the master's word gives action weight,
And what I framed in thought I will fulfill.
Ho, you my people, quickly come from rest.
Let the world see the fruit of bold behest.

Man all the tools, spade, shovel as is due,
The world marked out must straight be carried through....

To end the greatest work designed,
A thousand hands need but one mind.

(II, 266–267)

Master Faust would rather know nothing of Care, and continues to labor with grim determination to bring about her curse. He chooses blindness over disquiet—and over quietude. Rejecting all rest, forfeiting any possibility of retreat, he throws himself head over heels into a new and grandiose enterprise: to reclaim even more land, and to drain the marshes that threaten his conquest. But the thousands of strong arms that Mephistopheles the foreman has recruited for the task are malevolent specters, dead souls, and the ditch they dig is not a ditch at all, but Faust's grave. Faust, meanwhile, carried away by the clank of picks and shovels, which he commands Mephistopheles to multiply a thousand fold using all the means at his disposal—seduction, money, compulsion—dreams of the fertile fields that he hopes to wrest from the elements. Pure illusion. The reclamation project will be short-lived. Such considerations can make no claims on his attention. Faust is already (and always has been, in a sense) outside of time. In anticipation he contemplates the entranced multitude frolicking and bustling about in the new earthly paradise, and clearly sees that the moment will come when he can, at last, call out to the moment: "Linger you now, you are so fair" (II, 270). But the phrase, which he rejoices in being able to utter and which, under the terms of his pact with the Devil, leads only to his damnation. Faust dies without uttering it.

Faust dies, at once fulfilled, unsatisfied, and blinded. Neither dikes nor jetties, whispers Mephistopheles, can stop the sea from reclaiming what is rightfully its own; our monumental constructions are doomed to destruction. And, for the ultimate moment to which poor Faust has attempted to cling, his diabolical servant, gazing down upon his corpse laid out in the grave prepared for him, utters these pitiless words: "This wretched, empty moment at the last" (*Den letzten, schlechten, leeren Augenblick*) (II, 270). The accusation draws a definitive line through a contemptible life. The suspensive, the fatal phrase had not been spoken, but Mephistopheles, who can read the heart, concludes that Faust has whispered it to himself: proof enough for him. Not only has Faust's life been in vain, but, bedazzled by the moment, he has committed the unpardonable sin of believing that it has been a success. Mephistopheles has won. Faust cannot escape hell. And yet Mephistopheles will lose the final round; he will not take Faust's soul down with him.

At first glance, the scene in which heaven and hell argue over his soul seems curiously artificial. Though it purports to take up where *Faust I's* "Prologue in Heaven" leaves off, we get the impression that the poet is overdoing it, that he is making gentle sport of himself, or showing amusement at religious naïveté of a certain stripe. Unless he is winking in the general direction of the precisely inverse scene that ends Molière's *Don Juan*, and Mozart and Da Ponte's *Don Giovanni*: where Don Juan vanishes, sucked into the mouth of hell, Faust ascends to join the angels. But such a reading would be too simple. Its lightness, for starters, does not jibe with the serious, profoundly poetic character of the vast Faustian fresco—despite its entangled nature; the tragedy (let us remind ourselves once more that this is what Goethe calls his *magnum opus*) cannot end on a note of coarse humor or by the salvatory intervention of *angeli ex machina*. But above all, in a struggle that pits celestial against diabolical, an event of the greatest magnitude is being played out.

If Faust's soul has eluded Mephistopheles, despite the tight security cordon manned by horned and hoofed auxiliaries he has marshaled around the deceased, it can only be because he has been distracted by a new blaze that sears him from head to toe, and whose origin he realizes only when it is too late. This "element of super Devil / More sharp and keen than hell's own fire" (II, 276) overcomes him when he beholds the lascivious dance of the angels' chorus that envelops him. For the first time, Mephistopheles experiences the burn of love. For a split second he feels, on his flesh and in his heart, the passion he had so often mocked in Faust. Quickly he gets himself under control, disgusted at having vacillated under the influence of this "cursed flame" and comforted at having saved "the Devil's limbs by his control" (II, 278): a magnificent expression that reminds us of the value that God himself attaches to negation in the prologue. For all that, his brief moment of distraction has given the angels time enough to spirit Faust's soul away with them. But their victory, though seemingly unjust at first glance, is more than the fruit of a ruse; the world may owe a heavy debt to the power of negation (to formulate the question in Hegelian terms), but it indicates that love's ardor can vanquish the icy embers of hell.

Through Faust, and beyond his personal case, something other than the fate of the soul is being played out. That something is the victory of love; Margareta's return at the end of the drama, like Beatrice for Dante, accompanies (and welcomes) the spiritual elevation of her former lover and joins forces with the eternal feminine, which draws him higher, always higher.

Still, Faust's fate—the fate of his soul—is not merely an appendage of the inevitable victory of the celestial forces over those of the lower world. In a certain sense Faust must prove himself *worthy* of an elevation that cannot be justified by purely divine or cosmological considerations. The reason for his salvation is clearly stated:

> *Wer immer strebend sich bemüht,*
> *Der können wir erlösen*

> Saved is our spirit-peer, in peace;
> Preserved from evil scheming:
> "For he whose strivings never cease
> Is ours for his redeeming."

(II, 282)

Because he has never given up, Faust is ultimately saved. At the very beginning, let us recall, the Lord proclaims: *Es irrt der Mensch solang er strebt*: "For man must strive, and striving he must err" (I, 41). The success or the failure of a life cannot be measured by its accomplishments, but by its never ceasing to *streben*, an untranslatable verb that means, simultaneously, to reach for, to aspire to, to exert efforts, to seek, to desire. *Streben* is a being's striving for what it does not possess, for what it cannot, yet seeks to, understand; it is the work of Eros. Faust, in his striving, in the aspiration that constantly breathes new life into him, encounters love. Only in retrospect does his passion for Margareta, then for Helen, take on the appearance of a phase of spiritual love, as a first step toward the love of the beautiful in and of itself. One must approach such love, declares Diotima in Plato's *Symposium*, by degrees, beginning with the attraction we feel at the sight of carnal beauty. But Goethe's borrowings from Greek tragic form do not make Faust an admirer of Plato. The Faustian character is drawn much more by the uses of power than by contemplation of the beautiful. We can even affirm that in his case the former dominates, at the expense of the latter.

Seen in this light, Faust is a thoroughly modern figure, a man in constant motion; recovered from his amorous disappointments, he can find pleasure only in transforming the world. In Faust, the will to power takes form as he awakens from the dream of love. Little matter that the same dream had already expressed a desire for (sexual) power; little matter that entrepreneurial fervor, as we have already seen, merely channels erotic tension toward other objects. We know too that there is something Promethean in that near obsessive will to power of his, and that it functions at the expense of lucidity. Even though Faustian blindness ultimately benefits he who must endure it, his victory over Care is real enough. It grants him access to the paradise of the spirit, separated from the human condition by an unbridgeable chasm. Intervention by the supernatural, by the divine, by the angels must take place so that Faust, or more precisely, his soul, may cross it. In this sense, a *Deus ex machina* has indeed descended, one that leaves wide open the question: what does the earthly striving of Goethe's hero mean?

Faust's soul may well have ascended to the spiritual heights; Faustian man, modern man, still remains blinded by his ambitions; whatever he leaves behind him has all the appearances of purposeless destruction. Faust has expanded his empire to the detriment of his neighbor's peace and quiet, as embodied by Philemon and Baucis. Yet all the destruction he has wrought is futile, for the achievements that justify it, as Mephistopheles reminds us, are also doomed to vanish. All on earth is provisional; all is precarious; we are left to wonder whether, in the name of our ephemeral constructions, the violence inherent in the entrepreneurial spirit can be justified as it lays waste the garden of those who seek only fleeting happiness in the contemplation of the world—particularly since this conquering violence recognizes no limit. Faust can never have enough; his enterprise, had death not cut it short, would have gone on expanding. In a state of constant irritation at all that escapes his grasp, his ascendancy subsumes everything. Despite his contentment in imagining the bright future his gigantic projects promise to deliver, nothing can ever satisfy him; he must hitch the whole world to his megalomania. In *Faust* lurks a judgment, perhaps even the poet's premonition about the industrial civilization whose birth he has witnessed and helps make a reality: Faustian civilization knows no limits; it seeks to bend all to its will to mastery; nothing can escape the excess of its voracious appetite.

Here, in the space between transcendence and earthly life, the tragic nature of the Faustian epic stands revealed. Few works body forth, with such richness and with such intensity, the contradictory, wrenching tension that has split Western civilization in half. Perhaps it would be more accurate to speak of tripolar rather than bipolar tension. Our civilization is torn between Eros, Prometheus, and Christ. We desire everything: amorous fusion, the mastery of the world, and eternal spirituality in human brotherhood. If the first two are interchangeable and complementary, the third remains, in its deepest essence, incompatible with them. Spirituality (and even less so fraternity) in another world cannot be the *post mortem* reward for long, hard labor of a humanity thirsting for power and possessions. If we do not culti-vate spirituality in this life, the only life that, failing evidence to the contrary, we have even a remote certainty of enjoying, nothing, not even the sleight of hand of the greatest poets, can ever open its doors for us. But that may also the poet's way of asking a crucial question, one we are ill-prepared to answer: is it possible for man to give up building, transforming, and exploring, even at the price of his peace of soul? Is it possible even for us to ask such a question without a radical shift in our relationship with death?

Perhaps, when all is said and done, as Romain Gary so eloquently puts it, "The tragedy of Faust is not at all that he sold his soul to the Devil. The real tragedy is that there is no Devil to buy your soul. There is no 'taker.'"[52]

---

52. Romain Gary, *Promise at Dawn*, trans. John Markham Beach (New York: Harper, 1961), p. 113.

9

HEGEL:
THE INCARNATION OF THE SPIRIT

G RAPPLING WITH A WORK as fundamental—and as difficult—as the *Phenomenology of Mind* from a narrative perspective is an endeavor fraught with risk; the temptation was great to turn aside from a task I frankly accept as being beyond my powers. Considering that Hegel, rather like Descartes before him, relates an adventure of the mind, I might have been tempted to make full use the freedom inherent in my approach to emphasize the adventurousness of his enterprise, and relegate to the background that adventure's extraordinary conceptual requirements—and even more, all that gives it its particularity: its near-insurmountable challenge to both exposition and understanding. For all that, I claim for myself precisely such freedom, the same freedom that belongs to every reader: the freedom to approach the *Phenomenology of Mind* (and not—about this I must be perfectly clear!— Hegel's thought) as a narrative. There is, of course, a proviso attached: this particular narrative differs radically from all those that we have examined thus far, both in terms of its volume and in its relation to its predecessors, Plato and Descartes included. So much does it differ from all that comes before that to discuss reading it would be of scant interest unless our "discussion," with all its inherent risk of failure, were to attempt to tell what cannot be told.

So radically resistant to telling is the *Phenomenology of Mind*, that we are overcome with vertigo as we tread its precipitous path; so intense is the vertigo that the pressure we feel mounting in our stroke-threatened brain can express itself only in wild, liberating, restorative laughter. Why, then, even attempt to relate what cannot be related? Why undertake the task here; why not simply abandon it at philosophy's doorstep? To which I answer, as certain civilian authorities respond to certain military men: so as not to leave the *Phenomenology of Mind* to the philosophers. In fact, to take up this book dressed "in civilian clothes," with no bullet-proof vest for protection, no heavy artillery for support, may also provide the best opportunity to read it with a minimum of preconceptions, with the precarious advantage of the lightly-armored, mobile peltast over the hoplite. But the real reason that makes it impossible for me not to take up the *Phenomenology of Mind* in these pages has everything to do with the struggle that begins with Plato and continues down through the centuries, the clash of philosophy against fable. As I ventured in the introduction to *Truth or Death*, the *Phenomenology of Mind* stands forth as that altogether particular and exceptional moment in Western thought when narrative and philosophy attempt to conclude a marriage of reason that is under continuous threat from madness. Reason here stands as its motive, its pivot, its object, and its subject; madness is the motive force, the infinite spiral that, as it weaves together the narrative and the conceptual, carries them away in its dizzying ascension.

The reader of the *Phenomenology* runs an entire gamut of contradictory states: when he doesn't feel like a duck grounded by clipped wings, he may take himself for an eagle, or an Icarus soon doomed to lose his waxen prosthesis beneath the pitiless sun rays of truth. There are moments when he soars high in wonderment, but more often than not he recoils in terror at the abyss into which his reason threatens to plunge him. But we would betray Hegel if we were to remain at the level of perceptible immediacy. We can speak of the Hegelian enterprise only after a grueling battle with the concepts by which the philosopher would have us grasp the spiritual adventure he relates. For Hegel lays before us nothing less than the moments and the movements through which the universal mind, through schism and recomposition, achieves thorough self-knowledge. History is pregnant with the movement, with the coming into being that each individual unwittingly carries within himself. The task to which Hegel summons us, is to grasp those concepts that make it possible to illuminate the path along which time leads us in our blindness, to forge alongside it the conceptual tools that can lift us progressively toward effective knowledge of our own conscience; that is, the advent within us of the subject, which is at the same time the subject of Reason (or the spirit of history—the *Zeitgeist*) within us. In a nutshell, it is time to strap on Hegel's conceptual crampons and emerge from the Platonic cave. The difference is that our exodus will be, in a manner of speaking, as intimated by Kant in his writings on cosmopolitanism, on history's agenda.

But having assigned myself this mission, or rather, having assigned it to the *Phenomenology*, I have gone far beyond, in using expressions like "effective knowledge" and "advent of the subject," what is permissible to say without tumbling into the glaringly and patently obvious that Hegel has warned us against from the outset. I have already concluded, without the slightest basis, that the Hegelian project culminates in the spiritual and intellectual apotheosis that it holds out as a distant, shimmering possibility. I postulate the absolute I am called upon to attain and, in postulating it, instantly forbid myself access to it. Worse yet, I presume to understand what the *Phenomenology of Mind* proposes. And all the while, each of its pages, in its shadow and in its light, whispers that nothing of what they appear to convey can be entirely understood; that one must beware of those who pretend to have digested and successfully explained them.

Such is the fundamental contradiction embedded in the inception of the Hegelian approach itself—always understood restrictively here, as specific to the *Phenomenology of Mind* and not necessarily representative of the entire body of the philosopher's work. All that I, with some temerity, have elaborated above must then be considered, if not false, then at least as suspect, as null and void, or at best as premature. That initial contradiction, as presented in the work's lengthy preface, marks what we might conveniently call the zero (or first) degree of consciousness. But it also seems clear that such a zero degree does not exist. It would certainly appear not to exist for the philosopher. Even as he presents us (in a "preface" written after the fact) with a capsule summary of his work, he has already completed for himself—and inscribed for us—the itinerary that he proposes we follow. Even less does it exist for the reader, whom the philosopher rightly presumes to be caught up in the magma of preconceived ideas of which he is not even aware. To rid the reader of those preconceptions is the first task of "true" philosophy. Now, such a task looms as the most difficult of all, since most of the philosophies handed down by tradition (up to the *Phenomenology of Mind*, it is understood) are presented as systems whose vocation is to destroy or to supplant those that have preceded them, or even to refute in advance those that might eventually be used against them.

The task of the preface is to introduce the reader to an idea of philosophy different from how philosophy has accustomed him to conceive of it. In this way he may enter, free of prejudice, purged of the spirit of system, into the "true" philosophy Hegel propounds (which we can provisionally define, for simplicity's sake, as "dialectical"). In other words, the reader is being quite firmly requested neither to contradict nor to approve what is being proposed to him as a trail to be blazed, and whose destination he can only hope to comprehend when he reaches its end. Except that our intrepid reader is not armed with so much as a machete to hack his way through the thickets, and that the tools he needs to clear a passage probably lie hidden somewhere ahead of him, along the path that the philosopher has, in fact, already cleared for him.

This initial contradiction forces Hegel to lay down the fundamental contradiction that underlies the entire work to come: the contradiction between the absoluteness of the truth he promises to deliver, and the necessarily progressive deployment that leads to it. The *Phenomenology of Mind* can thus present itself only as the road at whose end the contradiction should ideally find its solution. But just as abruptly the very notion of "solution," necessarily premature at this stage, risks attaching the reader to an *a priori* certainty of a fixed preconception of the true, which would prejudice the experience (*Erfahrung*) of the movement that alone can lead to it. The absolute must be proclaimed as true philosophy's objective, yet at the same time it must be evoked in such a way that it appears unattainable: therein lies the contradiction.

> For the real subject-matter is not exhausted in its purpose, but in working the matter out; nor is the mere result attained the concrete whole itself, but the result along with the process of arriving at it. (69)[53]

Now, the process of arriving at it is not that which is sought, unless its purpose is never truly achieved. Failing which the truth toward which it reaches is in danger, in its fixed and "definitive" form, of being nothing more than a system like any other. If what is fixed and preconceived is fated to be obliterated under the blowtorch of the dialectic as a false, unfounded opinion, then as truth, whatever it may be, is attained it should promptly abolish itself in turn, lest it sink to the bottom, there to join the other wrecks that litter the watery graveyard of dogmatic philosophy. What is achieved abolishes itself. So extensively that, to be true to the movement of Hegelian thought as set forth in the *Phenomenology*, it is in a "definitive"—and not merely temporary— manner that we must understand the truth that it holds out to us as a perpetually unfinished, absolutely impracticable experience.

If I am raising this basic issue early on, at a time that might even appear premature, it is because for the *Phenomenology*, destination and intelligibility are indistinguishable. But if we then take these elements for granted, the

53. Georg Wilhelm Friedrich Hegel, The *Phenomenology of Mind*, trans. James Baillie (London: George Allen and Unwin Ltd., 1955). "Phenomenology of Mind" will be used throughout the text, although it can also be accurately translated as "Phenomenology of Spirit" (see note below).

tension that transforms its philosophical journey into a dizzying intellectual adventure promptly collapses. If both destination and intelligibility are posited at the outset, there is no reason to tussle with a text whose unrelenting difficulty now seems little more than a laborious mystification that can scarcely conceal its principial insufficiency. Truth to tell, I find it altogether improbable that a text of this kind, throbbing as it does with an almost palpable feverishness, could have been written in an attempt to mislead or to obscure. Its style would have inevitably betrayed it. But Hegel's writing is that of a man who, though he does not know precisely where he is going, does not despair of finding out one day, and even believes he will succeed. The nuance is a crucial one. There lurks in his mad endeavor, even beneath the appearance of self-assurance, a touch of magnificent desperation. Even in the prologue we find, to a particularly intense degree, the tension of uncertainty. The writing is that of a thinker who, despite or because of all the work he has already accomplished, has just *begun* to convince himself of the necessity of his *approach*. Not of the truth of his *result*. That result he may well proclaim, as if to reassure himself, but no certainty exists: that much we can attest as we follow his wandering course. "It [the mind] only wins to its truth when it finds itself utterly torn asunder" (93). A tearing asunder of such magnitude cannot be mended, unless we are prepared to accept the most mediocre of contentment, which Hegel promptly lashes out at. Evoking the "pitiful feeling of the divine," he adds: "By the little which can thus satisfy the needs of the human spirit we can measure the extent of its loss" (73).

Obviously, we can offset these quotes with other extracts that quite peremptorily express the exact opposite. In Hegel, tension and tearing asunder are often contradicted by insupportable assurance, even arrogance. There can be little doubt that one must choose one's Hegel, while at the same time not ignoring the Hegel that disturbs us. But what would be the point of a purely negative critique? Why bother to read him in the first place? Let us put it this way: this particular, high-voltage Hegel is the one that interests me, that urges me on to grapple with a work that, were it to take itself as certainty, would be simply indigestible and futile. If the *Phenomenology of Mind* still speaks to us today, it is largely because of what it leaves unsaid. It provides the reason why, daunted by the death-kiss that the certainty of absolute truth would in my view bestow upon it, I am wagering that I can approach it in the very state of indefinite suspension that sustains it.

One way for Hegel to imply, perhaps even unknowingly, that his enterprise may be an impossible one is to establish, in the first pages of his first chapter, direct knowledge as provided by the sense-experience (*die sinnliche*

Gewissheit) as absolute, unsurpassable wisdom, as the richest and the *truest* knowledge. But this incalculable richness is not simply imagined, and even less conceived; the knowledge thus acquired from sense-certainty remains the poorest. Sense-certainty, in other words, utters only pure "This." And by so saying, says nothing at all. It grasps the real but cannot take the measure of what it has grasped, for it cannot conceptualize its "approach." The word is wholly unequal to the task; certainty cannot advance, for it cannot understand itself. Sense-certainty is *by nature* hostile to concept; it can do no more than keep "mere apprehension (*Auffassen*) free from conceptual comprehension (*Begreifen*)" (149). There exists, says Hegel, a conceptual manner of grasping things that has no connection with their immediate, intuitive apprehension. An incommensurable space separates the two neighboring and opposing ways of grasping the real, confronted with which the *Phenomenology of Mind* proclaims itself as a kind of immense circle (*Kreis*) in which the mind will "come back," enriched by its conceptual experience, to its original starting point.

But "coming back" must remain wholly putative. The trajectory of the *Phenomenology* cannot, strictly speaking, "bring back" thought to a point of departure that cannot, by definition, be discovered. Whether or not Hegel is prepared to admit it, an incommensurable gap persists between the immediacy of sense-certainty and the lengthy mediation of conceptual reflection. As the immediate knowledge that sense-certainty can apprehend is essentially indescribable, its truth can neither be transmitted nor philosophically explained. On this ground, philosophy can do little more than throw up its hands. From the point of view of philosophy, let us repeat, truth finds form only in concept; sense-certainty, though, lying as it does beneath as well as above all concepts, remains both unusable and *irreducible*. Hegel may not admit it, but the conceptual effort in and of itself, no matter how promising at first glance, must necessarily lead to loss when measured against the absoluteness of an immediacy that refuses to decompose and that eludes at minimum the rational language of the philosophical *logos*, if not all language. The *Phenomenology of Mind* may well bend asymmetrically toward the absolute that it seeks to attain; we know it will never reach its goal. It stands as an almost despairing attempt to narrow the epistemological gap that separates our understanding from the absolute. And it can only begin this monumental task by breaking into its component parts the unconscious operation by which the subject grasps its object or—to proceed in orderly fashion, and to speak in general terms—by examining, one by one, the stages through which consciousness comes to know the world, and comes to know itself in the world.

If we look a bit closer, knowing of this kind is hardly a simple matter—let us examine more closely how Hegel reduces it to its component parts. Sense-certainty in act is always awareness of something: the subject of this awareness, the *I* (or the *this-as-I*) encounters an *object* (the *this-as-object*). Analysis of this encounter restricts itself, in the first place, to awareness that each of the two terms exists separately, then leads directly to the obvious conclusion that sense-certainty is made manifest only in the relationship that binds them. This linkage is necessary for knowledge of the *I*, which to exist needs an object. Knowledge necessitates an object as intermediary, but the object does not care whether it is known or not: "it remains and stands even though it is not known, while the knowledge does not exist if the object is not there" (151). It is thus the task of sense-certainty (or of knowledge, or of the *I*) to ask what, in its eyes, constitutes the object, or the this-as-object. Now, the object, which we have just defined as existing independently of knowledge, enjoys independent existence only in its particularity: we are looking at this particular tree, the one in front of my house, or at the tree I sawed down yesterday—such detail clearly illustrates that I must locate each of these objects (in this case, each tree) individually in time and space, through sufficiently developed circumstantial indications. Contrariwise, the object as concept, the tree in general, exists only in the knowledge that constitutes it; it can be grasped only by and in language—while language is powerless to provide a term that can define the singular tree I have in mind when I think back to the tree I used to climb as a boy. The power of the concept of *tree* lies in its power to capture, in a single cast of the net, all imaginable particular trees, without being able to designate any of them in its singular truth.

What I have just said about trees, or about any other general object (the *here*, the *now*, etc.) I may also say of the *I*: In the same way when I say "I," "this individual I," I say quite generally "all *I's*" (154)—just as the knowledge of which we speak, the knowledge of sense-certainty, is not the knowledge of any individual *I*. It belongs no more to you than to me in particular; it is the *I* of sense-certainty.

> Sense-certainty discovers by experience, therefore, that its essential nature lies neither in the object nor in the I; and that the immediacy peculiar to it is neither an immediacy of the one nor of the other.... We arrive in this way at the result, that we have to put the whole of sense-certainty as its essential reality, and no longer merely one of its moments, as happened in both cases, where first

the object as against the I, and then the I, was to be its true reality. (155)

The two moments nonetheless stand as necessary steps to extract this essential reality. Thus:

> It is clear from all this that the dialectical process involved in sense-certainty is nothing else than the mere history of the process—of its experience; and sense-certainty itself is nothing else than simply this history. The naïve consciousness too, for that reason, is of itself always coming to this result, which is the real truth in this case, and is always having experience of it: but is always forgetting it again and beginning the process all over. (158)

The task of the *Phenomenology of Mind* is to mend the forgetting, and to avoid beginning the process all over again in perpetuity. Just as consciousness (*Bewusstein*) discovers through the experience of sense-certainty that "truth is at home," it follows that the task of consciousness is to carry on as far as it can with the self-inscribed effort it has begun, that has put it on the trail of inner truth. That is why Hegel also presents the *Phenomenology* as the "Science of the experience of consciousness." We will do well to remember there is nothing individual about this particular consciousness—not unlike the *I* of all *I*'s, it is general (*allgemein*). Not only may each individual pursue his own course (the one that Hegel suggests we follow), but experience, in its diversity of moments and movements, is the stuff of universal history, which in turn, through all its vicissitudes, is essentially the creation of the mind (which is far more than consciousness and reason, for it is consciousness of self and of the world in their necessary relation, and thus consciousness and reason of oneself and of the entire world, that world of which they know themselves to be a part but, more than that, the most perfect, the loftiest and most complete, the sole true expression). The *Phenomenology* intends nothing less than to make itself the moment, the bearer or the translation of that coming-into-being, or, more precisely, of the succession of movements that lead to it and of which the philosopher in person, Hegel himself, is the lucid interpreter—it is the philosophical tool, the conceptual approach through which the mind gains full self-awareness, and emerges into the full light of its own truth. The *Phenomenology*, for all that, does not touch upon universal history (to which Hegel would later devote his celebrated courses, published under the title *Lectures on the Philosophy of History*), its dialectical movement whose element is "pure conception," whose content, a concept of itself, stands revealed as "something reflected into self, a subject" (84). The *Phenomenology* invites us to join the challenging progression by which consciousness, reflected in its relation to the world, is raised up to the level of concept, of the universal, and discovers itself as subject. It is this discovery that constitutes its truth.

On this exigent path there can be no short cuts. We must move forward step by step, guidebook in hand, without losing sight of our general direction. At the same time, we should keep in mind that Hegel, as he was preparing to revise the *Phenomenology* shortly before his death from cholera, had made known his intention to "rid his ship of its useless ballast." But what exactly does his "useless ballast" consist of? The danger is that each reader will judge arbitrarily, based purely on criteria and preferences that are his alone. Exactly how much ballast did Hegel not have time to rid his ship of? No one can claim to know what should be expelled from the *Phenomenology* in order to bring the submarine to the surface, particularly since it might breech keel uppermost. We must agree to cruise on through the near-darkness of the deeps. There exists no shortened version, no limpid reading of the *Phenomenology*, any more than there exists the possibility for us, here (or wherever else, for that matter) to replicate Hegel's own path in its smallest twists and turns, in its most discrete instants, except by rewriting the entire text word for word! Whoever attempts to interpret his work finds himself faced with an insoluble contradiction, which none of Hegel's readers, the greatest of them included, can escape. One of the best known French Hegelians, Alexandre Kojève, offers us telling confirmation: his luminous interpretation of the *Phenomenology* is too clear to be "true." In fact, one might well venture that Kojève, through his understanding of Hegel's entire *œuvre* (and not merely the *Phenomenology*) has constructed his own philosophy of history.[54]

In short, there is no such thing as a "valid" reading of the *Phenomenology*; it would be madness on my part to even try to summarize it. Such an attempt would assume, for starters, that I understood it! But is it really necessary to harp on just how incongruous such a pretension would be? We know that any text of substance (be it *The Odyssey*, the Gospels, or Goethe's *Faust*) ineluctably raises the question of interpretation. But here, a radical, crippling complexity precedes any attempted interpretation: it devolves instead upon the accessibility of what is to be interpreted, and raises its head at the very first level of reading. Rather like a miner who is not sure he has located the ore-bearing vein, the reader constantly wonders if what he is

54. Alexandre Kojève, *Introduction to the Reading of Hegel. Lectures on The Phenomenology of Spirit*, comp. Raymond Queneau, ed. Alan Bloom, trans. James H. Nichols Jr. (New York: Basic Books, 1969).

reading possesses the slightest *textual* intelligibility. Is there anything here to be grasped, or is he dealing with a verbal delirium that utterly defies comprehension?

At the risk of admitting my own intellectual weakness, I affirm without hesitation that this text, the *Phenomenology of Mind*, is partially, if not fundamentally, delirious. Let us say that, as for me, I can only read it as a work of delirium. If I do not simply set it aside, if I have not given up speaking of my experience of it, it is because I believe that the Hegelian delirium reveals an even greater delirium, one that is ours: *the delirium of the West*. More tellingly than anyone else, Hegel "betrays" the West, feverishly revealing its dreams and its nightmares, unveiling (perhaps in spite of himself) its subconscious. In the *Phenomenology*, the West tells its story as in no other text, and the thought that carries the story along is so powerful that, whatever the cost, I cannot do without it.

To treat the *Phenomenology* as delirium, far from being a way to sidestep it, is to meet its radical difficulty head on, and at the same time, to face up to the delirious dimension of our civilization at the roots, in the least simplistic, most demanding possible way. In his certainty that the West is synonymous with the advent of the spirit, Hegel posits our civilization as radical *exigency*. Only if it knows itself to be *invested* by the spirit can it be the advent he claims it to be: to be the bearer of the spirit is not enough; that civilization bears responsibility for its advent. The *Phenomenology* is the price Hegel's reader must pay in order to accede to the truth that he, Hegel, has already grasped. The reader must follow the same Way of the Cross.[55] In his book, Hegel wages a titanic struggle against himself. Though he may be aware of the outcome, such awareness is granted only to he who, Hegel included, ceaselessly travels along his path, for it—knowledge—is naught but movement. No sooner does it come to a halt or congeal than it dies. The *Phenomenology* is circular, in apparent contradiction with Hegel's linear conception of history. But the circle it describes is constantly moving, rising up from one level to the next, so that its progress can best be visualized as a spiral.

After surveying and identifying the successive moments of the certainty of senses (Chapter 1), the *Phenomenology* repeats the same procedure with respect to perception (Chapter 2) and understanding (Chapter 3). These first three levels follow a trajectory that we could categorize as inaugural, in that it relates and initiates the dialectic of the relationship between the subject

---

55. At the very end of the *Phenomenology*, Hegel asserts that history and the *science* of the ways in which knowledge appears "form at once the recollection and the Golgotha of Absolute Spirit" (808).

and its object, between consciousness and the world. Its method is one of dissociating, at each level, what in appearance is one, then of reunifying what thought, through its efforts, has deconstructed. But in speaking of the subject-object relationship, and in referring to their unity, I have already anticipated a great deal (just as Hegel does in his exposé, which shifts between tracing the movement of consciousness in its slow and laborious progression, and rushing forward to illustrate exactly the position of the current stage in relation to the whole of the pathway to be traveled).

Let us then follow the pathway from its inception, and take a closer look at what is going on at the sense-certainty level (Chapter 1). At this initial level, consciousness, in its immediate relationship with the world, is first and foremost in a state of fusion with it, indistinguishable from the great whole (rather like, we might imagine, a breast-feeding baby without access to speech—literally, the *infans*). But we already know that this fusion is devoid of meaning apart from the tautology *it is*. As *savoir-être*, it does not know of its own existence, asks not about itself; were we not beings of the world, we could certainly content ourselves with it. Man is the being who names things and speaks the world, as the second chapter of Genesis so succinctly relates. And once consciousness has named, it establishes a distance between itself and that which it has named, between itself and the world. It is then that the subject-object dichotomy appears as a fact of existence: as the most commonly shared vision of speaking beings.

That last assertion could very well lead to confusion, were it to strengthen in us the opinion that ever since man began to speak, he has always separated "words and things." Foucault, in his celebrated work,[56] claims that such separation emerges in its full power only with European classicism, in the first decades of the seventeenth century. Of course, Hegel's purview is broader: that of the apparently indisputable distinction between self and world. Even at this level of generality, on further reflection, we can see that such a distinction can by no means be assumed to exist in every culture; not, at any rate, in the same way. It is most probably recent in human history, and our "quite natural" way of conceiving of it is thoroughly modern.

This remark points to a first level of difficulty in reading the *Phenomenology*: though it implicitly (and sometimes explicitly) refers to what might be construed as historical evolution that, for the totality of human consciousness as Hegel conceives it, moves from sense-certainty to the accomplishment of the spirit, there is nothing historical about the pathway it

56. Michel Foucault, *Les mots et les choses: une archéologie des sciences humaines* (Paris: Gallimard, 1966); translated into English as *The Order of Things: an Archeology of the Human Sciences* (New York: Vintage Books, 1973).

would have us follow. In other words, in the *Phenomenology*, the onward march of consciousness toward the spirit is not at all "periodized" (as it would later be in *Lessons on the Philosophy of History*), and its stages (even though they may at times correspond to an easily identifiable period in history) are presented in the "pure" logic of the Hegelian dialectic.[57] Consciousness is shaped through an exceptionally destabilizing relationship with time; it is at all times *both* the dissociation of its successive elements (almost inevitably perceived in temporal linearity) *and* the intemporal summation of its diverse movements. Hegel frequently spends much time and effort developing what may seem graspable at a glance (in an *Augenblick*, literally, the twinkling of an eye) or, conversely, subsumes in a single brief assertion (generally because he has developed it somewhere else) what thought cannot grasp except through a lengthy process.

Separation between consciousness (or the *I*) and the world is thus brought about even before consciousness becomes aware of itself, and, above all, even before it clearly formulates it to itself. What this formulation implies is that the *I* (or consciousness) becomes conscious of itself as an object distinct from other objects. In other words, consciousness has set itself up as an object of investigation and reflection. In the process it becomes aware that distancing itself from itself as object only became possible by first examining other objects, objects that it considers primarily as being outside of itself, or, more simply put, by contemplation of the outer world. But, on reflection, worldly externality, the world that first appears to it as being outside itself, encompasses it as object: consciousness (the *I*) discovers itself as part of the world, as an object in the world. Further, this very discovery does not appear possible except by virtue of the double movement that is produced: from itself to the world, and from the world to it. Consciousness only comes to know itself through the world that reflects upon it, which, mirror-like, allows for its reflection as consciousness.

That said, the *I* forms relationships with objects and connects with the world through singular, discrete objects—the desk at which I am writing, the chair in which I am reading, the book I am holding—situated in singular and discrete places and moments, in a specific here and now. But these particular objects, this here, this now, this book, that writing desk can be postulated by consciousness as objects, and, further, assigned to another consciousness, only if behind the generic object, the concept looms in each of these singular objects: behind the *here* of that writing desk and the *now* of my reading

---

57. This is, let it be noted, the reproach that could be addressed to Kojève's interpretation of the *Phenomenology*: that of being too exclusively a historical reading of the dialectic that here, from Hegel's standpoint, is first and foremost a response to logical necessity.

stands the *here* and the *now* in their generality (or the concept of here and the concept of now), behind the book I am holding in my hands and about which I am speaking, the general idea of *book* or, to put it differently, all existing and imaginable books. The only term I can use to refer to the book I hold in my hands is this generality, this generic *book*, the word *book*, the concept *book* in its universality. If I were to describe it in its specificity, that is, to detail its title, its contents, the texture of its paper, the number of syllables it contains, how I acquired it, and so on, I would be undertaking an enterprise as exhausting as it would be inexhaustible. I would never be able to complete its description. Something would always be missing, including the most important detail: the reasons for my boredom or my passionate interest. The singular remains forever irreducible to all attempts to define it exhaustively. The singular is, strictly speaking, unutterable.

> They "mean" this bit of paper I am writing on, or rather, *have* written on: but they do not say what they "mean." If they really wanted to *say* this bit of paper which they "mean," and they wanted to say so, that is impossible, because of the This of sense, which is "meant" cannot be reached by language, which belongs to consciousness, i.e., to what is inherently universal. In the very attempt to say it, it would, therefore, crumble in their hands.... (157–158)

It is indeed well and good to *say* that language exists, but its vocabulary is necessarily limited in its possibilities: it can designate only the commonplace, the generic, the universal (*das Allgemeine* in German). So, the reasoning that the *I* has just applied to the objects that it situates outside of itself also applies to itself, taken as object — just as we concluded earlier with regard to this book, he who is reading it cannot say "I" unless, behind this singular ego stands a generic *I*. And, in any event, to *say* itself, to designate itself in its singularity, the singular *I* that is Monsieur Tartempion could well spend more than a lifetime in the attempt. Indeed, that is the reason why what we term literature exists and why, in literature, we unfailingly encounter the unutterable, to such a degree that it can be singled out and identified, and along with it all art, as the art of surrounding the ineffable.

> Sense-certainty discovers by experience, therefore, that its essential nature[58] lies neither in the object nor in the I; and that the immediacy peculiar to it is neither an immediacy of the one or of the other. For, in the case of both, what I "mean" is rather something non-essential; and the object and the I are universals, in

---

58. *Wesen* in German, which can also refer to being, to existence, to the way of being.

which that Now and Here and I, which I "mean" do not hold out, do not exist. We arrive in this way at the result, that we have to put the whole of sense-certainty as its essential reality, and no longer merely one of its moments, as happened in both cases, where first the object as against the I, and then the I, was to be its true reality. (154–155)

Through the experience (*Erfahrung*) of the singular, sense-certainty simultaneously attains the generality (or universality) of the objects it encounters and of the *I* that experiences it. So it is that this certainty, coming to know itself as generic and raising itself up to the level of concept, takes a first, decisive step toward truth. In like manner it becomes clear that the only truth to which the word, and thus philosophy, can accede, which they can intelligibly transmit to an Other, is the truth of the concept. But, once again, I am getting ahead of myself. The Other has not yet made its appearance, and will have a significant role to play only in Chapter 4. Before then, in examining this relationship, over and above what can be perceived by the senses, in terms of perception and understanding, the dialectic of the relationship between subject and object must be developed in its every movement, in its every moment. Yet these selfsame moments are, in a manner of speaking, embedded in what is perceived by the senses, and stand forth as soon as sense-certainty begins to reflect on what is becoming of it.

Perception (*Wahrnehmung*—literally, "taking as true") is observation, which, moving beyond the immediateness of sense-certainty, had already begun to rear its head when I undertook to illustrate this certainty or, in greater proximity with the German expression, to take into account what is true about it. Understanding (which, truth to tell, is present in the Hegelian discourse from the outset) merely draws a lesson from the path already traveled by positing that—if on one side lies the world, and on the other, perception—perception and understanding give us the world not as it is in itself, but as phenomenon (or as a cluster of phenomena), in such a way that our senses and our intellect can apprehend it. Hegel is referring here to the well-known distinction drawn by Kant in the *Critique of Pure Reason*, between the thing in itself (or *noumenon*—a concept quite close to the Platonic idea) and the thing as it appears (or *phenomenon*). The Kantian distinction seems at first glance indisputable: never will we be able to circumscribe exactly the real. But Hegel rightly observes that the affirmation itself forgets that understanding expresses itself thusly, excluding itself in an equally arbitrary fashion, from the world it is observing, a world that is itself being considered, in an equally arbitrary manner, in a kind of inertia.

Understanding thus displays its inadequacy in keeping alive without sufficient cause the caesura that separates it from the world, and points to its incapacity to overcome the subject-object dichotomy.

The source of this incapacity is clear: heretofore (until Hegel, that is), we have been examining the world and our own consciousness from the viewpoint of knowledge alone; we have yet to embrace effective reality in its unity. Even though, thanks to our understanding, we know the world (object) and knowledge (subject) to be in a state of interaction with one another, both remain (in the still-partial knowledge that is ours at this stage) distinct entities. Separation will persist (we must once more get ahead of ourselves) as long as consciousness does not understand itself in the world, and does not understand the world in itself. Such understanding would, strictly speaking, be that of Hegelian reason (*Vernunft*), whose purview, as we have already observed, goes far beyond simple understanding. But to speak of reason, consciousness must engage in the carefully thought-out experience of its subjective encounter with the Other, with a consciousness other than its own, activated by its own subjectivity (contrary to the inert object that consciousness had heretofore placed in opposition to it), which for all its singularity nonetheless participates fully in universal subjectivity, like the singular *I* of the *I* in general. Consciousness thus necessarily encounters itself in interaction with the other and, at the same time, with the other it will discover in itself, thus abolishing in one fell dialectical swoop the distance that once separated subject and object.

That encounter provides the material for Chapter 4, the most central, crucial chapter of Hegel's book—probably also the most abundantly commented on, and most often misappropriated of the *Phenomenology*, leading up, as it does, to the celebrated dialectic of the master and the slave. Up until this point (i.e., the point at which we had left consciousness at the end of Chapter 3), the other whom consciousness had encountered on its path had implicitly been considered neutral. But, as both Plato and Aristotle well realized, man is a creature of desire. If he finds pleasure and even, on occasion, full satisfaction in contemplating the world, the object *world* is also what he devours, what he consumes and consummates. Man enjoys the fruits of the earth and of all that his insatiable appetite craves, including the other's body. No sooner has he finished eating, or making love, than he is ready to begin all over again. If not then and there, the next day, or the day after that: whether slow or fast, his consumption is endless. Its inherent pleasure annihilates the object consumed (including in the sexual act that takes the other solely as an object, and which can lead, as in Sade, to its mutilation and to its death). But that pleasure can only be provisional at best. The belly or the flesh can achieve momentary satisfaction but consciousness can hardly be expected to follow suit. It may well even be that *for it*, for sensual gratification, which can best be described as biological (zoological, in fact) or animal, gratification as an idea remains devoid of meaning, as it has never been able to take full cognizance of its desire.

Nothing better illustrates the point than the sexual act: enjoying the other's body releases tension of the flesh (cerebral tension included), but no sooner has the act been consummated than the fruits of the ensuing pleasure dissipate if the act is not reflected in the other's gaze. Though Hegel does not speak of it in the *Phenomenology*, Kojève, like Lacan after him, are Hegelians to the core when they uphold that amorous desire is not so much desire for the other as desire for *the other's* desire: I desire of the other neither his or her mouth nor his or her sex, whatever I might claim. I desire to be desired by him (or her)—the reason why voice and eyes play such a decisive role in the attraction we generate or that we feel, since it is through them that desire is expressed so much more effectively than through any other organ. "Moral" (here meaning simple opposition to physical, animal needs) desire cannot arise in consciousness if that consciousness does not encounter an other. This is what makes it a specifically human desire. Only the encounter with a consciousness at once deeply similar in its essence and perfectly different in its individuality can stimulate the desire to be recognized by such an *alter ego*. "Self-consciousness attains its satisfaction only in another self-consciousness" (226). In the course of such redoubling, self-consciousness truly "comes alive":

> A self-consciousness has before it a self-consciousness. Only so and only then *is* it self-consciousness in actual fact; for here first of all it comes to have the unity of itself in its otherness. Ego which is the object of its notion, is in point of fact no "*object*." The object of desire, however, is only independent, for it is the universal, ineradicable substance, the fluent, self-identical essential reality. When a self-consciousness is the object, the object is just as much ego as object.
>
> With this we already have before us the notion of Mind or Spirit. What consciousness has further to become aware of, is the experience of what mind is—this absolute substance, which is the unity of the different self-related and self-existent self-consciousness in the perfect freedom and independence of their opposition as independent components of that substance: Ego that is "we," a

plurality of Egos, and "we" that is a single Ego. Consciousness first finds in self-consciousness—the notion of mind—its turning point, where it leaves the parti-colored show of the sensuous immediate, passes from the dark void of the transcendent and remote super-sensuous,[59] and steps into the spiritual daylight of the present. (236–237)

With this flight of poetic fancy—something that occasionally happens in the *Phenomenology*—Hegel pulls on his seven-league boots and, with a single bound, leaps across the entire space separating a still-inarticulate self-consciousness that has barely arrived at the threshold of the "native land of truth" (219) from its definitive advent in the effectivity of the spirit. By alluding to the end point of the adventure, Hegel takes the deliberate risk of shattering its charm. But he presents it enigmatically enough to sustain the mystery needed to intrigue the adventurer. Yet the philosophical distance that separates these two moments remains immense, and cannot be abolished except through a new series of movements which in turn, repeated at a higher level, lead us back to the moments explored in the first three chapters. Once again, our aim is not to trace Hegel's footsteps through all their self-referential loops, and even less so to reproduce the repetitive insistence he uses and abuses to describe the progression of a moving, disorienting thought that is constantly catching itself, redeploying and reintegrating exactly what it has just eliminated. Here we enter into a virtually infinite hall of mirrors: "Self-consciousness exists in itself and for itself, in and by virtue of the fact that it exists for another self-consciousness; that is to say, it exists only by being acknowledged or "recognized" (229).

Self-consciousness (*an sich*) cannot grasp itself. It exists without knowing it. Contrariwise, consciousness *for self* (*für sich*) remains closed in upon itself. It is a subjectivity that knows itself but that does not understand the world, which it is unaware of. The first part (A) of Chapter 4, entitled "*Independence and Dependence of Self-Consciousness: Lordship and Bondage*" (218) sets forth the successive movements through which "consciousness," now separated from itself, now separated from the world (and which is therefore never anything but partially or fragmentarily "consciousness"), achieves full awareness of itself in its relation to the world in becoming *at once* consciousness for itself, or "for self" (*für sich*), *and* self-consciousness in the world through factual recognition that emanates from other self-consciousnesses.

---

59. An allusion to the world of *noumena* (or things in themselves) in Kant, and to that of Platonic ideas.

Let us attempt to chart in more proximate detail the succession of instants that Hegel calls the "process of Recognition (*des Anerkennens*)" (200) and that he develops at the beginning of the justifiably famous Part A of Chapter 4. That is to say, an initial self-consciousness, which we call "ego" (and which we will here cause to speak in the first person), which encounters a second self-consciousness, which we call "the other." In my encounter with the other I step outside myself and, losing myself, find *my*self in the other, which in turn must be sublated in that it is not truly the other that I encounter but myself in the other, an *alter ego* in the strictest sense of the word: the position of the egotist. But the movement of my consciousness does not stop there: I must (a necessity to whose meaning we shall return shortly) sublate or move beyond that other that has become mine, a double shift of sorts that, in sublating me in him, refers me back to myself and reliberates the other in restoring him to his own being. As I come and go from myself to the other, and from the other to myself, awareness dawns that the other exists independently of me as consciousness (and not as a simple object) and that he is indeed able to follow the same course as I. And my self-consciousness (or my consciousness) is thereby altered: I henceforth know myself as an *I* fully conscious of the other, and of myself as an other for his self-consciousness of his own self, which is in turn self-consciousness and of the other consciousness that I represent for him.

Here begins a coming and going that, like the infinite reflection of two mirrors, might well never end. The image of mirrors is particularly eloquent. Unless one were to pierce a hole in the middle of one of them, their infinite reverberations can never be completely apprehended, nor even seen through the hole; the infinite images are lost to the gaze in the increasingly indistinguishable depth of their mutual reflection. In their imagined confrontation the two self-consciousnesses (I and the other) find themselves with regard to each other in a similarly mirror-imaged position. As in the case of our mirrors, the reciprocal movement that is generated from one consciousness to another is virtually infinite. It makes the head spin, and whatever we have been able to apprehend rapidly fades. Hegel himself, of course, writes neither of mirrors nor of infinity. But his dialectic (with particular power in this passage) is enough to make one's head spin: *there is no end to it.* The potentially infinite movement of the dialectic, were we to pursue it until the exhaustion of thought, would ultimately—to put it in Hegelian terms— sublate itself. Consciousness, in a state of collapse, would return to its starting point, the better to awaken from its nightmare and discover itself in its initial state. But Hegel is careful to bring our dizziness to an end, and to cover

over the abyss that he had earlier opened. It is precisely in the attempt at closure, at bringing to an end the very interminable movement that he has set in motion, that the philosopher of Jena slides from vertigo into delirium.

There is seemingly no escape from the contradiction: either consciousness exhausts itself in the endless hall of mirrors and sinks into stupor, or it brings the game to an arbitrary end, from which it can emerge "enriched," after a double (or quadruple) to-and-fro, from the dialectical adventure and conceive of itself as part and parcel of the universal consciousness it has experienced in the encounter with the other's self-consciousness, and that it may repeat (and must necessarily repeat) with any other. That is exactly what Hegel has chosen to do. It is a choice, however, that leads him straight to delirium. A richly instructive delirium, true enough; but delirium all the same: that very delirium we must now attempt to understand.

Having reached this point in the *Phenomenology*, we may, without tipping the exercise into the abyss where all thought annihilates itself, attempt to remain within the instability of the movement touched off by the Hegelian dialectic. For it has the immense merit of leading us to the fluctuating complexity of the simple, with all the ethical and political consequences that derive from a sense of ever-unfinished awakening. Anyone can experience without mediation and accept without demonstration, as a feeling of immediate certainty, that each person's consciousness participates (if only potentially, and often unbeknownst to him) in universal consciousness, and that the latter itself adequately reflects the world. But, as Hegel emphasizes, such a sensible attitude does not know what it is experiencing. Not only is it unable to address it; its blind enthusiasm is likely to lead to irresponsible attitudes and behaviors, inspired by the simple-minded notion that we are all brothers, united in the same truth, transparent to one another. In the name of this spiritual ecumenism, we run the risk of ignoring our differences, of reducing the other to oneself and, should he not wish to listen to reason, to exterminate him with a clear conscience. Such is the clear conscience of the altruist, whose posture Hegel ironically labels as appropriate to a "beautiful soul." In the beauty that it attributes to itself, the "beautiful soul" raises itself up in its own eyes in opposition to a world that it sees as corrupted, and its "heart-throb for the welfare of mankind passes therefore into the rage of frantic self-conceit" (297). The *Phenomenology* thus warns us that the universality of consciousness, being wholly *in and of* the world, being bodied forth *in* and *by* history, cannot cause the other's contrarian alterity to vanish. It is impossible to expel the other, even at his most radical, even in his eventual hostility, from the world, from humanity. Polyneices may well have fought his brother and against his city, but Antigone would not allow that he not be buried there, that is, that he be excluded from the order of human beings: an act of exclusion that no one, no power, no regime can pronounce.

It is hardly coincidental that, in the famous Part A of Chapter 4 of the *Phenomenology*, the dialectic of self-consciousness leads directly to the dialectic of lordship and bondage.[60] In Hegel's eyes, it is clear enough that the movement of recognition whose moments he has analyzed does not take place, concretely, in conditions of equality, as implicitly presumed above in the exposition of the dialectic. Necessarily, and first and foremost, the encounter of self-consciousnesses is the object or the occasion of conflict, of bloody confrontation; it occurs, consequently, in a state of inequality. In fact, in history, recognition of one self-consciousness by the other as an equal consciousness has not been gained by mutual agreement. Such recognition has instead been achieved by the use of force and, after confrontation, by the submission of the weaker party. For there to be effective recognition a victor and a vanquished are needed; the latter must submit to the former. Let the weaker die, and the victor gain only a corpse (if Hector's body has any significance for Achilles, it is only because he has torn it from the hands of living Trojans who will later come, in the person of their king Priam, to supplicate the victor for its return). It is at the cost of his human dignity that the vanquished, to preserve his existence, concedes victory to the victor and, in submitting to his new master, agrees to serve him as a slave. By his act of submission, the vanquished recognizes the victor—except that the victor does not recognize him; in the final analysis, recognition by the slave of his master, coming from a being who has been reduced to the status of object, is worthless in the master's eyes. Why, after all, should he value the recognition of someone he does not recognize?

Here, the dialectic of lordship and bondage, of master and slave, undergoes a spectacular reversal. Laboring for the master alone, the slave enjoys none of (or only marginally) the fruits of his labor. Conversely, the master is quite content to consume the goods produced by his slave, thus maintaining a relationship that posits the world as purely object—the very world where consciousness lay dormant before encountering, in Chapter 4, another consciousness, and when before it lay only objects. So, while the master remains entrapped in his passive, parasitical enjoyment, the slave is aware that he is working for the master, that is to say, for a self-consciousness that he recognizes as such. Such recognition, added to the consciousness that he

---

60. Hegel implicitly refers, in using the term *Knecht*, to bondage, or slavery, as it was practiced in ancient times: he who, in combat, prefers to save his life rather than risk it to defend his dignity as a free man becomes a slave, as Aristotle reminds us.

is producing much more than he is permitted to enjoy or, in other words, his consciousness of not being restricted to the production of only that which he needs to survive, creates a situation that awakens him to his dignity as producer (something the master cannot do). Through work, the slave contrives to escape object status and to claim for himself full status as subject in the face of an unmoving master, whose self-consciousness is frittered away in sloth and futility. In this way, the slave's progression toward claiming subject status, toward self-consciousness, *necessarily* constitutes the motor of history, and reinitiates the dialectical process that leads to the advent of the mind, the spirit—the necessity of which explains why, at the end of the day, masters cannot resist the emancipation of their slaves, nor withstand the claim that work is a source of dignity.

Hegel must surely be oversimplifying. Never in history has society been reduced to a simple two-sided relationship between master and slave; nor does our philosopher deal with the masters' relations with one another. The citizens of Athens may well have lived on the benefits of slavery; their material dependence, far from inhibiting their mutual recognition, allowed them on the contrary to exercise that recognition through the *isagoria* and the *isonomia* that united them in a collective civic consciousness. But we must recall that, even though the dialectic of lordship and bondage is one of the passages in the *Phenomenology* that refers most clearly to a certain historical period (the slave-owning societies of antiquity), Hegel is not propounding a philosophy of history, and even less so history in its more narrow sense. Were we to take him seriously, historically, we might well wonder if today we have not come to a point where, from the Hegelian perspective, we have all become slaves to a system that surpasses us. Leaving this question hanging for a moment, let us return to the essentially conceptual level of the *Phenomenology*. The master-slave dynamic is presented as being as disincarnate as a mathematical theorem, and must be understood as a moment of the greater dialectic of which it forms a part. This dialectic, in effect, does not end with the movement that transforms a servile consciousness into a consciousness that aspires to become master of itself, satisfied with continuing to live in the subjective certainty of its existence. Strengthened by its new certainty, that consciousness must return to—and discover its correspondence with—the world.

The task of reason (the topic of Chapter 5) is to make that discovery. Reason, *Vernunft*, is superior to mere understanding, *Verstand* (discussed in Chapter 3), for it raises consciousness to the level of concept and makes its truth accessible to it. Such a truth does not restrict itself to knowledge of itself in the world and in relation with other consciousnesses. No, it is the result of the effort by which self-consciousness ultimately contrives to conceive of itself, above and beyond its singularity, in its "unity with the universal" (272), as the truest expression of the world, as the highest (not to say unique) degree of reality of the world. Consciousness finds its ultimate truth in its perfect correspondence with the world, and the world, in its correspondence with consciousness. The difference between world and self-consciousness in the world is, in turn, sublated. At the same time, the absolute correspondence between world and consciousness preserves in itself all the moments, all the fractures that compose it. Self-consciousness is never at rest. There is nothing easy about its entry into reason's precincts. Its truth is never definitively gained; that same consciousness must once more travel the same circular path at the same superior level of movement. Such is the price of passage from certainty to truth.

Consciousness, having become "reason assured of itself" (273), ceases to see the world as a source of discontentment (as Christian consciousness does) and may thus take a positive interest in it. But, threatened by the danger that it will forget the path already trod, consciousness risks taking itself for "all reality"—an idealistic way of formulating the "principle of Reason" (272); that is to say, positioning itself with respect to the world as "observing reason" (281) though separate from it, an attitude that could be described as positivist. Yet it is no longer enough for consciousness, as it observes the world, to simply perceive; henceforth, it seeks to understand. No longer is it interested by the *this of the senses*, but by its underlying universality, that is to say, the essential: "Through this distinction into what is essential and what is unessential, the notion rises out of the dispersion of sensibility, and knowledge thereby makes it clear that it has to do at least quite as essentially with its own self as with things" (286). But Hegel's "declaration" points, with a touch of irony, to the separateness of world and consciousness. Consciousness still conceives of itself and examines itself as a knowing object, and not as the world *acting* upon itself, a conception to which one may not ascend except by rising to the realm of the spirit. The road it must travel is long, and reason cannot neglect the moments that remain for it to pass through, or the movements that it has yet to accomplish in order to reach its destination. As long as it restricts itself to observation, consciousness will remain outside the world, or remain aloof in its presence; it cannot grasp itself as action. In order to do so, it must act—as an actor whose position as observer diverts from its aim. By Hegel's own admission, consciousness is trapped in a circle from which it is very difficult to escape:

Consciousness must act solely as what it inherently and implicitly is, may be for it explicitly; or, acting is just the process of mind coming to be *qua* consciousness. What it is implicitly, therefore, it knows from its actual reality. Hence it is that an individual cannot know what he is till he has made himself real by action.

Consciousness, however, seems on this view to be unable to determine the purpose of its action before action takes place; but before action occurs it must, in virtue of being consciousness, have the act in front of itself as entirely its own, i.e., as a purpose. The individual, therefore, who is going to act seems to find himself in a circle, where each movement already presupposes the others, and hence seems unable to find a beginning, because it only gets to know by its own original nature, the nature which is to be its purpose, by first acting, while in order to act it must know that purpose beforehand.

The obstacle appears to be insurmountable. But Hegel slices off-handedly through it, adding:

But just for that reason it has to start straight away and, whatever the circumstances are, without troubling further about beginning, means, and end, proceed to action at once. For its essential and implicit (*ansichseyende*) nature is beginning, means and end all in one. (422)

The passage is striking—and typically Hegelian. All at once, the obstacle appears as the selfsame necessity that forces consciousness to overcome it, not unlike a jumping horse being driven at a gallop toward the bar. As if by magic, in one fell swoop, all the movements and circumambulations through which Hegel drives his individual (beginning, middle, end) are reduced to their "original essence."

Here we touch upon, through that particularly eloquent example, one of the essential characteristics of the *Phenomenology*: the permanence of the hypostasis that is most often implicit and sometimes, as above, explicit, according to which the spirit whose advent it reveals has always been *causa sua*—its own cause—that is to say, the motor that propels the series of movements that lead to its coming. The unity of the individual and the universal, of concept and action, of conscience and actual reality is always, and from the beginning, hypostatized. For Hegel, reality is one or, to paraphrase, not only do contradictory realities exist but, behind the interplay of their contradictions, and in the form of a "sum" or assemblage of their movements, lies *the* reality.

> It is the "absolute fact," which no longer suffers from the opposi-
> tion of certainty and its truth, between universal and individual,
> between purpose and its reality, but whose existence is the reality
> and action of self-consciousness. (440)

In this light, the *Phenomenology* can be seen as the repeated affirmation of an immense tautology, but a tautology of unequaled power, proportional to the immensity of all that it has embraced—a tautology that sets itself the paradoxical task of bringing transcendence down to earth as immanence (idealists will claim, conversely, that it attempts to raise immanence up to the heights of transcendence, but such an inversion is incompatible with Hegel's pitiless critique of idealism). Ultimately, despite the indisputable power of Hegelian speech, we end up wondering whether Hegel has *effectively* gone beyond affirmation of sense-certainty; whether he has truly managed to say anything more than, *the world is*. Indeed, he may have quite simply arrived at the immanence posited by Spinoza as one of the basic postulates of his ethics, when he proclaims: "REALITY AND PERFECTION (*realitas et perfectio*) I understand to be one and the same thing."[61]

Spinoza's appearance is no accident. He is the thinker of whom Hegel quite plainly states: "Spinoza or no philosophy." Peremptory though the judgment might seem, it does indicate that, for Hegel, Spinoza's ethics stand simultaneously for the best that philosophy has produced, for the highest point reached before him, and for an obligatory starting point: a thought that he nevertheless intends to surpass. Spinoza is the thinker of limitations within consciousness of the limitless. His central question is: how can the limited being that is man, incapable of understanding either the world or his own body, enhance his capacity for life, his joy? The knowledge that is accessible to man, and which at the same time constitutes his only liberty, cannot be knowledge of the world, but knowledge of that which, of the world, affects him. Man stands before the world like the swimmer facing the wave: he cannot cause the sea to cease its flux but he can, as Gilles Deleuze so delight-fully puts it, sport with and take delight in the wave instead of being its simple object, instead of letting oneself be swept away or dashed on the rocks. By learning to sport with the waves, man learns to feel himself a part of the sea, and acquires intuitive knowledge of the element in which he is floating. By contrast, and to remain within our metaphor, Hegel wishes to

61. Baruch Spinoza, *Ethics, "*Of the Nature and Origin of the Mind" (London: J.M. Dent, 1910), p. 38.

understand the sea; his *Phenomenology* sets out *by the use of reason* to grasp it in its totality: the sea *becomes* the swimmer, the swimmer *becomes* the sea and transforms it by swimming. The difference is not simply one of nuance; it is capital. Hegelian thought abolishes all limits, or assigns human thought a limit that it mistakes for that of a world which is itself limitless; here lies his delirium. Far from being "superceded," Spinoza has been ignored in his essential modesty.[62] Hegel is not alone in his ignorance; it is the hallmark of Western thought, as a whole, in which Spinoza, respected and admired though he may be, has to this day remained an outsider. We Westerners are, for the most part, Hegelians.

But most of the time we are Hegelians without knowing it. Not only have we forgotten what our vision of the world owes to the *Weltanschauung* of the philosopher of Jena; worse yet, in a general sense, we have no idea of what the *Phenomenology* conceals in terms of resources of critical power. His novel of the mind or of the spirit, having put in motion the repetition of movements that lead directly to it appears, at the same time, to undertake a phenomenal critical review of all the theological, philosophical, and scientific postures produced by the thought the West claims as its own, from antiquity up to the present day. Its critique is a radical one, radical to an extent almost as difficult to imagine as the *Phenomenology* itself is arduous to read. It proceeds from the point of view of the Hegelian spirit, i.e., the point of view of a spirit that unreservedly identifies itself with the world whose active principle it is revealed (to itself) as being. In the process, Hegel endorses unreservedly Spinoza's equation between perfection and reality. It would be utter vanity, unless one wished to wallow about in endless complaining, to wish the world other than it is. Consequently, nothing, unless one seeks self-annihilation in sullen withdrawal and insignificance, warrants being thought outside the world, to one side, above or below it. The invention of transcendence is a bad joke. We find ourselves in purest immanence.

From the Greeks to Kant—with the exception of Spinoza—the theology and the philosophy from which the West has drawn its nourishment have been almost entirely constructed alongside the world, if not against it; they have set up, atop the world, devices of evasion. In the process, these devices have taken on the appearance of positions that are quite simply untenable. They cannot be justified, nor understood, from Hegel's vantage point, except as moments necessary to the advent of the ultimate possible philosophy. The

---

62. I cannot forgo noting in passing that Kojève's interpretation of Spinoza's thought lies at the opposite extremity of that which I have sketched out here, with the aid of Deleuze. In his *Introduction to the Reading of Hegel*, Kojève insists: "As I have already said, Spinoza's system is the perfect incarnation of the absurd" (p. 117). Absurd, I venture to say, in that it pre-emptively destroys Hegel's ambitions to attain the absolute.

difficulty of the *Phenomenology* can now be more readily grasped: given that history (the past) forms an integral part of the world, nothing of what the world has produced can be ignored or denied; the erring of the past has not been error, but a necessary detour; it constitutes the raw material of the spirit itself, steeped in its own birth-pangs. The flour, the kneading trough, the oven (the matrix), and the bread together constitute the distinct yet indistinguishable moments of the sole and unique batch of bread from which Hegel the baker, as he tempts us with the odor of his golden-crusted, fresh-baked loaves, offers us the first bite.

The enterprise is pure madness, of course—neither greater nor lesser than Faust's, nor of all the alchemists before him. But his critical powers—of which we have yet to speak—are formidable indeed. If mind or spirit[63] *is* the world, knowledge belongs indiscriminately to both, and cannot be separated from things, from what we call "nature." The very idea of nature has become obsolete, inadequate. The world is no longer conceivable outside us, nor can it be treated like an object at our disposal, as human beings. It can only appear to us as the very essence that makes us what we are, and that we serve to *do* day in, day out. We are action in the world and the world *is* our action. If the spirit is already among us, or if it arrives before our very eyes; if, to put it succinctly, the soul of the world appears in 1806 in Jena astride its horse, nothing remains but to rejoice in its advent.

Our only possible reservation would be that Napoleon himself does not yet realize what he incarnates, and that he would need the philosopher who alone understands him to find out. To become the incarnation of the spirit, Napoleon need only abandon the battlefield to read the *Phenomenology* over Hegel's shoulder, ending his reading to the roar of his victorious cannons. Insofar as the *Phenomenology*'s language accomplishes the conjunction of the spirit's self-knowledge and the history that reveals it, it towers as the philosophical keystone that seals the arch of this triumphal advent. It is not because history (and Napoleon along with it) is still unaware of itself that it (and with it the spirit) is not in the process of coming into being, since quite precisely thanks to Hegel's thought, it is taking shape before our very eyes; since henceforth history itself now finds both its meaning and its fulfillment in the *Phenomenology* itself. But *insofar as all history since Hegel has given these triumphal claims the lie, and in the most unequivocal possible way*, we can only read the *Phenomenology* today as *an infinite task that remains entirely to be accomplished*, a task that is quite thoroughly impossible to bring to a conclusion.

63. Translator's note: for *esprit*, here, I use both mind and spirit.

Of Hegelian thought our civilization has retained only absolute power, only the absence of limits and not at all the consciousness which, if it were today even marginally Hegelian, would realize that as it devours the world it, like Faust, is hastening its own destruction. We are what we do, and what we do diminishes us, diminishes our capacity for being. We have all been reduced to bondage under a dynamic that eludes us. That is not my conclusion. It flows logically from a Hegelian reading of the real world. As for me, I line up with Spinoza on this issue: nothing can rule out that man (and the technique of which he is so proud) is not being manipulated by a world (by a kind of matter, etc.) that our understanding cannot fathom. But, instead of puffing up with pride at our illusory mastery, we can always attempt to sport with the wave that looms above us in its majestic immensity. Nothing, of course, permits me to rule out that matter, the better to know itself, has invented the human spirit. But nothing can assure me of it, either. If I sport with the wave I am not *obliged* to make decisions where none can be made, to rule upon what reason cannot resolve. Nothing allows me to affirm: this *must* come into being. Yet the *Phenomenology* is at every turn articulated by necessity.

Such necessity has a virtue. If the world *necessarily* is, if it is necessarily what it is and not an illusion in which we dream it is what it is, and if it is neither the antechamber of another world, then the consciousness (which is consciousness of that necessity) can neither reject, dissociate itself, nor hold it up as a simple object of its contemplation, of its theory. Only in the world, and in its relationship with it, can consciousness attempt to understand itself actively. In its attempt to understand, all dualism, all distinctions between materialism and idealism, all transcendence (pointing to whatever instance, whatever thing existing outside or above the world, or in any other position or situation), all such distinctions and divisions become preposterous, impossible, *false*. The world (and self-consciousness along with it) *is* what it becomes and *becomes* what it is. From that moment on, it is impossible for anyone, for any civilization and for humanity in general to believe itself to be master of the world, and the concept of *nature*, as defining the entirety of what should be at our disposal, evaporates. If the Enlightenment was right in bringing heaven down to earth (though the formula, which we will return to, seems to me unfortunate), if the Enlightenment justly dismisses the idea of transcendence, it has profoundly deceived itself by believing that this operation has placed the world at the disposition of men, in the discretionary power of the observing consciousness, seen as external utility in the service of science and technique. The world is, of course, utility, but utility for itself alone, insofar as it is subject, i.e., that it acts in and of itself upon itself. This all meshes perfectly with Spinoza's idea of reality as perfection, in which reality by definition cannot be anything other than what it is.

Hegel goes further. He says: the world and self-consciousness coincide. As the latter is necessarily human (if only through Hegel's thought), that would mean that human consciousness *is* or *becomes* the world's consciousness of itself. Nothing less. It follows that the sentient animals that inhabit the minuscule particle of dust that is the earth in the unimaginable immensity of the universe are the (exclusive?) bearers of universal consciousness. Hegel would surely laugh at the concern that the spirit be assigned a particular place; nothing could be less essential. It is enough for him than the identity of being and mind/spirit (or of matter and thought) be *thinkable*. The fact that Hegel himself could think as much is evidence enough. But Hegel has invented nothing. The identity of being and thought already exists in Parmenides. Hegel knows this; and he did not write that indigestible tome, the *Phenomenology of Mind*, to repeat in a thousand ways Parmenides' (avowedly) fragmentary aphorism. Hegel is saying something else, which Parmenides could not have said, for he hardly occupies the same place in history. In other words, the story Hegel tells us, which Parmenides could not have known, is the onward *march* that the world and the mind/spirit have accomplished in the course of history, at first in a state of ignorance, then in increasingly comprehensive knowledge of one another, before finally achieving full consciousness of their reciprocity.

What is most original about Hegel is his determination to show that the process of mutual recognition takes place in time: a potent affirmation that transforms philosophy into a historical discipline. Outside of history, it becomes incomprehensible, futile, without effect. Contrary to Heidegger's assertion that all philosophers are contemporaries, Hegelian philosophy cannot escape the idea of progress. In fact, it is the understanding of progress as it unfolds (if I may be forgiven the redundancy). From this perspective every important philosopher, from Heraclitus to Kant, constitutes a greater or a lesser moment. To a greater or lesser extent, each is cognizant of the progression of the spirit toward self-knowledge. The *Phenomenology* is the keystone that completes the arch of the edifice and ensures its cohesion. I am deliberately using, perhaps a bit disloyally, an architectural metaphor that suggests permanence in a domain where, strictly speaking, all is movement. Hegel constructs nothing; he enunciates that which is becoming. But as, in speaking it, he cannot help but present his own words as the crowning moment of this process of becoming, one wonders anxiously what could possibly follow in its footsteps. Nothing? Nothing significant, in any event;

and certainly nothing of any philosophical importance. Whether Hegel intended it or not, the *Phenomenology* brings philosophy to an end; it no longer has anything to tell us. Only science remains: the effectivity of the spirit and the world joined in action.

That philosophy "comes to an end" with the *Phenomenology* is not necessarily invalidated by the numerous twists and turns that it has experienced since then. Kierkegaard, Schopenhauer, Nietzsche, Bergson, Husserl, Heidegger, and Wittgenstein, to name but a few, may be little more than belated shoots on the Hegelian branch. Or, contrarily, they may be vain attempts, for all their beauty and courage, to resist its irresistible rise. Whatever the case, there can be little doubt that the *Phenomenology* sounds the death knell of every philosophical system — though it proclaims itself the first part of a *System of Science (System der Wissenschaft)* whose second part would never see the light of day. But, even should we admit that philosophy no longer has anything to say, its inutility or its muteness are necessarily connected with the evolution of history itself. Philosophy would tiptoe toward the exit, as man finally ascends to a state of *Befriedichkeit*, to the satisfaction with self and with the world that the advent of the spirit brings about. From that vantage point, as we have seen, the refutation pronounced by history seems implacable.

Unless, perhaps, in a violent effort at distanciation, we attempt to fathom, one by one, all the wars, the massacres, and the death camps that divide us from Jena in 1806 as the convulsions of history itself. What weight, after all, can the faltering attempts of two centuries have against the millennia that have preceded them, other than as the most recent failures? Perhaps some consolation might be gained from the accumulation of horrors were we able, even in the slightest, to convince ourselves that humanity has learned something. But the death, the suffering seem all to have been for naught. The dominant impression today is that we have inexorably returned, with a few minor variations, to our point of departure. In this pallid light, the end of philosophy looks less like a summation than a capital execution: philosophy, having too obviously failed to guide and to understand the world, has lost its head. Its impotence is double: it cannot return to the directive function that it enjoyed prior to the *Phenomenology* (as with Kant, for example); but it no longer seems to be in phase with the history whose spirit and finality it pretends to articulate. It can no longer say what should be, nor what is.

Hegel has swept us into an immense spiral of dementia. That is what it *must* be. But that which *is* should not be, so *insupportable* has the world in its current state become. Such is precisely the contradiction it would like to rescue us from by proclaiming the *good tidings* that in history there occurs a moment when man—consciousness—attains the *reasoned* certitude of understanding the world. He proclaims his faith in an advent (if not in each and every one of us, at least among those who understand the *Phenomenology*) that bears an uncanny resemblance to the second coming of a godless Christ. It is the deeply personal conviction that a reading of the *Phenomenology* can touch off within us, or reveal to us; that same revelation, however, is nothing more than reason can firmly establish. The opposite conviction, the conviction that neither the world nor history has the slightest finality, the tiniest parcel of meaning, is no more refutable than Hegel's conviction. The most striking thing about the *Phenomenology* is the idea that we alone can derive meaning from the world; the idea that because consciousness is present in the world we are obliged to locate ourselves at that most demanding level of meaning.

For the *Phenomenology* most probably draws its greatest strength in confronting us with a *requirement*. That terrible and magnificent requirement comprises the only tenable philosophical attitude possible after the definitive collapse of all metaphysics: TO SAY YES TO WHAT IS, to choose to become an integral part of the world, to become a subject in the fullest sense, the conscious *agent* of oneself and not merely a *patient*. Acquiescing to the world in this way is surely the only way for consciousness to understand itself in the world and in its relationship with the world, and for it to produce meaning for itself. That *understanding* can clearly not be reduced to knowledge of the world as something objective (the posture of knowing, positivist consciousness); that *understanding* is action in the world, action within the world and in intelligence with it (and not whatsoever the will to transform it "from without"—a perfectly illusory and logically impossible position). We are in the world what we do there. We are beings of desire that cannot attempt to understand their relation with the world except by engaging it, by testing ourselves against it and in it. But our unreserved attachment to the world cannot be interpreted as unreserved acceptance of all that takes place there, of all human action that depends upon us, of all action. The question of desire, and of its "content," or better, of its direction; the question of knowing what we desire of ourselves, we human beings, in the world, remains unchanged.

The equation between self-consciousness and the world (expressed as either certainty or as intention) can only envisage the world as that of human beings, as it concerns them: it is the world of consciousness for consciousness. The world is reduced or equivalent to (if the idea of reduction seems unnecessarily reductionist) what man thinks the world is or to what he desires the world to be. In this regard, the *Phenomenology* carries humanism to its furthest extreme: the world exists *for man and by man* alone. Man, a historical being whose destiny is death, is interested in history alone, is concerned by history alone, acts in history alone. Hegel would surely feel his views vindicated by the subsequent development of astrophysics: physicists comprehend and describe today the universe as having a history, whose genesis is the *Big Bang*. The modern account of the history of the sidereal world is quite Hegelian: in evoking its origins, the spirit achieves a new threshold of self-consciousness. But, at the same time, it indicates that, while he was cogitating in Jena upon the soul of the world, Hegel was engaged in the most audacious extrapolation or anticipation.

When all is said and done, the *Phenomenology* takes on all the appearances of an intuition as profound as it is inspired, an intuition that vainly seeks the keys to its own proof. Like a smithy at his forge, Hegel shapes and folds language in all possible directions, forcing it to say what it cannot, what will always elude it. German, in its nearly infinite capacity for self-generation, for lexical proliferation by the unlimited combination and recombination of terms, is probably the only modern European language in which such an enterprise could have been conceived, planned, and written. The *Phenomenology* is utterly untranslatable. Not in the commonplace (and often abusive) sense of the word, in which all texts are by definition untranslatable in their idiosyncrasies and most intimate nuances. No, it is untranslatable in the deepest sense: what the German text says—or attempts to say—cannot be rendered in any other language, in a form that is *assuredly* intelligible. One wonders, in fact, if this text, this *Phenomenology*, could even be translated into German! It may only be readable in Hegelian, a language that only Hegel could understand. That would be the sign that what it says can truly not go beyond the intuition that carries it.

The circle, or the spiral, that the *Phenomenology* describes, is no less revealing for all that. Retrospectively, and from the perspective of the historical philosophy whose trail it blazed, the distance that separates us from Jena means that we must read the *Phenomenology* as the tale of a failure of spirit. Spirit in fact appears to have thrown up its hands; that non-advent in turn beckons us so imperiously that the question that wells up upon reading is not whether or not history has "ended," as claimed by those who cannot imagine any other horizon than theirs. The question is one of knowing whether *this* history, that of spirit, has even truly begun. If we were to imagine that the eyewitness to the battle of Jena might today be an onlooker at the end of history that some have decreed in his name, he might well have concluded, never having known the *Shoah*, that the soul of the world was probably lost in the steppes of Russia, or sunk beneath the icy waters of the Berezina. It is almost certain that he would have seen little more, in self-styled postmodern consciousness, than the "bare empty unit of the person," the Roman term referring to the apotheosis of the emperors, designating "a contingent insubstantial process and activity that comes to no durable subsistence" and which constitutes in his eyes "an expression of contempt" (503–504). The vacuity he describes goes hand in hand with an equally vain sense of power, which reminds us of Faust's hysterical excitement at feeling thousands of arms toiling to carry out his will:

> The lord of the world becomes really conscious of what he is — viz. the universal right of actuality — by that power of destruction which he exercises against the contrasted selfhood of his subjects. For his power is not the spiritual union and concord in which the various persons might get to know their own self-consciousness. Rather they exist as persons separately for themselves, and all continuity with others is excluded from the absolute punctual atomicity of their nature. They are, therefore, in a merely negative relation of exclusion both to one another and to him, who *is* their principle of connexion or continuity. *Qua* this continuity, he is the essential being and content of their formal nature — a content, however, foreign to them, and a being hostile in character, which abolishes just what they take to be their very essence, viz. bare self-existence without any content, mere empty independent existence each of its own account. And, again, *qua* the continuity of their personality, he destroys this very personality itself. Juridical personality thus finds itself, rather, without itself noticeable as something distinct from and opposed to the indifferent medium into which it insinuates its way and hence cannot be averted. Only when the infection has become widespread is that consciousness alive to it, which unconcernedly yielded to its influence. For what this consciousness received into itself was doubtless something simple, homogenous, and uniform throughout it, but was at the same time the simplicity of self-reflected negativity, which later on also develops by its nature into something opposed, and thereby reminds consciousness of its previous state. (553–554)

As he sketches a portrait of Rome at the height of its imperial power, Hegel unwittingly directs our attention to our own era, to an era that has failed to accomplish its redemptive mission. The image of the all-powerful tyrant is no longer appropriate to our day and age, of course (except for certain scale models to be found in those countries that have not yet been fortunate enough to graduate to liberal democracy). Today's "lord of the world" can best be visualized as an impersonal dynamic or a social class, or a hegemonic country, rather than a readily identifiable despot. Otherwise, we might be reading a description of our "individualistic" society. What in Hegel's eyes represents, in the onward march of spirit, a stage long passed through (that of the Roman Empire), the portrait now seems to refer—two centuries after Jena—to *our* world. A world in full retreat from the *ideals* of the Enlightenment, whose limits Hegel has so eloquently illustrated.

Though the Enlightenment brought heaven down to earth, as I have already noted, it was aware of what it was doing. Hegel is quick to declare that in its struggle against religion, the Enlightenment "is entirely foolish; belief experiences it as a way of speaking which does not know what it is saying, and does not understand the facts of the case when it talks about priestly deception, and deluding the people" (569). It cannot see that the battle it has waged will immediately turn against it. If the Christian religion is a lie, and not a moment in the progress of self-consciousness toward its truth, then the Enlightenment suddenly finds itself without underpinnings. The "enlightened" declaration of belief becomes in turn a lie. In *Rameau's Nephew* (one of the rare texts quoted in the *Phenomenology*) the eponymous character impudently carries out an inversion of realities that is honest enough to present itself as farce. To the consternation of the philosopher (Diderot), Rameau's nephew leaves nothing standing, not even his own discourse: "*When all prejudice and superstition have been banished, the question arises, what next? What is the truth enlightenment has diffused in their stead?*" (576).

None. The Enlightenment brought no truth that had not existed before it. It acts as if it has destroyed all that came before it, including history, and seeks to rebuild it all. But such reconstruction is only possible in that the history it imagines it is abolishing is pregnant with all the moments that the spirit reintegrates into its advent. The Enlightenment cannot, however, bring about such an advent on its own, for it is blind to its own (Christian) foundations and thus incapable of acting. Yet it goes beyond ancient skepticism reduced to a mere philosophical attitude: it represents, in fact, a *social movement* that paves the way for action.

Indeed, only through revolutionary action can the subject accede to full self-consciousness in the world, can the advent of spirit truly come about. But a nagging question remains: is *revolutionary action* (even when captured and waged by Bonaparte) enough to enable the philosophy that has been able to see through its origins and its aims? If the revolutionaries themselves believe in the "values" of the Enlightenment as new, autonomous ideals, and not as the secularized expression of the Christian teaching, we are justified in fearing that they will be mistaken about the extent of their action, up to and including Bonaparte. This is the reason why—as we have seen—a Hegel was needed to reveal it to them. For, definitively speaking, it is Hegel himself and he *alone* who, with the full force of this thought, endows with meaning history and the civilization that accomplishes it. But what is to be done if the revealer dies without having been understood?

The *Phenomenology* reveals, after the fact, a persistent and insurmountable contradiction at the heart the West's imagined self-image. The West, accordingly, is the decisive moment, acting at the peak of universal history of which it alone possesses the key that, in order to carry out its mission (to bring about the advent of spirit), must absorb history within itself and efface all that constitutes it. Such an extraordinary accomplishment is only possible on the condition that the West surpass itself and achieve a degree of self-understanding that it persists, in point of fact, in demonstrating itself incapable of doing. Our civilization should, in other words, successfully abolish itself in order to strive, along with others, toward the universal. However, in the abbreviated version of Hegelianism that has continued to inspire it, the fact that the West takes itself seriously as the social, economic, and political incarnation of the universal, indicates that, from a strictly Hegelian perspective, we have not taken a single step forward from the time of the Enlightenment. That in our noble generosity we may admit that the incarnation may not yet be perfect fundamentally changes nothing; such a concession in no way modifies our certainty that nothing, for all the catastrophes that have marked the last century, can alter our certainty that we are on the right path, the only possible path. We have, in fact, kept the very worst of Hegel: the feeling that we have arrived (as "new money" puts it). This self-assurance is a grave hindrance to any significant movement of consciousness. Our civilization has retained only the technique and the accumulative logic of movement, while consciousness, though dissatisfied with itself, has resigned itself to the stagnation that has been its state ever since the burial of the *Phenomenology*, and of the mind/spirit whose story it relates, even though that story cannot be told.

What the *Phenomenology* ultimately tells us, despite its narrator; what it expresses in spite of itself and yet with such extraordinary power, is the possibility that *time*, historical time, may well accomplish no task, no task of the spirit. For the spirit, presuming that it exists of course, time does not exist. What a tragic defection! For the human is a historical being; the human being is the thinking animal cognizant of the past. The subject, the *I*, is consciousness of history. The *Phenomenology* has every appearance of being a desperate upheaval of thought confronted with the eventuality that history has no meaning; that it is, to use the celebrated Shakespearean formula, "a tale told by an idiot, full of sound and fury, signifying nothing." Should thought be alone in a world hostile or simply indifferent to it, no possible meaning can be produced. Meaning can exist for thought only on the condition that it conceives of itself in harmony with the universe of which it constitutes the reflecting mirror, with a world in which it discovers itself in action as consciousness of the world. But thought is also that curious flux capable of concluding that nothing allows it to take upon itself any coincidence whatsoever between itself and the world. Consciousness can never be entirely assured of the existence of the spirit, of the spiritual effectivity of the world. But it is in the experience of this hiatus that it becomes itself; it is in failing, and there alone, that it can fully attempt to attain self-consciousness; it is in this moment of vertigo that it remains *alive*. There alone it discovers what Hegel, in his preface, says of the spirit: [*conscience*] *only wins its truth when it finds itself utterly torn asunder.*

10

MOBY DICK:
PLUMBING THE DEPTHS

Cans't thou draw out leviathan with a hook? or
his tongue with a cord which thou lettest down?...

Cans't thou fill his skin with barbed iron? or
his head with fish spears?
Lay thine hand upon him, remember the battle,
do no more.

Job, 41:1–8

THE SEA: IMMEMORIAL, OMNIPRESENT. Timeless. The matrical sea, the primordial womb, smooth and taut of skin, heaving and pregnant with invisible multitudes, calm above the abyss. Contained fury forever unchained by the winds as if sounding, across the face of the waters, the retreat of the dark forces lurking in its depths. Through this sea swims Leviathan, the biblical monster; the evil time-bleached whale: Moby Dick. Atop the waters sails an ancient hunter thirsting for revenge, totally obsessed by the need to harpoon, to kill the unspeakable beast that has torn off his leg: Ahab, captain of the *Pequod*. Such is the structure, the red thread of the narrative; such are the two principal characters of Melville's celebrated novel: Western literature's last great epic, the Homeric tale of modernity.

Unlike other modern-day adventure tales, *Moby Dick* is not a story of unexpected twists and turns. Its adventure lies in expectation: in suspense sustained until the final resolution. The adventure proper—the actual hunt for the mythical whale—concentrated in the final three episodes, occupies only a tiny portion of the whole (three chapters out of one hundred thirty-five, for some thirty pages out of five hundred fifty).[64] It is merely the climax, the final outburst of a long-nurtured rage. *Moby Dick* sings the wrath of Ahab, as does the *Iliad* that of Achilles. Wrath is the toxin that contaminates the narrative tissue of both books. Ahab's single-mindedness weighs like a curse upon the closed world of the *Pequod*, as does Achilles' fury upon the camp of the Achaeans.

The worlds they describe are closed, yet they abound in incident. Like its Homeric model, the circumscribed world of *Moby Dick* depicts life in its inexhaustible diversity, boarding in its nets a prodigious catch of details far too numerous to count. Melville's masterpiece stands before us like a semi-ironic, semi-serious work of scientific genius on cetaceans and their preda-tors, on whalers, their techniques and their equipment. Indeed, whaling ships can be subsumed into a distinct universe of their own, quite distinct from the merchant marine. They carry sufficient supplies of water and food to stay at sea for years on end, never calling at port, abandoning the hunt only in extreme necessity. In fact, the *Pequod* encounters on its voyage only other whaling ships.

Isolation invests the desperate logic of the hunt with a prodigious power. All converges upon its grotesquely magnified object. The ritual of the hunt, whale morphology,[65] the minute preparations that must be made for capturing and butchering the prey, the entire apparatus that prepares the reader as well as the crew itself, is nothing more than the long, necessary prelude to defeat and death. As it lays before us the details that foreshadow the final shipwreck it can do no more than postpone the ineluctable fate it prefigures. The narra-tor, as he methodically pieces together the complex components that make it up, heightens the tension that permeates the venture upon which he has signed us. The obsession to find and to kill Moby Dick emerges with greater clarity at each stage of the voyage, in the form of the hunters' obsessive determination to pursue their own death, to set a trap for themselves.

Only the narrator escapes death. A voice must survive to tell the tale. But the survivor has little of his own to relate. And even less about his tasks on the whaling ship: a simple crew member, indistinguishable from the other sailors, and low enough in rank judging by his "salary" (in point of fact, his share of the catch calculated in terms of the estimated value of his work), with no specific function except that which allows him to be present and to

64. Herman Melville, *Moby Dick, or The Whale*, ed. Luther S. Mansfield and Howard P. Vincent (New York: Hendricks House, 1952).
65. The term "whale" refers to an entire suborder of cetaceans. All are not necessarily "true" whales in the narrowly correct sense of the word. Strictly speaking, Moby Dick is a sperm whale, boasting a powerful jaw armed with teeth.

recount what he has seen. We see nothing of him as an individual before his arrival in the thriving coastal town of New Bedford, where he must pay for a few nights' plebian lodgings while awaiting the Nantucket ferry. For it is from that island port, mythical and timeless locus of the whaling trade, that he must embark. This period of inactivity gives him the opportunity to reveal to the reader his mood, his fears, his vision of the world, allowing him, retrospectively, to lay down a succession of symbolic indicators for the events he will soon witness. The narrator cannot help himself from taking liberties with chronology. Indeed, he knows many things that the eyewitness is still not aware of, and in whom he makes great efforts to instill a sense of foreboding. To tell the tale is to reshape in the light of knowledge that which one has experienced, in the feigned ignorance of what must come. From its very first pages a fog-bound fatalism already enshrouds the book.

Call me Ishmael are its first words. Call me as I say, for you know nothing of my name, nor of my age, nor about what I have done thus far in my life, except that I have already knocked about on ships. Call me what you want, but preferably by the name I've just cast at your feet. It's not just any old name, either: that of Abram's (who is not yet Abraham) bastard son. Ishmael or Ismail, "God hears," is not the son of the promise (reserved for Isaac), but the mythical ancestor of the Arabs, the son set aside and yet blessed and circumcised, a member of the alliance that, through Abraham, and beyond the specific fate of Israel, unites all peoples. The narrator establishes his position, at once marginal to the world and at the epicenter of events. He knows whereof he speaks; he has not allowed himself to be carried away—except for a brief instant—by the dementia of the enterprise he relates. That is why he does not die from it. The narrator escapes the shipwreck not simply through narrative necessity (he could easily have pieced his tale together from a third-party survivor) but, more importantly, because he has remained lucid, like a quasi-scientific observer. His outlook ultimately immunizes him against the collective delirium into which Ahab has plunged the entire crew, and against which the only man who attempts to oppose him—his second in command, Starbuck—is helpless.[66]

Early on, said Ishmael receives from an extraneous source an ambiguous signal: his chosen whaler has been promised a far-from-ordinary fate. The signal takes the face and voice of a prophet of doom encountered near the harbor. Elijah is the old rag picker's name—that of the Old Testament prophet who opposes the idolatry of Ahab, king of Israel. "And Ahab the son of Omri did evil in the sight of the LORD above all that were before

---

66. Unlike the story of the mutineers of the *Bounty*.

him" (1 Kgs: 16–30). The captain of the *Pequod*, insinuates the prophet, is a king damned, but the narrator brushes off the curse: Elijah is either a madman who does not know what he is talking about, or a man unhinged, trying to frighten him.

And yet the narrator himself is not afraid to admit to a death impulse of his own, which, at first glance, hardly jibes with his role as detached observer.

> Whenever I find myself growing grim about the mouth; whenever it is a damp drizzly November in my soul ... then, I account it high time to get to sea as soon as I can. This is my substitute for pistol and ball. With a philosophical flourish Cato throws himself upon his sword; I quietly take to the ship. (1)

If the decision to get to sea seems like suicide, it also spares him the necessity of firing a pistol ball into his head. To take to the ship is to take calm flight: to flee the world, and guard oneself against it. And nothing, as we know, can better isolate us from the world than a whaler. Whatever the next task—to scale the rigging, swab down the deck, obey orders—we are all slaves of someone or something. What counts is to be able to breathe the salt air without paying passage, and better still, by earning a bit of that ostensibly despicable money all of us ceaselessly pursue.

Then comes the mystery of the whale:

> Though I cannot tell why it was exactly that those stage managers, the Fates, put me down for this shabby part of a whaling voyage, when others were set down for magnificent parts in high tragedies, and short and easy parts in genteel comedies, and jolly parts in farces—though I cannot tell why this was exactly; yet, now that I recall all the circumstances, I think I can see a little into the springs and motives which being cunningly presented to me under various disguises, induced me to set about performing the part I did, besides cajoling me into the delusion that it was a choice resulting from my own unbiased freewill and discriminating judgment.
>
> Chief among these motives was the overwhelming idea of the great whale himself. Such a portentous and mysterious monster roused all my curiosity....
>
> By reason of these things, then, the whaling voyage was welcome; the great flood-gates of the wonder-world swung open, and in the wild conceits that swayed me to my purpose, two and two there floated into my inmost soul, endless processions of the

> whale, and, mid most of them all, one grand hooded phenomenon,
> like a snow hill in the air. (5–6)

As hindsight or as premonition, the great white whale haunts the tale from the start. It is as though the eyewitness already knew the secret goal of the vessel on which he was about to ship out. As though the Fates had already assigned him his role, and his destination. Now, blithely caught up in his future shipmaster's obsession, he seems a stranger to himself. He does not know what makes him act: a will that is not his own and which he does not share, but which, under full sail, he can no longer elude. If the narrator himself is driven by the desire for flight, by curiosity about the unknown, by a vague vision, it is this curiosity that leads him willy-nilly to the extremes to which, along with his shipmates, Ahab will soon drag him down, driven by an imperious desire to overcome with which Ishmael has nothing to do. He attends, as a spectator, to another man's fate, and chances following the damned soul of the vessel's only master. Of course, to the extent that the master's fate—death—is that of all men, it also prefigures his own; he has already experienced it in a New Bedford chapel as he examined the marble plaques that commemorate the whaling ship crews lost at sea or to the jaws of a whale, that have preceded him on his perilous path:

> Yes, Ishmael, the same fate may be thine.... Yes, there is death in
> this business of whaling—a speechless quick chaotic bundling of
> man into Eternity. But what then? Methinks we have hugely mis-
> taken this matter of Life and Death. Methinks that what they call
> my shadow here on earth is my true substance. Methinks that in
> looking at things spiritual, we are too much like oysters observing
> the sun through the water, and thinking that thick water the thinnest
> of air. Methinks my body is but the lees of my better being. In fact
> take my body who will, take it I say, it is not me. (36)

Perhaps the narrator does not fear death because he seeks no victory. His acceptance, before the fact, of death keeps him from sinking into the collective madness that so rapidly overwhelms the *Pequod*.

No sooner has the narrator boarded ship, no sooner have the anchors been weighed, than his actions, and even his feelings, practically cease to exist. What he is witnessing, and what he knows are all that matter. And he knows plenty: about the cetacean order, about whaling, its history, its dangers, and its tools. Thanks to a few introductory whaling scenes, he brings to life his knowledge with a dramatic touch that, through a recitation of the ordinary perils inherent in the act of harpooning a whale, hints at the danger to come. For an entire world separates Moby Dick from his fellow creatures. Here, cetology has the function of separating the commonplace from the ineffable. The narrator undertakes more than a few encyclopedic incursions into the cetacean universe not simply to ridicule the way most people represent those great beasts, and the false assurances of the zoologists (a pleasure he is happy to indulge), but above all to delimitate the borderline between the known and the unknown, the visible and the invisible. Moby Dick is never described, only evoked in his monstrous whiteness. The narrator does no more than sketch out a portrait of the whale in the most general terms, making no attempt to conceal the incompleteness and inadequacy of his description. For "any way you look at it, you must need conclude that the great Leviathan is that one creature in the world which must remain unpainted to the last" (265).

Even whales of an "ordinary" size are of such weight and bulk that they cannot be pulled aboard. Some of them may in fact be so heavy, so massive that they threaten to pull down the vessel that has lashed them to its side. The only way to properly examine the monster is to hack it to pieces, to form an idea of its overall structure from the components of its gigantic skeleton once the flesh has been entirely removed and its fat boiled down to oil and stored away in barrels. Science, then, cannot examine the great cetacean in its natural element, nor even arrive at a proper idea of its corpse, given that the technology needed to extract it from the sea does not exist. At best, a whole corpse is available when by luck a baby is harpooned. What better metaphor for modern knowledge, which can only seek knowledge by killing, mutilating, and dissecting? Scientific efficacy is necessarily reductionist.

Following the same train of thought, it is impossible for the casual observer to tell where the whale's head ends and where its body begins. The point where the two are joined can be determined only by cutting deep into the flesh while the animal is still submerged, under dangerous conditions. The operation is critical: the sperm, that precious substance that gives its name to the most sought-after species, is found in the head of the whale. As the name Moby *Dick* would indicate, sperm is omnipresent in *Moby Dick*: it is the essential substance, the white gold—its market value and spiritual-ized merchandise combined—that lies at the heart of the hunt. That rule should apply, at any rate, to any normal whale hunt, including that of the *Pequod*, were it not for the mad objective of its captain who, the better to annihilate the elusive and insubstantial, not only disregards the greater good of the hunt, but ignores its symbolic aspect; he ignores, in the final analysis, the Holy Grail. As such, he stands revealed as a resolutely modern knight. Of the inheritance of knighthood he incarnates only the furious will to victory: this fury, as we shall soon see, blinds him to the meaning of his mission. Blind though he may be, Ahab is also searching, a harrowing search for all that lies beyond his reach, and that he will intuit belatedly on the eve of the final hunt. But before venturing into the ineffable, let us turn once more to zoology.

Close examination of the whale's head (Chapter 74) leads us to the brutal conclusion that the monster is faceless. We know it has a head that is externally indistinguishable from the elongated mass of the body, and that accounts for fully one third of its length. The massive head, viewed from the front, presents not the slightest irregularity, not the tiniest orifice, be it ocular, auditory, or nasal. The blowhole located atop its skull, from which it expels air in the form of water vapor, takes the place of the nose. Its minuscule eyes are set back so far on each side of its head that the whale cannot see straight ahead or directly behind but only laterally, each eye distinct from the other. Its redoubtable jaw is set so deeply recessed that it could better be described as opening "under the chin"—except that the animal possesses nothing resembling a chin. The whale's "face" (in sharp contrast with the mobile, contorted face of the baleen whale) is a smooth, blind wall—in the image of captain Ahab. Covered by a hard, rubbery texture, impenetrable to the sharpest of harpoons, the sperm whale's head, seen from the front, looks like a powerful battering ram. The lack of a nose, the central element of any face, constitutes a crippling aesthetic deficiency: "Dash the nose from Phidias's marble Jove, and what a sorry reminder!" And yet, seen head on, the whale's head provides a sublime spectacle:

> Human or animal, the mystical brow is as that great golden seal affixed by the German Emperors to their decrees. It signifies— "God: done this day by my hand." But in most creatures, nay in man himself, very often the brow is but a mere strip of alpine land lying along the snow line. Few are the foreheads which like Shakespeare's or Melancthon's rise so high, and descend so low, that the eyes themselves seem clear, eternal, tideless mountain lakes; and all above them in the forehead's wrinkles, you seem to track the antlered thoughts descending there to drink, as the Highland hunters track the snow prints of the deer. But in the great Sperm Whale, this high and mighty god-like dignity inherent in the brow is so immensely amplified, that gazing on it, in that full front view, you feel the Deity and the dread powers more forcibly than

in beholding any other object in living nature. (344–345)

The "awful Chaldee of the Sperm Whale's brow" remains indecipherable, and the narrator, altogether too pleased to pass himself off as "unlettered," can never hope to read it. He merely draws it to our attention: "Read it if you can" (345). Before it we stand, like Adam on the first day of creation.

Our unlettered eyewitness has consulted books of zoology, and the accuracy of his descriptions reveal a truly scientific understanding of the animal. Yet in the final analysis, faced with the essence of a thing, science can at best hold its peace. The whale's essence eludes the narrator not because he is unlettered, but because none can read it. "Thou shalt not see my face," YHWH warns man. Scientific investigation and surgical dismemberment only deepen the mute enigma of the great sphinx of the seas. No Œdipus will ever know its secret. Perhaps that is why it must be harpooned. Seen in that light Ahab is hardly more unreasonable than his crew. He simply carries the impulsive logic of the hunt to its extreme; despite all appearances, profit is only a secondary motive. The hunt's unspoken, primary, unconscious motivation is to kill, to eradicate, and to massacre whatever we cannot understand. Ahab is alone in having grasped the imperious need to eliminate the enigma at the source. Understandably enough: the enigma has already cost him a leg, an amputation that is itself the painful wage of an obsessive logic reaching back to before his first battles. Why did he take such risks against an overwhelmingly powerful adversary when there are thousands of other whales to hunt? It can only be that, hoping to penetrate the mystery, he must attack its unique and principal figure: "That inscrutable thing is chiefly what I hate" (162). Ordinary sperm whales are but lesser, mortal divinities compared with the white eminence of the only god that truly matters. The only god whose killing, because of its invincibility, would constitute a decisive victory.

If the secret to even a defeated and dismembered whale cannot be found, what can we hope to know of the beast that all, with the exception of Ahab, have given up hope of fighting? Not much. Size and whiteness aside, we only know of its few identifying features from what the captain of the *Pequod* tells his crew: a wrinkled brow and a crooked jaw, with three holes punctured in his starboard fluke (175). Otherwise, the great white whale is simply a rumor. A rumor that takes full form only in Ahab's hatred, and in the power his hatred wields over those around him. Even the narrator, despite his distance from the events he relates, cannot escape it. Following the captain's fiery speech to the assembled crew, in which he reveals to them the avenging mission that he commands them to make their own, the narrator is astonished to find himself caught up in the collective madness:

> I, Ishmael, was one of that crew; my shouts had gone up with the rest; my oath had been welded with theirs; and stronger I shouted, and more did I hammer and clench my oath, because of the dread in my soul. A wild, mystical, sympathetical feeling was in me; Ahab's quenchless feud seemed mine. (175)

So begins the chapter entitled "Moby Dick," that directly follows Ahab's harangue. Only through him can Moby Dick exist. The white whale has long been spoken of, of course; many a whaler has seen it; some have even touched its remarkable malignity, but its presence—and its comings and goings—are those of a phantom. Legend tells of sightings on the same day in opposing latitudes, as if it alone knew the secret submarine sealanes that allowed it to overturn all calculations and to move from one antipode to another in the space of a few hours. Its legendary omnipresence is not merely spatial; it is also temporal. The great white whale is immemorial, eternal. Its whiteness, the sum of all colors blended together and quintessential color of the sacred, is also the pallor of fear. Clothed in its sepulchral whiteness, the sacred—the divine and the damned—inspires awe. Moby Dick is the incarnation of God, the Devil, and death all at once. He possesses all the essential attributes of God: omnipotence, immortality, eternity, ubiquity; he cannot be depicted, cannot be described. He has the Devil's power of temptation, malice, and ferocity. To those who would draw too near, he promises death. If they persist, a watery grave awaits.

As the promise of death spares no one, Moby Dick embodies not only the obsession of his pursuer. We are all pursuing death, whether we are fully aware of it or not. It is this death impulse that Ahab touches off and darkly mobilizes among his crew. He is so successful that even Starbuck, whom we know to be the least susceptible, ends up succumbing in desperation. It is already too late, when his captain unexpectedly wavers, that he believes for a moment that he might dissuade him. On the eve of the final hunt, in the chapter that immediately precedes the account of its first day, entitled with tender irony "The Symphony," the captain's soul and that of his first mate find themselves almost miraculously in tune for a brief instant.

The time is ripe. Everyone senses that the hour of decision is at hand, that nothing can stop it, and the day promises to be exceptionally fine. With the brilliance of steel and the softness of azure, sea and sky commingle, sun-blessed, in a deliberate kind of orgasm. Unbending and tight-knotted in the morning light, Ahab leans over the rail and observes his shadow vanishing into the water, untroubled by the premonition of his imminent shipwreck. Instead, he is carried away by the sudden sweetness of the world, forgetting for a moment the cancer that is eating away at his soul:

> That glad, happy air, that winsome sky, did at last stroke and caress him, the step-mother world, so long cruel—forbidding—now threw affectionate arms round his stubborn neck, and did seem to joyously sob over him, as if over one, that however willful and erring, she could yet find it in her heart to save and bless. From beneath his slouched hat Ahab dropped a tear into the sea, nor did all the pacific contain such wealth as in that one wee drop.
>
> Starbuck saw the old man, saw him, how he heavily leaned over the side; and he seemed to hear in his own true heart the measureless throbbing that stole out of the centre of the serenity around. Careful not to touch him, or be noticed by him, he yet drew near to him and stood there.
>
> Ahab turned.
>
> "Starbuck!"
>
> "Sir."
>
> "Oh, Starbuck! It is a mild mild wind, and a mild-looking sky. On such a day—very much such a sweetness as this—I struck my first whale—a boy-harpooner of eighteen! Forty—forty—forty years ago!—ago! Forty years of continual whaling! Forty years of privation, and peril, and storm-time! Forty years on the pitiless sea! For forty years has Ahab forsaken the peaceful land, for forty years to make war on the horrors of the deep! (533–534)

Starbuck does not see the tear well up in his eye, but he feels, wishes to believe that his captain has reached a turning point, or that there may still be a turning point. On hearing Ahab's pathetic account of his life, of the young woman and the child he left behind that the older man glimpses for a split-second in the first mate's eyes, Starbuck makes a final attempt to sway him, to persuade him that there is still time to turn back, and head for Nantucket.

> But Ahab's glance was averted; like a blighted tree he shook, and cast his last, cindered apple to the soil.
>
> "What is is, what nameless, inscrutable, unearthly thing is it, what cozening, hidden lord and master, and cruel remorseless emperor commands me; that against all natural lovings and long-

> ings, I so keep pushing and crowding, and jamming myself on all
> the time, recklessly making me ready to do what in my own proper,
> natural heart, I durst not so much as dare? Is Ahab, Ahab? Is it I,
> God, or who, that lifts this arm? But if the great sun move not of
> himself, but is as an errand-boy in heaven; not one single star can
> revolve, but by some invisible power; how then can this one small
> heart beat; this one small brain think thoughts; unless God does that
> beating, does that thinking, does that living, and not I. (536)

Without a word, "but blanched to a corpse's hue" (536), Starbuck abandons
the captain to the ineluctable. Ahab himself curses his madness, yet is
powerless against it. The necessity of victory overwhelms the sweetness of
life. But victory is impossible, its object as chimerical as it is destructive. If
the great, mythical whale possesses the attributes of God, if indeed it is the
marine metaphor, the modern-day Neptune, then God himself is the inspiration, the driving force and the ultimate objective of his dementia. Zeus and
Poseidon have become one, uniting in the unnamable, becoming YHWH, for
the destruction of man. God has entrapped man in a vicious circle: He
punishes him with the very murderous passion that He has inspired. "He
alone commands; He alone also fulfills," writes Luther tellingly in his
Concerning Christian Liberty.[67] The paradox exists only for the non-believer
however; the Christian finds liberty, the only liberty he can call his own, the
freedom of the soul, in faith and in sacred word. But Ahab is quite precisely
the man who listens to no word, be it from without, or within. Trapped by his
hatred, he is not free but simply enslaved by his unconsidered need for
triumph, for revenge.

His punishment, so it seems, is the fruit of a fundamental impiety. Even
before meeting Ahab we learn of his transgression from the mouth of Peleg,
one of the *Pequod*'s two owners, a retired shipmaster whom Ahab had served
as first mate. "He's a grand, ungodly, god-like man," he tells the narrator,
"much above the common" (79). Peleg, himself a non-believer, clearly identifies with his former first mate against his bigoted associate Bildad, another
former captain who is named for one of the three friends who comfort Job in
his trials. "So are the paths of all that forget God; and the hypocrite's hope
shall perish: Whose hope shall be cut off, and whose trust shall be a spider's
web" (Job, 8:13–14), affirms the biblical Bildad.[68] There can be no doubt that
Ahab is among the miscreants; Peleg, in turn, represents him to the narrator,
who vainly asks to see him. For at that moment, Ahab is not on board his

---

67. http//www.gutenberg.org.files/1911/1911-h/1911-h.htm
68. It must be noted that YHWH castigates Bildad and his two friends: "Ye have not spoken of me the
thing which is right, like my servant Job" (Job, 42:8).

vessel. He is confined to his home by a malady, an unidentified malaise; he will only board ship at the last minute, unseen by the crew. Like YHWH, Ahab remains concealed in the sacred cavern of his quarters, to which only his mates have access. Aboard ship a troubling atmosphere of subterranean transcendence prevails that creates the conditions, after several days sailing southward, for what must literally be termed an apparition. On a less frigid but still dark morning, as the narrator goes up to the quarterdeck, he shudders with an ill omen:

> Reality outran apprehension; Captain Ahab stood upon his quarter-deck.
>
> There seemed no sign of common bodily illness about him, not of the recovery from any. He looked like a man cut away from the stake, when the fire has overrunningly washed all the limbs without consuming them, or taking away one particle from their compacted aged robustness. His whole high, broad form, seemed made of solid bronze, and shaped in an unalterable mould, like Cellini's cast Perseus. Threading its way out from among his grey hairs, and continuing right down one side of his tawny, scorched face and neck, till it disappeared in his clothing, you saw a slender rod-like mark, lividly whitish. (120)

Ahab bears the mark of lightning; perhaps it is the sign of a scission that may have traveled the length of his body and, ultimately, his very being. Each time he casts his eye over the quarterdeck, erect, motionless, his ivory peg leg anchored in a specially-bored hole, he hangs fast to the shroud (in both meanings of the word) as though clutching the rope of death itself. His secret "malady," as we learn almost at the end of the book, must remain hidden as long as possible: it is the result of a mysterious crack in the whalebone that now serves as a leg. In the wake of an inexplicable nighttime accident that befalls him in his own home, Ahab was found unconscious, wounded in the groin by a splinter of his shattered appendage. Even before returning to the hunt, Ahab has once again been brought low by the very species he is pursuing, and from which the prosthesis that would repair his amputation has been fashioned. But the wound is incurable. Now he carries within him the bone of the very species to which belongs the monster he pursues in hatred. Ahab is a vulnerable god, to whom God grants no peace, whom God casts into an impious search, as if to punish him for his lack of piety.

Is his impiety as rigidly determined as the movement of the stars? Is Ahab free to be impious, free to be Ahab? For all his phantasms of omnipotence[69] he feels himself a helpless prisoner of overwhelming forces. But his feelings of impotence may well be punishment for a life insufficiently reflected upon. Ahab is the one who acts without attempting to know himself. More precisely, in ignorance of who he is, Ahab *is acted upon* by his impulses. Unlike Œdipus, he remains to the bitter end blind to his own self, and obstinately refuses to turn his gaze inward. We will never know anything more about him than his passion for whaling and his thirst for revenge. What dark forces drive him onward in his murderous pursuit of Moby Dick? Of them, we know nothing. God provides us with not a shred of explanation; he stands for the simplest, the most acceptable manner for naming ignorance. The object of Ahab's passion may be metaphysical instead of material; unlike his fellows, the *Pequod*'s master may prefer absolute murder to the far more lucrative revenues to be derived from ordinary whaling: everything points to the excess of his ambition. What his mediocre colleagues toil for day after day Ahab seeks in the absolute. But his excess is also representative, and his appetite, like that of those who practice his trade, insatiable. Where others tack against the wind, hoping to escape it, Ahab sails steadfastly toward failure, his course set straight for death. For all his psychic blindness, Ahab *sees* his madness. But he refuses to seek out its roots in himself, preferring to accuse God. Yet he intuits the dementia that drives him on, where others imagine that they are simply going about their business. For the everyday killing in which they participate is endless, without measure. Never will there be enough spermaceti, never enough gold.

Ahab incarnates to an ultimate degree the onrush of a civilization unbound—*the all-grasping Western world*—which, in its refusal to call its own boundless greed into question, toils feverishly to be itself devoured by the monstrous voracity of its own folly. Moby Dick is the devouring chimera that turns against those whom it entices, and who pursue it. The whale is white, as is the man who leads the hunt to track it down, with no thought for the lives of the non-white members of his crew. The whale hunt, taken generally, is an allegory for industrial capitalism that obliterates whatever it exploits. In Chapter 105, ironically entitled "Does the Whale's Magnitude Diminish?—Will He Perish?" (455), the narrator echoes the fear that, by inconsiderate hunting, the whales, like the bison of Illinois and Missouri,[70]

---

69. "I'd strike the sun if it insulted me," Ahab exclaims to the assembled crew.

70. I cannot resist the temptation to reproduce here a sample of the narrator's sense of humor. In his comparison between the disappearance of the bison and the eventual extinction of the whales, he reminds us that where once the buffalo in their tens of thousands could cause the earth to tremble, now stands a populous capital where "a well-bred realtor sells you land at one dollar per inch."

are inexorably destined for extinction. But even he, all things considered, does not believe it. The vast frigid expanses beneath which they can seek refuge, he claims, will protect them from men and their harpoons. Whether the narrator's arguments are pertinent is of little import. For him, the immortality of the whale is essential, and proceeds from a biblical, quasi-mystical vision of the world:

> He swam the seas before the continents broke water; he once swam over the site of the Tuileries, and Windsor Castle, and the Kremlin. In Noah's flood he despised Noah's Ark; and if ever the world is to be again flooded, like the Netherlands, to kill off its rates, then the eternal whale will still survive, and rearing upon the topmost crest of the equatorial flood, spout his frothed defiance to the skies. (459)

For all its predatory character and its destructive consequences, Western civilization, when compared with the millenary longevity of whales, is nothing but an accident of history, a mere ripple on the surface of the ocean. No more than Ahab's frenzy can best Moby Dick, industrial civilization cannot seriously threaten, in the long term, the immortality of the god that rules the sea's great depths. Yet again it is quite exactly consciousness of this smallness, of man's impotence against Leviathan, which enrages the *Pequod*'s master. The West, for all its destructive fury, for all its unrelenting exploitation, by no means represents the world's destiny, and Ahab is not simply the emblematic figure of a civilization thirsting for conquest.

Above and beyond Western civilization, Ahab shoulders the burden of all humanity. In his eyes Moby Dick embodies not only all the suffering, not only the malevolent forces that have been visited upon him. No, "[h]e piled upon the whale's white hump the sum of all the general rage and hate felt by his whole race from Adam down" (181).

How tempting it would be to read *Moby Dick* as an allegory for triumphant America. And, in its quotidian upheavals, that is undoubtedly what the whaling adventure represents. The risks are high, but the beast is hunted and killed, and the spermaceti extracted; success is possible, even if some whalers return from their exhausting expeditions frustrated and empty-handed. Yet that very predatory normalcy, with its balance sheet of risks and benefits that can be nicely calculated in the end, leaves Ahab indifferent. His indifference to what others may do with their butter (or whale oil) lies at the root of his lack of faith (cost-benefit analysis). He wants more—much more; in fact, he wants something entirely different: the immortal glory of killing immortality.

The glory of achieving much more than Achilles ever did. To the warrior ideal of the hero of antiquity he adds a distinctly modern immoderation. For all the excessiveness of his wrath (which is, in any event, the result of a divine manipulation beyond his control), Achilles remains bound by moderation: his goal is to kill Hector, a mortal, an act that will cost him his life, out of friendship for his comrade Patroclus. Ahab seeks to kill God; his wrath is mystical, and his mysticism destroys all that it feeds upon. This ungodly man's belief in God is stronger than the believers', for believing he can reach him, annihilate him. God is not dead—quite the contrary. He lives in insolent fashion, defying a humanity that he continues to draw toward him, to lacerate it with wounds. Disaster has befallen all ships that stray too close to him; only those who flee in time have escaped being dragged down with all hands.

Ahab's desire is to go down with all hands: anything but to survive God's insolent perversity. In the process he achieves, to a depth where others cannot follow, the secret destiny of the West: he spurs on within himself the onrushing fury of a civilization that has unconsciously taken death as its horizon, and we know it. The adventure and its ineluctable failure are metaphysical. In attempting to carry out the supreme murder, the murder of transcendence, Ahab can only drown in his bitterness, a bitterness as deep as his despair, an oceanic bitterness.

In Chapter 45, entitled "The Affidavit"—presented as distinct from the story, but as necessary as the others for its understanding—, the narrator takes extraordinary pains to show, by assembling a variety of credible eyewitness accounts, the accuracy of all that he, as a whaler, attests: all the exceptional attributes ascribed to Moby Dick exist in other great whales; furthermore, from highest antiquity, whales have suffered similar disrepute, and accomplished exploits comparable to his. So, it is Ahab who has constructed his enemy, has raised him up to the full stature of an idea to be destroyed. By doing so, he becomes a tragic emblem of the species he believes he must avenge. The whaler, under constant threat of being strangled, mutilated, or thrown into the sea by the taut-stretched web of his own lines,[71] represents the human condition. We are all threatened by our own harpoons, by our own lines; we all bob along atop the surface of the unplumbed depths that are life, so many Columbuses sliding across the infinite, above the innumerable, questing for our superficial America.[72]

---

71. The narrator masterfully describes the complexity of his situation in Chapter 60, entitled "The Line," concluding: "All men live enveloped in whale lines" (270).

72. Columbus is described as a conqueror: "Columbus sailed over numberless unknown worlds to discover his one superficial western one" (267).

Ahab's shipwreck is a fair match for all that he has refused to seek out and to understand within himself. If the Other—and if need be, all the tiny others that may lie across the pathway leading to that impossible murder—must be killed, it is because the source of human unhappiness is everywhere else than within him. But, against his will, Ahab proves that his misfortune comes only from within himself, from himself alone. For Moby Dick is not God, but simply a whale that is larger, stronger, and more resourceful than any other, magnified to the divine power.

11

BOUVARD AND PÉCUCHET:
KNOWLEDGE AND ITS LAMENTS

Thus everything has come to pieces in their hands.

DEATH DID NOT PERMIT Flaubert to finish his work. It came upon him as he was writing the final chapter of *Bouvard and Pécuchet*, just before his eponymous couple had come full circle. The story of the two cronies can be summarized easily enough: two friends, who share a curiosity about the world and a taste for life, are bored with their work as copyists; they withdraw to the countryside, where they dabble in most of the fashionable scientific activities of the day until, disenchanted by each, they return to their original occupation: copying.

Through the two pen-pushers' repeated attempts to experience life, and their flirtation with science, the narrator fashions an image of the world, of a particular world: the world of friendship, of life as a couple, of rural pre-Revolutionary France under Louis-Philippe, and the post-Revolutionary days of the Second Empire; of the scientific, modernist, and reactionary nineteenth century, and beyond it, of the great issues of metaphysics, religion, and the human condition. All these worlds encapsulated within one another can never entirely convey the *world*, for it eludes, in and of itself, all attempts at capture; but they do produce its mirror-image, its ever-changing, ill-defined projection, its less than faithful copy. Copyists to a fault, copyists Bouvard and Pécuchet will remain throughout their fruitless tribulations, "returning" in the end to what they have never left. Never do they contrive to taste life to the full, to get to the heart of things. As if the habit of copying, of being so long and so far removed from what they transcribed had made it impossible for them, in their maturity, to create, to invent, to produce, or even to dream.

And yet, throughout their long years of copying, dreaming was exactly what they never ceased to do; their retirement—they hope—will finally allow them to make their dreams come true. No dream, of course, can come literally true. But Bouvard and Pécuchet's successive disenchantments owe more to their inability to accomplish anything substantial, no matter how impassioned they may become at times. Everything falls apart in their hands. Whatever they undertake they prematurely abandon; when their endeavors encounter setbacks, they give up; they are waverers, amateurs to the end.

In terms of narrative structure, their repeated failures clearly express the need to keep the protagonists constantly moving, in the image of the civilization to which they belong. As he hustles them along from one activity to another, from one fad to another, the narrator lays before us—not without irony—an exposition of the knowledge, the behavior, and the enthusiasms of the day. But if Bouvard and Pécuchet were nothing but puppets in an encyclopedic demonstration, their efforts, their desires, and their whole lives would be of little interest. Yet, in spite of everything, the two characters touch us: therein lies the puzzle that forms the umbilicus of the narrative, the puzzle without which there would simply be no novel.

Just over forty-seven years old, in the prime of life, Bouvard and Pécuchet meet in the overwhelming emptiness of a summer Sunday afternoon:

> There was a temperature of ninety degrees, and the Boulevard Bourdon was completely deserted.
> Lower down, the Canal St. Martin, enclosed by two locks, showed the straight line of its inky water. Midway, there was a boat filled with timber, and on the banks two rows of barrels.
> Across the canal, between the houses separated by timberyards, the clear expanse of sky was cut into segments of deep blue, and as the sun beat down, the white fronts, the slate roofs, the granite quays dazzled. A confused murmur rose far off in the sultry air; and everything seemed lulled in the Sunday quiet and the sadness of summer days.
> Two men appeared. (17)[73]

So begins the novel, with the encounter of two idle solitudes in the afternoon of their lives, on the banks of dead calm and against the ultramarine background of an unattainable dream. Having sat down at the same time on the same bench, they bare themselves, both literally and figuratively, of their

---

73. Gustave Flaubert, *Bouvard and Pécuchet*, trans. T. W. Earp and G. W. Stonier, with an introduction by Lionel Trilling (New York: New Directions, 1954).

hats and their names. They have had the same idea. Together, they will have still more. They strike up a friendship. The inkiness of the Canal St. Martin links them like an ironic hyphen. As they keep assiduous company their affinities are revealed, their curiosity stimulated and their intelligence sharpened. But ideas increase their suffering, as their brief excursions into the countryside does their sorrow at being in the city:

> The monotony of the office became hateful. Always the scratching penknife and the sand-sprinkler, the same inkpot, the same pens, and the same companions!...
>
> At one time they had been almost happy; but now they had a higher opinion of themselves, their work humiliated them, and they made common cause in this disgust, exciting and spoiling one another. Pécuchet acquired Bouvard's roughness; Bouvard took on something of Pécuchet's misanthropy. (27)

Three years after their meeting, thanks to an unexpected inheritance from Bouvard's natural father, they leave their "abominable situation" behind and take up residence in the countryside, on an estate of thirty-eight hectares, with farm buildings, a kitchen garden, and a residence at Chavignolles, in the Calvados, between Caen and Falaise. Breathing deeply, from his balcony, the air of his last night in Paris as he looks out over the quays, Bouvard "felt a sinking of the heart, a sadness which he dared not confess" (33). As for Pécuchet, he takes leave of his apartment with relief. But the long, sodden voyage that leads him and his furniture to Chavignolles goes badly. It is full of the unpleasant and the unexpected, of gusting winds and rain squalls, through a countryside "spread out in great slabs of cold, monotonous green" (34); while Bouvard, who has left two days later, having sent his belongings ahead, takes the wrong coach and wakes up in Rouen. His nine days of wandering, of miscues and delays prefigure the nine chapters of their new life, their nine fruitless attempts to invest it with meaning.

Yet they awaken from their first night in the country, calm, quiet, and moonlit, with untrammeled delight. In perfect tune with Bouvard's freshly lighted pipe and Pécuchet's first pinch of snuff, that first morning might well have been "the best they had ever known" (37). The best and the last. No other would reach the pinnacle of simple happiness that flows from taking possession of the immediate world that surrounds them. The vegetable garden, the arbor, the espaliers, the orchard, the tree-lined path, the copse, the rural landscape: all combine to create a harmonious setting for the virgin existence that is about to begin. The décor of their dreams is now in place. It does not begin to disintegrate immediately. The two boon companions do all they can to protect it. They begin, in fact, where Candide left off: by cultivating their garden.

But only vegetables grow in that particular garden. There is nothing philosophical about its yield. As the yield seems satisfactory, they are emboldened to aim higher: "Now that they were skilled in gardening, they ought to succeed at agriculture—and they were taken with the ambition to develop the farm themselves" (40). The idea seems all the more necessary considering that, ever since their first visit, master Gouy, the farmer, has been constantly denigrating the soil and the farm buildings, and seems ill-inclined to upgrade the estate—a strategy one might expect from a cunning tenant who is trying to lower the rent. The two beginners proceed with caution, by observing *in situ* how others till the soil, reading farming manuals, wearying their tenant with advice, and finally informing him that his lease will not be renewed. "After that Gouy was stingy with the manure, let weeds go, ruined the soil" (44). Reinvestment in apparatus, animals, and personnel cost them four times the rent of the farm; the farmhands are none too anxious to work; they invite their cousins to come and live on the farm; they pilfer the grain; clearing the fields of stones adversely affects the wheat crop; the grain is beaten down by hailstorms; the fodder ferments and, in a splendid apotheosis, goes up in flames. Financial ruin threatens; they must sell and, while awaiting a buyer, entrust the farm once more to Gouy at one-third the previous rent. No matter! They will grow fruit crops, "not for pleasure, but as a speculative venture!" (54).

> Bouvard tried to train the apricot trees; they rebelled. He forced their stems down to the level of the soil; none of them grew up again. The cherries, on which he had made notches, produced gum.
>
> First they pruned a long way down, which did away with the buds near the base, then too little, which produced water shoots; and they often hesitated, unable to distinguish wood buds from fruit buds....
>
> Sometimes Pécuchet would draw his handbook from his pocket and study a paragraph, standing there, with his spade beside him, in the pose of the gardener who adorned the frontispiece. The resemblance greatly flattered him. It gave him a high opinion of the author. (56–57)

Striking the right pose is no less important than successful grafting and pruning. Still, pears and plums finally ripen, and then a storm destroys the crop. The drumfire of hailstones brings the "lucrative" and "productive" phase of their avocation to an abrupt halt. All things considered, a good financial investment yields more than any agricultural or fruit-growing venture. After having considered giving up everything in a moment of discouragement, the two friends turn to more aesthetic, domestic activities: landscape gardening and preserving. The garden is remodeled according to the high canons of kitsch; the results are a source of consternation for their guests. The preserves rapidly go bad, and must be discarded. And, in a climactic event, their attempt to set up a still ends with an explosion that could well have cost them their lives. "Perhaps it is because we never studied chemistry" (73), concludes Pécuchet.

After the applied arts come the hard sciences: chemistry, anatomy, and physiology—under the sardonic gaze of Dr. Vaucorbeil. Our sorcerer's apprentices hasten to put their newly-acquired medical knowledge to the test. To the astonishment of the physician, they wield their stethoscopes, effect a cure or two, and then, when their treatments turn dangerous and then fail, they give up. Their incursion into medicine has given them insight into the workings of their bodies. They develop a concern for their health, delve into hygiene and submit themselves to dietetic discipline until, confronted with the evidence that their diets are destroying their lives, they return to their late nights, to their drinking, smoking, and snuff-taking.

Bellies full, digesting their meal in the garden, their heads in the stars, Bouvard and Pécuchet slip into a state of cosmic intoxication, transported by the infinite depths of the nebulae and the speed of light, transfixed by the emptiness that lies between the visible and the invisible, and the possibility that other worlds may be inhabited.

> Some shooting stars fell suddenly, describing what seemed the parabola of a gigantic rocket on the sky.
>
> "Look!" said Bouvard, "there are worlds vanishing."
>
> Pécuchet replied:
>
> "If ours in its turn made a plunge, the citizens of the stars would not be more moved than we are now. Such ideas check one's pride."
>
> "What's the object of it all?"
>
> "Perhaps there's no object."
>
> "And yet—"

Pécuchet repeated: "And yet—" two or three times, without
finding anything to say.

"All the same, I should greatly like to know how the universe
came to be made." (94)

Their meditation foreshadows metaphysical concerns, and awakens in
Pécuchet a religious tremor that Bouvard does not share. But the enigma of
beginnings sends them veering off into geology and paleontology. They study
the strata of the earth and collect rocks which they accumulate in their
quarters; they extract so many fossils that the cliff face threatens to collapse,
which in turn earns them a brief arrest and a warning from the court. They
read Cuvier, Lamarck, Saint-Hilaire; they engage the vicar Jeuffroy in a
dispute over Scripture, whose truth is challenged by science; they tremble in
terror at the disappearance of the continents. At the foot of the cliffs at Étretat,
the thought of an earthquake beneath the Channel suddenly overwhelms
Bouvard with a panic that Pécuchet cannot assuage. Soon, "tired of the
Eocene and the Miocene" (112), disenchanted by the mineral realm, our
geologists remake themselves as archeologists, scouring the countryside,
plundering churches, and rapidly transforming their house into a museum.
Among their choicest pieces, a ceramic Saint Peter with a drunkard's face, and
a seashell-encrusted commode vie for top honors in the bad taste sweepstakes.

The passion for old objects leads them to History. They consider writing
the biography of the Duke of Angoulême, a secondary figure who, though
according to Bouvard was an imbecile, nonetheless had some impact on
affairs of state. But History soon reveals itself to be even more defective than
geology, and their best attempts at biographical restitution seem vain, in the
light of the two men's total inability to manage what goes on in their own
house—there is no way of knowing whether the governess or the carpenter
has emptied the bottle of Calvados, left the garden door ajar and let a stray
cow destroy the wooden chest and damage the statues. All things considered,
the historical novel, plunging us as it does straight into the action as if we
were there, is much truer to life. So off they charge, hot on the heels of Sir
Walter Scott and Alexandre Dumas, whose methodology rapidly leaves them
cold. As long as we are creating fables, they reason, why not stride out into
the broad field of art and literature? Bouvard and Pécuchet now try their hand
at the classics: Racine strikes them as artificial; Molière, cold and calculating,
but *Hernani* sweeps them off their feet—they declaim whole soliloquies. The
craving to write torments them like an itch.

> In the end they resolved to write a play.
> The difficulty was to find a subject....
> At times they felt a tremor, as though it were the waft of an idea; as they grasped at it, it vanished.
> But there are ways of finding subject. (161–152)

None of the ways work, of course. Then, too, there's more to it than the subject; a plot line is needed; feelings; rules! But without genius, what is the use of rules? Even genius itself "is not enough" (163). Nor can it be recognized on short notice. Today's successes quickly wither, and great works remain long unappreciated. "Plays are a commodity like anything else" (163). Style is often sacrificed to the desire to entertain, to amuse. The narrator steps in to offer a succinct treatise on literature and grammar, which reminds one of the lesson in "philosophy" from the *Bourgeois gentilhomme*. The two friends, unable to impart their literary enthusiasm to their entourage, lament its prejudices, its narrow-mindedness, and its utilitarian morality. Marescot the notary would have literature be edifying. "Vaucourbeil, too, considered that art should have an aim: to try to improve the masses!" (171). The count uses the occasion to distribute pamphlets promoting universal suffrage.

The February 1848 Revolution breaks out. Suddenly, History with a capital *H* comes bursting into everyday life, enlarges its theater, and leads Bouvard and Pécuchet into electoral politics. What an opportunity to venture into political thought, and to force liberalism in all its variants, then socialism, through the meat-grinder of ridicule. Rousseau, Saint-Simon, Fourier, Proudhon are expedited in a few sentences. "Your socialists," says Bouvard, "are always asking to tyrannize" (199). Pécuchet protests. For all their ridiculousness, the utopians "deserve our love," because they have paid a high personal price. "The hideousness of the world appalls them, and, in the hope of making it better, they have suffered all" (200). The world, says Bouvard ironically, will not be changed "thanks to some gentleman's theories" (200). Pécuchet believes in the possibility of a better system, and insists that he has discovered it. Bouvard bursts out laughing; his friend slams the door. "The squabble was over; they recognized that their studies lacked a basis—political economy" (200)—perhaps that is why nothing is said of Marx. Whatever the theory, in the real world, the reaction is not long in coming. Revolutionary enthusiasm gives way to the fear of rioting, and to the Party of Order. No sooner acclaimed than abandoned, the Republic is replaced by authoritarianism. In his vexation, Pécuchet bitterly salutes the tyranny of the providential man.

"Since the middle classes are hooligans, the workers jealous, the priests servile, and since, after all, the people accept every sort of tyrant, so long as he leaves their snouts in the trough, Napoleon[74] is right! Let him gag the mob, stamp it under foot, crush it! That will never be too great a penalty for its hatred of the right, its cowardice, its ineptitude, its blindness!"

Bouvard was thinking: "Progress—what a joke." He added, "And politics—a fine mess!"

"It's not a science," replied Pécuchet. "Military tactics is better: one can at least foresee what it going to happen. Suppose we start on it?"

"No, thanks," answered Bouvard. "I'm sick of everything. Let's sell this shanty and go, 'to the sound of God's thunder, among the savages!'"

"As you please!" (203)

Amidst the inactivity that follows their political embarrassment, amorous adventure blooms. While Bouvard is discreetly courting and proposing marriage to Madame Bordin, Pécuchet loses his virginity in the cellar, where he has his way with Mélie. The serving wench returns the favor by passing on to him a venereal disease. Madame Bordin, meanwhile, seeks nothing from Bouvard but her own advantage, and mocks his pot belly. Having first kept their love lives a secret, the two friends reveal their misfortunes to one another, and perorate on women, uttering "all the well-known commonplaces" (214). They swear never to touch another woman, and renew, in a tender embrace, their briefly suspended friendship. The chapter on love (the seventh) is far and away the shortest of the book: all is wrapped up in twelve pages.

In the next two chapters (8 and 9, the last that Flaubert could complete) Bouvard and Pécuchet take up, in order, gymnastics, magnetism, hypnotism, and spiritualism. Again, they pretend to cure the sick; again they dabble in magic. They speculate on matter and spirit, on good and evil, weighing the pros and cons of materialism and idealism; they plunge into philosophy, question the concept of the *etendue* in optics, are terrified by death, argue violently over broken dishes, decide to hang themselves and then, each lacking a last will and testament, change their minds; faced with the emptiness of their existence, they draw closer to religion. Hoping it will give them belief, they seek grace: Pécuchet ardently; Bouvard slowly, grumbling at first, then attempting to believe in spite of himself. But Christianity's pretense that it

74. The Napoleon referred to is Charles Louis Napoléon Bonaparte, nephew of Napoleon I, who, first as president of the Republic, ruled as emperor under the name of Napoleon III.

alone possesses salvation revolts them; the hypocrisy of religious institutions repels them. Like everything that has come before, their religious quest ends in frustration. Only education remains, the subject of the tenth and last chapter, which Flaubert could not complete. From his synopsis we know that their ultimate effort will also end badly, in a scandal touched off by a public lecture by the two friends in Chavignolles: "They are accused of undermining Religion, public order, inciting to Revolt, etc." They end up admitting to each other, simultaneously, the project that each has been mulling over for some time without having said a word about it: to copy everything down. This they proceed to do. But the authorities, judicial and medical alike, wonder if they should not simply be locked up.

For all its appearances of triviality and harmlessness, concealed by the extreme economy of the narrative, the odyssey[75] of Bouvard and Pécuchet is, in the final analysis, mad. The madness that possesses them parodies the beginning of *Faust*, and situates them squarely at the antipodes of the passion that burns in Balthazar Claës in Balzac's *La Recherché de l'absolu*. Flaubert knows his classics, and the boundless curiosity of his couple of amateurs offers us a revealing contrast with their illustrious predecessors.

Like Dr. Faust, the two friends dabble in all disciplines, but far more superficially than he, and in the twilight of their existence, while Goethe's hero begins by exhausting the charms of study, and devotes the first half of his lifetime to science before throwing himself, rejuvenated by Mephistopheles, into a new life of passion and action that drive him to a state of exaltation that is finally cut short only by death.

Balzac's hero is a man of passion as well, but his passion leads in a single direction, as precise as it is invariable: to transform matter in the crucible of chemistry. Everything: his love, the health of the wife who adores him in spite of everything, the well-being of his children, whom he thoughtlessly plunges into destitution. He cannot resist: beyond the confines of his laboratory, of chemistry, he languishes. Perpetually on the verge of achieving the chemical transformation that will make him rich and famous, Balthazar Claës, with the assistance of his faithful servant Lemulquier, is always falling short of his goal by a hair's breadth, and always for lack of resources: just one final investment, one final expenditure, and success will be assured—a hope constantly postponed; a hope that, from failure to fiasco, never materializes and in the end exhausts his resources. Only the death of his wife and the

---

75. Raymond Queneau, in an unfinished draft preface, includes *Bouvard and Pécuchet* among the odysseys.

energetic intervention of his daughter ultimately halt Claës, and even then, not completely: the secret of matter will haunt him until the bitter end.

Unlike him, Bouvard and Pécuchet are mired in boredom, and will stop at nothing to relieve it. They experience bursts of enthusiasm; novelty's short-lived enthusiasms chip away at their fortune but do not completely ruin them. They have no experience of the devastation that can accompany passion. Their only passion, if it can be described as such, is the friendship that binds them. But even those ties of friendship are the product of a curious kind of passivity. It is enough for the two to chase a few skirts for their companionship to suffer. But no amount of passion can breathe life into their amorous enterprises; these too are failures, just like everything that has gone before. Only after involuntarily witnessing a harrowing lovers' quarrel, only after having seen the lover devastated when her partner cynically abandons her, does Pécuchet experience feelings he had never known before:

> What he had just surprised was, for Pécuchet, the discovery of a new world—an entire new world—which contained dazzling radiances, riotous bursts of blossom, oceans, tempests, treasures and abysses of infinite depth. What matter that it was charged with terror! He dreamed of love, was eager to feel it like her, like him to inspire it…. He considered Heaven unjust, felt himself an outcast, and his friend no longer loved him. He was deserted every evening. (207–208)

The betrayal he witnesses reminds the unhappy Pécuchet of his abandonment at the hands of his friend, who has taken off to conquer Madame Bordin. No doubt that the sight of Mélie's curvaceous loins and of her shapely calves as she draws water at the well has already turned his head to some small extent, but it is primarily out of dissatisfaction and by imitation (not of Bouvard, of whose enterprise he is not aware, but of the lovers whom he has just surprised) that Pécuchet, mustering all his courage, resolves to seduce Mélie. Even their amorous initiatives are copies. A copy of the past for Bouvard; for Pécuchet, a copy of someone else's passion. Even in love, the two friends experience nothing that they can authentically call their own. They know only, and experience only, the self-love that they are constantly passing back and forth to one another.

The only thing amorous about their friendship is its specular quality. The successive objects of their enthusiasm are essential to the play of mirrors in which they contemplate themselves; as a result, they are interchangeable. The two are not at all interested in science for itself, but for what their mutual admiration of the sciences fosters between them; it lends them stature in their own eyes; they stand apart from others, raise themselves above their condition, and above their fellow citizens. From the very beginning, and despite their disagreements, what drives their friendship is their feeling of superiority over their work mates—as it does, later on, over the society in which they live. For the same reason, their ostensible goodwill notwithstanding, religion, that school of humility *par excellence*, cannot in the long run satisfy them: faith would relegate them to the rank of mere mortals, and they cannot deprive themselves, no matter how pathetic and miserable they may be, of the sweet sin of pride.

Bouvard and Pécuchet are intelligent enough to know that they are mediocrities. But it is precisely this knowledge, this complacent lucidity that, with each successive setback, elevates them in their own esteem. Each failure is followed by another incursion into a field as yet unexplored, where their inexperience guarantees them failure anew. That unending process leads them logically to pedagogy: where they have failed now they must teach, must "train" disciples who may succeed in their place. But failure, in their eyes, cannot simply be the result of their ineptitude; it also reflects the failure of the social system: a disaster that the chapter of politics complacently displays. It is not Bouvard and Pécuchet who fail at every turn, but the society that surrounds them, a brutish, narrow-minded society that is little inclined to understand what they understand, and even less able to countenance their aspirations.

> Bouvard and Pécuchet enunciated their abominable paradoxes on other occasions. They held up to doubt the probity of men, the chastity of women, the intelligence of the Government, the good sense of the people—in fact, they undermined all foundations.
>
> Foureau became disturbed, and threatened them with prison if they continued such discourses.
>
> The evidence of their superiority gave umbrage. As they upheld immoral points of view, they were surely immoral themselves; slanders were invented about them.
>
> Then a pitiable faculty developed in their spirit, that of perceiving stupidity and no longer tolerating it. (258)

Scorn for stupidity ends up being contaminated by its object: it becomes stupidity in turn. Do Bouvard and Pécuchet look down pitilessly upon their entourage? It will not be long before said entourage reciprocates. The physician is insupportably self-important (though he entertains few illusions about the scientific, or even systematic dimension of his craft), but he is not wrong in ridiculing our two sorcerer's apprentices' twaddle about magnetism. Even though the two of them irritate, even though they challenge the social and political order, they themselves cannot avoid fashions and prejudices, not even—could anything be more ridiculous?—the ambition to become members of parliament. All their ventures they undertake vicariously, consulting inaccurate textbooks, or seeking the advice of charlatans—whom they are quick to copy. Their credulity and their pretensions are no lesser, and no less laughable, than those of the very people they turn up their noses at. They explore nothing in depth; far from drawing lessons from their failures, ever-newer chimeras sway them. Except at the end, when they make up their minds to return to copying: the sole moment of wisdom and of authenticity they can claim as their own.

Curiously, that moment of authenticity redeems everything: their errors, their impenitent amateurism, their foolishness, and their ambition. In mysterious ways, which we have already noted and which we must examine more closely, we end up becoming attached to Bouvard and Pécuchet. If, in the end, they move us more than they irritate us, it is probably because our two copyists are themselves a caricatured copy of what we all are vaguely conscious of being, with all our pretensions and our foibles and our imbecilities, all so curiously representative of the illusory condition of modern man—of that man condemned to prove his originality, his value, his idiosyncrasy. They are two Don Quixotes who yearn to find in reality the singularity that Cervantes's hero seeks in fiction, and in dreams.

Paradoxically, the only way for them to affirm their singularity is to return to the copyist's desk. Only thus, through the sole competence they can claim as their own, can they unconsciously give shape to their desires, to their need to leave a mark. What is richest in meaning is their *return*, and not simply copying as an activity. When copying was nothing but a means for our two pen-pushers to earn their daily bread, their occupation had no symbolic dimension. And yet, the decision to *return* to writing at the end of their encyclopedic adventures is a gratuitous act that reflects no need to earn a living; its significance surely warrants closer attention. It is not enough to say that they return to their original occupation out of force of habit, or for want of anything better to do. We must attempt to understand their turnabout as a kind of relapse, for which they themselves do not seek the reason.

We might begin by examining exactly what they intend to copy. This material is available to us, a portion of it at least: it consists of a collection of quotes classified under a variety of headings ("The Collection of Foolish

Quotations," "The Marquise's Album," "The Dictionary of Accepted Ideas" and "The Catalogue of Chic Ideas") that Flaubert had intended to bring together in what would have been the "second volume," the "copy" of *Bouvard and Pécuchet*. At first glance, the two friends seem intent on conveying the inexhaustible treasure of human stupidity. The impression that arises on reading these definitions, these pearls of wisdom, is not entirely one-sided. Not everything is blatantly stupid: more than a few stupidities contain a grain of truth; inversely, any aphorism can end up looking stupid, if only because of the "definitive" tone its absolute formulation gives it. Many proverbs can be reversed with no loss to their evocative power. "Appearances can be deceiving," write the authors of the "Dictionary."[76] They could well have added that they need not be. A formula, any formula loses its effectiveness when it is applied again and again. But, as Baudelaire puts it, "It takes genius to create a commonplace."

But the *Dictionary of Accepted Ideas* can often be disappointing, because of its lack of humor, because the ideas in question are no longer "accepted," or because the entries only confirm such banal, widespread use that that they are no longer a source of mirth. Truth to tell, the ridiculous, the laughable— like the tragic, like the poetic—can only deliver their full charge when seen in their natural context. That context is often cruelly missing in the *Dictionary*. Is this an accident? Our two friends also seem to suffer from the same lack of context. Not that the social, historical, and political context of their existence is lacking; on the contrary, we know now that it is powerfully underlined. In fact, it is their very existence here—and not the world in which they come and go—that lacks consistency and credibility. Bouvard and Pécuchet's behavior may be "human," but their behavior as human beings seems improbable, so excessive do they ultimately appear in their banality. By distilling in themselves stupidity and intelligence, generosity and small-mindedness, vanity and modesty, knowledge and ignorance, lucidity and blindness, skepticism and credulity, they become little more than caricatures, stick figures, an interminable enumeration of all possible defects and qualities. Our two experimenters experience nothing in full, complete no task. Their every attempt comes to them from outside themselves. Events wash over them, leaving no trace but lassitude. From that lassitude they never emerge, except to take up some new foible. For they remain unaware, perpetually unaware, of what they love, of what keeps them alive. They can claim no life of their own, no life that is theirs and theirs alone.

---

76. Flaubert was assisted in the writing of the *Dictionary* by Edmond Laporte, who also contributed entries of his own devising.

But their "life experience" and their "authenticity" (terms that could be added quite nicely to the famous *Dictionary*) hark back to the most hackneyed commonplaces. In their lack of authenticity, Bouvard and Pécuchet are perhaps "truer," more pathetically "authentic" than their contemporaries. Perhaps, unbeknownst to themselves of course, they express an indigestible truth: not only are we all, to a greater or lesser extent, nothing but imitators, copiers; life itself may well be little more than *mimesis*, airs and graces. Whatever we might attempt to *say* about life may well be mired in banality. That would transform the *Dictionary* into a demonstration of the radical deficiency of all vocabulary, would transform vocabulary itself into a grimace that masks the unutterable, that masks all literature; would transform it into a lie. Like silence, the authenticity of life experience cannot survive its invocation.

In the *Dictionary of Accepted Ideas*, under the entry PHILOSOPHY, we read simply: "always snicker at it" (71)—a masterwork of concision that embraces both philosophy and its denigrators. Flaubert snickers at the snickerers. But the snickering hardly begins and ends there. The pages devoted to our two wood-lice's[77] philosophical flights of fancy (principally at the end of Chapter 8) are no less ferocious than those that, a few pages previously, describe their spiritualist experiments. In a flight of derision the narrator connects those questionable practices to their impact upon how matter and spirit are conceived, upon the materiality or immateriality of the soul. Bouvard endorses the former, Pécuchet the latter. But the controversy leads them to a remarkable encounter: they read Spinoza's *Ethics*, or, more precisely, "the places marked with a pencil" (243) in the copy loaned to them—another sign that they are only able to follow a trail that has already been marked out. No matter; what they grasp (and what the narrator succeeds, in a veritable *tour de force*, in presenting in a single page) is neither ridiculous nor simplistic, nor does it betray Spinoza. What they read makes their heads swim:

> All this was like being in a balloon at night, in glacial coldness, carried on an endless voyage towards a bottomless abyss, and with nothing near but the unseizable, the motionless, the eternal. It was too much. They gave it up.
> And wanting something less tough, they bought the Course of Philosophy for the use of schools, by M. Guesnier. (244)

---

77. One of Flaubert's first titles for what was to become *Bouvard and Pécuchet* was *The Story of Two Wood-lice*.

Here we have one of the rare occasions when the two friends come to grips directly with the text of a great creative spirit, even though they read only a few passages. The confrontation is an arduous one; there is nothing banal about the moment of truth it leads to: "it was too much." Spinoza threatens to carry them further than they are prepared to venture. This time, their decision comes neither from failure, nor from some intellectual intricacy, for they understand the better part of what they read. They comprehend enough of it, in fact, to grasp that at their feet lies an abyss of sorts, the gaping void of the inexpressible where all thought is in danger of losing its bearings. Spinoza makes them shudder; he eludes all irony, all the contradictory systems by which other philosophers confuse or simply leave them behind. They turn their backs on philosophies, on systems, but not on philosophical inquiry.

It, in fact, remains fully intact and surges violently to the surface just when, weary of dogmas and yearning to rediscover the simple joys of life, they go out for a stroll, and encounter the carcass of a dog:

> The four legs were dried up. The grinning jaw revealed ivory fangs beneath blue chops; instead of the belly there was an earth-colored mass that seemed to quiver so thickly did it pullulate with vermin. It stirred, beaten by the sun, under the buzzing of flies, in that intolerable stench—a fierce, and as it were, devouring odor.
>
> But Bouvard wrinkled his brow and tears damped his eyes.
>
> Pécuchet said stoically: "One day we shall be like that."
>
> The thought of death had taken possession of them. They talked of it as they went back.
>
> After all, it does not exist. We depart in the dew, in the breeze, in the stars. We become part of the sap of the trees, the sparkle of jewels, the plumage of birds. We give back to Nature what she lent us, and the void before us holds nothing more awful than the void behind us.
>
> They tried to imagine death in the form of a very dark night, a bottomless pit, a never-ending swoon—anything at all was better than this monotonous, absurd and hopeless existence.
>
> They recited their unsatisfied desires. Bouvard had always wanted horses, carriages, the best Burgundies, and beautiful yielding women in a splendid mansion. Pécuchet's ambition was philosophical knowledge. With that, the most vast of problems, that which contains all others, would be resolved in a twinkling. When would he get so far?
>
> "As well finish at once."

"As you like," said Bouvard.

And they examined the question of suicide.

"Where is the evil in rejecting a burden that crushes you, in performing an act that harms nobody? If it offended God, should we have the power to accomplish it? It is not a cowardice, in spite of what is said; rather a noble insolence, to flout, even to one's own hurt, what men most prize." (260–261)

They ponder the available methods, choose death by hanging, install two nooses and two chairs in the attic, and allow some time to pass—the time needed to convince themselves to carry out their plan. On Christmas Eve, with nothing to eat in the house, Bouvard downs an entire carafe of *eau de vie*; Pécuchet drinks tea. An argument erupts over a peccadillo—a broken cup—and tempers flare. Pécuchet, at wit's end, affirms that he prefers death, leaves his companion and climbs up to the attic. Bouvard follows; he finds him there, standing on his chair, rope in hand.

Bouvard wanted to follow suit.

"Wait for me!"

And he was climbing on the other chair, when suddenly, stopping:

"But ... we've not made our wills."

"My word! That's true."

Sobs swelled in their breasts. They went to the little window to breathe.

The air was cold and many stars were shining in a sky as black as ink.

The whiteness of the snow that covered the earth was lost in the mist on the horizon.

They perceived, close to the ground, little lights which, approaching and growing larger, were all moving towards the church.

Curiosity impelled them there.

It was the midnight Mass. (262–263)

The two friends bungle even their death, in a scene that is by turns grotesque, then touching, in one of those rapid-fire modulations of mood so typical of the narrator's brusque, pared-down approach. The redemptive effect of the religious celebration brings to mind the instant, in the first *Faust*, where, just as he is about to swallow poison, the eponymous hero changes his mind, soothed by the Easter canticles that remind him of his childhood.

Except that in the case of *Bouvard and Pécuchet*, the same effect follows failure, like balm on a pitiable renunciation. The pretext—that of a last will and testament—is particularly pathetic; they have no heirs and nothing to will. Nothing to hand down to future generations.

That void, the absence of any possible testament, is precisely what keeps them from dying, as though they could not kill themselves, as though they were unworthy of death unless they could leave something behind. But what can one leave behind when one believes in nothing, and when religion itself, which in a moment of communion could make them feel "as though a dawn were rising in their souls" (264), stands revealed in its turn as shallow, false, mercantile, deceptive ...

If the world, and things, can only be copied; if life, and death itself, can only be imitated, as Bouvard's mimetic impulse illustrates—he mimics the action of his friend ... only to notice the absence of a notarized authorization that would give them license to see things through to the end!—; if it is impossible to create and to invent, then nothing can be handed down to posterity. It is no coincidence that the two men have no heirs, no coincidence that their final attempt, before they return to copying, to educate two young orphans, also ends badly. Their final failure is the most serious in its signifi- cance; it reveals, after all the failures that have gone before, that Bouvard and Pécuchet are themselves orphans, life-cripples who have never once in their entire existence achieved a thing. Unable to depart from the register of repetition, the best they can do is consult guidebooks, instruction manuals, and, when all else has been attempted, take up the pen to rewrite the already- written. The sterility of repetition condemns their dictionary of foolish quotations to insignificance. The critical spirit has been frittered away, it has no further use. Everything becomes futility; nothing can transform what has been borrowed from others. Not that Bouvard and Pécuchet are fools; they often show themselves to be perspicacious, and have a keen nose for the stupidity that is everywhere around them, but they lack that vital inner energy, that indescribable quality nothing from outside can replace, that alone makes it possible to marvel, to tell a tale, to transmit. They are barrels riddled with holes, utterly unable to hold any of what is poured into them. Of the world they demand everything; of themselves, nothing. If they have come full circle, it is because their odyssey has not changed them.

If we are to posit that Bouvard and Pécuchet, above and beyond their particular quirks, personify the individual of our Western civilization—that orphan who believes he is constantly innovating yet merely repeats himself, Flaubert's novel shines a cruel light on the far greater infirmity of modern times. Does this civilization of ours have anything to transmit? Everything would seem to indicate that it does, for today, as in Flaubert's day, things are changing at a dizzying rate; no other civilization has innovated, transformed, overturned as has ours. But it may well be that these incessant revolutions, as Marx noted apropos of the bourgeoisie (whose mission, he writes, is to revolutionize modes of production without respite); it may well be that all these changes may ultimately be the deceptive tawdriness of one and the same reproduction—to employ the Marxian vocabulary. This reproduction may well "expand," may well lead to an ever-increasing accumulation; it may well also be, above all, a repetition of the same thing, the circular movement of an unceasingly amplified exploitation and devastation.

But this incessant movement is possible only in the presence of its corollary: a necessary and undeniable inventiveness. That is precisely what Bouvard and Pécuchet so manifestly lack. From that perspective, there is nothing modern at all about the two friends; in the final analysis, they are not even critical of modernity. They are merely users, consumers of modern inventiveness. In this regard, yet again, they are disagreeably like most of us, who remain passive in the face of all that changes us, who are more often objects than subjects of a change imposed from outside ourselves. That passivity varies from one individual to another, depending on his or her character, social position, education, trade or profession. But what we call "individualism" is most frequently mindless mimicry, produced by a near-automatic transmission whose mechanism we cannot grasp. In our day, the inheritance of one generation is handed down to another via the unconscious. In fact, the essence of what is transmitted ends up eluding the critical spirit we take such pride in cultivating.

There is nothing terribly new here; such it has always been: culture, in the strong sense of the term, is that which is transmitted unconsciously, that of which we are unaware, so much is it a part of ourselves. The celebrated definition of culture as "what remains when all else has been forgotten," expresses something profound. The difference between the modern-day transmission of culture and that of the traditions of the past is that the unconscious portion of whatever is being transmitted increases as its ritualized, symbolized portion decreases. Bouvard and Pécuchet are orphans; beyond their life as copyists they have no points of reference. Of the former, we know that he does not have a legitimate father; of the latter, that he never knew his mother, and that his father was a small merchant. Nothing else. No childhood from which, like Faust, they could draw sustenance. From the outset, under the burning sun of Boulevard Bourdon, they encounter one another in the desert of their lives. For all their best efforts, they will never be able to make that desert bloom.

They are sterile, and they know it. But even that knowledge remains without effect; it cannot help them to live. It is a doleful, disenchanted knowledge that cannot be transmitted to anyone; a knowledge that makes all literature futile, insipid. *Bouvard and Pécuchet* is, in itself, a non-novel: written down, in a deliberately dry style, but not without power—and with flashes of beauty; a novel of the absence of the novelistic, of the impossibility of writing anything new, of telling something that is worth being told. Insofar as it is a *copy*, it is, at the same time, a reflection of a world about which everyone must ask: is this the world we wish to live in?

12

THE BROTHERS KARAMAZOV:
AN ODOR OF SANCTITY

THREE BROTHERS, PERHAPS FOUR, born of the same father, Fyodor Pavlovich Karamazov. Three legitimate sons of two different wives, both deceased: Dmitri Fyodorovich (or Mitya) of the first, and of the second, Ivan Fyodorovich and Alexey Fyodorovich (or Alyosha), respectively twenty-seven, twenty-three and nineteen at the beginning of the events related in the book. To them add a likely bastard, a valet in the service of his presumed father, who has named him Smerdyakov. The two other elements of his name, Pavel Fyodorovich, are, for all intents and purposes, never spoken. He is known only as Smerdyakov. The name, meaning "stench" in Russian is an attribute of his mother, the flea-ridden, half-wild idiot girl called Stinking Lizaveta, who Fyodor has never entirely denied impregnating, and who has come to give birth in the garden of her putative progenitor, where she dies immediately thereafter. All of which leaves us with a constellation of five males, a "primitive (and womanless) horde," with the sole exception of Maria Ignatievna, wife of the watchman of the paternal home, Grigory Vassilyevich Koutouzov. And with the exception of the second-hand girls that pass through Fyodor Pavlovich's hands.

The Brothers Karamazov, Dostoevky's last great novel (1880) tells a tale of parricide. The actual murder of a parent unworthy of the name of father. But also, at another level, and at the same time, the murder of God. "We only need to destroy the idea of God in man, that's how we have to set to work" (738)[78] whispers the Devil, who comes to haunt Ivan in his nightmare. Meanwhile, the little she-devil Liza, a destructive young woman smitten with Alyosha, insists on the collective nature of the crime. Speaking of the trial of

78. Fyodor Dostoevsky, *The Brothers Karamazov*, trans. Constance Garnett (New York: The Modern Library, 1996).

the alleged murderer, she observes: "every one loves crime.... They all declare that they hate evil, but secretly they all love it" (665). Alyosha, speaking with the honesty that Liza so appreciates in him, is obliged to recognize that there is "some truth" in her verdict: "You wouldn't believe how I respect you, Alyosha, for never telling lies" (665).

The name "Karamazov" falls halfway between heaven and earth, between the animal sensuality of the father, and divine spirituality. The author discreetly slips us the keys as we go: it is made up of a Turkish word, *kara*, black (in Russian, *chorny*), and the suffix *mazov*, from *maz*, unction. The Karamazov family is anointed in black, governed by the ambiguity of a dark unction; damned and simultaneously blessed. On the side of the damned stands Fyodor, the father, his first two sons (at least a portion of each of them, to which we will return) and, a slave among the damned, the stinking Smerdyakov. On the side of the blessed stands Alyosha, the tragic hero.

Yet he is a hero with whom the narrator is ill at ease:

> In beginning the life story of my hero, Alexey Fyodorovich Karamazov, I find myself in somewhat of a quandary. Namely, though I call Alexey Fyodorovich my hero, I myself know that he is by no means a great man, and hence I foresee such unavoidable questions as these: "What is so remarkable about your Alexey Fyodorovich, that you have chosen him as your hero? What has he accomplished? What is he known for, and by whom?..." I say this because unhappily I anticipate it. For me he is remarkable, but I doubt strongly whether I shall succeed in proving this to the reader. The fact is, if you please, that he is a protagonist, but a protagonist vague and undefined. (xv)

Alexey Fyodorovich's heroism cannot be immediately "read," his character lacks the maturity necessary to stand forth in its full "brightness." Yet his entire being seems to radiate light: excessively; perhaps preternaturally. There is something abnormal, even irritating perhaps, in so much intelligence, so much moderation in a lad who has just emerged from adolescence. There lies its disturbing strangeness: everything about this Alyosha of ours appears calculated to irritate—excessive faith and compassion, suspicious sweetness and purity, and wisdom that seems too precocious by half. And yet our too-perfect young man is neither mawkish, nor pretentious, nor laughable—for the simple reason that he is blissfully unaware: he has no idea of his qualities; unlike his brother Ivan, there is nothing cerebral, nothing self-regarding about Alyosha's intelligence. Alyosha draws his charm, his strength, and his beauty from the perfectly amoral nature of his innocence. His amorality is like his brothers', but it is the amorality of another world, Alyosha inhabits a universe all his own; he has no need to pass judgments on anything or anyone.

Furthermore, among the four sons of Fyodor Pavlovich, only Alexey does not wish for his father's death. Though abandoned in childhood, he is unscarred by the experience. As the narrator rather confusedly explains in his introductory note, the novel he lays before the reader deals with only half the hero's life, the essential part, that in which we see him in action. Behind it lies hidden a "first tale," which "takes place thirteen years ago." In fact, "it is hardly even a novel, but only a period in my hero's early youth." Two novels then, for a single life, a problem that requires something to be said of the first one: "I cannot do without this first tale, because much in the second tale would be unintelligible without it" (xvi). But the first novel is reduced to the most meager share, covering only some fifty pages of a work numbering 880. Of our hero's early childhood, orphaned at age four, all that remains, alongside his mother's face and caresses, is a strange and unforgettable memory:

> Such memories may persist, as everyone knows, from an even earlier age, even from two years old, but scarcely standing out through a whole life-time like spots of light out of darkness, like a corner torn out of a huge picture, which has all faded and disappeared except that fragment. That is how it was with him. He remembered one still summer evening, an open window, the slanting rays of the setting sun (that he recalled most vividly of all); in a corner of the room[79] the holy image, before it a lighted lamp, and on her knees before the image his mother, sobbing hysterically with cries and moans, snatching him up in both arms, squeezing him close till it hurt, and praying for him to the Mother of God, holding him out in both arms to the image as though to put him under the Mother's protection ... and suddenly a nurse runs in and snatches him from her in terror. That was the picture! And Alyosha remembered his mother's face at that minute. He used to say that it was frenzied but beautiful as he remembered. But he rarely cared to speak of this memory to any one. (17)

With regard to Alyosha, the first of the two novels can be reduced to the slanting rays of the sun that bathe in their light a scene of terrifying, brutally

---

79. We encounter this same mutilated geography of babyhood memory in Proust, where the narrator can recall (before chance intercedes to develop the rest of the passage) only that narrow section of the house at Combray that is connected to the painful memory of the absence of a mother's kiss.

interrupted beauty, of which he remembers only the splendor. In his memory the beauty of his mother's trance-filled face overcomes the hysteria and the violence that were to tear her from him. One wonders, of course, with what unfathomable workings trauma has strengthened, in the child, the absolute need for the beauty that rescues him from terror. For all that, his salvation, to rephrase Hölderlin, has indeed sprung from the very locus of danger. In a dark and magnificent flash, this primitive novel points to the existence, in the hero, of an inner emptiness about which we shall never know a thing. All we know is that, at any moment, it can engulf him and that, against such a threat, the hero carries a powerful talisman: his mother's face. Poison and antidote in one, it is the *pharmakon* of his love, a drug that to his good fortune Alyosha has learned naturally to take in judicious doses, the better to protect himself from the father whom he need not detest.

Of all the sons, both legitimate and natural, Alexey alone has not been destroyed, nor gravely stricken (not yet, at any rate) by the family poison, by the karamazovian blackness. The calamity of the father weighs heavily on the other three. Dmitri, the eldest, shares his father's unbridled sensuality, his obsession with the money necessary to satisfy it. He is the only son whose mother possessed a personal fortune of her own, an inheritance he believes is his by right, just as he believes his father has stolen most of it. Worse, the father has used the money he owes to impress Grushenka (Agrafena Alexandrovna), the woman whom Mitya dreams of making his mistress, and perhaps even his wife. Of the three, his interests are most clearly opposed to the father's. Father and son covet the same prey. The thirst for gold and sex that sets them against each other fosters in the son a hatred whose violence is exacerbated by the father who reminds him of his own moral decay. For, unlike his progenitor, Dmitri is prone to bouts of self-importance; the noble impulse has not entirely been extinguished in him. He knows that he is scum, and is proud of the fact. But he also knows that the old man is even worse. Fyodor is villainy, concupiscence, and baseness in human form. In his moments of self-loathing, Dmitri Fyodorovich begrudges his father for being their likeness, and rages against his utter lack of dignity. Of the three sons trapped in the father's evil skein, Mitya is the one who, for all intents and purposes, has the best reasons to wish his death. He makes no effort to conceal it. Raising the possibility that his father will attempt to lure Grushenka to his house, he tells Alyosha:

> "How can you say you'll kill our father?"
> "I don't know, I don't know ... Perhaps I shall not kill him, perhaps I shall. I'm afraid he'll suddenly be so loathsome to me at

that moment. I hate his double chin, his nose, his eyes, his shameless grin. I feel a personal repulsion. That's what I'm afraid of, that's what may be too much for me." (445–446)

Ivan appears protected from such temptations. Having recently returned, like his brothers, to his birthplace, he is the only one of the three legitimate sons to reside in his father's house, where the two of them, to the narrator's astonishment, get along "on the best possible terms" (15). But his education has distanced him radically from the old man. Ivan is the educated one, the well-read scholar, and the family philosopher: the most Westernized of the Karamazovs. Though his knowledge goes hand in hand with a disenchanted view of the world that borders on his father's cynical pragmatism, he does not share his father's unbridled lecherousness. But since, as he likes to repeat, "everything is permitted," he has no justification for condemning Fyodor Pavlovich's behavior. Still, at this point, we know only superficially about Ivan: he has a brilliant mind, but is a man of few words—a closed book, unforthcoming.

As for Smerdyakov, we already know that he is a kind of sub-being, something scraped from the bottom of the garbage can, prone to violent epileptic fits, lurking in the darkness of general opprobrium; his sole usefulness is his ability to cook, and to serve his putative progenitor scrupulously. Toward his master he demonstrates a combination of servility, honesty, and simple-mindedness that, as we will later learn, is a matter of cold calculation. In the first place, that servile humility seems to coincide with his most immediate interests: the master (his father) needs him, and were he to disappear, his situation would only worsen. With no claim on the succession, he has no interest in seeing the old man dead.

The first two parts of the novel put all the circumstances of the murder in place. That in turn involves the closed circle of the Karamazov family (including Smerdyakov). But the core family is inscribed in the broader context of the small town where the tragedy takes place. The town is not simply the location where the action occurs; it emerges as its necessary condition, as its matrix. Each character, no matter how minor, to a greater or lesser degree contributes to the assassination that, as Liza notes, suits everyone. In this tiny world, there is no rejoicing at the death of Fyodor Pavlovich—nor does anyone express deep regret. But because he dies at his son's hand, because of the act of parricide—at last!—something has happened where normally nothing does. The murder and trial attract the attention of all Russia; it is written about in the Moscow and St. Petersburg papers. The arrival of the celebrated defense lawyer Fetyukovich promises a courtroom debate from which the local prosecutor intends to derive maximum advantage in the hope of breaking out of the provincial obscurity where he has long been confined by the injustice of the authorities. In a tasty detail, the town's sudden celebrity forces the narrator, in spite of himself, to step out of the anonymity he had successfully maintained up until now, by quoting the title of an article published in the newspaper *Gossip*: "The Karamazov Case at Skotoprigonyevsk. That, alas! was the name of our little town. I had hitherto kept it concealed" (655). The name means something like "wild animal reserve," and brings to mind a substance that draws flies,[80] another element of the stink which we will have occasion to return to.

On the roster of external factors, outside the family core, appear two women rivals: Grushenka, the bone of contention, who cares not a whit for either father or son, and Katerina Ivanovna. Dmitri, in the small town where he was serving as an officer, out of frustration at being ignored by her, had once attempted to humiliate this proud young woman by forcing her to beg to save her father. But at the sight of the supplicant's nobility and beauty, Mitya had abandoned his plan and gave her the money, asking for nothing in return. Struck by the unexpected gravity of their encounter, Dmitri and Katerina are soon engaged. But the engagement has more to do with the challenge one represents to the other than with genuine romantic attraction. Each would have his or her pride prevail: Katerina wants to save her savior, to elevate the debauchee to the level of the gesture that she has made. Dmitri does not want to owe her anything, to prove that he has no need of her and her devotion, the better to surpass her in nobility.

All for naught: the encounter with Grushenka throws him into the jaws of Eros. Grushenka is a wild beast whose contemptuous bite will not let him rest. The beast will, in the end, come to love her tamer: *after* the murder. As though the final act had to take place before she could accept Mitya—though her change of heart may also be related to her disappointment with the Polish seducer whose return she has been awaiting for five years. She encounters him on the night of the murder: his behavior is nasty; he has squandered his fortune, gone to fat. Whether or not Mitya has committed the murder, it has made him a greater man; innocent or guilty, she will love him all the same. Not only that, the guilty party, she insists, is she: she, and she alone is responsible for all that has happened, for having encouraged the rivalry between father and son. Come what may, she will stand side by side with the man

---

80. *Skotoprigonyevsk* derives from *skot*, cattle, beasts, and *prigon*, the place to which they are brought or herded. It is also difficult not to detect the Greek root *skato*, genitive of *skor*, excrement.

accused of having killed his father for her sake, the man whose greatness of soul she has discovered.

Katerina, as a matter of principle, operates in quite the opposite way. If Grushenka embodies perdition, Katerina is the pathway to salvation. She is determined to save her fiancée, even if that means saving him from himself. Knowing him to be short of funds, she asks him to send to Moscow the sum of 3,000 rubles that she has secretly handed over to him. There is no hurry, she assures him: such is her discreet way of advancing, perhaps even giving him, the money. What she asks of him is but pretext for what she wishes to do for him. Mitya hastens to squander the money in one wild night with Grushenka—who, by a way of reward, allows him to kiss her foot. The gift that was to have rescued him contributes to his downfall. Mortally shamed by this flagrant misuse—theft in his eyes but, as we will only learn later, only half consumed—Dmitri refuses to show himself before Katerina. His indignity has irremediably separated him from the only person with both the means and the desire—however ambiguous—to help him.

Worse yet, obsession with the debt drives him to his wit's end. He is prepared to stop at nothing to lay hands on the 3,000 rubles he so desperately needs to repay Katerina and restore his honor. If he cannot repay it, he can reconquer neither his self-esteem, nor the new life he dreams of for Grushenka. Everything, when the time comes, will point to him as the culprit. From Smerdyakov he has learned that his father is keeping 3,000 rubles in an envelope to impress that selfsame Grushenka. Two days before the crime, in a moment of drunkenness, he sends Katerina a note warning her that if the situation becomes desperate, he might well even kill his father to get his hands on the money. In her first deposition, Katerina, who is concerned to protect Mitya, conceals its existence. But after Ivan's gibbering testimony, with his sudden confession of responsibility for the murder (we shall soon see why), she makes up her mind, out of love for Ivan, to recant her testimony and to produce the incriminating letter in court. At the same time she reveals that the 3,000 rubles she had entrusted to Mitya were, in her eyes, a test; or worse, a trap:

> "How, how could he have failed to understand that I was practically telling him to his face, 'You want money to be false with me with your creature, so here's the money for you. I give it to you myself. Take it, if you have so little honor as to take it!' I wanted to prove what he was, and what happened? He took it, he took it and squandered it with that creature in one night ... But he knew, he knew that I knew all about it....

> "That's true, Katya," Mitya roared suddenly. "I looked into your eyes and I knew that you were dishonoring me, and yet I took your money. Despise me as a scoundrel, despise me all of you! I've deserved it!" (784–785)

Instead of the agent of salvation that she seems at first, Katerina ultimately stands revealed, by her own admission, as a far more devastating instrument of perdition than even her rival. The manner in which she acknowledges having put Mitya to the test has all the appearances of an act of implacable vengeance. She exploits his weaknesses, of which she is well aware, to bring low a man who had once attempted to humiliate her, knowing all the while that this same man—has he not demonstrated it by turning back from the humiliation he had attempted to inflict upon her?—is, for all his debauchery, still capable of true nobility of soul.

The two feminine rivals exacerbate Mitya's despair, and lend credence to the appearance of guilt, but they have no bearing on a murder he did not commit. Or, more precisely, they are no more responsible than anyone else. Once the eventuality of crime is in the air, no matter what hand strikes the final blow, each individual's responsibility is proportional to his or her capacity to stop it. Collective responsibility looms even more forcefully in the course of an attempted conciliation that ends in confrontation and confusion. Not without malice, Fyodor Pavlovich has invited his eldest son to discuss their differences with elder Zossima, Alyosha's mentor, pride of the monastery where the youngest son resides in pursuit of his novitiate.

> What was such an elder? An elderly one who took your soul, your will, into his soul and his will. When you choose an elder, you renounce your own will and yield it to him in complete submission, complete self-abnegation. This novitiate, this terrible school of abnegation, is undertaken voluntarily, in the hope of self-conquest, of self-mastery, in order, after a life of obedience, to attain perfect freedom, that is, from self; to escape the lot of those who have lived their whole life without finding their true selves in themselves. (*Elders*, 27)

Alyosha excepted, the members of the Karamazov family who gather in the cell of the elder Zossima (Fyodor, Ivan, and Dmitri) are there as a result of a misunderstanding; nothing could be further from any intention of self-mastery. The narrator describes it as "An Unfortunate Gathering"—the title of the second book, which is entirely devoted to that strange meeting.

Unfortunate it is, and doubly so. First of all, in the literal sense. The idea had been to pluck father and son from the everyday surroundings of their quarrel and to bring them together on ground metaphorically situated at the halfway point between earth and heaven. Secondly, in the figurative sense: the meeting quickly veers off into scandal, not only because the participants, abandoning all measure, all sense of the sanctity of their surroundings, trade insults, but also, and even principally (chronologically) because God himself is called into question.

While awaiting Dmitri's late arrival (due, he insists, to the poor instructions he'd received from Smerdyakov, thus indirectly implicating the valet), Ivan must defend, before the assembled monks, his ultramontane theses on the primacy of the Church in the administration of justice. Those who know him are not fooled. First among them is a certain Pyotor Alexandrovich Miüsov, Dmitri's mother's cousin (whose short-lived tutor he had once been), who through a kind of unhealthy curiosity has joined the Karamazovs in their monastic *excursus*. Ivan always enjoyed cultivating paradoxes, Miüsov reminds them, making it known to whoever cares to listen that for unbelievers like him, egoism is all, and crime should be permitted; that it is even necessary "as the inevitable, the most rational, even honorable outcome of his position." (*Why Is Such a Man Alive?*, 75) Dmitri, who has arrived as the debate has already begun, is reminded of the necessity of crime to ensure that he has heard correctly—and for him to draw his own conclusions: "I'll remember it." The elder, however, refuses to be caught up in Ivan's rhetoric:

> Meanwhile, in your despair, you too divert yourself with magazine articles and discussions in society, though you don't believe your own arguments, and with an aching heart mock them inwardly ... That question you have not answered, and it is your great grief, for it clamours for an answer. (75)

Father Zossima is content to listen, intervening only to reveal. He replies to the forced antics of old Karamazov by enjoining him to stop feeling such shame for himself, for "that is the source of everything." As the invective and the accusations fly back and forth between father and son, the elder's interventions become less and less frequent, as though he were "waiting for something," "as though trying to make out something which was not perfectly clear to him" (77). Though he had come to pardon, Mitya, caught up in the Fyodor's loathsome farce, rediscovers the repugnance and the scorn that his father's incurable baseness inspires in him: "'Why is such a man alive?' Dmitri, beside himself with rage, growled in a hollow voice.... 'Listen, listen monks, to the parricide!' cried Fyodor Pavlovich" (77). It is as if the whole meeting had been dreamed up by the father with the sole purpose of provoking the son, of making his criminal intentions clear for all to see.

It is at that instant, as the unspeakable reaches its climax, that the totally unexpected occurs. Without a word, the elder rises and moves toward Mitya:

> Father Zossima moved towards Dmitri and reaching him sank on his knees before him. Alyosha thought that he had fallen from weakness, but this was not so. The elder distinctly and deliberately bowed down at Dmitri's feet till his forehead touched the floor. Alyosha was so astounded that he failed to assist him when he got up again. There was a faint smile on his lips.
>
> "Good bye! Forgive me, all of you," he said, bowing on all sides to his guests.
>
> Dmitri stood for a few moments in amazement. Bowing down to him, what did it mean? Suddenly he cried aloud, "Oh God," hid his face in his hands and rushed out of the room. (78)

Only the following day would Alyosha learn the significance of the elder's bow, whose reason he dares not immediately ask: the monk has bowed down "to the great suffering in store for Dmitri," adding, "I seemed to see something terrible yesterday ... as though his whole feature was expressed in his eyes." Finally: "A look came into his eyes—so that I was instantly horror-stricken at what that man is preparing for himself" (*Father Zossima and His Visitors*, 317). The incident at the monastery seems indeed to have saddled Dmitri with a curse; Father Zossima's bowing down before him has now lent him a Christ-like aura. It appears that the eldest of the Karamazov brothers has been designated as the expiatory victim of the coming evil. Sensing the nearness of death, the elder enjoins Alyosha to immerse himself in the sorrow of the world:

> "When it is God's will to call me, leave the monastery. Go away for good. ... This is not your place for the time. I bless you for great service in the world. Yours will be a long pilgrimage. And you will have to take a wife, too. You will have to bear *all* before you come back. There will be much to do. But I don't doubt of you, and so I send you forth. Christ is with you. Do not abandon Him and He will not abandon you. You will see great sorrow, and in that sorrow you will be happy. This is my last message to you: in sorrow seek happiness." (*A Young Man Bent on a Career*, 81)

The sorrow Alyosha will be called upon to bear is the sorrow of the world. The sorrow before which the elder bows down is Mitya's individual sorrow. Zossima commands Alyosha to look after him above all others, as though the youngest brother's mission were to help the elder bear the cross that awaits him.

But the most acute of sorrows, as unexpected as it is unforeseeable, befalls Alyosha himself, above all others, with the death of his beloved master. That sorrow has nothing to do with the sadness of his departure; it emanates, instead, from the overwhelming presence of his corpse. The death of the elder is a major event that draws pilgrims and is accompanied by divine signs, even by miracles. But behold, as though it were the sole sign, Zossima's body begins to stink. With scandalous rapidity the odor of sanctity becomes the stench of rotting flesh.

His premature decomposition functions as a powerful scouring agent. Cruelly it strips faith and the love of Christ of their institutions and their traditions. God, constantly rejected, including within the Church, no longer responds to human aspirations. The stench of Zossima's corpse is less a condemnation of the elder himself, than of the importance that the monks and the people have attached to the institution (which, the narrator has earlier taken pains to explain, is the recent and controversial reappearance of an ancient, long-lost practice). But the stupor that has afflicted Alyosha will only be short-lived, as if the hero has instinctually understood this ignominious sign as an extension of the order that has returned him to the sorrows of the world. Emanating from the body of a near-saint, the malodorous humor that oozes from the death chamber through the entire monastery, and from the monastery to the town (whose name the narrator has not yet revealed), the selfsame stench, bloated by rumor, takes on a metaphysical dimension.

The world stinks. The town, the monastery, and the Karamazov family: all of them stink. The stench of the cadaver floats through the air, the symbolic emanation of the tragedy that has been played out in the dying man's presence. Ratkin, an ambitious novice who is Alyosha's cynical companion if not his unconscious double, takes advantage of the latter's inner upheaval to attempt to lead him, who is still a virgin, into the pleasures of the flesh. To his own astonishment, he has no trouble convincing him—having vainly attempted to turn his head once before—to accompany him to Grushenka's. Alyosha's capitulation bolsters his claims about the terrible destructiveness of love, of which the tribulations of the Karamazov clan provide such a pitiable spectacle. After all, he tells Alyosha:

"You're a Karamazov yourself; you're a thorough Karamazov—no doubt birth and selection have something to answer
for. You're a sensualist from your father, a crazy saint from your
mother. Why do you tremble? Is it true, then? Do you know,
Grushenka has been begging me to bring you along. 'I'll pull off
his cassock,' she says." (84)

At this point the elder is not yet dead; Alyosha refuses. Two days later,
sweeping aside all restraint, as though the putrefaction scandal had now
infected him, he allows himself to be led to the all-devouring Grushenka. But
she does not correspond to the image that surrounds her in the town. More
innocent than her reputation, she bends low before Alexey's innocence.
Touched by his caring, fraternal attitude toward his brother, she abandons
whatever intention she might have had to devour him. The meeting ends in
confusion for the would-be pimp and Alyosha returns, at peace, to the
monastery to stand vigil over the corpse of the elder who, in a dream, invites
him to attend the wedding at Canaan and drink the wine of joy. Three days
later, obeying the command of his deceased master, he will leave the
monastery.

Meanwhile catastrophe has struck, in the form of the meeting between
Alyosha and Grushenka. Here, once more, each seems oblivious to the
destruction they are rushing toward. Now reconciled with God's world,
which the anti-miracle had caused him for a moment to loath,[81] led to the
wine of joy by none less than the "sinful woman" herself, Alyosha forgets
Dmitri, introduced to the dream of faith by the very person who had expressly
recommended, before his death, that he look after his older brother.
Meanwhile Grushenka, who has concealed from him her comings and
goings, who had left (immediately after the meeting with Alyosha) for a
secret tryst at Mokroïe with the same wretched Pole who had seduced and
abandoned her five years before, now plunges Dmitri deep into despair, and
forces him, distraught and jealous, to stalk his father's house to see if she is
there. As if that were not enough, his extraordinary efforts to raise the sum he
needs exacerbate his unrest and anxiety and contribute powerfully to accredit
the thesis of a violent, premeditated crime.

The father has indeed been murdered, but in a way that remains obscure.
Torn by jealousy, Mitya calls at the old man's house to see if *she* is there.
From the garden, he can see only the old man, sad and alone. But to be
absolutely certain, in full knowledge of the code, he taps on the window and
then conceals himself. The old man opens the window, imagines that the

81. Alyosha briefly rebels, not against God, but against God's world.

signal has come from her whom he has been expecting. He calls her name aloud. She is not there. He should be relieved but as at every turn in the story, something else, something as predictable as it is unforeseeable, happens:

> Mitya looked at him from the side without stirring. The old man's profile that he loathed so, his pendant Adam's apple, his hooked nose, his lips that smiled in greedy expectations, were all brightly lighted up by the slanting lamplight falling on the left from the room. A horrible fury of hatred suddenly surged up in Mitya's heart. "There he was, his rival, the man who had tormented him, had ruined his life!" It was a rush of the sudden, furious, revengeful anger of which he had spoken, as though foreseeing it, to Alyosha, four days ago in the arbour, when in answer to Alyosha's question, "How can you say you'll kill our father?" "I don't know, I don't know...."
>
> The personal repulsion was growing unendurable. Mitya was beside himself, he suddenly pulled the brass pestle out of his pocket.
>
> "God was watching over me then," Mitya himself said afterwards. At that very moment, Grigory waked up on his bed of sickness. (*In the Dark*, 445–446)

That blank space, that space "in the dark" (the chapter title) along with the long suspension that interrupts the critical moment, raise doubts about the possibility of the murder. It is as though a psychological blank had, at that very moment, blinded Mitya; as though his arm had struck without him being aware of it—the selfsame divine providence that he will later plead is hardly more than an indicator, within him, of a necessary act of forgetfulness. The narrator does not categorically affirm that Grigory's unexpected arrival in the garden has stayed Mitya's murderous hand; we deduct it only from the latter's testimony. Grigory sees only the open window and a fleeing shadow that he manages to overtake and catch just as Dmitri, now recognized and denounced as a parricide, attempts to scale the fence, striking him a blow to the head with his pestle to force him to let go. Such is the terrible consciousness of the act beneath which Mitya, not knowing whether Grigory, to whom he turns for an instant to wipe up the blood, is dead or not, leaves the scene of the crime.

Much later, on the eve of the trial and only a few hours before killing himself, Smerdyakov will relate to Ivan how, by turning to his advantage circumstances that pointed to Dmitri, he himself killed Fyodor Pavlovich and absconded with the 3,000 rubles whose hiding place he alone knew, in order to begin life all over again in Moscow or abroad. In the light of this revelation, Ivan's role takes on a new dimension. Other conversations with Smerdyakov, both before and after the crime, have already given us substantial indications.

Of the three brothers, Ivan is the most complex, the most secretive, and the hardest to understand. His apparently untroubled cohabitation with his father conceals an underlying hostility: of the three, he is secretly the most anxious to get rid of him. He has little more affection for his brother Mitya, whom he judges severely: "one reptile should devour another" (*First Interview with Smerdyakov,* 697) he confides, in a rage, to Alyosha following a violent argument that ends with Dmitri beating his father. Enamored of Katerina (who is not called Ivanovna for nothing), Ivan finds himself, in relation to her, in a position of false rivalry with his brother, who would like nothing better than to pass her on to him. But that is precisely what he cannot bear. Ivan would like to conquer the beautiful Ivanovna on his own merits, and envies her ambiguous feelings toward her unworthy "fiancé." Katerina loves Ivan, but her love cannot release her from her compulsion to "save" Mitya by enslaving him to her, a domination she knows she can never wield over Ivan.

Ivan adopts a wait-and-see attitude toward his youngest brother. But, thanks to the crisis, reconciliation begins. His relationship with Katerina has now reached an impasse; Ivan decides to return to Moscow. As his departure is imminent, he lowers his guard: "It's always best to get to know people just before leaving them" (*The Brothers Make Friends*, 254–255). Ivan confesses to Alyosha that his hesitations have made it hard to approach him. Soon he realized that his brother was not begging, that he was standing "straight in his boots," that Alyosha loved him. Thanks to fraternal love, Ivan can display himself to advantage and to profess his faith, without boasting. To display his unbelief so ostentatiously is a provocation: "Of course, I am just such a little boy as you are" (259). Man, with his three-dimensional, Euclidian vision of the world, has no way of understanding God. Yet at the same time, as though by a miracle, the idea has occurred to him: "And what's strange, what would be marvelous, is not that God should really exist; the marvel is that such a idea, the idea of the necessity of God, could enter the head of such a savage, vicious beast as man. So holy is it, so touching, so wise and so great a credit it does to man" (260). Ivan confides to his brother what Alyosha will himself repeat when faced with the horrifying distress that follows the death of the elder: "It's not that I don't accept God, you must understand, it's the world created by Him I don't and cannot accept" (261).

Ivan does not believe in the order of things, and yet he wishes to live—and does live—"in spite of logic" (256); he has the Karamozovian thirst for life. That thirst, in the enthusiasm of the friendship that forms between him and Alyosha, is noble, lofty, disinterested. But it soon encounters the hard realities of the world—as Christ does the Grand Inquisitor: a tale he relates to his brother, a tale of his own invention that depicts Jesus as having returned to earth, been arrested by the Grand Inquisitor, and set free on condition that he undertake never again to return among men. Unlike his Inquisitor, however, Ivan is fascinated by Alyosha's Christ-like charisma. No sooner has he left the tavern where the two have spoken, no sooner has he approached the paternal home, than the charm ceases to function. A sense of anguish overcomes him, one he cannot define. "For so many years I've been silent with the whole world and not deigned to speak, and all of a sudden I reel off a rigmarole like that." (*For Awhile a Very Obscure One*, 295). Later, on that same evening, Ivan resents Alyosha for having confided in him: "His head ached, and there was a painful throbbing in his temples. He felt his hands were twitching convulsively." (*The Third and Last Interview with Smerdyakov*, 707). Meanwhile, Ivan has had an enigmatic, meaningful conversation with Smerdyakov that, as we will later realize, was setting the stage for the murder.

Like everyone else, but perhaps even more than everyone else, Ivan feels boundless contempt for the sub-human valet. Occasionally he casts before him, like a bone before a dog, scraps of his philosophy—particularly the idea, which remains etched on the servant's mind, that in the absence of God "all is permitted." If, in Ivan's eyes, Alyosha reflects the Christ-like part of his being, Smerdyakov represents all that is damned.

As he returns to his father's house to prepare for his departure, Ivan encounters Smerdyakov:

> On a bench in the gateway the valet Smerdyakov was sitting, enjoying the coolness of the evening, and at the first glance at him Ivan knew that the valet Smerdyakov was on his mind, and that it was this man that his soul loathed.... "Is it possible that a miserable, contemptible creature like that can worry me so much?" he wondered, with insufferable irritation. (*For Awhile a Very Obscure One*, 295)

An ambivalent dialogue begins. In a succession of allusions, the valet suggests to the master's son that his departure has left the door to the crime fully ajar. Smerdyakov even sketches out the scenarios that Ivan's absence will enable. In fact, he sees in it a signal, even an authorization countersigned by his interlocutor's decision to leave. The departure comes at an opportune (or very inopportune!) time; Smerdyakov feels an epileptic fit coming on, but he does not know when it will begin, or how long it will last. Ivan refuses to understand him but his suspicions are raised; he warns the lackey:

> Ivan took a long look at him.
>
> "You are talking nonsense, I see, and I don't quite understand you," he said softly, but with a sort of menace. "Do you mean to pretend to be ill to-morrow for three days, eh?"
>
> Smerdyakov, who was looking at the ground again, and playing with the toe of his right foot, set the foot down, moved the left one forward, and grinning, articulated:
>
> "If I were able to play such a trick, that is, pretend to have a fit—and it would not be difficult for a man accustomed to them—I should have a perfect right to use such a means to save myself from death. For even if Agrafena Alexandrovna comes to see his father while I am ill, his honor can't blame a sick man for not telling him. He'd be ashamed to."
>
> "Hang it all," Ivan cried, his face working with anger. "Why are you always in such a funk for your life? All my brother Dmitri's threats are only hasty words and mean nothing. He won't kill you; it's not you he'll kill!"
>
> "He'd kill me first of all, like a fly. But even more than that, I am afraid I shall be taken for an accomplice of his when he does something crazy to his father."
>
> "Why should you be taken for an accomplice?"
>
> "They'll think I'm an accomplice, because I let him know the signals of a great secret."
>
> "What secret? Whom did you tell? Confound you, speak more plainly." (298–299)

The lackey explains that father Fyodor, torn between the fear of opening his door at night to Dmitri and of keeping it closed to Grushenka, had agreed with Smerdyakov upon a set of signals known to him alone, which would alert him to the visitor's identity. The valet adds that he had also informed Mitya of the 3,000 rubles that were awaiting the young woman: even if she did not come, there would be motive enough for him to break into his father's house. As Ivan raises more objections, Smerdyakov disposes of them, one after the other. Smerdyakov encourages Ivan to leave—precisely for the criminal to be able to act with impunity, as Ivan soon concludes:

"If I go away, you see what will happen here." Ivan drew his breath with difficulty.

"Precisely so," said Smerdyakov, softly and reasonably, watching Ivan intently, however.

"What do you mean by 'precisely so'?" Ivan questioned him, with a menacing light in his eyes, restraining himself with difficulty.

"I spoke because I felt sorry for you. If I were in your place I should simply throw it all up ... rather than stay on in such a position," answered Smerdyakov, with the most candid air looking at Ivan's flashing eyes. They were both silent.

"You seem to be a perfect idiot, and what's more ... an awful scoundrel too." Ivan rose suddenly from the bench. (303)

A scoundrel he may be, but he is nobody's fool—far from it. In fact, he plays his pseudo-simplemindedness to the hilt, and Ivan knows it all too well. Just as he knows that by leaving he will cause the trap set by Smerdyakov to spring shut on his father and his brother. "One reptile should devour another," were his words. He, Ivan, is the scoundrel. The scoundrel's work is to let someone else do the dirty work: something worse than simply criminal; criminal and cowardly. Just as his train is entering the Moscow station, Ivan suddenly becomes aware of the impact of his departure: "I am a scoundrel," he whispered to himself (*It's Always Worth While Speaking to a Clever Man*, 511). Whether Dmitri or Smerdyakov kill the father, Mitya will be accused and Ivan, in full knowledge, will reap the benefits: two, rather than three, will divide the inheritance. Alyosha will also be a "beneficiary" but he is indifferent to money, has never wanted it, never known about it, has never considered what he might do with it.

The murder perpetrated, Alyosha will instinctively grasp that Mitya is innocent, that Smerdyakov is the executioner and that Ivan, judging by his behavior, is the instigator and the real guilty party. Even before Smerdyakov reminds him of their earlier conversation, and reveals in detail how he carried out his threat, Ivan rejects what he already knows too well, clinging helplessly to the idea that Dmitri is guilty. Not that this hypothesis absolves Ivan of all guilt, but even were it true, his complicity with Smerdyakov remains indirect. But if, on the other hand, the lackey has struck the deadly blow, then that piece of excrement has simply acted out his will. That is why Alyosha, "obeying some irresistible command," in a feverish attempt to relieve Ivan of the guilt he knows is tearing him apart, cries out: "You have accused yourself and have confessed to yourself that you are the murderer and no one else. But you didn't do it: you are mistaken: you are not the murderer. Do you hear? It was not you! God has sent me to tell you so" (*Not You, Not You!*, 686).

Alexey here speaks in the name of God. In the name of divine charity he absolves Ivan of a crime that his brother had truly wished to commit, or deliberately allowed to take place, but for which society cannot punish him. Ivan cannot be formally accused of instigation, or of complicity. He never instructed the lackey, "Kill," or "Organize the murder." He is only complicit, an instigator by omission, in absentia. And now his brother wishes to absolve him before the only tribunal to which his conscience must eventually answer. The act of absolution flows from brotherly love. But in the same perspective, nothing obliges the narrator to make Alyosha God's messenger. Surely it is Alyosha himself who claims such powers, the better to lend more weight to his words. But God, in this case, cannot be invoked for simple reasons of commodity, and certainly not by such a pure believer, by someone as profoundly, as authentically convinced as Alexey. No. In this tale of murder, God, as we know, is present from the very beginning, and the uttering of His name at the most crucial moment, when each man's ultimate responsibility is at stake, has a much broader, much deeper meaning than as a mere tool of persuasion—or, furthermore, to convince an eventual unbeliever. While everything points to shared responsibility, that of the victim himself, that of the sons whom he fathered then held up to ridicule, that of the wider community that surrounds them, we see Alyosha assigning it, in the name of God, to the lackey alone, upon the sole offspring who is *unworthy of being called son or brother.*

All unfolds as though Smerdyakov were the only person for whom the God of Alyosha, and Alyosha himself, holds no compassion. True enough, Alyosha does not openly display his contempt, shows neither hate nor disdain. But this normally compassionate soul makes not the slightest effort to help him, to understand him. Twice he finds himself in the lackey's company; neither time is there the slightest desire to make his acquaintance.

The first time, Smerdyakov is holding forth in the presence of Fyodor, Ivan, and Grigory. He puts forward, echoing Ivan in the presence of the elder, a paradoxical thesis on the abjuration of the Christian faith under threat of torture. Instead of raising the legitimate fear of such a threat, Smerdyakov—too clever by half—argues that the renegade has not renounced his faith at all, since God had already willed (or allowed) him to do so even before he opens his mouth. As a result, said renegade, when he denies having been baptized, is no longer a Christian. Those present greet his twisted reasoning with derision and sarcasm. When the father asks Alyosha, who had arrived just a few moments earlier, whether he thinks Smerdyakov's argument—which has now been transposed to another ironic tirade on the faith that supposedly moves mountains, a faith that perhaps two or three obdurate hermits possess, and when Fyodor wonders aloud whether, in his speech and in his mannerisms, the lackey is not entirely representative of the Russian faith, Alyosha corrects him, saying in all seriousness: "No, Smerdyakov has not the Russian faith at all," admitting that only the idea is "purely Russian" (*The Controversy*, 145).

The second encounter is even more inadvertent, and thoroughly unpleasant. Alyosha has hidden in the arbor of the garden of the house where Dmitri is a lodger, in the hope of surprising him, but it is Smerdyakov who turns up, taking a seat on a bench that is invisible from the arbor, alongside the house-owner's daughter, whom he attempts unsuccessfully to seduce. The girl may well call him Pavel Fyodorovich, but Alyosha *believes* that he can recognize the valet by his voice, and not by his patronymic. Betrayed by a sneeze, Alyosha has no choice but to show himself: a brief, cold exchange between the two brothers follows, about where Dmitri may be and what he may be doing. Disdainfully, Smerdyakov declares that he is not his brother's "keeper" (*Smerdyakov with a Guitar*, 251). The hero keeps none of the other characters he encounters at such a distance. Alyosha crosses Smerdyakov's path twice, and both times, with perfect politeness, denies him. First, by excluding him from faith (an exclusion that, in comparison, he does not extend to Ivan), then by ignoring his true name. For Alyosha, as for almost everyone else, the lackey is merely Smerdyakov. He stinks. He is distasteful to God.

Yet it is God who causes (or who allows) the corpse of the elder to stink prematurely. One can only conclude that the stench, which has spread throughout the little town, foreshadows the murder and symbolically implicates the entire community. In the same register, the malodorous Smerdyakov represents something more than himself. His stench is not merely his own, but that of everyone; he is merely their representative. The silent one, whom Ivan dismisses as "excrement"—without drawing the slightest remonstrance from Alyosha—is described by the narrator as "the contemplative," in reference to a painting by Kramskoy:

> There is a remarkable picture by the painter Kramskoy, called "Contemplation." There is a forest in winter, and on a roadway through the forest, in absolute solitude, stands a peasant in a torn caftan and bark shoes. He stands, as it were, lost in thought. Yet he

is not thinking; he is "contemplating." If any one touched him he would start and look at one as though awakening and bewildered. It's true he would come to himself immediately; but if he were asked what he had been thinking about, he would remember nothing. Yet probably he had hidden within himself the impression which had dominated him during the period of contemplation. Those impressions are dear to him and no doubt he hoards them imperceptibly, and even unconsciously. How and why, of course, he does not know either. He may suddenly, after hoarding impressions for many years, abandon everything and go off to Jerusalem on a pilgrimage for his soul's salvation, or perhaps he will suddenly set fire to his native village, or perhaps do both. There are a good many "contemplatives" among the peasantry. Well, Smerdyakov was probably one of them, and he probably was greedily hoarding up his impressions, hardly knowing why. (*The Controversy*, 159)

The portrait depicts a certain type then prevalent among the Russians. The narrator, in linking the Contemplative and Smerdyakov, suggests that the latter is a representative of this type; representative, too, despite Alyosha's rather peremptory negation, of a certain Russian *faith*, one capable of both the best and the worst. Smerdyakov, who advocates the principle that "all is permitted," as preached by Ivan, is by no means a believer. The lackey's unstable, ill-defined nature reflects the ambivalence that pervades virtually all the characters of Dostoevsky's tale. They pervade Russia, the Church, and even God Himself. Smerdyakov, in the image of Kramskoy's contemplative, inhabits a chasm of solitude. This solitude may well be that of the Russian people, the little people of immense Russia, whom God has threatened to forsake.

We find ourselves here faced with an enigma we are unlikely to solve. By scouring from the gutter of received ideas clichés reduced to meaninglessness by overuse, we might suppose that the subject is the illustrious enigma of the "Russian soul." But let us leave the soul to its uncertain essence. Let us call it instead the enigma of Russian being. For the enigma of Russian being pervades, silently, imperceptibly, the entire *Brothers Karamazov*. It believes yet does not believe; it throws itself into love and into hatred with the same fervor; it adores and abhors everything with the same impulsiveness: God and the Devil, life and death, drunkenness, neighbors and friends, as well as enemies, money, sensuality and asceticism, reason and madness. Ready to believe everything, to reject everything. At times it can even loath love and love hatred. A mere nothing can prod it into justifying its madness, can throw reason into a panic, but can also bring reason to its madness. Such violent contrasts are visible throughout the novel, and in the unpredictability that governs its protagonists. Things seem, invariably, to happen *contrary* to their expectations, in spite of themselves, as though they were driven by forces that they can neither understand nor master.

Even Alyosha, the most moderate of the lot, the most reasonable, the most peaceful, seems impelled by such forces—the only difference being that, in his case, the force is called God, or love of God, or even love, period. But God is more than simply love. God remains incomprehensible, bewildering, diabolical almost. To speak bluntly, God himself at times smells bad. Or seems responsible, at minimum, for the stench of the world. The ambivalence is not determined by the narrator's (not to mention Dostoevsky's) unbelief. The narrator believes in God, but he also believes God is threatened by the decomposition of all that He has wrought, and, primarily, by those who profess to defend and protect it. His faith—identical in its fundamentals, minus the purity, with that of his hero Alyosha—displays not a shred of pity for the message of religion. Conservatism and modernism, Orthodoxy and the West, are thrown up against one another, and then dispatched to the same hell. The narrator is indisputably Christian, and a fervent believer; but he is also a Christian beset by worry and even anguish, who believes in the possibility that God may eventually vanish, drowned in the sewers of the world, exhausted by the evil of the world He has created.

Alyosha's presence suddenly takes on another dimension. The salvation of humanity (Russian, but not solely that) depends on one man alone. One man is enough, one man like him, for God not to die. And yet, this near-Christ-like figure, the very one that the Church would seek to expel (as the Grand Inquisitor does Jesus) is exposed to the same forces that threaten all men. Like all men, love of life awakens his sensitivity to the bite of sensual beauty. It is a bite at once magnificent and terrible; for it, man may raise himself up to the supreme nobility, or sink into the most sordid baseness; for it, he may be prepared to sacrifice his life or to kill, even go so far as to renounce his faith. Alyosha, far from being insensitive to the flesh—he is a Karamazov, after all—resists all the vileness and degradation of its attractions. *For the time being*. The narrator (or the tale) takes leave of him as his adult life begins. We have no way of knowing what he may become.

But we do know the limits of his compassion. Even in his pure eyes, cleansed of all prejudice, Smerdyakov is not wholly a part of humanity; he stands excluded from the Christian fraternity. The just man upon whom humanity must depend for its spiritual salvation is fallible. Through that fallibility and directly into the heart of that man, of that matchless man, drips the poison of exclusion: that of the other, up to and including the other within him whom he has never truly confronted. Let us remember the narrator's opening advice: his hero is "vague and undefined" (*From the Author*, xv). Alyosha has not yet realized the extent of the darkness that lurks within him, of the stranger that slumbers deep inside him. He, and with him the entire world, up to and including God Himself, is in great danger. God is not dead, but he is vulnerable; he may well decompose.

God's vulnerability, the very real danger that He may decompose, is a universal peril. Russia has no protection against its impact. But the evil wind that, in the narrator's eyes, has swept across Russia at this, the end of the nineteenth century, is blowing from the West. Western nihilism is nourishing Smerdyakov, though he does not know it. In the final analysis, nihilism's effect upon the Contemplative kills the father—whose indignity (or weakness, in the case of God) cannot justify parricide.

There is nothing mysterious about Dostoevsky's anti-Western sentiments. Much more intriguing is the fascination his novels, and particularly *The Brothers Karamazov*, hold for Western minds. It is as if, from the vastness of a Russia thus far spared the worst of modernization, but whose first, deleterious effects are beginning to be felt, now blows an easterly wind that wafts back to us the stink of our own decomposition. As if, from the Russia of the Karamazovs, the repressed upheavals of our subconscious return, in all their violence and disorderliness, to haunt us.

But the two-way flux of thoughts far surpasses any mere cultural antagonism. Be it East or West, humanity as a whole, that part of humanity that claims the monotheist tradition as its own, cannot avoid the question of evil. Against evil, the ideals of the Enlightenment have proven themselves impressively impotent (and we are far better placed than was Dostoevsky to assert as much). Nothing, today, indicates that the capacity to overcome it has increased in the slightest. The power and the universality of *The Brothers Karamazov* spring from the fundamental question that the book leaves hanging. That burning, intolerable question is placed by the narrator in the mouth of Ivan, the coward, the cynic, the "modern," in what must surely be the most bitter, most implacable passage of the entire novel, during his only long discussion with Alyosha.

Ivan tells the story of a general who orders an eight-year-old child torn to pieces by his hunting hounds for having, at play, injured the paw of a favorite dog. The child is thrown naked to the dogs, like a piece of game; looking on are the assembled domestics. The executioner has placed the child's mother in the first row. The child is made to run in the bitter cold of an autumn morning, and the hounds are let loose. Ivan asks his brother what should be done with the general:

> "Well, what did he deserve? To be shot? To be shot for the satisfaction of our moral feelings? Speak, Alyosha!"
>
> "To be shot," murmured Alyosha, lifting his eyes to Ivan, with a pale, twisted smile.
>
> "Bravo!" cried Ivan delighted. "If even you say so ... You're a pretty monk! So there is a little devil sitting in your heart, Alyosha Karamazov!..."
>
> "Why are you trying me?" Alyosha cried, with sudden distress. "Will you say what you mean at last?"
>
> "Of course, I will; that's what I've been leading up to. You are dear to me, I don't want to let you go, and I won't give you up to your Zossima."
>
> Ivan for a minute was silent; his face became at once very sad.
>
> "Listen! I took the case of children only to make my case clearer.... Is there in the whole world a being who would have the right to forgive and could forgive? I don't want harmony. From love for humanity, I don't want it. I would rather be left with the unavenged suffering. I would rather remain with my unavenged suffering and unsatisfied indignation, *even if I* were wrong. Besides, too high a price is asked for harmony; it's beyond our means to pay so much to enter on it. And so, I hasten to give back my entrance ticket, and if I am an honest man I am bound to give it back as soon as possible. And that I am doing. It's not God that I don't accept, Alyosha, only I most respectfully return Him the ticket."
>
> "That's rebellion," murmured Alyosha, looking down.
>
> "Rebellion? I am sorry you call it that," said Ivan earnestly. "One can hardly live in rebellion, and I want to live. Tell me yourself, I challenge you—answer. Imagine that you are creating a fabric of human destiny with the object of making men happy in the end, giving them peace and rest at last, but that it was essential and inevitable to torture to death only one tiny creature—that baby beating its breast with its fist, for instance—and to found that edifice on its unavenged tears, would you consent to be the architect on those conditions? Tell me, and tell the truth."
>
> "No, I wouldn't consent," said Alyosha softly. (*Rebellion*, 271–272)

The admission is not enough for Alyosha. Returning to Ivan's previous question—does there exist a being that has the right to pardon all—, he reminds his brother that such a right belongs to the unique being who shed his blood for all, and upon whose sacrifice the entire edifice rests. Ivan has not forgotten; he is surprised, in fact, that it has taken Alyosha so long to respond, for it is this being whom his family members are constantly invoking. It is at this point that Ivan, in response to those who refer to Christ, tells the story of the Grand Inquisitor whose ultimate secret is not to believe in God, and who seeks to construct humanity's illusory and servile happiness upon the precepts of a Christ whose presence he finds intolerable. The Inquisitor, unbeliever that he is, must dismiss him whom he invokes, and in whose existence he does not believe.

Though the hero himself never allows himself any doubt, the question of God, the question the elder tells Ivan, "clamors for an answer" (*Why Is Such a Man Alive?*, 75) remains unanswered. In the event, it transcends civilization, place, and time. Modernity, which believes it has settled the issue, has never touched it. One of the principal reasons for our fascination, up to the present, with *The Brothers Karamazov* lies in the way the novel intertwines a criminal intrigue of exceptional richness and intensity with the fundamental question asked by metaphysics: the meaning of our presence in the world. The narrator asks the question in the most radical of all possible ways, all the while giving no answer. He asks it against the backdrop of the great myths that have sustained Western civilization (Genesis, Prometheus, The Gospels) at the very instant that this civilization believes it has ceased to believe. In returning to these myths, and in asking once more, particularly through the Christ-myth, the question of our presence in the world, Dostoevsky imparts to his novel a mythical dimension that, in the European literature of the nineteenth century, has already ceased to be possible, that has already lost its power to sway the mind and the heart.

13

ZARATHUSTRA:
THINKING THE UNTHINKABLE

R EADING NIETZSCHE'S *ZARATHUSTRA* is an existential ordeal.[82] It is not the kind of book one plunges into blithely. Its style roils the stomach as it does the mind. Its dual nature makes it particularly difficult to decode: as poetry, it eludes all attempts at rational analysis; as philosophical discourse, it is susceptible to judgment. Attempting to make sense of this text creates, for me, an unusual risk: of deep dissatisfaction with my own efforts; of betraying a body of thought that is beyond my grasp. In his preface to *Ecce Homo*, Nietzsche writes:

> Within my writings my *Zarathustra* stands by itself. I have with this book given mankind the greatest gift that has ever been given it. With a voice that speaks across millennia, it is not only the most exalted book that exists, the actual book of the air of the heights— the entire fact man lies at a tremendous distance beneath it—it is also the profoundest, born out of the innermost abundance of truth, an inexhaustible well into which no bucket descends without coming up filled with gold and goodness.... One has above all to hear correctly the tone that proceeds from this mouth, this halcyon tone, if one is not to do pitiable injustice to the meaning of its wisdom.[83]

82. That it is a personal ordeal for me harks back to the difficult circumstances in which I first read this book, at age eighteen; circumstances that, in returning to it forty years later, I have rediscovered between the lines. They still impinge on my reading, down to the present day. They are more than a handicap: they make me particularly sensitive to the book's emotional charge. I would like to thank Dalie Giroux, who has been kind enough to comment on this chapter, for encouraging me to overcome my fears. I must admit that I have not entirely succeeded. But her precious remarks have made it possible for me to bring a measure of nuance to my views, though in a way, I fear, that will not do full justice to their quality, which proceed from the deep understanding of Nietzsche's work that I do not possess. In my own defense, I can only offer that I do not intend to deal with the entire Nietzschean oeuvre, but with one of its formative texts, that which is closest to the narrative form, *Thus Spake Zarathustra*. This is the limitation inherent in my approach.
83. Friedrich Wilhelm Nietzsche, *Ecce Homo*, trans. R. J. Hollingdale (London: Penguin Classics, 1992), p. 4.

At first glance these outrageous claims seem to concern a book written by someone else, perhaps by Zarathustra himself, rather than Nietzsche, as if the latter were merely the interpreter of a timeless message whose loftiness and profundity totally escape him ... In any event, "not everyone is free to have ears for Zarathustra"[84]; what assurance do I have of the quality, or the sensitivity of my hearing? And yet I boldly presume to read it, in full knowledge that my own experience of this matchless text risks having none of its ponderousness, its seriousness, its grace and lightness. I lack the air of the High Engadine. But I also refuse to be paralyzed by the writer's claims for his work. I am reading the poet and the philosopher, not the commentator. Since Zarathustra himself cautions his disciples to be on guard against him, I do not believe I am betraying Nietzsche by daring to read him against himself.

Thus Spake Zarathustra is "a book for all and none"[85]; anyone can read it, no one possesses the key to its understanding. Zarathustra may ultimately be speaking to himself alone. But he tirelessly addresses himself to others. That address must navigate the Scylla and Charybdis of language, it must appeal to common sense, something that the hero partially rejects. As a result, everything he attempts to say risks being seen as obscure, murky. The interplay of light and darkness, and even turbidity, has been deliberately built into the text. The narrator (who most of the time is Zarathustra himself) has set up a self-destructing discursive apparatus. It is as though he could not speak to his own kind except by repeatedly negating his own message. What manner of speech can he possibly claim as his own? The question is anything but rhetorical. Like Homer, but in a totally different register, Zarathustra is a life-hunter. He seeks to articulate the conditions that make life a living adventure. There is a whiff of despair about the effort, but he continually sports with that very despair. The playfulness undoubtedly can be located in the minor tonality that underlies everything that, in Zarathustra, is in contradiction with itself.

Philosophy, in its concern with generalities and with concepts, seems at first glance perfectly unsuited to speak of life. This is the task of poetry and of literature, whose evocative powers derive precisely from the fact that they approach life by way of the particular. Which is why Zarathustra, herald of life, seeks his path between poetry and philosophy. The path is grueling, even impassable perhaps. Is it possible to be the bard of life in general? Faced by the magnitude of the task at hand, we can imagine to what supreme necessity the self-destructiveness we have just discussed responds: the incessant affirmation of life, *in and of itself*, grows wearisome, and in the end,

84. Ibid., p. 4.
85. *Ein Buch für Alle und Keinen* is the German subtitle.

abolishes itself. *Zarathustra* strives to deflect the threat by pre-empting it: by burning its own pages one by one. Implicitly, it stands as the last book, the book that proclaims, in a deep and resonant voice, the end of all books—unless from its heap of ashes, phoenix-like, is to rise anew the unwritten book that each of us bears within him or herself ...

Zarathustra's message resonates like an anti-discourse; its fulsome words intone anti-philosophy. It can hardly be unintentional that the narrator uses fable, the age-old enemy of philosophers; it cannot be out of simple derision that the fable draws upon the Gospel. In fact, it is evangelical in two ways: both in its parody and in its objective. Zarathustra continuously poaches in Jesus' preserves. He speaks continuously in the name of truth (punctuating his harangues with *wahrlich*: "verily"), expresses himself in parables, encounters the mocking hostility of the crowd, and even incurs the non-comprehension of his disciples. None of which stops him from proclaiming, against the Christly message, his own glad tidings, according to which the Superman (*der Überrmensch*) is nigh. "Man is something that is to be surpassed" (*Der Mensch ist etwas, das man überwinden werden soll*); the refrain returns time and again, with increasing power. *Soll* becomes *muss*; wishes, and expectations, are transmuted into necessity. The indispensable advent of this surpassing can only come about with the destruction of all that obstructs it: fear, religion, spirit, goodness, happiness, seriousness, prejudices, scorn for the body, expectations of an afterlife. Everything climaxes in the intransigent quest for the vital force; in the quest for that which no one should have to search for. For it is assumed that such a force is a gift that each one of us receives at birth in substantial increments. But it is a gift that vanishes under the impact of culture (*Bildung*) and morality. Coming to life is as hard as walking a tightrope strung high above a dizzying drop. "Man is a rope stretched between the animal and the Superman—a rope over an abyss."[86]

Zarathustra is a tightrope walker who knows exactly how difficult is the challenge that awaits him. His enthusiasm may be childlike; it is not naïve. It is often overshadowed by his acute awareness of the abyss he must cross. Periodically he must draw fresh strength from his two loyal companions—the eagle and the serpent: respectively the proudest, most celestial of all creatures and the earthliest, and wisest. One floats high above everything, a symbol of synthesis. The other slithers, insinuates itself into the heart of things—and sometimes curls affectionately around the neck of he who soars, symbol of analysis. Like them, and between the two extremes they embody, Zarathustra rises and falls, moving from the invigorating mountain breezes to

86. Friedrich Nietzsche, *Thus Spake Zarathustra*, trans. Thomas Common (New York: The Modern Library, 1997), p. 8.

the leaden atmosphere of the plains and of the cities, torn between the thirst for solitude and the need to speak.

At thirty—the age at which Christ withdraws to the desert—Zarathustra leaves the lake of his birth and takes to the mountain peaks. "There he enjoyed his spirit and his solitude, and for ten years did not weary of it" (3). After ten years of life in a cave, Zarathustra feels the need to return among mankind, and begins his descent (*Untergang*).[87] But men want none of what he has brought them. They are too proud of their culture, dazzled by their mindless entertainments. The crowd quickly wearies of Zarathustra's haranguing; it is impatient to watch a true tightrope walker who is chafing to begin. But the tightrope walker is too slow; he is rapidly overtaken and passed by a leaping rival, and plummets into the crowd below. The spectators recoil from his point of impact. Zarathustra alone stands motionless. He assumes responsibility for the body that has fallen at his feet, a symbol of the people's response to his message, and carries it off to the forest where he lays it to rest in a hollowed-out tree trunk. The episode of the tightrope walker convinces Zarathustra that he is "not the mouth for these ears" (10). He needs friends, disciples he can speak to, fertile ground in which he can sow his message—as in the parable of the sower.

Having completed his sowing, Zarathustra now feels impelled to follow his path alone, and takes his leave of his disciples:

> Verily, I advise you: depart from me, and guard yourselves against Zarathustra! And better still: be ashamed of him! Perhaps he hath deceived you.
>
> The man of knowledge must be able not only to love his enemies, but also to hate his friends.
>
> One requiteth a teacher badly if one remain merely a scholar. And why will ye not pluck at my wreath?...
>
> Ye say, ye believe in Zarathustra? But of what account is Zarathustra? Ye are my believers: but of what account are all believers!
>
> Ye had not yet sought yourselves: then did ye find me. So do all believers; therefore all belief is of so little account.
>
> Now do I bid you lose me and find yourselves; and only when ye have all denied me, will I return unto you. (82–83)

So, full of expectation Zarathustra returns to the mountains, and to the solitude of his cave, "like a sower who has scattered his seed" (87).

---

87. The word can mean descent, decline, setting (particularly of the sun).

Months pass, then years; a child appears to him in a dream, holding up a mirror in which he sees his own face grinning back in diabolical sarcasm, a sign that his enemies have "disfigured the likeness of my doctrine" (87–88) and caused him to lose his friends. Swept along by the torrent of his love he goes down to the sea, and rejoins them in the Happy Isles, where he resumes his teaching. But it is far beneath what has been expected of him. In another dream a voiceless murmur rebukes him for silencing his deepest thoughts, for not daring to take his teachings to their ultimate extreme, for rejecting the most difficult task of all: to command great things. "Thy fruits are ripe, but thou art not ripe for thy fruits!" (162). Heartbroken, Zarathustra once again resolves to take leave of his friends; he returns to his solitary path. Having crossed the sea and returned to the continent, making his way amongst the peoples, pursuing his teachings as he goes, he seeks out his cave.

Zarathustra sojourns in his cave for months, years, torn between revulsion, expectation and lethargy, until the day when his totemic animals enjoin him to leave it and explore his estate. Summoned by a cry of distress from the superior human being, he encounters, not too far from his home, a variety of personages (including two kings, a sorcerer, the ugliest of men and killer of God, the last Pope, a voluntary beggar, and Zarathustra's own shadow). In turn he invites them to visit him in his cave, where he welcomes them all that very evening for a copious supper. But they are not the superior humans whom he expects; they are not his true companions. And he exclaims: "But still do I lack my proper men!" (366). The next morning, as his guests slumber on in the cave, Zarathustra steps out and meets a mild-tempered lion that roars and smiles, a sign that the time has come. Not to aspire to happiness, but to aspire to the task at hand.

> Well! The lion hath come, my children are nigh, Zarathustra hath grown ripe, mine hour come: —
> This is my morning, my day beginneth: arise now, arise, thou great noontide!" — — (368)

As the energy of early morning swells up resurgent within Zarathustra, his tale ends, and with it, the book. The story itself, the story of his comings and goings, and of the events that accompany them, occupy a modest space at best—the essence of the book is to be found in its language, and in the inner murmurings of the narrator. But reduced though they may be, the events that demarcate Zarathustra's path nonetheless reveal something of that essence. His path is a cyclical one, and Zarathustra is always passing through—including through his own cave. Despite his long periods of residence there, he seems ultimately to abandon it to his guests, provisionally at least. Whether for good or not, no one can tell. Zarathustra's new morning departure brings the book to a close, but not necessarily the cycle.

His beginning again echoes the eternal return foreshadowed by his animals, which are concerned about the immense discouragement that has come over him after the journey that has brought him back from the Happy Isles. They encourage Zarathustra, devastated by the malady of disgust, to cure his soul through new songs:

> For thine animals know it well, O Zarathustra, who thou art and must become. Behold, *thou art the teacher of the eternal return*,—and that is now *thy* fate!
>
> That thou must be the first to teach this teaching—how could this great fate not be thy greatest danger and infirmity!
>
> Behold, we know what thou teachest: that all things eternally return, and ourselves with them, and that we have already existed times without number, and all things with us....
>
> And if thou wouldst now die, O Zarathustra, behold, we know also how thou wouldst then speak to thyself:—but thine animals beseech thee not to die yet!
>
> Thou wouldst speak, and without trembling, buoyant rather with bliss, for a great weight and worry would be taken from thee, thou patientest one!—
>
> "Now do I die and disappear," wouldst thou say, "and in a moment I am nothing. Souls are as mortal as bodies.
>
> But the plexus of causes returneth in which I am intertwined,—it will again create me! I myself pertain to the causes of the eternal return.
>
> I come again with the sun, with this earth, with this eagle, with this serpent—not to a new life, or a better life, or a similar life:
>
> —I come again eternally to this identical and selfsame life, in its greatest and its smallest, to teach again the eternal return of all things,—
>
> —To speak again the word of the noontide of earth and man, to announce again to man the Superman." (247–248)

Eternal return, in *this* passage, must *above all* be taken literally. For it constitutes one of the central elements of Zarathustra's teaching. If the animals—the only creatures to which he has nothing to teach—turn to him to comfort him in his hour of greatest discouragement, it is because in it there is something redemptive, something that restores to this world the hope that Christianity defers to the hereafter.

As he strides from seas to peaks, from cities to forests, Zarathustra exhausts himself as he teaches a love beyond words whose essence, even for his closest disciples, remains inaccessible. One must be superhuman to gain full access to it, and the path to self-excelling remains beyond men's grasp; even the "superior men" among them cannot envision the horizon where boundaries are surpassed—to say nothing of the "last man" who, having discovered bliss, blinks his eyes in bedazzlement and delight. The fateful recurrence caused by his misunderstood words—words always anticipated but never truly spoken—periodically plunges Zarathustra into a despond from which the idea of the eternal return functions powerfully to rescue him. But that redemption, in its necessity, illuminates the love of life in all its contradictions.

The repeated affirmation of that love, as we know, ultimately collides with an insurmountable obstacle. By dint of constant harping, it provokes a sense of satiation, of disgust. Disgust may well be disgusted by itself, but even this double negation cannot bring back life's magic. His words having been reduced to impotence, the narrator can do no more than shift evil about, from place to place. A process of coming and going has begun, and may well go on forever. Disgust with wisdom sends Zarathustra out into the world; disgust with the world sends him back to his cave, time and again. Everything happens as though there is no way to escape the impasse in which the message that seeks to elevate life, to make life not only a value, but *the* supreme value, has been trapped—except in the cosmic perspective of limitless repetition. But at this level, Zarathustra encounters an even greater contradiction.

If everything ultimately returns to itself, if it becomes exactly what it has always been, not to another new life resembling the life it had lived, but to the same, identical life that is being related to us, then everything we find in it we will unfailingly find once more. And not only that: the eternity of return implies that it has already been repeated an infinite number of times, so that the journey narrated here is being narrated for the *umpteenth* time. *Thus Spake Zarathustra* may well burn one thousand times, and one thousand times rise from its ashes; but it will not have changed one iota. The impossible task of harping incessantly on the primacy of life never steps back from the edge of the precipice it threatens incessantly to hurtle over. What at first may have seemed salutary is as desperate as the message it repeats; the mere idea of the incessant reproduction of itself may well become a source of despair carried to the infinite power.

Since *everything* returns, the eternal return is neutral. We are left, in the end, with a never-ending loop: neither, *a priori*, a source of hope nor of despair. Having abolished the linear nature of time, the eternal return looms before us as the most powerful possible expression of *presence*. It is enough to visit Prague once to never have left—one night is enough to love the city forever; one painful experience is enough to suffer until the end of time. In this light, Zarathustra, in spite of himself, has a touch of the Hegelian about him: he is, and becomes, as does each one of us, the infinite addition of all the moments and movements that combine to construct him in his relations with the world. That construction has always been present, and yet is eternally unfinished, just as the present, in its eternity, is never-ending. In Zarathustra's unending struggle for life, everything is always pre-established; nothing is ever finally determined. Between the "already here" and the "not yet," only the eye that sees the world, only interpretation, only thought are still "in play." Events repeat themselves, but can be read in an inexhaustible number of ways. If, above and beyond the repetition of phenomena, the eternal return subsumes the unchanged return of the thought that interprets them; if, then, it implies the strict impossibility of thinking the already-thought in a different way; if even the freedom to read anew is abolished, then Zarathustra's teaching is reduced to a repetition of all that has already been said, of all that is already known, and, finally, of all that has not been understood. In that reductivist vision, the eternal return—and the recurrence of things—can be nothing more than the interminable repetition of ignorance of them. Zarathustra's path leads to no liberation whatsoever; it holds out no succor.

Only a liberating perspective could possibly hold out some small interest; should we wish to follow our hero, it is the only one acceptable. But the pathway is steep, crooked, and poorly marked. It has no clear goal, no conclusion. What must be overcome remains ill-defined; the superhuman remains indefinable. We know only that the distance that separates the human from the superhuman is incommensurable, like that which separates the "real" world from Zarathustra's dream world. He is all too aware of the fact, nor does he overlook the magnitude of the obstacles that lie in his path. Indeed, he concentrates all his destructive fury on pulverizing them. But as in life, so in negation: the message of negation, constantly repeated, ends up negating itself, and dribbles away into impotence. Even in revolt, Zarathustra senses the danger of disgust with his own speech; he despairs of perhaps losing even the possibility of innocence he has invoked from the beginning of this teaching.

Innocence is the subject of the celebrated parable that, following hard on the prologue, opens the first part of Zarathustra's speech, entitled "The Three Metamorphoses." The parable sets forth "how the spirit becometh a camel, the camel a lion, and the lion at last a child" (23). The spirit seeks, first, to be "well laden" like the kneeling camel; it cries out for the "heaviest thing"; the spirit then becomes a lion, "freedom will it capture, and lordship in its own wilderness" (24). By uttering, "I will" it shatters the "thou wilt" etched in gold on each scale of the mighty dragon that lies in its path. The spirit needs the lion's power "for the most formidable" conquest of all, to earn the right "to create new values—that even the lion cannot accomplish." That, only the child can do.

> But tell me, my brethren, what the child can do, which even a lion could not do? Why hath the preying lion still to become a child?
>
> Innocence is the child, and forgetfulness, a new beginning, a game, a self-rolling wheel, a first movement, a holy Yea.
>
> Aye, for the game of creating, my brethren, there is needed a holy Yea unto life: its own will, willeth now the spirit; his own world winneth the world's outcast. (25)

Childish acquiescence in the game of creation requires us to expunge the scribblings of culture (*Bildung*), that we erase from our faces the motley colors of the past, those very costumes and beliefs that the inhabitant of the "country of man," daubed with the many brightly colored paints, believes himself done with. To achieve solitude, to protect oneself from others is not enough, for "the worst enemy thou canst meet, wilt thou thyself always be" (67).

> Thou lonesome one, thou goest the way of the creating one; a God wilt thou create for thyself out of thy seven devils!
>
> Thou lonesome one, thou goest the way of the loving one; thou lovest thyself, and on that account despisest thou thyself, as only the loving ones despise.
>
> To create, desireth the loving one, because he despiseth! What knoweth he of love who hath not been obliged to despise just what he loved!
>
> With thy love, go into thine isolation, my brother, and with thy creating, and late only will justice limp after thee.
>
> With my tears, go into thine isolation, my brother. I love him who seeketh to create beyond himself, and thus succumbeth. (67–68)

There is a poignant grandeur to this passage, in which Zarathustra calls for the loss that saves, a barely concealed echo of the words of Jesus: "For whosoever will save his life shall lose it: but whosoever shall lose his life for my sake and the Gospel's, the same shall save it" (Mark, 8:35).

The only difference—and it is a fundamental one—is that for Zarathustra, each man can only promise himself the loss that saves, and must reap its fruits in this life. Indeed, *Zarathustra* stands before us like an exclusively terrestrial version, an even more radical version, if such a thing is possible, of the Gospel message. Jesus' "suffer the little children to come unto me" (Mark, 10:14) takes on a sweeping new form in the injunction to become the child of the third metamorphosis. "Love thy neighbor as thyself" becomes: "your bad love to yourselves maketh solitude a prison for you" (64); "not the neighbor do I teach you, but the friend" (64). The eternal return, meantime, gleams in the light of the Gospel like a kind of permanent resurrection, and the cross that each must bear leads to renewal in the here and now. Nietzsche once more, involuntarily, rejoins Hegel: each offers us his earth-bound version of the salvation Christianity promises for the world beyond. There is an inevitability about salvation for Hegel; it "would suffice" (!) to seize the concept in its fullness in order to attain the spirit. But for Nietzsche, though the spirit is always at work, we cannot mistrust it enough: it is endlessly falling into the traps it sets for itself; it seeks refuge in mediocre consolations; it even imagines that it can cut itself free of the body.

Nothing, for all the promises of eternal return, is assured. Almost inevitably we begin to feel that all is lost and gone forever; nothing, in the cycle of eternal return, can ensure intelligence that metamorphosis—even mentally—of that which must be changed is enough. Zarathustra, almost in spite of himself, becomes the bard of loss in whose vertigo the idea of an unachievable superhuman finally creates the only possible intoxication. "Let the world be lost," writes Marguerite Duras in *Le Camion*. Let us at least feel the extraordinary sensual delight of our inevitable fall into the abyss, like that of Antigone into the absoluteness of the *até* her acts have summoned forth. Zarathustra has administered the medicine of damnation. The price of life's exaltation is the sorrow of being in the world. As in the tragedies of Sophocles, man takes his pleasure in understanding, in ultimately understanding what has struck him.

The unending dimension of Zarathustra's wanderings, so often bodied forth in his speech, do possess a salutary counterpart: the effort, continually begun anew, to strip away layer after layer. The garments of fear, of shame, and of falsity are cast, one after another, into the abyss. The abyss is deliverance.

Into it is cast the human being in his most rudimentary nudity, as are cast all his values. As an advocate of the process of denuding, of stripping away, Zarathustra (and behind him, Nietzsche) stands revealed as the spiritual father of what today, in philosophy and the social sciences, is known as "deconstruction." Fashionable as an academic term, the word refers to a cautious, orderly operation, one that stands in sharp contrast with the violent uprooting that Zarathustra, in his overweening hypersensitivity, has undertaken. The notion of deconstruction removes the painful overtones from the unceasing self-labor that consists of tearing oneself away from oneself. But that labor cannot bring about the leveling of values. Zarathustra nowhere affirms that all values are equivalent; quite the opposite, he proclaims that each value is worth only what it costs me in terms of the effort needed to conquer it, to make it authentically mine. Such a conquest is made possible only by shedding, by leaving behind—like a snake its old skin—the myriad scales of *received* values—those that glitter like so many "thou shalt's" on the dragon that confronts the lion before it is transformed into a child. Child here communicates fragility. But we cannot rid ourselves of our received values all at once, once and for all; the shedding of our skin that Zarathustra summons us to *begin all over again* can only make us extraordinarily vulnerable.

For the human being cannot live without values. The human being is a creator of values:

> Values did man only assign to things in order to maintain himself—he created only the significance of things, a human significance! Therefore he called himself "man," that is, the valuator.
>
> Valuating is creating: hear it, ye creating ones! Valuation itself is the treasure and jewel of the valued things.
>
> Through valuation only is there value; and without valuation the nut of existence would be hollow. Hear it, ye creating ones!
>
> Change of values—that is, change of the creating ones. Always doth he destroy who hath to be a creator.
>
> Creating ones were first of all peoples, and only in late times individuals; verily, the individual himself is still the latest creation.
>
> Peoples once hung over them tables of the good. Love which would rule and love which would obey, created for themselves such tables.
>
> Older is the pleasure in the herd than the pleasure of the ego: and as long as the good conscience is for the herd, the bad conscience only saith: ego. (61–62)

It would be wrong to assume that Zarathustra is advocating the short-sighted egoism that today, with hardly a second thought, goes by the name of "individualism," and is nothing but the mimetic appetite for "always more"—irrespective of what "more" might be. Never, perhaps, beneath the glistening and variegated surface, have the herd instinct and conformism been so prevalent than at the dawn of the twenty-first century. We have seen how the Ego can aspire to shed the gaudy accouterments of the past, of habit and of collective belonging only through a process of stripping away. In the light of these preconditions, the individual is not simply young; his advent has not yet taken place. Nor will it take place as long as each people continue to hammer out its own collective values, as long as there remain as many goals as peoples:

> A thousand goals have there been hitherto, for a thousand peoples there have been. Only the fetter for the thousand necks is still lacking; there is only one goal. As yet humanity hath not a goal.
> But pray tell me, my brethren, if the goal of humanity be still lacking, is there not also still lacking—humanity itself? (62)

Zarathustra's call for the destruction of all accepted values, and the effort of reconstruction incumbent upon the individual have as their goal the emergence of a common project for humanity: a humanity to come. There is something frankly terrifying about recomposing individual values within an overarching whole. But the context rules out all totalitarian interpretation. Though it is not formulated in the passage, the project, the goal in question can be nothing else than the surpassing of the human in the march toward the superhuman. It is to the necessity of this process that Zarathustra constantly returns as he continues on his journey. The above passages are taken from the chapter entitled "The Thousand and One Goals"; the chapter that follows it takes up "Neighbor Love." We now know that it contains an embedded warning against the biblical precept, and a call to the thorny and intricate love of self.

The goal that Zarathustra would assign to humanity can only be the opportunity for self-surpassing, a process hindered by the prejudices constructed by peoples over time. It is through the effort that each Ego, its scales fallen, must exert to become itself that humanity may eventually be impelled by one sole desire, a desire that follows as many paths as there are individuals. That which each person may well discover as he or she follows his path, that which consists of personal fulfillment, is up to each of them to discover in a solitude from which friendship is not excluded. Zarathustra, in the rising sun of his last departure, does not yet know what his path will be, nor what he will find, nor even if he will encounter those whom he expects. He knows only that he *wants*.

So it is that the affirmation of life, for him, is first and foremost a matter of life-wish, that is—in appearance contradictorily—the wish for that which exists and for that which had been. "'Will to existence': that will—doth not exist" (125). What we have before us is the notorious "will to power" that would later give rise to a multitude of contradictory interpretations. As expressed in the chapter entitled "Self-Surpassing," will to power is opposed to "will to truth" against which Zarathustra lashes out as the vain desire of the wise to begin by "making thinkable" all being. For want of understanding the nature of all being:

> Ye would still create a world before which ye can bow the knee: such is your ultimate hope and ecstasy....
>
> The living thing I did follow; I walked in the broadest and narrowest paths to learn its nature....
>
> But wherever I found living things, there heard I also the language of obedience. All living things are obeying things.
>
> And this I heard secondly: Whatever cannot obey itself, is commanded. Such is the nature of living things.
>
> This, however, is the third thing which I heard—namely, that commanding is more difficult than obeying. (123–124)

In this chapter, the will to power is first and foremost *inward* listening and obeying. It becomes commanding only toward he who proves unfit to obey himself. In this way, the weaker "steals the power" of he who obeys himself in commanding—a commanding that he must expiate. For life has revealed its secret to Zarathustra—a secret we already know to be constituent of humanity: "'Behold,' said she, 'I am that *which must ever surpass itself*'" (125). Further on, in a chapter on redemption, Zarathustra gives a starting definition of that deliverance[88]: "To redeem what is past, and to transform every 'It was' into 'Thus I would have it!'—that only do I call redemption." (153) "All 'It was' is a fragment, a riddle, a fearful chance—until the creating Will saith thereto: 'But thus would I have it'" (155).

The will to power here stands forth as redemptive, creative: in obedience to life, and in surpassing itself as does the very life it obeys, it creates and saves the world *from all that it was*. We could even go so far as to say that, by listening carefully to the world (rather than wishing to explain it in the

---

88. *Erlösung* can mean both redemption and deliverance.

manner of the wise, or to master it by technique), the will to power rescues it from the past, from oblivion. Life-affirmation thus ceases to be pure tautology. It becomes acquiescingly active and instinctual to the world—close, in fact, to Spinoza's joy, to Spinoza's desire to increase the world's capacity for being. As such, as an inner movement that espouses the world, the will to power stands forth as a desire for knowledge incompatible with a conception of the eternal return understood as a strict repetition of the same thing. For that will to be done, if only as an interpretive force for a world that is never completely given, always to be invented, always to be unveiled (even to the slightest extent), the eternal present must preserve a portion of the undecidable, conserve something of the indeterminateness so dear to Anaximander. The will to power and the eternal return can only be intelligently read in their dialectical relationship, in the mutual limits they impose on one another, bestow upon one another. The eternal return is the interpretation of a will whose liberty is not absolute. If we are to attempt to be free, we must see the world as it is reproduced in its perpetual dynamism.

Even our best attempts to invest Zarathustra's pronouncements with coherence have their limitations. Nothing in the tale allows us to assert such coherence with the slightest assurance. Zarathustra is enmeshed in contradictions from which he does not necessarily seek to extricate himself, but which return periodically to taunt him, like the slobbering idiot who holds up to him the deforming mirror of the disabused judgment that he, Zarathustra, has made against mankind, and who, dismayed by the caricature of his own despair, the narrator finally silences.

My need to find coherence in the teachings of Zarathustra proceeds, I must confess, from the necessity to hold back the surge of nausea that intense reading can at times arouse. For me, at least, Zarathustra's message has a powerful effect: it impels me, in an almost physical sense, to want to free myself from the ties with which it has bound me. Another, more radical measure against the destabilizing effect of *Zarathustra* is to consider it as evidence of sickness. But by ducking the issue in that way, I only aggravate what I am attempting to protect myself against. For if indeed there is sickness, it is not simply Nietzsche's; it is that of humankind—a generalized sickness, congenital to the species, to which such individuals as Zarathustra or Nietzsche, who place no constraint on their thought, prove to be extraordinarily sensitive. *They*, in their exceptional acuity, have diagnosed the human being as illness. The human being is an illness that thought cannot cure. Worse yet, thought is the cause, the principle: thought itself is the sickness that has irremediably afflicted human beings.

Zarathustra violently displays all its symptoms: he sings the body, but his song remains despairingly cerebral; in him, it is always the spirit who speaks. He extols friendship but finds no friends or must leave behind those he does encounter. He places the highest value on social ties, but can live only in his teachings or in solitude, sharing nothing with anyone. Love surges forth in the form of a torrent rushing down the mountains to the sea only to vanish. The herald of the body appears to know neither sex nor sensuality, nor—except at the very end—tenderness. The brief chapter in which Zarathustra takes up the question of chastity is brutally revealing of that particular infirmity:

> I love the forest. It is bad to live in cities: there, there are too many of the lustful.
>
> Is it not better to fall into the hands of a murderer than into the dreams of a lustful woman?
>
> And just look at these men: their eyes saith it—they know nothing better on earth than to lie with a woman.
>
> Filth is at the bottom of their souls; and alas! if their filth hath still spirit in it!
>
> Would that ye were perfect—at least as animals! But to animals belongeth innocence.
>
> Do I counsel you to slay your instincts? I counsel you to innocence in your instincts.
>
> Do I counsel you to chastity? Chastity is a virtue with some, but with many almost a vice.
>
> These are continent, to be sure: but doggish lust looketh enviously out of all that they do....
>
> Verily, there are chaste ones from their nature; they are gentler of heart, and laugh better and oftener than you.
>
> They laugh at chastity and ask: "What is chastity?"
>
> Is chastity not folly? But the folly came unto us, and not we unto it.
>
> We offered that guest harbor and heart: not it dwelleth with us—let it stay as long as it will!—(56–57)

Should the "innocence of the senses" belong to animals, how can it be counseled for man, except to wish that man turn his back, yet again, on the symbolic dimension of his nature? But such renunciation is quite impossible, and Zarathustra knows it. That is why he cannot counsel greater chastity to those who cannot endure it. He is content to congratulate himself for receiving it as a shared gift. But the gift is a perfectly sterile one. He who lashes out at those who are contemptuous of the body himself lives outside his body. Once more, thought displays its impotence in overcoming the radical contradictions that it inflicts upon itself: Zarathustra's "choice" of chastity is not a choice, it is a folly of external origin; nothing can justify it except fear of the body, and more specifically, fear of woman's body, which in turn looks suspiciously like fear of life. Woman's body is an open wound at the heart of a thought that reveals itself as tragically impregnated in spite of itself, contrary to all that it pretends, by an iniquitous love of life. In Zarathustra, we hear distant echoes of Augustine.

Love of life remains refractory to all thought. And so it is that Zarathustra finally reaches the most insupportable of all paradoxes: thought cannot save—it is this obvious conclusion that he ceaselessly mulls over, upon which he ruminates, from every possible angle. What is unique in man also brings about man's perdition; it is for this reason that we cannot expect anything from the spirit. But it is the spirit that *thinks* despair; it is the spirit that affirms it. The spirit cannot divest itself of its critic's task by pleading its enthrallment to the body, its subordination to life. Such subordination would be little more than another preconception: the simple inversion of the opposite received idea. As does the body, the spiritual proceeds from life—*a fortiori*, the distinction between the corporal and the spiritual is another of those prejudices that must be overcome. The spirit may be fully justified in making sport of the loftiness of its pretensions, but deprecate as it may, it cannot be dispensed from thinking; it shows, instead, that Zarathustra cannot, to his dismay, just like everyone else, stop himself from thinking. In denying its superiority, the spirit can suppress nothing of its function; it exercises it supremely, even though it may be dragged through the muck. If the spirit were to radically negate itself—a contradiction in terms—Zarathustra would need only fall silent. Thought cannot save, nor can life. We are condemned to thought in the same way as we are condemned to life—and to death.

Whoever turns his back on thought, turns his back on life, on *human* life at least, insofar as humans are those beings who, knowing themselves to think, cannot but gaze upon life—irrespective of the quality of their gaze. The matter of quality has, indeed, an impact upon our way of living. As Nietzsche puts it: "All that interests me is what helps me to live." There are many passages in *Zarathustra* that furnish us with this precious asset. But these breaths of liberty, of lucidity, are stifled by a discourse that promises no exit. With *Zarathustra*, Nietzsche may well have attained that point in his thought where the exaltation of surpassing despairs of itself, flounders and spreads like a mortal poison through the narrator's veins. It is all well and good for him to rise one fine morning and leave behind him, in his grotto, those who he never expected in the first place; no one can foretell how long the sunlight of his solitude will sustain him in his onward journey. Fully recovered from his earlier exaltations, the reader asks, puzzled, as he closes the book: "But where can Zarathustra joyfully turn his steps, if not toward the abyss of Dionysian sensuality?"

In his quest for the impossible, Zarathustra may well come to resemble a kind of Don Quixote. But there are radical differences: he refuses to invent a distinct world, to create for himself a hideaway in the imaginary. Zarathustra is firmly anchored in the real, in madness, that is, in a world ordinary people can never know. Ordinary people, people like you and me, believe that they are living in what they call reality, simply because they know nothing of their madness. They are wise enough to believe that they are not mad, without realizing that wisdom is madness that does not know it is madness. Zarathustra is fully aware of his madness; his wisdom is the knowledge that he is mad, that is, defenseless against the real. From that state of realness, his speech sends to us ordinary mortals a series of incandescent fragments, torpedoes that blast gaping holes in the heavy armor plating that guards us against life.

Life is a threat. That is the price it exacts from us. Consciousness of that constant threat, awareness of life's threat to *derange* us, is the price we must pay to strive to become (once more) living beings—meaning in a state of rebellion against all forms of abdication of our being. And then, perhaps, like Zarathustra on the last morning of his tale, we will no longer need to protect ourselves against the birds that will alight with infinite tenderness atop our heads.

14

MOSES:
FREUD'S LAST WILL AND TESTAMENT

FREUD HAS A STRANGE, almost obsessive fascination with Moses. His study of the celebrated sculpture by Michelangelo that represents the prophet seated, wrathful, and tormented, the Tables of the Law under his arm, offers us eloquent testimony. In the statue's mouth he places a tale the likes of which the artist may never have dreamed. At the end of his life, the founder of psychoanalysis returned to the founder of Judaism in a text full of foreboding, a composite rehashing of older material, lengthened, and patched together like Harlequin's costume from scraps of material that, instead of concealing the various stages of fabrication, deliberately displays its every stitch. In it, Freud seems intent on inflicting upon his readers the laborious process of composition, on drawing attention to his hesitations, on begging pardon for the audacity and incongruity of his work. It is this complexity that makes *Moses and Monotheism* (1939),[89] along with *Totem and Taboo*, the greatest source of embarrassment for Freud's disciples.

Totem and Taboo can be explained away, if need be, as a simple error. But with *Moses*, Freud trumpets his impenitence, revisiting the very theses that he had published twenty-five years earlier. Some would like to downplay the gravity of his second offense; they attribute it to its author's intellectual decline. That version depicts a great man weakened by illness, alarmed about the fate of his people, a disabused and bitter man who has been overwhelmed by historical speculation totally secondary to the essence of his work and the core of his theory. My own view is radically different: *Moses* reveals, instead, the fundamental concerns that were to haunt Freud until his dying breath. He had lost none of his intellectual agility; on the contrary, his spirited defense

---

89. Sigmund Freud, *Moses and Monotheism*, trans. Katherine Jones (New York: Vintage Books, 1967).

of his earliest theses shows a pitilessly self-critical mind at work. What was to be his final major book was also, for him, a work of the highest value.

Central to those concerns was the founding of psychoanalysis. Exiled in London and feeling the end to be near, Freud published, with great urgency and without self-censorship, a work begun several years before in Vienna, where he had been proceeding with extreme caution, almost under surveillance. Like a painter constantly adding new brush strokes to his canvas, Freud constructs a portrait of Moses from disparate biographical elements he well knows are uncertain. He employs these elements freely enough to assemble a vision of his principal figure that, by his own admission, seems uneven. Yet he continues to buttress it, laying out new arguments and fresh hypotheses, each one more unverifiable than the last. The historical Moses is unknowable. To reconstruct another figure, no less fictitious than the biblical figure, one need only agree that the Torah account is necessarily incomplete, that it is primarily a legend. For him to compose a new *novel*,[90] a new *theory* of Moses, his reconstruction need only be no more implausible than the prophet portrayed in Exodus. The goal of the father of psychoanalysis is theoretical, as are the key issues of his novel.

Put brutally, Freud topples the figure of the Commendatore from his pedestal. First things first: Moses and his monotheism are Egyptian; the Jews do not yet exist as a distinct people before following their leader in the exodus. The Mosaic Law and their desert wanderings will give them form and shape. They are believers, but they do not yet form a people, until they mingle with the other tribes of the region, quite likely in the vicinity of Madian, long after the death of their leader—a death for which they are responsible. Moses the Egyptian had been assassinated by this own people, who were no longer prepared to submit to the rigors of the Law, and no longer wished to wander in the wilderness. Then, another Moses, a Madianite of unrefined ways, belonging to one of the tribes with which the exiles had joined forces, a prophet of the angry god of volcanoes, symbolically replaces the assassinated father as reparation for the unpardonable act committed much earlier. From the fusion of its diverse elements, and from the combination of veneration and repressed murder represented by the person of the second Moses, arises the Jewish people, now reconciled with the specter of its founder. The duplication explains the double personality, both of the biblical prophet and of the god he serves—or whom he makes use of.

---

90. I treat this disconcerting book as a novel, in full knowledge that Freud had at first entitled his essay *Moses: a Historical Novel.*

For Freud, the monotheism introduced into Egypt by the Pharaoh Akhnaton, and carried on after the fall of the new religion by a dissident Moses, may indeed constitute progress. It still remains, as do all religions, the expression of a collective neurosis, a neurosis that springs from the murder of the father of the primitive horde that he had analyzed a quarter century before in *Totem and Taboo*. Freud returns, at the end of his life, to the very anthropological and historical considerations that psychoanalysis supposedly no longer had need of, or worse, that might adversely affect it. The discipline now seemed firmly established in the West; the master's disciples could not understand what he meant by returning to the kind of unsound, dangerous theories that threatened to discredit the Freudian theory rather than consolidate it.

But Freud had never simply intended to devise a new clinical method for the treatment of individual neurosis. His ambition was to construct a theory that would encompass all psychic phenomena, ranging from the individual to society at large; a theory that would take the collective psyche of peoples (phylogeny) or that of individuals (psychogenesis) into full account. At first glance, the need for such a correspondence might seem irrational and counterproductive. Clinical activity can manage quite nicely without it; the problems of the individual psyche are more than enough to keep psychoanalysts' purses full. But for a mind as curious and as wide-ranging as Freud's, that fleeting satisfaction was not enough. Moreover, the ultimate pertinence, the force of psychoanalytic theory itself, would ultimately suffer.

From his first halting steps in existence, a human being involuntarily absorbs the surrounding culture, which in turn exerts a powerful force in giving shape to what he is to become. We could even venture that the impression left upon him by that culture will form, from his earliest infancy, a vital part of his subconscious. Culture, society, its norms, and its history are an integral part of the subconscious that we bear within us. The collective psyche being part and parcel of the individual psyche, the validity of psychoanalytical theory depends, in fact, on the need to provide a unified explanation of the various levels of that psyche. The theory must be able to explain, using the same principles, how both have evolved. The system of religious representation prevailing in so-called primitive societies corresponds with the infantile stage, and so on, and so forth—hence the notion that monotheism constitutes collective progress in comparison with animism or polytheism, just as awareness of duty represents individual progress in the adult in comparison with the irrational fear of the father, or of the Super-Ego, in the infant.

Our task is not to discuss the validity of such correspondences, which I have sketched out with a brevity that some readers may find appalling. No, our main concern is to understand how vital they are for Freud. For it is directly to this question that the story of his fictitious Moses speaks. And if we must compare fictions, Freud's is by far the better, and the more useful, for it confirms and consolidates the basic premises of psychoanalysis. Exactly what does it consist of? To put it with extreme bluntness—quite unlike Freud's prudent, gradualist approach in *Moses and Monotheism*—it is the matter of the Œdipus Complex and the configuration of the psyche in its two successive, superposed and complementary topics: the unconscious-preconscious-conscious sequence elaborated in *The Interpretation of Dreams* (1900) and the topography of the psyche laid out in *The Ego and the Id* (1923). It is nothing less, in fact, than the central core of Freudian theory, upon which we must linger for a moment.

The essentially diachronic sequence laid out in *The Interpretation of Dreams* takes into account the work of time upon an individual's psychism. For its part, the topography of *The Ego and the Id*, which tends toward synchronicity, describes the way in which these instances, separated from one another by the scars of time, cohabit within the space of the psyche. The resulting caesuras are as plural as they are complex: the mind is not simply divided between two monolithic instances, the Ego and consciousness on the one hand, and the Id and subconscious on the other. A portion of the Ego and the Super-Ego plunge deeply into the subconscious, while a portion of impulses make their way toward the conscious, by way of the preconscious which, through dreams, "Freudian slips," and other acts of absence, comes knocking on the door of the conscious. In both schemes, as in the Œdipus Complex, *latency* possesses a crucial function. It represents the time needed for the repressed to pass from the subconscious to the preconscious, and from the preconscious to the conscious. The repressed thus designates that which, in the individual, may well emerge later in life from the founding experiences of its earliest existence, relegated either consciously or more probably unconsciously to oblivion—oblivion here meaning a dormant segment of emotional memory, and not its definitive erasure. Repression does not affect only the forbidden urges contained in the Id, but also those very impulses that, in the Ego, can take the form of moral precepts gathered together in the Ideal Ego, which Freud also termed the Super-Ego.

Now, these impulses and their accompanying prohibitions are linked, at the most fundamental level, to the sexual and emotional life of the child in his relations with his mother and father—in what can be termed the Œdipal triangle. The child seeks to supplant his rival of the same sex in the affections of the parent of the opposite sex, but identifies at the same time with him or her whom he seeks to push aside. Conflict arises between impulses, prohibitions, and identifications. The way in which the child experiences these conflicted feelings, and the way the parents handle them, generates traumas of varying gravity, which, because of their unpleasant nature, are thrust deep into the subconscious. After a certain age (around five years old) the infant's sexual activity ceases, and it enters into the period of latency so essential to the creation of the neurosis that will later return to haunt the adult in his or her erotic and emotional life. The period of latency thus designates in the individual the "incubation period" that, by separating the trauma from its resurgence, allows the neurosis to take root and to function. All human beings forget, at least partially, the traumatizing infantile sexual experience that, with the onset of adolescence, threatens to rise to the surface.

As we can already observe from reading *Totem and Taboo*, Freud clearly seeks to demonstrate that, *mutatis mutandis*, the same process takes place at the collective level: religion, a kind of collective Super-Ego, proceeds from the inchoate necessity experienced by peoples to transform the traumas they have inflicted upon themselves in a past so distant that it is partially obscured. Among these traumas stands one that, in one way or another, has left an indelible mark on the development of most societies and that *Totem and Taboo*, as we know, identifies as the murder of the father of the primitive horde. Limited in numbers at first, the earliest groups of humans were dominated by the absolute power of the chief, who could claim all the clan's females for himself, until his sons finally revolted against him and put him to death. Whatever the subsequent stages of social organization (which we need not agree on here),[91] the distant, nearly forgotten figure of the assassinated father returns as the divine father, and wields, at the symbolic level, a power as great as that exercised by the executed tribal chief. Religious sacrifice unconsciously commemorates this initial murder—that of Moses, in the case of the Jews—as though the scene should be restaged to remind us of the respect due the victim, henceforth elevated to divine stature. That particular religious rite, and with it religion as a whole, is unaware of its traumatic origins, which lie at the root of its neurosis. The image of the tyrannical father as an obstruction to be brought down in order to gain access to his women here assumes capital importance: it indicates that, as for the individual, the tragedy being played out and that continues to be commemorated is Œdipal

91. Summarizing the content of *Totem and Taboo*, Freud suggests the following sequence: "brother clan, matriarchy, exogamy, and totemism" (169) to describe the extremely lengthy period that separates the era of the primitive horde from the victory of monotheism.

in nature. The difference being that the process that covers between seven and eight years in the life of an individual can extend over as many decades, or even longer, in the life of societies.

The analogy between individual and collective neurosis nonetheless presents what Freud himself identifies as "two difficulties." The first is that the analogy rests on the study of a single case, that of the Jews, to which we will return. The second, which is of much greater concern to the narrator, raises a fundamental problem: "In what form is the active tradition in the life of the peoples still extant?" (119). It cannot be in the form of conscious communication, since that which is being transmitted is by definition repressed. The difficulty consists precisely in demarcating an unconscious transmission.

To make the unprepared reader's task easier, Freud ventures to "place the result of the following investigation at the very beginning," asserting: "the concordance between the individual and the mass is in this point almost complete. The masses, too, retain an impression of the past in unconscious memory traces." For him, "the case of the individual seems to be clear enough" (120). He goes on, in a few pages, to present the two topics just outlined, and concedes that the concordance is simply postulated. But it is a postulate that weights the balance in favor of the Freudian thesis. For, after all, the history of individuals, in and of itself, does not always provide enough evidence to explain the power and persistence of the Œdipal triangle over time:

> The behavior of a neurotic child to his parents when under the influence of an Œdipus and castration complex is very rich in such reactions, which seem unreasonable in the individual and can only be understood phylogenetically, in relation to the experiences of earlier generations. (127)

So, not only a simple analogy exists, but also an organic link between collective and individual neuroses: a powerful correspondence whose unifying force can be evaluated on the theoretical level. The irresistible attraction of this conceptual unity for the founding father of psychoanalysis casts fresh light on how important the case of Moses is for Freud, and upon his growing vehemence in defending his version of Exodus: the universality and the coherence of his theory are at stake. If the theory holds equally for peoples and individuals, if it is valid for all humanity, then psychoanalysis would decisively bolster its heuristic capacity—hence the capital importance, in *Moses and Monotheism*, of the matter of periodicity. The span of time that separates the murder of Moses from the encounter between the two groups that go on to constitute the Jewish people *must* cover several generations in order that the re-emergence of the Egyptian monotheism that Moses communicated to his first faithful followers can be seen in the new religion; and the confusion that unconsciously arises in the biblical imagination between the noble Egyptian and the Madian priest be explained. This precise return of the repressed, this particular superposition and their manifest proof, are indeed indispensable to the central core of the Freudian theory. But since the theoretical reconstruction invoked in support of the theory is not only unverifiable, but even rather daring, we can understand Freud's desire to formulate it piecemeal, hesitantly at first, almost excusing himself as he goes, until he can transform the hypothesis that will be called upon to justify his theory into the event whose necessity the theory demonstrates, and whose certainty it attests. Only surreptitiously and very gradually does the narrator reverse the meaning of the proof, and finally derive from the theory what it, the theory, had demanded of history in the first place.

The theory confirms itself by explaining what history cannot relate. The circularity of that tautological explanation refers back to the first of the two difficulties pointed out by the narrator, and to which we must now return: the uniqueness of the historical case upon which narrative speculation rests. Since the theory makes it possible to draw conclusions that are more certain than history itself, its uniqueness has ceased to be a handicap. Not only does the search for other examples no longer seem indispensable, the remarkable longevity of the Jewish people makes it an exemplary case study, and confers upon it an exceptional revelatory capacity. In its capacity as the founding people of monotheistic religion, its history is by definition exemplary. Thanks to its prodigious timelessness, we can behold, in this people more than in any other, the religious evolution of all humanity.

The meaning of its chosen status is thereby illuminated: not at all as God's favorite people, but as leading to a higher level of spirituality, which constitutes its "precious treasure" (134). Better than any other, the history of the Jewish people allows us to observe the sequence that leads from the father of the primitive horde to the advent of monotheism. Seen in this light, the murder of Moses is not an inaugural act; it is, in fact, the repetition of the original murder related in *Totem and Taboo*. Precisely because the Jews have reinflicted the archaic ritual upon a person as eminent as Moses are their denial of the act and their subsequent devotion to monotheism so intense. The case of the Jews illustrates in the liveliest possible way a general truth specific to the human animal, to wit, "that men have always known[92] ... that

---

92. The knowledge referred to here is unconscious, repressed.

once upon a time they had a primeval father and killed him" (129)—a killing that would, much later, be echoed by that of Christ.

Before Moses there was the murder of the father of the horde. After him, the sacrifice of Jesus: a fantasy of expiation "welcomed in the form of a gospel of salvation." (110) Freud's interpretation of Christ's passion gives his theory ample room to deploy its unifying power. The "original sin" that the crucifixion of the son redeems, and that only a son can redeem, is nothing more than Paul's vague and brilliant denomination designating the murder of the father. In giving his life, the son replaces the "enrapturing feeling of being the chosen ones" by "release through salvation" (174). The Last Supper and the Holy Communion that keep alive his memory now appear as a watered down version of the primitive killing, the prohibition against repetition,[93] the redemptive sacrifice of the Son and the new fraternity that the act inaugurates.[94] But the "religious innovation" that the preeminence of the Son represents is fraught with ambivalence:

> Meant to propitiate the Father Deity, it ends by his being dethroned and set aside. The Mosaic religion had been a father religion; Christianity became a Son religion. The old God, the Father, took second place; Christ, the Son, stood in his stead, just as in those dark times every son had longed to do. Paul, by developing the Jewish religion further, became its destroyer. His success was certainly mainly due to the fact that through the idea of salvation he laid the ghost of the feeling of guilt. It was also due to his giving up the idea of the chosen people and its visible signs— circumcision. That is how the new religion could become all-embracing, universal....
>
> In certain respects the new religion was a cultural regression as compared with the older Jewish religion; this happens regularly when a new mass of people on a lower cultural level effects an invasion or is admitted into an older culture. The Christian religion did not keep to the lofty heights of spirituality to which the Jewish religion had soared. The former was no longer strictly monotheistic. (111–112)

---

93. We should bear in mind that, in the Freudian interpretation, the totem is taboo in that it is forbidden to eat, except on solemn and exceptional occasions where the prohibition is ritually replicated by the opposite act: its sacrifice, that subconsciously commemorates the killing of the father and reaffirms its prohibition.
94. On this fraternal aspect, and on the ambiguity of the death of Christ, which is in a sense the death of God himself, I refer the reader to what I call the "Story of the Death of God," *Truth or Death*, Chapter 8.

But there is one point on which, according to Freud, the Christian religion represents an advance over Judaism. That advance is a significant one. Where Judaism continues obstinately to deny the murder of the Father, Christianity admits the founding sin, and restages it in the form of expiation, the better to absolve humanity. Where the murder of the first Messiah, Moses, remains obscure, the killing of the second, Christ, is displayed, proclaimed, and openly commemorated. So much so that in his resurrection "there is some historical truth ... for he was the resurrected Moses and the returned primeval father of the primitive horde as well—only transfigured, and as a Son in the place of the Father." Thus the crime imputed to the Jews, "if correctly translated" is not the murder of Christ (for, in the final analysis, Jesus *consents* to his sacrifice) but their refusal to confess to their earlier killing of God. Christianity's avowal buttresses Freud's thesis and confirms, as though it were necessary, that the murder of Moses "becomes an indispensable part of our reasoning" (113)—so clearly that the new dispensation has no hesitation about killing him, on the symbolic level, a second time. But it also shows that a vital element of biblical history has eluded the People of the Book themselves. Where Christianity makes it possible, even unbeknownst to it and against its will, to take another step toward the anthropological and psychoanalytical significance of monotheistic religion, Judaism fully intends to keep the religious meaning of its chosen status intact.

Herein lies the "treasure" whose secret Freud profanes. Not only has he kidnapped Moses from his people, as he proclaims in the celebrated first sentence of his novel, to which we will return, but its religion *in toto*, declaring without hesitation, in quite a Hegelian vein, that the advent of Christianity has reduced it to the "fossil" state.[95] Freud shows not the slightest sensitivity toward the religion of his ancestors, as if his theory would derive additional credibility were he not to show any indulgence toward the mythical foundations that had enabled his people to endure. His program of destruction is as radical as was Paul the Apostle's. But it serves an entirely different cause.

As he reviews the obvious contradictions of the biblical narrative, Freud lets drop: "The distortion of a text is not unlike a murder. The difficulty lies not in the execution of the deed but in the doing away with the traces" (82). But this is exactly what our scriptural killer of Moses deliberately fails to do: not content with putting a great man to death a second time, he makes every effort to leave the traces of his murder as visible and numerous as possible. In confessing his crime, he is following the Christian approach, as against

---

95. "And yet Christianity marked a progress in the history of religion: that is to say, in regard to the return of the repressed. From now on, the Jewish religion was, so to speak, a fossil" (113).

Jewish tradition. It is not enough for him to burn the precious treasure of his people. It is as though he is telling us: "Look closely at what I am burning, and the determination with which I am doing it." His insistence is even more fascinating: in telling the story of his Moses, Freud is also telling his own story. He tells it not only by revealing his scholarly hesitations and torments, but also, as a subtext, as a great but partially misunderstood man, who identifies, and knows himself to be identified, with the cause he defends. So staunchly does he do so that it is far from unthinkable to wonder whether, in the murder as committed by Freud, there does not lurk—unbeknownst to him—a suicidal element.

At first glance, the hypothesis seems unfounded. The only truly new element we find in the last part of his work is a ringing apology for the lone, great man. In attributing to such a man the ability to determine the fate of an entire people, Freud is well aware that he is moving against the modern historical trend, which favors "more hidden, general, and impersonal factors" (changes in economic circumstances, changes in food supply, progress in the use of materials, changes in climate, demographic shifts), in which individuals play no other part than as "representatives of mass tendencies" (136). But the magnitude of those underlying factors cannot eliminate the feeling that some individuals do play a more prominent role, and are recognized as far more gifted and influential than the mean. This is indeed what Freud finds most intriguing about the notion of the "great man." What causes us to bestow this honorific title on some men, and not on others? Not for what they have truly accomplished, as one might think, but for their impact on the collective imagination:

> We know that the great majority of people have a strong need
> for authority which they can admire, to which they can submit, and
> which dominates and sometimes even ill-treats them. We have
> learned from the psychology of the individual whence comes this
> need of the masses. It is the longing for the father that lives in each
> of us from his childhood days, for the same father whom the hero
> of the legend boasts of having overcome. And now it begins to
> dawn on us that all the features with which we furnish the great
> man are traits of the father, that in this similarity lies the essence,
> which so far has eluded us, of the great man. (140)

Moses looms large as the supreme father figure. But, in the light of what we have just argued, his stature, like that of all great men, has suffered yet another mortal blow: our veneration for him is purely infantile. Freud places the great man high atop his pedestal the better to topple him from a greater height. He does not shrink from calling Moses the *Führer* of the Jewish people. There is nothing innocent, in 1938, about his choice of the very term that the Nazis had already been using for several years to designate their venerated and all-powerful chief. If this had been a "Freudian slip" on Freud's part (which seems almost unthinkable), it would have been more revealing still. It would have indicated that, deep in his subconscious, the desire to overthrow the statue of the father is at work. But, I believe, his attempt at subversion is a perfectly deliberate one, and the comparison with the German dictator, in its discretion, must be seen as voluntary. The comparison reflects the pitiless lucidity we know Freud to be capable of. For, the least we can say is that, whatever portion of his motivation may be unconscious, he never retreated from the extreme consequences—in his eyes—of his theory.

To the extent that the father of psychoanalysis identifies—no matter how minimally—with Moses, his deconstruction of the great man can only turn against him. The narrator may not be the object of popular adulation, but he knows that he is to a certain extent venerated by his disciples—to which he has himself contributed. He is probably no less aware that his contribution is justified in his eyes by the need to avoid, at all costs, having the discipline he has founded driven aground by stormy seas. But discipline can only be maintained by imposing the paternal authority that he owes, like it or not, to his status as creator. Freud cannot but be torn between the exigencies of discipline and his sharp distrust of anything resembling a personality cult, between the need to maintain order—in society as in psychoanalysis—and the theoretical demystification of a paternal function we can hardly imagine abolishing.

To the theoretical necessity of *Moses and Monotheism* must then be added whatever testamentary concerns are intimately connected with it. What Moses had achieved for his people, Freud has accomplished for all humanity. From this perspective, the attempt to deconstruct the biblical Moses may initially seem contradictory. Freud, at first blush, would have little to gain from toppling the founder of Judaism from his pedestal. But it is precisely, as we have suggested, by the audacious affirmation of that very act that his book begins, and that we must now directly quote: "To deny a people the man whom it praises as the greatest of its sons is not a deed to be undertaken lightheartedly—especially by one belonging to that people" (1).

But Freud's identification with Moses is ambiguous. In fact, he would rather cast himself, *mutatis mutandis*, in the role of a new Paul. Not, of course, that he wishes to become the apostle of a new religion. But he is well aware of being the founder of a scientific doctrine that has assigned religion to its proper place, that considers it in the light of its true function: as the necessary symbolic representation of collective neurosis. So, all things considered, the operation that would extract Moses from his people obeys a double logic. Firstly, Freud always feared that the discipline he founded would remain "Jewish." Its founder could in absolutely no way be compared to the man reputed to have founded a religion defined above all else by its particularism—which explains why Freud can so readily identify with an Egyptian Moses. But—secondly—Paul provides an even more satisfying, less ambiguous figure. Freud has every reason to identify with a Jew who is reputed to have spread Judaism throughout the world. Following the example of the Apostle Paul, Freud, a Jew like him, used his Judaic heritage to universalize the new doctrine destined to explain, then to replace all religion.

The question of the great man remains. Above and beyond the de-judaization of Moses, who at one stroke ceases to be the father of monotheism, we have seen that the founding father of psychoanalysis has set out to demystify the great figures of history. His goal is to overthrow the father. In this way he pursues the work begun by Christ: once more he kills the father, this time in a more effective way, by replacing the father cult with the confraternity of the sons. In so doing, he assumes the role of the last father, or first son. Freud claims to dispossess the Jewish people of "the greatest of its sons" and not of its "father." But that abduction, above all, makes it impossible for anyone after Freud's death to use his name or to appropriate his authority and claim to speak in his name.

The testamentary work that is *Moses and Monotheism* thus emerges as a semi-conscious attempt, tinged with desperation, by the progenitor of psycho-analysis to protect the solidity and the integrity of his theory, while at the same time dethroning a father figure—whether it be his own, or any other dominant figure to come who might attempt to reclaim the authority of the founder—who must die. At the same time, he has also contrived to ensure that psychoanalysis will never have a father—even if he is deprived of his throne in the process. Even more radically, it is his way of indirectly affirm-ing that psychoanalysis must forgo all fathers.

Now, the book's celebrated opening sentence can be heard in a different key. At the beginning of the narrative, the narrator deprives his hero, and him-self, of paternal stature for the sake of a fraternity to be built: Freud and *his* Moses are already Christ-like and fraternal. The question can no longer be one of removing the son. On the contrary, he must be set up in place of the father, with all the ambiguity such a shift in roles implies. The eldest son is necessarily the greatest; behind him lurks the possibility of another father. Not so easily can paternal authority be abolished.

Freud thus stands before us as a new Moses. A Moses who, having killed the old, and along with him all Jewish claims to chosen status based on religion, leads his new people, the numerically limited people of psychoanalysis, out of the desert and into the world. But, having sacrificed his person, he is also, and perhaps even more so, a new Christ—and at the same time, he who elucidates everything: Paul. Should we view him as Moses, we begin to wonder what kind of pact the "people of psy" must conclude with the other tribes in order to perpetuate the cult of the great man that "people" will have unknowingly killed, and for whose murder they will never be able to assume responsibility. If we view him as Christ, we find ourselves doubting that the new Church can avoid the sectarian divisions and the terrible fratricidal quarrels they nourish, for all of Paul's attempts to bring about a semblance of order. Ultimately, Freud emerges as a Trinitarian figure in which the person of the founder, Moses, is linked with that of the redeemer, Jesus, and that of the apostle and organizer, Paul—as though the meeting of these three powers were enough to ensure that the Œdipal trinity would be handed down without idolatry.

In his lifetime, Freud was haunted by the question, and the presence, of the father. His obsession, updated with *Moses and Monotheism*, stands confirmed as both central and critical to his *œuvre*. There can be little doubt that it constitutes a vital part of the complex self-knowledge our civilization must strive for: this is the painstaking task it must accomplish to reach adulthood, and from which it appears to shrink back still.

To what at first glance might have seemed a purely psychoanalytic concern is now added a civilizational dimension. That Freud's *Moses* could be produced by a mind so apprehensive about his legacy to humanity indicates that his thought intersects—in reverse—with Hegelian delirium. We are far indeed from Plato and his gardens of the written word. Rather than accept the diversity of interpretations to come, rather than allow the thoughts of future readers to cultivate the most variegated blooms long after the seeds of the text have been planted, Freud goes to extraordinary lengths to ensure that his work is understood, and that its interpretation is strictly circumscribed. His unremitting effort mirrors the *Phenomenology of Mind* in its excess, though under quite different appearances. Unlike Hegel, Freud seems straightforward; he tells his story in simple language. But this very simplicity never stops calling itself into question—complicating itself by additions that cast doubt upon what has just been asserted (*Moses and Monotheism* is an example taken to the point of caricature). Freud even sometimes appears hesitant about the pertinence of his own discipline. His hesitations are real enough, momentarily, in his mind. They are not strictly rhetorical. But in the end, when the core of the theory is at stake, they almost invariably integrate into its structure all they had first doubted. Freud is a past master in the art of turning the objections he has raised into arguments for his views.

Here we come at last to the fundamental paradox of psychoanalysis. It is a discipline that claims to shed light upon that dark side of us, which by definition eludes our conscious and cannot be grasped by reason. It brings reason to bear upon that which is non-reasonable. There can be little doubt that Freud, aware of the paradox, possessed the genius to invent the concept of the preconscious, that semi-obscure zone of the psyche where the unarticulated rises close enough to the surface that it can be apprehended and interpreted by reason. But the portion that reason can apprehend and analyze will always remain infinitely small in comparison with the incommensurability of all that remains forever buried in the depths of subconscious, for the precise reason that its depths are, strictly speaking, unfathomable. Who can doubt that Freud has performed yeoman service by making it possible for our culture to put some distance between itself and triumphal reason? His achievement has been to reveal, partially, the power of impulse and of the repressed that dwell within us. He has done it by divesting the Ego of its presumptuous vanity, by silencing its deafening chatter. He found a way to let speech flow, allowed it to puncture the façade of ego-centered discourse.

But in his attempt to explain the hidden mechanisms of that speech he has also helped, in spite of himself, to restore the Ego to its position of dominance, to popularize the idea that the thinking subject can, in spite of everything and with modest effort, restore the empire of the self and obey its reason—or that of society. Today many Freudians justly decry the egocentric reappropriation of psychoanalysis. Psychoanalysis has little value except as a process of destitution; but it is the conscious that must contrive to survive among the shards of Ego that it has dashed to earth. Freud, whatever his intentions, has abandoned us just as our self-corroding civilization, which can never fully recognize the virulence of its critical spirit, tears itself apart—our civilization that always seems, in times of crisis, to put aside its abrasive spirit and put on a reassuring face, to mask its disquiet with the triumphal face of rationalism. Freud's *Moses*, the culmination of a prodigiously fecund intellectual life, stands as the unconscious avowal of that anxiety. Between doubt and continuity, continuity must prevail. Certainly, psychoanalysis must continue on without a master; it must also do so in such a way that each person becomes, to the greatest possible extent, his own master: the principal incarnate of an uncertainty sufficiently certain of itself to hold angst in abeyance—quite exactly as the Hegelian consciousness has devised a thousand stratagems to heal the gaping wound it claims to countenance.

15

JOYCE:
WRITING EXCESS[96]

JAMES JOYCE'S *ULYSSES* opens on a view to the sea, from the summit of a tower, in an instant of elevation that is purely pagan in its power:

> Stately, plump Buck Mulligan came from the stairhead, bearing a bowl of lather on which a mirror and razor lay crossed. A yellow dressinggown, ungirdled, was sustained gently behind him on the mild morning air. He held the bowl aloft and intoned:
> —*Introinbo ad altare Dei.*
> Halted, he peered down the dark winding stairs and called out coarsely:
> —Come up, Kinch! Come up, you fearful Jesuit!
> Solemnly he came forward and mounted the round gunrest. He faced about and blessed gravely thrice the tower, the surrounding land and the awaking mountains. Then, catching sight of Stephen Dedalus, he bent towards him made a rapid cross in the air, gurgling in his throat and shaking his head. (I, 9)[97]

Buck Mulligan, the scalpular apprentice, summons Stephen Dedalus, wielder of the pen, mocking in high humor the absurdity of the latter's Greek-sounding last name, which, he adds, has nothing on his own—Malachie. It is his own way of holding up to gentle ridicule the kind of double reference—GreekJew or JewGreek—the learned love to boast of and, at the same time, to make sport of the dangers of the labyrinth that lies in wait for them. Mulligan admonishes his friend in no uncertain terms for having refused to

---

96. An earlier version of this chapter was published as "Ulysses en personne" in *Conjonctures*, no. 39–40 (2005), pp. 245–272.
97. James Joyce, *Ulysses* (London: The Bodley Head, 1960). References in parentheses are to part and page.

perform the simple act that his mother had asked of him in her dying breath: to kneel beside her death bed. Doing so, in his eyes, would have lent too much importance to death, which must be left in its pitiful triviality. He knows all there is to know about cadavers and dissections. Life lies before them, broad as the sea, as snot-clotted as the filthy handkerchief he extracts from Stephen's pocket to wipe his razor. "Give up the moody brooding," (I, 18) Mulligan commands him. Why, the two of them would Hellenize Ireland if they put their minds to it.

Alone now at the top of the Martello tower—like Nerval's *tour abolie*[98]—Stephen muses on fragments of his mother's life and death. No, he will no longer ruminate on "love's bitter mystery." No, he will not bend beneath the spectral glare of her vitreous eyes, he will not be Hamlet.

> *Her eyes on me to strike me down....*

> Ghoul! Chewer of corpses!
> No, mother! Let me be and let me live. (I, 19)

Right he was to have not knelt, and wrong the villainous Mulligan to accuse him of resisting; wrong to think it possible to kiss the sea, to embrace life, to dismiss that bothersome intruder, death, to bow down in the ritual that would so solemnly and imperiously sanctify him. He hastens downstairs to join Mulligan and Haines, a passing Saxon, to sink his teeth into the fat of things, to drink strong, milk-redolent morning tea.

Thus begins Joyce's celebrated novel. With life's sharp and ironic bite, with the salt tang of new morning on Dublin Bay. Or, later, after having taught class and instructed his pupils in the certainties and uncertainties of history, Stephen abandons himself to the fast-flowing chain of free association. His mind is like a rag picker, gathering up everything that catches its eye. "Ineluctable modality of the visible," thinks Stephen. The remains of a shoe protruding from the sand, the slime-green silvery blue sea, the solidity and the fluidity of all things visible bounded by the diaphanous and the opaque, shells snap crackle and popping underfoot. Fragments intermingled with reminiscences, images scattered in memory whose growing chaos, like the dog he watches zigzagging across the strand at low tide, lead him in his solitude to invoke the gentle caress of a captivating woman: "Touch me. Soft eyes. Soft soft soft hand. I am lonely here. O, touch me soon, now. What is that word known to all men? I am quiet here alone. Sad too. Touch, touch me" (I, 83).

---

98. "Le prince d'Aquitaine à tour abolie" is an enigmatic line from Gérard de Nerval's poem "El Desdichado," recycled by T. S. Eliot in *The Waste Land* (1922).

He watches the flooding tide flow landward, filling the hollows. *And no more turn aside and brood*, goes the refrain, though there is much to brood about, much seaweed swirled to and fro by the tide. Can't find his kerchief; must have left it where Mulligan's thrown it. Stealthily scrapes the booger extracted from his nostril on the edge of a rock.

The dreamy appetite of Stephen, the Dublinesque stand-in for the adventurous Telemachus, the son whom death—he believes—has released from its womb, feeds on the motley dazzle of the world. We have been duly warned: the ripe fruit is not about to drop off of its own accord into the reclining reader's gaping maw. Thought strikes out on a rocky, uphill path and follows precipitous meanderings. Life is a sorrow, life is a joy, and both have a price. This odyssey will be no simple matter. With Homer, we revel in the trials of Ulysses; with Joyce, we suffer with the pleasures of Bloom. Difficulty, like the treacherous wine-dark sea, is rich in the unexpected, fertile in discovery. We have now reached the end of Book I. The eponymous hero can now make his appearance.

When the Homeric Leopold Bloom—Poldy for those who know him intimately—steps onto the stage, it is as if the day has begun all over again. Breakfast and its priceless gastronomic moments. Daily life, less young than a few pages earlier, takes on new, more intimate detail. The hero's insatiable appetence for fried mutton kidneys leads him toward a surrogate:

> Ham and eggs, no. No good eggs with this drouth. Want pure fresh water. Thursday: not a good day for a mutton kidney at Buckley's. Fried with butter, a shake of pepper. Better a pork kidney at Dlugazc's. While the kettle is boiling. (I, 83)

Follows an eight-page return trip to the corner butcher's, during which a succession of petty details trip and stumble over one another: the sleepy mutterings of his wife Molly, who wants nothing in particular, the master key he decides not to rummage through the pocket of another pair of pants for, so as not to wake her—carefully closing the door not to rattle the latch, warm day in prospect in the morning sunlight, greetings for Mr. O'Rourke followed by mental calculation of the irregularities that make it possible for publicans to get rich overnight, the rump of the neighbors' maid whose energy gives him ideas—alas! no more than that—but who now threatens, as she bobs from side to side in front of the butcher's counter, to prevent him from acquiring the one remaining kidney that Bloom, alarmed, sees oozing fat, and that he finally pockets, wrapped and tumefacient, for a mere three pence, plus a brochure on investment possibilities in Palestine, not for me thank you, followed by a brief discursion into the immemorial history of a vagabond people washed ashore on the banks of a dead sea. Mail in the entry hall, the word "metempsychosis" elucidated in the moist odor of the conjugal bed, while up from the kitchen floats the vengeful whiff of burning kidney. Saved *in extremis*, the kidney accompanies him bite by bite as he reads a letter from his daughter, one short page read and reread in the resigned joy of a father distantly concerned for her virtue, after which, comfortably ensconced on the throne, he turns to relieving himself with the same scrupulous attention that he had paid his breakfast. And then, true enough, there's the funeral. What time is it? "Poor Dignam!" (I, 103). Enough of the preliminaries. Let the journey commence.

It will be a long day of extensive perambulation in mourning clothes— those damned funerals!—through the pocket handkerchief that is Dublin. In his peregrinations, Bloom runs into a blathering fool who inevitably expounds on poor Dignam's terrible fate, and who prevents him from quietly rejoicing in the shapely silhouette of the young lady just stepping into a cabriolet. The best moment lost, blotted out by a passing tram. A bit later, Bloom circumspectly enters a post office to claim, under an assumed name (false visiting card concealed in his hat) an unhoped-for letter from Martha, his (future?) mistress, which he takes great pains to read far from inquiring eyes. The cool and hallowed odor of old stone draws him into a church, such a fine place for a tryst—if only at this moment she could slide over close against him, where some pitifully attended service is being celebrated. Eucharistic ritual: bread for the commoners, wine for the priest. Clever. No risk of drawing drunkards. The priest makes his way along the line of the faithful with his softened hosts. "Look at them. Now I bet it makes them feel happy. Lollipop. It does. Yes, bread of angels, it's called. There's a big idea behind it, a kind of kingdom of God is within you feel" (I, 119).

No music; too bad. Molly is so fine in Rossini's *Stabat Mater*. "Mozart's Twelfth Mass: *Gloria* in that. Those old popes keen on music, on art and statues and pictures of all kinds" (I, 120). Drop by the chemist's, some lotion for Molly, *Peau d'Espagne*. All the scents. Curative, all you have to do is sniff them. Like ringing at the dentist's. Chose a lemon-scented soap. He'd gladly stop off at the Turkish baths for a good scrubbing and a massage.

> Nicer if a nice girl did it. Also I think I. Yes I. Do it in the bath. Curious longing I. Water to water. Combine business with pleasure.

Pity no time for massage. Feel fresh then all the day. Funeral be
rather glum. (I, 125)

Refreshed by his bath, Bloom joins the funeral procession in the
Hippomobile alongside three other friends, Dedalus-père included.
Haphazardly the cortege encounters the living and the dead. Bloom points out
Stephen crossing the street to his progenitor, who lashes out at that wretch
Mulligan, the worst kind of influence. "Full of his son. He is right. Something
to hand on" (I, 130). Lost in nostalgia, Bloom daydreams about the son, dead
in infancy, which he would have accompanied through existence. A fleeting
glimpse of the silhouette of Blazes Boylan, whom we quickly understand is
Molly's lover. Just what Bloom was thinking—what can she possibly see in
him? A child's casket heading in the same direction, hearses in the other, on
their way back from the cemetery. Close by his house they pass, never step
in on a woman applying her make-up, the immense structure of the hospital
for the indigent, death's antechamber. Pause. Cows heading for the slaughter-
house block their path. Poor Dignam, gone so suddenly; left an entire family
behind him. The goodly Mr. Power turns the discussion to the indignity of
suicide, never suspecting that Bloom's father killed himself by swallowing
poison. We need a tram for the dead, from the town to the graveyard, where
despite encumbrances we all end up. The graveyard, where we always
manage to end up. What a job, blessing corpses all day long; what an honor,
reciting prayers over the dead. The bedraggled funeral procession that has
accompanied the deceased to his last rest (now you're talking!) throws
Bloom into a lengthy meditative waltz about birth, death, rot: from the umbil-
ical cord to the pallbearers, with a subterranean digression amongst the
micro-organisms. Digression by way of what, exactly? As he leaves the
cemetery Bloom rediscovers his zest for life, bringing to the attention of one
of the gentlemen present that his hat has suffered a reparable dent. Remedial
measures are called for. The acid tone of thanks leads the do-gooder to take
his distance from the beneficiary of his good deed. He will be magnanimous:
"How grand we are this morning" (I, 170).

Comes a series of snapshots, sketches, and fleeting images of Dublin life,
tramways, din of rolling beer-barrels and rotary presses in the print shop
where we encounter Bloom as he plies his trade: classified ad salesman.
Those selfsame ads no newspaper can be without, not only as a matter of
financial survival, but because of the true life they contain: morsels of desire,
of dreams, of exchanges inserted or clipped, whose fragmented forms, as
Bloom suggests to his customers, the narration adopts. It is as though we find

ourselves in a Renoir film (did he ever read Joyce?),[99] with its quick cuts and its fast-flowing sequences, as if drawn from real life. Moments of existence sewn into a perpetually recomposing patchwork, the narrative constructs and deconstructs itself at a frantic pace. A writing style with one guiding principle: constant movement. Nothing else can capture the startling intensity of things. Rare, in any event, is the writing that does so with such verve, with such truculence.

Here now is Myles Crawford, editor-in-chief of the *Evening Telegraph*, holding forth on what journalism, real journalism, stood for in his time. Amidst laughter and jokes good and bad, caught up in the roil of daily life, the two boon companions decide, at Stephen's suggestion, to stop off at Mooney's, the pub just down the street. Crawford summarily dispatches Bloom, whom he has encountered in the street on his way back to the office with a classified ad. The advertiser would like his name mentioned in return.

> He can kiss my royal Irish arse, Myles Crawford cried loudly
> over his shoulder. Any time he likes, tell him.
> While Mr. Bloom stood weighing the point and about to smile
> he strode on jerkily. (I, 212)

Alone again, Bloom resumes his wanderings and his thoughts. Life, death, birth, follow one another called up by images, encounters; return redoubled by the pangs of childbirth—poor Mrs. Purefoy has been in labor for more than three days now, she can endure no more. Unbelievable how they've not been able to find a thing to relieve the travails of delivery. Hunger begins to gnaw at him, despite the cost of the slaughterings, the murders, and the dismemberments that he turns into meat products on which he gorges himself. Not to mention the oysters, those trashcans of the seas that no one would touch if their prices weren't out of sight. Restaurant. Men and only men, wolfing down their food and slurping their soup as if their lives depended on it, amidst the stench of overcooked vegetables and spit-thick sawdust. Bloom beats a hasty retreat. Assuages his hunger in a nearby pub, with a glass of Burgundy and a Gorgonzola sandwich. The sunlit touch of the wine sets him thinking about an afternoon of love in the undergrowth—rich fleshy lips and breasts full, swelling in her blouse of nun's veiling.

---

99. I am alluding precisely to the film *Le Crime de Monsieur Lange*, directed by Jean Renoir in 1935, in which the action takes place in a print shop in the Marais, in a series of rapid-fire scenes that seem to have been taken from real life. We find this same spontaneity, to an even higher degree, in *La régle du jeu*, filmed in 1939 by the same Renoir. There is a clear family connection between the film style of the son, and the painting style of the father, Auguste Renoir, visible in his famous painting of the *Moulin de la Galette* (1876).

Abandoning Bloom temporarily on the steps of the museum where Mulligan will swear that he's seen him deep in admiration of the callipygian Venus's median cleavage, the narrator (but who is he, really?) slips into another sanctuary, another locus of collection, a library. Stephen, in his peroration, orchestrates a high-falutin' disquisition, spiced by the arrival of Mulligan, on art, literature, the Trinity, paternity, and filiation, in which Shakespeare and Hamlet, who appear in leitmotif, constitute the pivot point. Is he Shakespeare himself? Is he Hamlet and his phantom father? He is the father of all his characters and, at the same time, are not all the characters, up to and including the most warped of them, directly drawn from his family history? Behind the irony of these academic debates, Stephen alludes to an aesthetic that might well be that of *Ulysses* itself.

> As we, or mother Dana, weave and unweave our bodies, Stephen said, from day to day, their molecules shuffled to and fro, so does the artist weave and unweave his image. And as the mole on my right breast is where it was when I was born, though all my body has been woven of new stuff time after time, so through the ghost of the unquiet father the image of the unloving son looks forth. In the intense instant of imagination, when the mind, Shelley says, is a fading coal, that which I was is that which I am and that which in possibility I may come to be. So in the future, the sister of the past, I may see myself as I sit here now but by reflection from that which then I shall be. (I, 280–281)

Consubstantiality is no longer made manifest as the delirium of Christian theology, delirious as it can be, might one add, but also as the profoundest way of addressing, via the question of paternal transmission, continuity itself. What of oneself continues on in oneself? The question accompanies and sheds light upon the mystery of filiation, of which consubstantiality may well be the highest, most enigmatic expression. The least one can say, declares Stephen, is that the enigma of fatherhood may well be the founding mystery of Christianity:

> Fatherhood, in the sense of conscious begetting, is unknown to man. It is a mystical estate, an apostolic succession, from only begetter to only begotten. On that mystery and not on the Madonna which the cunning Italian intellect flung to the mob of Europe, the church is founded and founded irremovably because founded, like the world, macro and microcosm, upon the void. Upon incertitude, upon unlikelihood. Amor matris, subjective and objective genitive,

may be the only true thing in life. Paternity may be a legal fiction.
Who is the father of any son that any son should love him or he any
son? (I, 299)

Upon being told by Mulligan of the oratorical exploit he has missed,
Haines the Saxon concludes simply that "Shakespeare is the happy hunting
ground of all minds that have lost their balance" (I, 357). A sharp jab to the
chin of anyone tempted to take all the theological and literary theorizing
seriously.

Another sequence of scenes follows, like snapshots from life. Fragments
of the day gleaned at random from diverse, increasingly numerous individuals, elements and instants of which intersect at an increasingly jolting
rhythm. The hastily assembled pieces of a puzzle that, even though they do
not quite fit together, end up by creating a landscape of sorts. Against the
backdrop of this landscape unfolds a multi-voiced musical score. We move
from painting to music, from dots of color to melodic lines, or to hold to a
pictorial language, from Fauvism to Cubism. Having lined up all the characters and their photographic images side by side, now to display them together
in their multiple aspects. Counterpoint, fugue, conversations incessantly
repeated, themes, wanderings, as we see Bloom popping up here and there,
leafing through books, taking a seat in a café, snared by his appetites like a
fly in molasses, while Boylan, "with impatience" and shod in canary yellow
spats, runs endlessly off to meet a lady whom we can no longer refuse to
recognize as Bloom's flower, alias Penelope: Molly in person.

Now a mid-afternoon migration toward a tavern that evokes the
Cyclopean cavern, to Barney Kiernan's where, like Polyphemus, a hairy,
brawny giant called the Citizen with his mastodon of a dog lays down the
law. A nameless narrator (we will never know who is the *I* that tells the tale)
turns up in the company of a man named Joe, and the two pillars of the pub
in their scorn leave no one unscathed. Each launches into his tirade, the
marketplace, the international situation, Irish patriotism, the greed of the
hangmen who, for five guineas, would set their own fathers jigging at the end
of a rope, a consideration that leads into sexual erection among the hanged,
the exact physiology of which the pedantic Bloom explains to an audience he
could not care less about. Against a background of drinking-hole triviality
shine sparks of epic, magic and allegorical bravura; laid before us are pomp
and circumstance combined in a duly noted almanac whose nomenclature
alone calls for another round. Tantric communication with poor Dignam—
him again—instructs us that the residents of Pralaya enjoy the best in modern

comfort, "talaphana, alavata, hatakalda, wataklasat" (I, 434). The all-too-recently departed, addressing the living, exhorts "all whom were still on the wrong side of Maya to acknowledge the true path for it was reported in devantic circles that Mars and Jupiter were out for mischief on the eastern angle where the ram has power" (I, 434).

A chapter that is *Ulysses'* most political. Among its many episodes and anecdotes weaves something that vaguely reminds us of resentment over all that has been inflicted from without upon Ireland. It is with this without that Bloom finds himself insidiously associated. Bloom, seen from without—seen by the others, and outside their den—, sniffing about the entrance to the cave, seems irksome, suspicious. His admission into the drinkers' circle, he who refuses to drink and contents himself with gnawing on a nasty cigar, is anything but equivocal. In the mind of the Citizen, who has not the slightest hesitation in handing him over to mob justice, this Jewboy with the borrowed name—Bloom is Jewish and his Hungarian-born father was called Virag (I, 487)—this Jewboy Bloom is thrown in, over his vehement protest, amongst the cohort of predators of this once flourishing isle, which history and the human species, to wit *the British Empire*, have shamelessly pillaged. The worthy Bloom, for whom a nation is "the same people living in the same place" (I, 487), a definition that brings hoots from his listeners, insists he is no foreigner; he was born in Ireland. Which makes him doubly persecuted: as an Irishman, and at the same time, just now, as a Jew. Then follows a plea for universal love the anonymous narrator makes gentle sport of:

> Love loves to love love. Nurse loves the new chemist. Constable 14A loves Mary Kelly. Gerty MacDowell loves the boy that has the bicycle. M.B.[100] loves a fair gentleman, Li Chi Han lovey up kissy Cha Pu Chow. Jumbo, the elephant, loves Alice, the elephant. Old Mr. Verschoyle with the ear trumpet loves old Mrs. Verschoyle with the turnedin eye. The man in the brown macintosh loves a lady who is dead. His Majesty the King loves Her Majesty the Queen. Mrs. Norman W. Tupper loves officer Taylor. You love a certain person. And this person loves that other person because everybody loves somebody but God loves everybody. (I, 481)

Love or not, the Citizen will not relent: Bloom, that dispossessor of widows and orphans, son of the perverse Virag, is a "wolf in sheep's clothing" (I, 488). The discussion turns sour. Bloom reminds whoever might care to hear that Mendelssohn, Marx, Spinoza, Christ, his father or his uncle, your

100. Most probably Marion or Molly Bloom, wife of the above.

God, when you come right down to it, are all Jews. Backed into a corner the Citizen seizes, as Bloom moves majestically on, the first thing he can lay hands on: the final scene of this deluge of feats ends with the prodigious fling of a bisquitbox with seismic consequences that, like the immense stone cast at Ulysses' ship by Polyphemus, narrowly avoids killing the hero.

The day is coming to an end. Along the shore. "The summer evening had begun to fold the world in its mysterious embrace" (II, 9). A faraway embrace is indeed taking place. A beautiful — and purely visual — love scene is slowly, subtly, tenderly, and bestially unfolding, between Gerty MacDowell of whom we have just spoken, and a mature man dressed in mourning, who looks upon her unmoving with ever-greater insistence. In a moment of immodesty fraught with innocence, Gerty reveals herself, offers herself up wholly to his gaze, bends over and opens to him right down to the tender crotch of her body, as though the man were penetrating her from a distance with all the power of the fireworks that, at that very instant, arch explosively skyward from the shore. Bloom, for it is indeed he, may well have soiled himself; she has remained immaculate. Taken and yet intact, tapped yet spotless, a spirit-impregnated virgin like Danae by Jupiter's golden shower. Life's sacred ejaculation. Their only tactile contact is in the form of a child's ball that rolls, as if to prefigure, right up to the young girl's legs. "Every bullet has its billet" (II, 47) Bloom utters, meditating *ex post facto* (in Stern's celebrated formula) on that instant of wordless love that refers, magnificently, to "the word that all men know." And that so few know how to experience. Bloom has experienced intense sensual pleasure beyond any touch, while Stephen had daydreamed early that morning of infinite caresses. "Love's bitter mystery" (II, 48) winds its way through a labyrinth altogether as complex as that of thought, altogether as tortuous as that of *Ulysses* itself, and the upsurge of lubricious communion, late in the fading light of a day filled with nothings comes, frothy white spindrift on the sand, as an unhoped-for reward. Something like a pinnacle has been reached, from which we must now climb down.

The descent promises to be as long as it is arduous. It begins with a return to the sources: the trial-fraught emergence of the child from the mother's womb. In pseudo-archaic style, Bloom the noble and valiant knight steps across the threshold of Lord Horne's maternity clinic metamorphosed into a medieval castle. Its vast wards hum with strutting, utterly self-possessed young coxcombs, among whom we find Stephen and Mulligan, joined later by the inevitable Haines who, popping up like a *diabolus ex machina* through a hidden doorway, agrees to play the villain of the piece. Pitiless age, spouting forth hell-bent for leather on the subject of entering and departing this world and, specifically, about the identity of the man (husband, confessor?) who has impregnated the lady who languishes in labor's travails (none other than our Mrs. Purefoy) for three days running in this very place. Once again, in a veritable "epitome of the course of life" (II, 111), the pompous and unruly, ethylic and scientific argument blazes up, stretches out, turns back upon itself and after innumerable twists and turns ends as the mutterings and blusterings of drunkards, in an increasingly repulsive out-spewing of verbiage. All's well that ends well, mother and child are fine and well. The merry troop flees the field in a state of total disorder.

The descent continues in Mabott Street, the red-light district. Here are the scenes everyone talks about. Straight out of the theater, with their actors and dialogues, their edifying soliloquies and breathtaking changes of costume. The downfall picks up steam, through Hades, then Circe, packed with episodes of all possible variety. Impossible to explore every nook and cranny of its infernal labyrinth, to keep track of the boundless comedy of the "pornosophical philotheology" (II, 131) brewing and stewing there. Traditionally, the kingdom of Hades is a place of transition, like the whorehouses of yore, where sons would be brought to learn from their fathers, as does Stephen from Bloom. But it is also a place of judgment. Bloom, who narrowly escapes being crushed beneath a tram, is a father unworthy. Soon he will become involved with the town's law-enforcement agencies, and with the judiciary: nocturnal vagrancy, obstructing circulation, plagiary, sexual harassment, repeated indecent exposure and defamation of honorable women, public indecency. Bloom, the accused, amidst the hubbub of the courtroom, pleads not guilty, invokes his outstanding services to the Empire, protests his undying loyalty to the Crown, and paradoxically promises to mend his ways. His attorney whitewashes him, after the accused boasts that, in serving under the flag, he has done "all a white man could"[101] (II, 155–156). The members of the jury having declared themselves convinced of his guilt, the sergeant-at-arms thunders: "Whereas Leopold Bloom of no fixed abode is a wellknown dyna-mitard, forger, bigamist, bawd and cuckold and public nuisance to the citizens of Dublin and whereas at this commission of assizes the most honorable ... " (II, 169).

The prosecutor demands imprisonment until such time as he shall be hanged by the neck until dead. They take him away. As the hangman announces his price—five guineas per jugular, and begins to toll the bell—the desperate Bloom swears that the bomb he is accused of throwing was

---

101. "I regard him as the whitest man I know" (II, 156) argues the defense attorney.

nothing but a pig's head thrown to a stray dog, and that he had been attending a funeral. Upon which Paddy Dignam, once again, popping up like the ghost in *Hamlet*, testifies to his death, to his funeral, and that, unable to get enough whey to drink, he must make do with a call of nature.

Hard on the heels of the irrevocable verdict comes apotheosis. Bloom, locked in Zoë's embrace and gaze, imagines himself sweeping along to the sound of pealing bells, as the Lord Mayor of Dublin, in all the pomp and circumstances of a coronation ... only to slip from dream back into nightmare, which declares him Public Enemy Number One. Called to the rescue, Dr. Mulligan exonerates him on grounds of mental illness, explains his onanistic abuses as the result of hereditary epilepsy and, after intravaginal examination, declares this "perversely idealistic" man to be *virgo intacta*. But the medical report, read out by Dr. Dixon, quickly sets things aright:

> Professor Bloom is a finished example of the new womanly man. His moral nature is simple and lovable. Many have found him a dear man, a dear person. He is a rather quaint fellow on the whole, coy though not feebleminded in the medical sense. He has written a beautiful letter, a poem in itself, to the court missionary of the Reformed Priests' Protection Society which clears up everything. He is practically a total abstainer and I can affirm that he sleeps on straw litter and eats the most Spartan food, cold dried grocer's peas. He wears a hairshirt of purest Irish manufacture winter and summer and scourges himself every Saturday. He was, I understand, at one time a firstclass misdemeanant in Glencree reformatory. Another report states that he was a very posthumous child. I appeal for clemency in the name of the most sacred word our vocal organs have ever been called upon to speak. He is about to have a baby.
>
> (General commotion and compassion. Women faint. A wealthy American makes a street collection for Bloom. Gold and silver coins, blank cheques, banknotes, jewels, treasury bonds, maturing bills of exchange, I.O.U.'s, wedding rings, watchchains, lockets, necklaces and bracelets are rapidly collected.)
>
> BLOOM: O, I so want to be a mother.
>
> MRS. THORNTON: (In nursetender's gown) Embrace me tight dear. You'll soon be over it. Tight dear.
>
> (Bloom embraces her tightly and bears eight male yellow and white children.) (II, 190–191)

We are then treated to Bloom's genealogical lineage, that takes after Christ's. Saucy and orgiastic biblical tableaux, Donjuanesque and Faustian scenes tumble over one another in rapid succession, full of the unexpected, minced, interminable, until Bloom falls under the spell of a whorish mistress, Bella Cohen, the muscular and mustachioed matron who, soon addressed as Bello (II, 222), consents to be the slave of his phantasms and to drag her/himself, lower than a sewer rat, down into depravity where sadomasochist kitsch trades blows with bazaar-style metaphysics. Having reached the depths of his degeneration, Bloom must face his daughter and his wife, while Stephen Dedalus, having joined his adoptive father on the thirty-sixth floor below in a state of dead drunkenness, encounters the hideous specter of his mother come to warn him against hellfire and exhort him to repent. Stephen sends his "chewer of corpses" (II, 271) packing with a ringing *non serviam* (II, 271). The statue of the Commendatore cannot be far away. In fact, under the benevolent ægis of Edward VII, a battle to the death between Stephen, champion of Ireland, and the soldiers of His Gracious Majesty, is in preparation. The Homeric confrontation turns into a street fight, and the hellish night of Walpurgis ends pathetically on the sidewalk. So concludes the second part (Book II).

Part 3 (or Book III) opens on Bloom in a state of perplexity, indecent in his sobriety, wondering how he will drag Stephen's rag-clad body to cover. Bloom finally succeeds in getting his protégé to walk, half-pushing, half-dragging him, drunk and gasping for breath, to the coachmen's coffee house, the establishment at nearest remove from Stephen's place of collapse. Suddenly, décor and style shift. The beverage that claims to be coffee is revolting, but people there are chatting animatedly, telling tall tales in quiet voices altogether happily. A self-styled sailor buttonholes his fellow-customers and regales them with his exploits while the proprietor looks on with a mixture of vigilance and indulgence. It is not long before the excess and incoherence of his stories fade into the quiet indifference of his listeners. In total contrast with the riotous, surrealistic epic of the night in Mabott Street, people slowly return to normal in the dark expectation of dawn's first light. The quotidian takes on a truculent density while life, life as the regulars and the passers-by speak, invent and live it, throbs with an irresistible force.

In a similar vein Bloom invites Stephen, who has nowhere to go, to sleep it off at his place. The account of their return is cast in the ironic form of a police investigation, or interrogation, during which the narrator (perhaps on his own behalf) testifies to the accuracy of the facts, by way of restoring a certain distance from events without lessening their intensity. Still without his key, which he had left in his other trousers that morning, the husband sneaks like a thief into the conjugal domicile. Again and yet again daily life in its tiniest details—a place for everything and everything in its place—are invested with succulent truthfulness and finely nuanced funniness. Stephen duly fed and departed, Bloom slips between his wife's bed sheets where he feels the warm-still imprint of the just-departed lover. The book ends with the marvelous and justly famous monologue in which Molly reminisces about her meeting with Leopold and her life with him. For all his faults, she celebrates their love and renews her acquiescence in their marriage, in a magnificent hymn punctuated by a series of reverberating, life-affirming yeses.

> O that awful deepdown torrent O and the sea the sea crimson sometimes like fire and the glorious sunsets and the figtrees in the Alameda gardens yes and all the queer little streets and the pink and blue and yellow houses and the rosegardens and Jessamine and geraniums and cactuses and Gibraltar as a girl where I was a Flower of the mountain yes when I put the rose in my hair like the Andalusian girls used to shall I wear a red yes and how he kissed me under the Moorish wall and I thought well as well him as another and then I asked him with my eyes to ask again yes and then he asked me would I yes to say yes my mountain flower and first I put my arms around him yes and drew down to me so he could feel my breasts all perfume yes and his heart was going like mad and yes I said yes I will Yes. (II, 538)

So ends *Ulysses*. So powerfully do its final three chapters, simple and suggestive in their verve, immerse us in existence that we almost end up regretting that the entire narrative has not been made of the same stuff. But the third part would not perhaps have its full evocative force, its prodigious effect of truth, were it not preceded by what we can only call the delirium of prose progressively unchained. Its very excess fulfills a function. But that having been said, the exaggeration cannot be reduced to its functional aspect alone; its sole aim is not to sound the rising scale of the fantastic, the grotesque, and the surreal. The splitting asunder of the narration, the explosion of narrative prose, and the mocking laughter they convey are in fact the book's true subject; they form—or deform—the core message of *Ulysses*.

For this book is, first and foremost and perhaps definitively, a farce of monumental proportions, a swift kick in the behind at literature, and to an even greater extent, at literary criticism. Starting with the title: a masterstroke whose impact quickly exceeded the author's wildest dreams. Who will be able to establish, incontrovertibly and in absolute seriousness, buttressed with the minutest detail and the most solid references, the parallels between the adventures of Ulysses and the misadventures of Leopold Bloom? Balderdash! As Raymond Queneau has judiciously observed about *Bouvard and Pécuchet*, all great works of fiction can be seen as an Iliad, or as an Odyssey, or even, one is tempted to add, as a mixture of both. Joyce's novel is no more, and no less, Homeric than a whole slew of others, and several passages excepted (including the earthshaking throw of the biscuitbox), substantial amounts of indulgence, patience, and inventiveness are needed to establish the correspondences certain critics seem to take for granted between *Ulysses* and its "model." But Joyce's masterwork draws its subversive power from the fact that those points of correspondence cannot be taken for granted, that they do not resist close examination, that a yawning gap separates the two works.

Still, even in a reading that attempts to free the text to the maximum possible extent from its author's ghost, it is hard to ignore Joyce's original intention to head each of his novel's eighteen "chapters" with a title drawn from an episode or a character from the *Odyssey* (*Telemachus, Nestor, Proteus, Calypso*, etc.)[102] There is every reason to believe that those references were vitally important to him, that he did not lightly suppress them, and that the parallels between Ulysses' journey and Bloomsday, far from being critical inventions, were as deliberate as they were necessary. Necessary for Joyce in constructing his book: the Homeric plot-line underlies and encompasses an unbridled enterprise that threatens to run out of control, a precaution not necessarily shared by the reader. But Homer functions as more than a simple rein; his epic provides the frame of reference that liberates Joyce's novel from the restraints of realism; with it he can deploy his entire palette, and lend the fullest possible relief to his principal character who, in his feminine, mild-mannered self-doubting masculinity, torn by doubt about his own paternity, stands at furthest remove from a tribal chief or a warrior. In fact, he is their exact antithesis. All he can lay claim to from Ulysses is the alias with which the Homeric hero deceives the Cyclops: Bloom is *no one*. And as he is no one in particular he is everyone; because he is also unlike anyone else, and fundamentally inimitable he is no less deceptive than his namesake in his peaceable marginality. Only those who choose not to see will be misled by his emblematic insignificance.

Only in a spirit of gentle mockery can the story of Bloom's peregrinations assume the name of the *Odyssey*'s namesake—precisely because the two

---

102. A complete and useful listing of these references can be found on page xxxiii of Declan Kiberd's introduction to the Penguin edition used here.

journeys are so utterly unlike, in their form and in their place, in the events they relate, and in its characters. In truth, the two tales resemble one another only in the stratagems they employ. Ulysses, after all, is the man of a thousand wiles; Joyce, by the same token, is just as wily with regard to his readers — and perhaps even with regard to himself! The ruse is so effective that we can recognize in Bloom a kind of anti-Ulysses, a townsman who, in his own way, must marshal a thousand wiles, mental as well as geographical. In like manner, Molly makes a paradoxical Penelope who, for all her unfaithfulness, still remains fundamentally faithful to her plucky husband. Bloom flirts with life like Ulysses with danger and both, each on his own level, are lovers of existence, of its unexpectedness, and of its light. But the analogy can only be carried so far, and can only stand by virtue of its contrasts and antimonies. There is nothing glorious about Bloom, and everything about his odyssey is frankly ridiculous. Above and beyond the facetious reference to Homer, however, the meaning and the extent of the banality, of the ridiculousness, are the elements in *Ulysses* that warrant reflection.

As with every great story death hovers constantly over *Ulysses*. But the desire to tell the tale — Joyce himself excepted, of course — has very little to do with the need to leave one's footsteps behind, to survive in the memory of men. It is for this reason that death, which surges to the surface repeatedly in the course of the day, returns again and again like a pathetic, petty refrain, in the form of the conventional regrets expressed by everyone for that poor man Dignam, who will soon be, or who has just been, buried. Each one will utter his bit of doggerel, sighs Bloom after his first encounter, with a banality that gives a foretaste of the thinness of the human relationships that lie in wait for our solitary walker. In a more general sense, the restraint of the often-elliptical dialogues stands in sharp contrast to the effusiveness of the interior mono-logues that, of necessity, rub shoulders yet never cross-pollinate. There are times, of course, when a character will run on, like Stephen in the library, or blather on, like the self-styled sailor in the coachmen's pub, but those set-piece speeches, those unordered narratives are nothing but the audible extension of all that their speakers are constantly ruminating upon in silence.

The subject of our silent ruminations cannot, however, be grasped from a single viewpoint, or, more precisely, from a lone listening post. The narra-tion that carries them to our ears can be no less disjointed and discontinuous than life itself. An absence at first imperceptible, then increasingly visible and startling, emerges: the absence of a *single* narrator. There are, of course, *several* narrators, who often take up where the other has left off before the reader has even noticed. But it eventually becomes clear that now the hero, now another of the leading characters, and sometimes no one (another possible wink at Ulysses) is telling the story. Someone is telling a tale, or telling his own story; someone who says, "I" and, for all intents and purposes, participates in the scene he is witnessing, but whose identity we will never know. That *I* is not the author. The author does not tell the story, he causes the story to be told; he delegates, as if the reader himself were being called upon to become an eyewitness to the events, the spoken and unspoken thoughts in constant circulation; as if he himself, the reader, must reconstruct from the fragments of the scene that he is reading, as though he possesses the magical capability of entering into other people's minds. This perpetual fragmentation and disorganization of the narrative is an invitation to the reader to create. He, in fact, is the only one who can lend a certain coherence to a narration totally lacking in it. We may even venture that the author has done everything he can to make the task impossible. No other novel before it, to my knowledge (except perhaps Sterne's *Tristram Shandy*), makes the reader work so hard. That work can, over time, take its toll.

Ulysses, for all the corrosive humor that pervades it, contains passages that are frankly exasperating. Curiously, from one reading to another, we do not always find exasperation in the same place, but it will unfailingly arise; if not now, later on. Fast flowing associations (often of a jubilatory richness and accuracy), elisions, overlappings, enumerations (that induce gales of laughter), puns ... all end up losing their freshness from repetition. What was at first bracing ends up numbing the intellect. I would have great difficulty believing the person who would tell me he had never experienced such feelings on contact with *Ulysses*, especially at first reading; I know more than a few open-minded, time-tempered, and alert readers who, with all the good will in the world, have never made their way past page thirty.

It may well be, as an iconoclastic British critic has recently claimed,[103] that Joyce put his immense talent to immensely bad use. But it is hard for me to believe that, coming from a writer of such immense ability, while not seeking at all costs to absolve him, we are dealing with an immense case of shenanigans. Nor do I believe that we hold in our hands the uneven product of a crippled genius, even though I long flirted with the eventuality. Joyce could have written a wonderful book, a fabulous book if only ...

No. The difficulty of its reading, including all that is arbitrary and mind-deadening about it, is deliberate, willed. I cannot, of course, make such an assertion with full certainty. Joyce may well have been overwhelmed by his astonishing inventiveness, trapped by his own delirium. Were that the case, we

103. Dale Peck, "It all went wrong with Joyce," in the *Daily Telegraph*, London, August 2, 2004.

would be dealing with an overblown reputation sustained by an extraordinary degree of intellectual snobbery. But this hypothesis interests me not at all, for it casts not the slightest light on the work; furthermore, that same work has undeniably had—and continues to have—a considerable, though hard-to-measure impact on the course of Western literature. I begin with the hypothesis that Joyce consciously brought his entire talent to bear on destabilizing his readers; to that end, he took the premeditated risk of irritating them, of making them stop reading. No other hypothesis makes sense.

Seen from that perspective, what are we to make of *Ulysses*? An enterprise of erudition and rigor, as bizarre as the resonance of its words, that offers nothing less than the destruction of all narrative coherence. Not the end of the modern novel, but the systematic annihilation of a certain—let us call it classical (modern included)—form of narrative. Insofar as narrative generates meaning, it necessarily constructs or reconstructs something readable, something coherent from the formless magma that make up, in their unrefined state, human thought and action—the "tale told by an idiot, full of sound and fury, signifying nothing" that Shakespeare invokes at the beginning of *Macbeth*. It is not for nothing that the specter of Shakespeare, far more than that of Homer, hovers over *Ulysses*. For it is Shakespeare who is constantly torn between the two worlds, poised on the razor's edge that separates madness from reason, order from disorder, coherence from incoherence. We might even venture that Shakespeare attempts, paradoxically, to lend coherence to an inherently untenable situation, to render readable the threatening imbalance that constantly threatens to drive man into insanity.

Joyce goes one step further. The Shakespearean endowment of meaning remains strong; coherence eventually triumphs, if only because Shakespeare helps us to understand madness while at the same time setting out the often indistinct boundaries that separate it from reason. *Ulysses* attempts to escape the chalk circle that imprisons life, or that, more exactly, divides it into two opposing parts. Life cannot be arbitrarily divided: in it, both madness and reason, meaning and non-meaning, are indissolubly interrelated. Here, and here alone, from afar, like a profound but distant sense of kinship, the fading echo of Homer's tale reaches our ears: Ulysses, let us remember, is by no means the master of his fate; as "nursling of the gods" he is dependent entirely upon them, and for all his power, for all his wiles, can achieve nothing without the help of Athena.

But the world of *Ulysses* is most assuredly a world without gods; a world in which the Homeric hero, who is totally lost, can do nothing more than accept his fate. Accepting fate is precisely what Joyce's prose violently, joyously, irrevocably refuses to do. Life, life itself as we endure it, as we bite into it, as we spit it out, as we consume it, and as at the end we lose it without further recourse, but also life as we dream of it, the life of our minds above all else, does not accept fate. The cruelty and magnificence, the vivacity of life can only be grasped in its disorder, and any attempt, literary or otherwise, to bring order to it, to classify it into categories, that knowingly seeks to invest it with meaning, is either a falsehood, or is bound to fail before it has even begun. *Ulysses* thus stands before us as a novel whose intention is to breathe life into life, to render life in its newborn disorder, in its principalian discontinuity and disorganization, to reproduce life in all its rawness; in its chaos, and its incoherence.

But life in the raw, if the expression is to mean anything, cannot by definition be grasped; any attempt to reproduce it is illusory—particularly by the word. By the written word! Speech and writing are part of life; life produces them. But that portion of life that life produces cannot reproduce the life in whose living complexity and lively disorder it is a full participant. All language, unless it ceases to be language, that is to say, ceases to be comprehensible for any and all including the speaker; all language, all words, constitute an attempt, with varying degrees of success, to impose order. *Ulysses* has nothing to say about life in the raw; it is circumscribed, like any poem, by the unspoken. For all its verve, it can provide only the faintest reflection of life. But its subversive power remains great—I am tempted to say intact—when we compare it with more conventional ways of telling the tale of life. *Ulysses* comes alive in and of its own internal life, as a novel; it confronts us as a prodigious upsurge only *by virtue of the fact that literature exists*. It is a book that feeds—permanently—precisely upon what it attempts by all possible means to destroy. We can only deconstruct that which has been constructed. Deconstruction, like it or not, is necessarily reconstruction. Joyce knows this better than anyone. Yet another reason why, as he moves from one style to another, he has not the slightest fear of writing *well*; he hasn't the slightest hesitation at making himself perfectly and magnificently readable; in a word, almost classical, and finally, coherent. Not only is there coherence in his incoherence, but incoherence itself is organically distributed in such a way that the book as a whole holds together. On second reading, the way in which his destructuring has been organized is more readily apparent. It is quite possible to demonstrate, and there can be little doubt that the critics have done their utmost to do so, Joyce's extreme attention to detail in structuring his novel—quite independent of any Homeric references. Scenes, words, images, and associations continuously call out and reply, in visual and aural reverberations that make the head spin.

Truth to tell, so intensely does the head spin that the reader often feels like a boxer who has lingered too long in the ring. Whether or not this was Joyce's intention is of secondary importance. Nothing can force the reader to read the book at one sitting (even though such an experience, assuming it to were possible, might well have great richness). Every reader is free to take a breather, and then step back into the ring to resume the match. Then, too, we must know how to take pleasure from the struggle without attempting to win. To wish to "vanquish" *Ulysses*, to get the best of it, read it from cover to cover, to attempt to understand it in its superabundance, is an enterprise doomed to failure. *Ulysses*, like any great novel, should be read for the simple pleasure of reading. But this pleasure, like life itself, is not easily acquired. Like any intense joy, it does not come without suffering.

Far from killing the modern novel, *Ulysses* has opened boundless space before it. A risk-fraught venture itself, an opening of such breadth can carry with it disillusion or even bitterness. In those passages where the narrative may seem excessively excessive in its excess and then drop off into insignif-icance, it may well have a truly destructive effect: it may kill the desire to read, the desire to write, and finally, the desire to live. But the bitterness of such a state of nullity, paradoxically, can only affect those who praise Joyce and his work to the skies, who make of it the *nec plus ultra* of all literary endeavors. No author, not even the most ferocious—and Joyce no more than anyone else—warrants such an excess of honor. To claim *"après lui le deluge"* is to assert that Joyce has killed literature. Yet that would be beyond any mortal's ability to achieve. But to say such a thing would be to condemn his work to death. Worse yet, we would be depriving ourselves of the liberty it lays before us.

There can be little doubt that *Ulysses* is a thorny thicket where one can easily lose one's way, can become easily entangled. If its true hero is language itself, as is often claimed, we are reminded that all language is a kind of labyrinth from which one cannot extricate oneself, a succession of infinitely multiplying references in which it is easy to lose one's mind. The tool of reason can become the instrument of its loss. Such loss, a threat that spares no one, is not the property of any particular work of literature. One can similarly not extricate oneself from Joyce's novel, as one cannot from language itself, whatever language, whoever might attempt to exhaust it. Whether we are talking about *Ulysses* in particular, or language in general, such an achievement—against which the quest for the Holy Grail seems like mere child's play—would amount to dismissing the unspeakable. It is because the ineffable cannot be reduced to any particular kind of expression, that all language is simultaneously dearth and hidden abundance, constraint and liberty. Indeed, we should read *Ulysses*, but we should do so freely, joyfully, eager to venture into the infinite maze of its words, free to leap from page to page, free to take it as we wish, free to relish it as we would a prism that makes visible the inexhaustible spectrum of colors immobilized in each ray of light.

Ours, as readers, is a liberty that has no other goal than itself. But gratuitousness and the enjoyment of the game have their limitations. It might be possible, even desirable to live life as a game; to live in a state of constant high humor is far from self-evident, and can only be achieved with rigorous discipline. "Game" does not mean facility; easy games leave us cold. The game of life holds out cruel surprises for even the best tempered souls, even the most detached minds; it reveals unexpected, poignant beauties that are difficult, if not impossible, to ignore. But one day the game will end, and when that time comes, no one can be certain that he will be able to accept it.

No one knows what his last moment will be. It is no accident that fear of death weaves its way like a red thread through *Ulysses*. Mortal uncertainty slumbers wakefully even in the wisest among us. In it originates the tragic unrest that rises to the surface in moments of trial. Those moments, and the way we deal with them, place us four-square before what we have made of ourselves; they prod us with the question of what we call, for want of a better term, the meaning of our life. That is why literature exists. For life is in constant search of meaning; and meaning, under constant threat, can never be taken for granted. Literature must do far more than indulge in mockery or gratuitousness. Literature, even when it is making sport of its own pretensions, and perhaps particularly at such times, cannot go on, cannot exist except by relating something grave or marvelous, something beyond itself. Literature owes its vitality to its refusal to turn its back on all that escapes it. What better reason—in spite of his best efforts—for us not to turn our backs on Joyce.

16

PROUST:
THE ABOLITION OF TIME

A N INSTANT; A KISS. Everything turns on an instant that never comes. Or comes too late, as the poisoned reward of sickly anticipation. Downstairs, the adults are dawdling over their meal, and are only now sampling the pistachio ice cream. Upstairs, in his room, the child waits, yearns; he appoints Françoise as his emissary to carry a note that will never be answered. Years pass; the narrator still awaits the moment when mother will come to kiss him goodnight. No, not really the narrator; not just yet. He who waits is the failed author.[104] And yet someone else—Albertine, the love of his life—is the object of his desire. But the teller of the tale, he who speaks in the first person singular, already knows what the reader does not. He speaks; he has found the words by grasping something that we will learn only at the end, a discovery that remains concealed in the very writing that has made it possible. In the interval between waiting for his mother and waiting for his mistress (Albertine), time has unwound its sterile spindle and, were it not for the torments of jealousy, the mistress herself would little more than embellish the futile passing of days and years, which owe what little consistency they possess to the amorous anticipation that courses through them.

---

104. As we will see, the use of the term "narrator" may be a source of confusion. He who speaks, even though he has already completed the journey that he invites us to complete along with him, narrates it as though he were discovering it at the same time as the reader. For reasons of simplicity, to avoid weighty paraphrasing, I will be using the word narrator to designate the "I" of which the narrator speaks, and who is not, strictly speaking, the "I" who is telling the tale. For the same reasons, I will occasionally use the first name Marcel, which is only rarely employed in *Remembrance of Things Past*, as being that of the narrator, to distinguish the character "being told" from he who, later, will write. In this perspective, "Marcel" never refers to Proust himself, but to the diversity of "I's" that comprised the narrator before the act of writing.

In time's flow, however, arise those rarest of occasions when marks, signs[105] of that inexpressible object, which when sighted will confirm in the child, the young man, and ultimately the adult, each in turn, to understand that literature has passed him by, that he will never write. He is preceded on the path toward dilettantism by a certain Swann, an aesthete appreciated by the high society of the Faubourg Saint-Germain, the same person whose presence had deprived the child of his mother's kiss. Involuntarily Swann points out to the young Marcel the vanity of the world that awaits and draws him to it. But what draws him is only incidentally the social whirl; when all is said and done it is love that dangles its irresistible bait. Between two moments of what will become his passion for Albertine, the young man is taken with the image of Madame de Guermantes, just as Swann, that devoted admirer of the duchess and of the Guermantes family, had once been smitten with the figure of Odette. The difference is that Swann will win Odette, while the narrator will lose Albertine. The winning is illusory; the loss, necessary. Swann marries Odette after having ceased to love her, while the death of Albertine plunges the narrator into mourning, then into a void where the signs can rise once again to the surface and, at last, swanlike spread their wings.

Swann, which lengthens "swan" by a single consonant, is a deceptive and ambiguous sign. From (almost) the beginning his presence is capital. Everything begins and ends with him. Above all else he is the world, the great world present incognito in the little world of Combray, where the narrator's family regularly vacations. The family members know nothing of their occasional visitor's worldly success; in their eyes he is a failure, a man who has contracted a bad marriage, whose wife has betrayed him with a certain Monsieur Charlus (Swann's first name is Charles) who, like Swann himself, will reappear in the narrator's life in an entirely different light. Swann is indeed a failure, but in a way that only the narrator will much later be able to grasp. For the time being, Swann is a social success of whom little is known, and an unconscious instrument. His presence in the narrative is that of an obstacle and an intermediary. As a visitor, he is an obstacle: his presence restricts the mother's availability; the gift of the kiss, or more properly, its absence and its impossibility, depend upon him. As an intermediary, it is through his good offices that art and the world of letters enter into the young Marcel's life. Through him, as well, arises his first love Gilberte, Swann's only child with Odette.

---

105. Signs masterfully analyzed by Gilles Deleuze in *Proust and Signs, The Complete Text*, trans. Richard Howard (Minneapolis: University of Minnesota Press, 2003).

In Search of Lost Time (Remembrance of Things Past) opens along *Swann's Way*. Along this way, as along the Guermantes' way, a longer stroll that one could take when the weather is fine, we encounter all that nourishes the narrator's childhood: the smells of the countryside and the colorations of time, the intensity of emotion and the zest of reading, the joy of writing and the incurable feeling of powerlessness with which his literary ambition collides. His first loves—women, flowers, churches, walks, books—are interrupted, leading into a lengthy, apparently unrelated episode inserted into the text: a novel within a novel entitled *Swann in Love*. Many read it separately, while others prefer to pass over it completely. But as a timesaving strategy, it carries no weight: it is Charles Swann's passion for Odette de Crécy that casts its light over *Remembrance*, looking both forward and back into the past.

Ahead lies the narrator's adolescent and adult lives. Behind him, as we have seen, lies the childhood kiss denied; long has it saturated in its distress the sole portion of the house at Combray to remain alive in the narrator's emotional memory: that narrow vertical section connecting the garden, the salon, and the staircase leading to the bedroom. The remainder of the décor exists only in the pain-free memory that transmits exact information about the past, and that " preserve nothing of the past itself" (47).[106] Only by way of a gustatory rediscovery, a chance encounter with the long-forgotten taste of a madeleine dipped into a cup of the linden tea that his aunt prepares for him, only on contact with the textured fragrance that had kept alive within it the vividness neither time nor habit could tarnish, do the rest of the house and the surrounding countryside spring back to life.

But that very experience of memory finds itself imprisoned in the confusion of half-sleep and half-wakefulness that hovers so disconcertingly over the waltz of bedrooms in which the narrator has fallen asleep. *Remembrance* begins in the half-light where night and day, consciousness and oblivion are mingled. The sleeper, who often has just closed his eyes on the book that has slipped from his hands, holds "in a circle around him" (3) the worlds in which he has lived and simultaneously confuses them, throwing them together like the elements of the nest he has woven "out of the most diverse materials" (7): a corner of his pillow, the hem of his blanket, an end of a shawl, the edge of his bed, and a copy of a children's paper, *Les Débats roses* (7). In the semi-consciousness of drowsiness, time veers this way and that, blends into itself,

106. Marcel Proust, *Remembrance of Things Past*, trans. C. K. Scott Moncrieff, Terrence Kilmartin, and Andreas Mayor (New York: Random House, 1981), herein referred to as *Remembrance*. In 1995, a new translation, by several distinguished translators, appeared under the Penguin imprint entitled *In Search of Lost Time*. This translation of *Empire of Desire* uses the Scott Moncrieff translation as revised by Terence Kilmartin in homage to its pioneering achievement, but does so without any judgment on the quality of subsequent translations of Proust's masterwork.

superimposes itself, doing and undoing itself until, with the coming of daylight, the sleeper can restore things to their accustomed places in the room he is certain he occupies.

> But scarcely had daylight itself—and no longer the gleam from a last, dying ember on a brass curtain rod which I had mistaken for daylight—traced across the darkness, as with a stroke of chalk across a blackboard, its first white, correcting ray, then the window, with its curtains, would leave the frame of the doorway in which I had erroneously placed it, while, to make room for it, the writing-table, which my memory had clumsily installed where the window ought to be, would hurry off at full speed, thrusting before it the fireplace and sweeping aside the wall of the passage: a little court-yard would occupy the place where, a moment earlier, my dressing room had lain, and the dwelling-place which I had built up for myself in the darkness would have gone to join all those other dwellings glimpsed in the whirlpool of awakening, put to flight by that pale sign traced above my window-curtain by the uplifted forefinger of dawn. (203–204)

Combray (the first part of *Swann's Way*) takes place entirely within the immense parentheses of the waking dream where childhood memories are reconstructed as though between the two segments of an arch that together prefigure the architecture of the work to come.

Not for the simple pleasure of digression does the narrator, at the end of that first reconstruction, having related his first literary delight, his first aesthetic euphoria at the sight of the belfries of Martinville along the banks of the Vivonne, or at the sight of the rustic front porch at Saint-André-des-Champs, summon as though in passing "by an association of memories" that which, years after having left Combray, he had "been told ... of a love affair in which Swann had been involved before I was born, with a precision of detail which is often easier to obtain for the lives of people who have been dead for centuries than for those of our own most intimate friends" (203). By introducing a novel about Swann, in setting aside his own story for someone else's, the narrator, without letting go the thread of his concerns, departs the domain of pure subjectivity to step into history. For he well knows that Swann's love affair can only be the result of an investigation (the primary Greek meaning of the term *historia*). The investigation is wholly fictional, in the event: we are dealing with a novel. But by asserting his identity as a novelist (or fictional biographer), by claiming the right to speak in detail of another's life, the narrator has provided himself with the master key that will enable him, as his own story unfolds, to open the secret doorways of all his characters. *Remembrance* thus affirms in the clearest possible terms that it is not autobiography. It is invention.

But *Swann in Love* responds to another imperative as well. It prepares the reader for the world into which the narrator himself will be led, in part by Swann: the world of love, the fine world of the Faubourg Saint-Germain, and the little world, the "little clan" of the Verdurins, whom Swann begins to cultivate the better to insinuate himself into Odette's confidence. Swann is to the narrator what the narrator would have been had he never written. But the dandy does not merely embody the vanity of the social whirl and the false plenitude of amorous anxiety. He also introduces the theme of the artistic life, brought together in its two contradictory aspects in the Verdurins' salon where art, in its reflection of the camaraderie that welds the little clan together, is at once counterfeit and authentic. The first is that of a loutish and uninteresting painter named Biche, whom we will later find transformed, as we do many characters in *Remembrance*; the second is a promising young pianist who prefigures Morel the violinist, of whom the Verdurins become enamored during the narrator's presence among them. Painting and music are presented in this warm-hearted, caricature-like circle in the form of worldly baubles and as moments of truth.

Biche, the house buffoon and appointed portrait painter to the little clan, will become Elstir, will shape the young Marcel's aesthetic sensibilities and will lead him to see the world in a different light. The pianist plays the *andante* of a sonata in D-sharp by an unknown composer, a certain Vinteuil, whose gloomy silhouette the reader has already encountered near Combray, and whom he knows as the failed musician to whom his daughter's licentious attitude brings only heartache. Swann himself, who convinces Odette that he is at work on a study of Van Meer de Delft he had long abandoned, has "squandered his intellectual gifts on frivolous amusements and made use of his erudition in matters of art only to advise society ladies what pictures to buy and how to decorate their houses" (209). His frivolousness (even in his area of expertise) does not stop him (in a register he has not mastered) from being entirely caught up by the sonata, in which he recognizes a work he had heard the preceding year, performed on two instruments (piano and violin) and from which upon hearing had suddenly emerged a phrase, a harmony "that had just been played and that had opened and expanded his soul, as the fragrance of certain roses, wafted upon the moist air of evening, has the power of dilating one's nostrils," and for which he had been filled "with a new and strange desire" (227–228).

As *Swann in Love* begins the musical theme that will become throughout *Remembrance,* Vinteuil's "little phrase" appears for the first time in the form of an intimate thread that winds its way through the entire work. It becomes the "national anthem" of Swann's and Odette's love affair. Albertine will play it on the piano. Again and again it will rise to the surface, as if to recall amorous suffering and opportunities missed. For what it evokes is not simply lost love but another, far more substantial loss. On hearing it for the first time, before hearing it once more at the Verdurins', even before he had learned of its origins, Swann feels in it, like an organic change taking place within him, "the presence of one of those invisible realities in which he had ceased to believe and to which, as though the music had had upon the moral barrenness from which he was suffering a sort of recreative influence, he was conscious once again of the desire and almost the strength to consecrate his life" (230). Yet this same strength is insufficient to make Swann seek out the source from which it sprang; he will soon cease to think about it. It is reborn in the chance amorous encounter that brings him to the Verdurins'. And the same phrase will return, later, to toll the knell for his love when, expelled by the little clan and let drop by Odette, Swann rediscovers its melody in the high society salons his passion had momentarily caused him to set aside.

The little phrase signals the beginning and the end of the amorous sentiment that Swann believes he detects in Odette. It frames the narrative of his love. But it also points to that object along whose way the high society aesthete continually travels; it betrays the capricious, unpredictable, arbitrary character of the signs that point to its ephemeral presence. "Invisible realities" often arise when we least expect them; they can just as well shimmer in the light reflected from the waters of the Vivonne, glitter from a tile roof, echo from one belfry to another as they can unexpectedly bob to the surface of a society reception at which no one, were it not for an *I* who finds itself present only because of lack of anything else to do and whose thoughts are immersed in an entirely different world, makes the effort to capture them.

The principal themes of *Remembrance* are thus contained, in embryonic form, in the false parentheses of *Swann in Love.* Among them, of course, is the central question of time. Several of the characters we will encounter have already appeared in *Combray.* There is Swann, of course, Vinteuil and Odette herself, in the form of a lady in pink, a troubling *demimondaine* whom the young Marcel meets at his uncle's, and who will continue to bedazzle him. Even more numerous are those we will later encounter in his adult existence, figures like Dr. Cottard, who appears to have stepped across the threshold that separates Swann's time from that of the narrator with as much ease as one steps into the Verdurins' salon. Like the worthy doctor, virtually all the characters we have already encountered reappear years later without so much as an apparent wrinkle—an immutability that accentuates the signs of ageing that the narrator suddenly discovers on their faces at the end of the tale. Above and beyond creating the effect of a sharp break, this improbable chronology surreptitiously introduces a first abolition, a first dislocation of time. Insofar as they do not die, as the prolonged absence of the narrator does not suddenly reveal in them the decrepitude of advancing years, the characters of *Remembrance* exist in a kind of eternal present, in a state of indeterminate and near-suspended time. Not immune to change, the changes they undergo are less due to age than they are the fruit, in the narrator, of the slow maturation through which he had perceived the traits already inscribed upon their faces well before he could read those same traits.

Inevitably, between witness and narrator, there is a constant foreshortening at work: the latter knows what the former still does not, and cannot reveal. But it is impossible for the narrator to ignore what he already knows, since the truth that both motivates and guides his novelist's venture is to be found in this very knowledge. He must then use it cautiously, so as not to divulge prematurely the denouement that reveals it. So it is for time. Time past belongs to the narrator alone, and the *I*, who witnesses both the present and the past that has preceded him, is swept along by the current of a stream whose course and destination are unknown to him. Only the event not yet known, the event to come that—by way of anticipation—will make it possible for him to begin writing, only this event will lead him to understand the workings of time, which the artist he senses at last being born in himself is led to measure and to undo. It is the decisive experience acquired that, suddenly investing art and literature with meaning in his eyes, enables the narrator to take liberties with time, veer off on short cuts and undertake associations whose full scope nothing, at this stage, makes it possible for the reader to understand. The reader will come upon it only at journey's end when the narrator discovers, long after having abandoned the search, the key to his work.

If Swann is the unwitting cause of the child's separation from his mother, the story of his affair with Odette points to the caesura that separates his childhood at Combray from young Marcel's first love for Gilberte, their daughter, whom he encounters along the Champs-Élysées. Yet continuity between the two periods does exist. Indeed, it is at Combray where, in an instant of overpowering attraction, he recognizes his name, hears it spoken for the first time through a hedgerow of hawthorn that borders Swann's way. She casts him a glance that has every appearance of disdain, and gestures indecently in his direction in a way he takes as insolence before she is sharply reprimanded by "a lady in white whom I had not seen until that moment, while, a little way beyond her, a gentleman in a suit of linen 'ducks,' whom I did not know either, stared at me with eyes which seemed to be starting from his head" (154). The young Marcel grasps, from a scornful remark by his grandfather that the lady is Swann's wife who has remained alone with "her Charlus," a character whose same rapacious gaze he will re-experience, as an adolescent, fixed upon him, during his first bathing holiday at Balbec.

What a locus of intense condensation is this hawthorn hedge, whose full ramifications still elude the *I* that strolls along it. The instant combines the inimitable and fragile beauty of flowers, the fierce, and initially painful ordeal of love, the mistaking of the feelings of the love object, the misleading appearances of social life, with the predatory gaze of the Baron de Charlus, where the homosexuality he still believes he has concealed from the eyes of the world has already reared its head. Marcel can no better understand the stare of this gentleman, clad in linen duck, than he can Gilberte's, which will only reveal its significance decades later: the crude gesture, precipitated by the fear that it will be seen by his parents, was an invitation to the audacity in which he could not yet believe and which, judging by the hostile glance that she receives in return, she believed that he had not wished for. Up to and including those critical moments that can transform the course of their existence, human beings cannot understand one another; they fail to meet one another half way. Or they only understand one another much later, when the amorous ego for which such-and-such a gesture, such and such a glance has ceased to exist, replaced by an ego that has become indifferent to the person that his distant predecessor once loved. Yet another example of the kind of narrative impossibility in which the narrator constantly finds himself in relation to the person he was and in whose shoes he never completely succeeds in placing himself. What he relates, on principle, is not and cannot be what he has experienced.

The story told by *Remembrance* is, in other words, untellable. *I* cannot tell the story of my *ego*. The same holds true for individuals, and for peoples as well: their lives cannot, strictly speaking, be narrated. As the narrator himself repeatedly cautions, the ego that lives is separated from the ego that is telling the story by all the intermediary egos of which he knows nothing, and which eventually join one another in awareness of their succession, of their irreducibility and of their problematic unity only in the face of death. Not only do we wrongly decode the signals sent by others, neither do we know what it is exactly that we have experienced; we do not know this life that, with so little thought, we claim as our own, and which we imagine ourselves to possess only through a kind of unconscious swelling of the ego that believes, at every turn, that it subsumes within itself all those that have preceded it. We cannot rule out that *Remembrance*, in its attempt to capture something resembling the essence or the permanence of the ego, does not in fact lay bare before our eyes its dispersion and its inanity. For all that, the narrator wishes to believe that continuity is possible and, consequently, that there may be something enduring about the person. But neither endurance nor unity are self-evident nor can they be taken as given; they must be conquered, and can only be achieved at the cost of a long struggle: a struggle with oneself, with the multiplicity of egos drawn up at regular intervals in time, a struggle against time itself in which events, other people, nature, and the world send out signals as enigmatic as they are contradictory.

The only apparently indisputable, immediate truth that the young Marcel receives and retains from the stroll that leads him now along Swann's way, when rain threatens, now along the Guermantes way, when the sun is shining, is raw, unwrought truth that owes much to his bedazzlement by nature. But nature itself remains vague, ephemeral, confused; it leaves behind nothing enduring, nothing to satisfy the spirit as long as we do not pay it our undivided attention, as long as thought makes no effort to delve into its manifestations. No more than do humans, nature does not speak for itself, and its beauties, like the flowering hawthorn hedge, are by no means devoid of cruelty. Vegetables, minerals, and landscapes send us indecipherable messages that we do not know how to answer, and which we will only be able to understand years later after painstaking effort that may well go unrewarded. All by way of saying that *Remembrance* does not tell the narrator's (or narrators') life story. It tells the story of the effort to achieve the inner truth to which the beauty of the world summons him and which nothing can promise him, like Saint Augustine's grace, that he will receive.

That truth is precisely what Marcel despairs of ever attaining. The sense of his incapability grows stronger over time as chance places along his path powerful indications whose importance he cannot fail to realize, and yet whose meaning he can never determine. For all that, the first of them (first not in terms of the chronology of events, but in terms of the narrative), the episode of the madeleine dipped into the decoction of lime-blossom—the most celebrated, most clichéd piece of the entire *Remembrance*—opens a breach that seems in many ways decisive. It administers a vital lesson in memory to the young man who has not yet entirely abandoned the idea of becoming a writer. By bringing to life the "forgotten" details of life at Combray, it directs our eyes toward the abyss that separates conventional from emotional memory, which lies dormant where the quotidian has left it at rest. If the sight of the madeleine awakens nothing, it is because it has repeatedly displayed its "severe, religious folds" on the trays in pastryshops' windows.

> But when from a long distance past nothing subsists, after the people are dead, after the things are broken and scattered, taste and smell alone, more fragile but more enduring, more unsubstantial, more persistent, more faithful, remain poised a long time, like souls, remembering, hoping, amid the ruins of all the rest; and bear unflinchingly, in the tiny and almost impalpable drop of their essence, the vast structure of recollection. (51)

The ego that rediscovers in the taste of the madeleine this vast structure makes no attempt to deepen the raw, inexplicable happiness its flavor awakens in him above all else, as though he lacked the strength to carry on the sustained effort that he has already expended to connect his sense of taste with the places and events that play randomly across his palette before extracting "town and gardens alike" (51) from his teacup. What has been lost is not time, but the enduring understanding of a mysterious joy that from the very first bite, before even the concrete resurgence of memory, delivers up a vital part of its secret:

> An exquisite pleasure had invaded my senses, something isolated, detached, with no suggestion of its origin. And at once the vicissitudes of life had become indifferent to me, its disasters innocuous, its brevity illusory—this new sensation having had on me the effect which love has of filling me with a precious essence; or rather, the essence was not in me, it *was* me. I had ceased now to feel mediocre, contingent, mortal. (48)

A like feeling floods over the child at Combray when, seated next to the coachman on the return home in late afternoon, he contemplates in the fading light the dance performed, at every turn and rise, by the two steeples of Martinville and the belfry of Vieuxvicq. In the intoxication of the moment, the child sets down as he goes a page describing the scene of enchantment, making no particular effort to separate the pleasure of words from the pleasure of things, and experiences at that moment his first literary joy. Having completed his composition, *I* "so filled with happiness, I felt that I had entirely relieved my mind of its obsession with the steeples and the mystery which lay behind them" that, as though he "were a hen and had just laid an egg," he beings to sing at the top of his voice (198–199). That page, which the narrator copies almost without modification is striking in its descriptiveness. The images are beautifully drawn, precise, suggestive, but aside from a metaphor in which the steeples become "three maidens in a legend, abandoned in a solitary place over which night had begun to fall," nothing of what they conceal, not even the simple fact that they might conceal something, rises to the surface.

When, later on, this prose poem is shown to Monsieur de Norpois, a friend of his father's and a career diplomat invited to dinner at his parents', the important personage will detect the negative influence of the young Marcel's favorite author, Bergotte, whose superficiality and decadence he deplores. It is then that a double misunderstanding takes root. On the one hand, the diplomat encourages the father to allow his son to seek a career in the promising path of letters by depicting it in a utilitarian and opportunistic light, where the selflessness of art for art's sake has no place. On the other, several of Monsieur de Norpois's criticisms of his young friend correspond, before the fact, with the narrator's reflections, as a mature man, on the "literature of description" as practised by the Goncourt brothers, for which he will feel, once again, such a sad lack of talent.

The youthful future narrator's only attempt at literary creation meets with the disapproval of the very person who encourages him to pursue a literary career, but above all, there is something as incomplete as it is superficial in his display of virtuoso writing. It goes no deeper than the surface of things, expends no effort to delve deeper into his mysterious headiness at the sight of the three steeples. Young Marcel is happy enough to have prettily jotted down his impressions, happy to be *relieved* of the enigma and of the effort of digging deeper. He bursts into song, as proud as the hen with her egg, satisfied in the end, at having laid down almost exactly the opposite of that which writing requires. Free, for once, of regrets at having passed the essential by, he has unconsciously missed it once more.

His satisfaction is passing, and altogether exceptional. Disappointment, the feeling of absence, and the sadness of loss dominate most of his aesthetic emotions. The most tragic manifestation of that impotence is expressed in the enigmatic, despairing gesticulation of the three trees that the narrator encounters during an outing by coach with his grandmother and Madame de Villeparisis in the environs of Balbec.

We came down towards Hudimesnil; and suddenly I was overwhelmed with a profound happiness which I had not felt since Combray, a happiness analogous to that which had been given me by—among other things—the steeples of Martinville. But this time it remained incomplete. I had just seen, standing a little way back from the hog's-back road along which we were traveling, three trees which probably marked the entry to a covered driveway and formed a pattern which I was not seeing for the first time....

I looked at the three trees; I could see them plainly, but my mind felt that they were concealing something which I could not grasp, as when an object is placed out of reach, so that our fingers, stretched out at arm's-length, can only touch for a moment its outer surface, without managing to take hold of anything. Then we rest for a little while before thrusting out our arm with renewed momentum, and trying to reach an inch or two further. But if my mind was then to collect itself, to gather momentum, I should have to be alone. What would I not have given to be able to draw aside as I used to do on those walks along the Guermantes way, when I detached myself from my parents! I felt indeed that I ought to do so. I recognized that kind of pleasure which requires, it is true, a certain effort on the part of the mind, but in comparison with which the attractions of the indolence which inclines us to renounce that pleasure seem very slight. That pleasure, the object of which I could only dimly feel, which I must create for myself, I experienced only on rare occasions, but on each of these it seemed to me that the things that had happened in the meantime were of little importance, and that in attaching myself to the reality of that pleasure alone could I at length begin to lead a true life.... Where had I looked at them before? There was no place near Combray where an avenue opened off the road like that. Nor was there room for the site which they recalled to me in the scenery of the place in Germany where I had gone one year with my grandmother to take the waters. Was I to suppose, then, that they came from years already so remote in my life that the landscape which surrounded them had been entirely obliterated from my memory and that, like the pages which, with a sudden thrill, we recognize in a book that we imagined we had never read, they alone survived from the forgotten book of my earliest childhood?... And meanwhile, they were coming towards me; perhaps some fabulous apparition, a ring of witches or of Norns who would propound their oracles to me. I chose rather to believe that they were phantoms of the past, dear companions to my childhood, vanished friends who were invoking our common memories. Like ghosts they seemed to be appealing to me to bring them back to life. In their simple and passionate gesticulation I could discern the helpless anguish of a beloved person who has lost the power of speech, and feels that he will never be able to say to us what he wishes to say and we can never guess. Presently, at a cross-roads, the carriage left them. It was bearing me away from what alone I believed to be true, what would have made me truly happy; it was like my life.

I watched the trees gradually recede, waving their despairing arms, seeming to say to me: "What you fail to learn from us today you will never know. If you allow us to drop back into the hollow of the road from which we sought to raise ourselves up to you, a whole part of yourself which we were bringing to you will vanish forever into thin air." And indeed if, in the course of time, I did discover the kind of pleasure and disquiet which I had just felt once again, and if one evening—too late, but then for all time—I fastened myself to it, of those trees themselves I was never able to know what they had been trying to give me nor where else I had seen them. And when, the road having forked and the carriage with it, I turned my back on them and ceased to see them, while Mme de Villeparisis asked me what I was dreaming about, I was as wretched as if I had just lost a friend, had died to myself, had broken faith with the dead or repudiated a god. (771–773)

A loss that is utter, irredeemable. The *for all time* of the fastening affirmed cannot overtake the *too late* that it has just irrevocably fled. The three trees will never return from the emptiness in which their impotent observer has allowed them to vanish, and will keep forever the secret he could never extract from them. No matter how superficial the object of his reverie might seem—three trees alongside a country road—the sense of loss here reaches a peak of absoluteness that transforms it into the umbilicus, the black hole of *Remembrance*. The blissful feeling of immortality experienced by the *I* at the taste of the little madeleine is, at the sight of the trees of Hudimesnil, inverted: *I* there perishes of itself. A death that is almost certainly short-lived, but one that foreshadows that definitive death from whom none will return.

The impact of loss is barely mitigated by the furtive indication that, at some point in time the happiness lost in those trees will be rediscovered lastingly in other circumstances. We have been reminded. From early on, with the experience of the madeleine, the narrator announces that the discovery will be postponed "until much later." From the outset, he leads the reader to expect a decisive event. But the madeleine episode is already one such decisive event, opening as it does a previously restricted narrative space. The evocation of this initial revelation, located at the turning point of the kiss refused and of all Combray brought back to life, launches the story into the totality of the universe of *I*, into his multifaceted existence. Without it, the narrator's memories would have remained trapped in the narrow vertical corridor of pain. Amorous suffering, to which we will return, is one of the most powerful driving forces of the *Remembrance*, but it alone is not enough. There exists as well a secret joy that palpitates and hovers in time and space, that draws the future narrator out of his tribulations and his daily cares toward something far greater, far more powerful, raising *Remembrance* up as it does so to its full stature.

The search for the essence of the elusive happiness that underlies the entire narrative places it under tension as between two poles, as between two founding moments. The first of them we know well, at the beginning of the novel: the flutter of unexpected delight awakened by the famous madeleine dipped into the decoction of lime blossom. The second comes near the end of the story: the stumble caused by the two irregular paving stones at the Guermantes residence, which reminds the visitor of a similar moment of vacillation experienced in the Piazza San Marco, in Venice. At the risk of doing injustice to the indescribable, inexhaustible richness of *Remembrance*, of which only close, repeated reading can convey the merest idea, of which each new reading discovers, in delight, new dimensions, we must now make an immense and near sacrilegious leap to the second moment, in which the narrator, finally realizing what has heretofore escaped him, discovers the meaning of life.

To experience the full importance of this moment, we must have undertaken the long journey of the person who, at the moment when he least expects it, becomes aware of the work to be accomplished. After many years spent in a sanatorium far from society, cut off from the salons he had long attended, after years of medical care about which the narrator is content only to say that he has not been cured, he returns to high society by paying a visit one morning to the Guermantes'. Virtually certain that he will never undertake the task of writing that he has been constantly postponing until the morrow, he reassures himself that there was no point in "forgoing the pleasures of social life."

> This reasoning was, it is true, completely negative and merely deprived of their force those other reasons which might have dissuaded me from going to this fashionable concert. The positive reason that made me decide to go was the name of Guermantes, absent long enough from my mind to be able, when I read it upon the invitation card, to reawaken a ray of my attention, to draw up from the depths of my memory a sort of section of the past of the Guermantes, attended by all the other images of seigniorial forest and tall flowers which at that earlier time of my life had accompanied it, and to reassume for me the charm and the significance which I had found in it at Combray, when, passing along the Rue de l'Oiseau on my way home, I used to see from outside, like some dark laqueur, the window of Gilberte the Bad, Lord of Guermantes. For a moment the Guermantes had once more seemed to me to be totally different from people in society, comparable neither with them nor with any living being, even a reigning prince, creatures begotten of the union of the sharp and windy air of the dark town of Combray in which my childhood had been spent with the past which could be sensed there, in the little street, at the height of the stained-glass window. I had had a longing to go to the Guermantes party as if in going there I must have been brought nearer to my childhood and to the depths of my memory where my childhood dwelt. (887–888)

By an enchantment that the Guermantes cannot, in his eyes, decant into the new mansion that they have built in the Avenue du Bois, and that has an effect today only on their new guests as once did their former mansion on the young Marcel, and by the magic linked for him with that name, the narrator, finding himself in the wrong world, is soothed by the sounds of the old France of his infancy as he makes his way by carriage toward a modern residence of wealthy parvenus. The carriage trip takes him through the long-forgotten streets that he had once traveled with Françoise to the Champs-Élysées, and ends up transporting him like an aviator taking off "toward the silent heights of memory" (890). Those heights, that return to the past, lay the groundwork for the stunning reversal he will experience in the new and incongruous place where it is least likely to happen: in the antechamber of the artificial world that is his destination.

His preparation has been unconscious. As he steps down from the carriage (and from those heights) shortly before the courtyard gate, the narrator meditates upon the lassitude with which no later than the previous evening he had attempted to "note the characteristics of that line which, in a countryside reputed one of the loveliest of France, had separated upon the trunks of the trees the shadow from the light" and recalls ironically Bergotte's advice about his good fortunate, despite his illness: "You have the joys of the mind"— "How mistaken he was about me! How little joy there was in this sterile lucidity!" (898).

> But it is sometimes at the moment when we think that everything is lost that the intimation arrives which may save us; one has knocked at all the doors which lead nowhere, and then one stumbles without knowing it on the only door through which one can enter—which one might have sought in vain for a hundred years— and it opens of its own accord. Revolving the gloomy thoughts which I have just recorded I entered the courtyard of the Guermantes mansion and in my absent-minded state I had failed to see a car which was coming towards me; the chauffeur gave a shout and I just had time to step out of the way, but as I moved sharply backwards I tripped against the uneven paving-stones in front of the coach-house. And at the moment when, recovering my balance, I put my foot on a stone which was slightly lower than its neighbor, all my discouragement vanished and in its place was that same happiness which at various epochs of my life had been given to me by the sight of trees which I had thought that I recognized near Balbec, by the sight of the twin steeples of Martinville, by the flavor of a madeleine dipped in tea, and by all the other sensations of which I have spoken and of which the last works of Vinteuil had seemed to me to combine the quintessential character. Just as, at the moment when I tasted the madeleine, all anxiety about the future, all intellectual doubts had disappeared, so now those that a few seconds ago had assailed me on the subject of the reality of my literary gifts, the reality even of literature, were removed as if by magic. (898–899)

His ruminations upon failure and its accompanying distractions plunge the narrator into a state of unexpected happiness that has cost him not the slightest effort. Where the previous day it had been all he could do to note down an aesthetic impression that left him despairingly cold, the simple physical act of stepping aside now accidentally lays before him that which the full attention of his intellect had been unable to grasp. But it is this very attention that must now be put to work, to locate the source of a felicity from which the narrator has, this time, resolved not to turn aside, as he had so resigned himself in the face of all that the madeleine had given him in adjourning the search for its deepest causes. He attempts first to repeat the movement that had just made him trip from one paving stone to another. For naught.

> Every time that I merely repeated this physical movement, I achieved nothing; but if I succeeded, forgetting the Guermantes party, in recapturing what I had felt when I first placed my feet on the ground in this way, again the dazzling and indistinct vision fluttered near me, as if to say: "Seize me as I pass if you can, and try to solve the riddle of happiness which I set you." And almost at once I recognized the vision: it was Venice, of which my efforts to describe it and the supposed snapshots taken by my memory had never told me anything, but which the sensation which I had once experienced as I stood upon two uneven stones in the baptistery of St. Mark's had, recurring a moment ago, restored to me complete with all the other sensations linked on that day to that particular sensation, all of which had been watching in their place—from which with imperious suddenness a chance happening had caused them to emerge—in the series of forgotten days. (899–900)

Though he plays the role of invited guest, and enters into the Guermantes' mansion, our visitor has decided that this time he will not let go. Other warnings, in the solitude of the library into which the maître d'hôtel escorts him and serves him food while he waits for the musical selection that is being played to end, strengthen his resolve to persist in his efforts. The tinkle of a spoon against a plate brings back to life the ring of the railway worker's hammer striking against the wheel of the carriage while, the day before, he had observed from the train the unremarkable line of trees that today had seemed to him so pleasant to look at. The stiffness of a napkin recalls the pure, saline azure of Balbec where, on the day of his arrival, as he attempted to dry his face at the window with a similarly starched towel, fatigue and sadness had prevented him from reveling in the blue-green hue of the ocean that, now, filled him with delight. Not only have impressions located at far differing points in time lost nothing of their freshness, but above and beyond that, he only savors that freshness to the fullest when it returns to him cleansed of the attenuating circumstances that had once deprived him of the opportunity to enjoy it to the fullest: the preceding day's dark ruminations over his lack of a literary disposition, his concern, then at Balbec, at the prospect of acquainting himself with a new place. The third warning occurs shortly thereafter, upon contact with George Sand's *François le Champi*, noticed in the prince's library, which he leafs through distractedly.

This time, the impression is a disagreeable one. Like an intruder, the book insinuates itself into thoughts he appears at first glance to disagree with, until the narrator finally understands that the sadness it evokes carries him back to Combray, to that delectable moment of guilt when, to console him for the sadness of not having come to kiss him in his bed his mother, capitulating to the father's unexpected indulgence of the child's unhealthy need for affection, sadly relents and spends the night reading that very novel with him:

> My first reaction had been to ask myself, angrily, who this stranger was who was coming to trouble me. The stranger was none other than myself, the child I had been at that time, brought to life within me by the book, which knowing nothing of me except this child had instantly summoned him to its presence. (919–920)

The reminder, at this critical moment in the novel, of the painful event from which to a certain extent it springs, has a dimension that the narrator leaves, for the moment, in the shadows; it forms a part of an economy of sorrow to which we will return. For the moment, our first order of business is to get to the bottom of the understanding of happiness brought about by the unexpected resurgence of a fragment of the past. It is a happiness that depends not only on the extraordinary vividness that forgetfulness lends to the feeling encapsulated in this fragment; it is also the result of the unexpected linkage, brought about by its resurgence, of two moments in time far removed from one another. That same vividness, that same confluence, call forth in mutual reinforcement an immediacy whose truth is as physical as it is unassailable. In abolishing time, destructive time, time that depreciates all things if it does nothing else, those two factors make us feel as though we have touched, however briefly, upon the "essence of things" and as though we ourselves are immaterial, immortal, shielded from the ravages of time. Time becomes that malleable substance, that dough in which all associations are possible; they can, in turn, cancel each other out, be condensed, inverted, and presented as a portion of eternity that subsumes and annihilates all others, shreds of time "in the pure state" (905) where, in the image of the moments it encounters, the ego can fancy itself for an instant eternal.

Yet that fleeting immortality is sensorial, saddled with the perishable body that experiences it. Like the decomposition to which it is sooner or later vouchsafed, like life itself it lasts no longer than a brief flash. The telescoping of time is an ephemeral optical illusion that willed memory vainly attempts to prolong, "requiring no more exertion on our part than turning over the pages of a picture book" (906). Yet it is from that deceptive, carnal, and perishable moment that the spark of truth that intelligence must grasp springs to light. It is that illusion, truer than any organized thought can be experienced in the flesh, that provides the mind's lever with its Archimedean fulcrum, with the illusion that constitutes the firmest springboard of the spiritual life, the surest starting point of the artist's task. For if those brief moments of illumination, like faint echoes of Augustinian grace, have the power to make us attentive to the essence of things, they do not allow us to conserve it. Only through the work, only through the effort of creation can we approach in any enduring way the slow and complex appropriation that is never complete, that must always begin anew.

Time is never abolished except in the resurgence of the moment; it is constantly, daily, inexorably being worn away. If we fail to interpret the signs, we may well, like Swann, spend the time allotted to us without attempting to understand what we have made of it, living idly in the midst of superficial, aesthetic pleasures, and in the illusory permanence of our habits. Such an aesthetic facility finds its literary expression in the "literature of description" which, for all its descriptive capability, has nothing true to say, remaining as it does inattentive to "the little things" (a taste, the line of a steeple, the sound of an airplane) from which it is incumbent upon the writer, the poet, and the artist to extract *reality*.

> Gradually, thanks to its preservation by our memory, the chain of all those inaccurate expressions in which there survives nothing of what we have really experienced comes to constitute for us our thought, our life, our "reality," and this lie is all that can be reproduced by the art that styles itself "true to life," and art that is as simple as life, without beauty, a mere vain and tedious duplication of what our eyes see and our intellect records, so vain and so tedious that one wonders where the writer who devotes himself to it can have found the joyous and impulsive spark that was capable of setting him in motion and making him advance in his task. The greatness, on the other hand, of true art, of the art which M. de Norpois would have called a dilettante's pastime, lay, I had come to see, elsewhere: we have to rediscover, to reapprehend, to make ourselves more fully aware of that reality, remote from our daily preoccupations, from which we separate ourselves by an ever greater gulf as the conventional knowledge which we substitute for it grows thicker and more impermeable, that reality which it is very easy for us to die without ever having known and which is, quite simply, our life. (931)

Against the redundant, dreary, and fallacious "reality" of the "realists" stands that reality that we may well die without ever having known. But Proust formulates it in a breathtaking syntactical abbreviation that transforms the verb *to die* into an impossible transitive. In fact, it is reality itself that stands at risk of dying, and we shall be putting it to death by, in dying, having never known it; we will have condemned it to death for having failed to seek to know. But in designating *that reality as that which it is very easy for us to die without ever having known*, by that most audacious twisting of words, Proust brings out the total strangeness of that reality that is so at odds with that of the realists, of that other reality with which we may stand in proximity our entire lives without ever grasping. What we are at risk of missing *is quite simply our life itself*. It is our life that is at risk of being lost, of never being understood. The simplicity is bottomless, in total contrast with the "as simple as life itself, without beauty" of which it is said earlier that art "lived" is nothing but a duplicate. There may well exist a "life" (but is it worth the name?) that is nothing but the repetition of that which is not reflected upon, and *a life* that is never given beforehand where, in depths that can never be plumbed without effort, throb moments of truth.

> Real life, life at last, laid bare and illuminated—the only life in consequence which can be said to be really lived—is literature, and life thus defined is in a sense all the time immanent in ordinary men no less than in the artist. But most men do not see it because they do not seek to shed light upon it. And therefore their past is like a photographic darkroom encumbered with the innumerable negatives which remain useless because the intellect has not developed them. But art, if it means awareness of our own life, means also awareness of the lives of other people—for style for the writer, no less than colour for the painter, is a question not of technique but of vision: it is the revelation, which by direct and conscious methods would be impossible, of the qualitative difference, the uniqueness of the fashion in which the world appears to each one of us, a difference which, if there were no art, would remain for ever the secret of every individual. Through art alone are we able to emerge from ourselves, to know what another person sees of a universe which is not the same as our own and of which, without art, the landscapes would remain as unknown to us as those that may exist in the moon. Thanks to art, instead of seeing one world only, our own, we see that world multiply itself and we have at our disposal as many worlds as there are original artists, worlds more different one from the other than those which revolve in infinite

space, worlds which, centuries after the extinction of the fire from which their light first emanated, whether it is called Rembrandt or Vermeer, send us still each one its special radiance. (931–932)

There is nothing inward-turning about the ego whose permanence we know the narrator seeks; we know, in fact, that in its own way it becomes one with the awareness of all others. The everyday ego whose outward appearance each of us spends inordinate amounts of time to preserve is exactly what the work the narrator urges upon us breaks down.

> This work of the artist, this struggle to discern beneath matter, beneath experience, beneath words, something that is different from them, is a process exactly the reverse of that which, in those everyday lives which we live with our gaze averted from ourself, is at every moment being accomplished by vanity and passion and intellect, and habit too, when they smother our true impressions, so as entirely to conceal them from us, beneath a whole heap of verbal concepts and practical goals which we falsely call life. In short, this art which is so complicated is in fact the only living art. It alone expresses for others and renders visible to ourselves that life of ours which cannot effectively observe itself and of which the observable manifestations need to be translated and, often, to be read backwards and laboriously deciphered. Our vanity, our passions, our spirit of imitation, our abstract intelligence, our habits have long been at work, and it is the task of art to undo this work of theirs, making us travel back in the direction from which we have come to the depths where what has really existed lies unknown within us. And surely this was a most tempting prospect, this task of re-creating one's true life, of rejuvenating one's impressions. But it required courage of many kinds, including the courage of one's emotions. For above all it meant the abrogation of one's dearest illusions, it meant giving up one's belief in the objectivity of what one had oneself elaborated, so that now, instead of soothing oneself for the hundredth time with the words: "She was very sweet," one would have to transpose the phrase so that it read: "I experienced pleasure when I kissed her." (932–933)

The emotion of love here imparts a particular tinge to the work that the narrator now intends to undertake. But in the short term, the raw material that the artistic intelligence encounters in him—as opposed to the abstract intelligence that threatens to devour that same intelligence—is the variegated, glittering social whirl with which he will once more mingle behind the doors of the salon where, the music having ended, he must now make his appearance.

What a prodigious moment of condensation, in which the narrator's each and every temporal reference mingles with all the others, calling out and answering back in the slowly-revolving vortex of the masks of age worn by most of the faces he encounters, and that he recognizes only with greatest difficulty, rather like in the waltz of the doors, the furnishings and the windows which, at the beginning of the narrative, rearrange themselves according to the successive rooms in which the sleeper believes he has awakened. It is at this point that the immense trajectory of *Remembrance* comes not to a close, but brings together the two extremities of the full circle it has described: not simply because the novel ends at the moment when the narrator no longer doubts his powers to begin his work, but also because the extent of time lost, accentuated by the narrator's lengthy estrangement from the social world, is finally—and brutally—bodied forth in the cruelty inflicted upon the flesh, his like that of the others, by the passing years, while at the same time he feels himself spiritually abstracted from time's tyrannical and destructive order. Only death can henceforth prevent him from carrying out the task that the moments of immortality he has just experienced, and the short-lived abolition of time, have set in such profound motion.

But death itself remains life's great unknown, and those fragments of eternity captured by our spirit while we live may well belong to an unknown world far beyond our understanding and our flesh-and-blood existence, like "the little patch of yellow wall," that Bergotte carries away with him when he dies. From the time when he still lived with Albertine, the narrator relates how the author, whose works had so charmed him in childhood, had dropped dead of apoplexy in front of Vermeer's *View of Delft*. He who, for years, no longer left his house, had gone out of his way to visit the exposition of the Dutch master to have a closer look, in that "picture which he adored and imagined that he knew by heart, a little patch of yellow wall" that one critic had pronounced "so well painted that it was, if one looked at it by itself, like some precious specimen of Chinese art, of a beauty that was sufficient in itself" (185). In the growing severity of the dizziness that accompanies his visit, Bergotte perceives in the weight-pans of a celestial scale his own life in perfect balance with that little patch of yellow wall. Sensing that he has "rashly sacrificed the former for the latter," he twice utters, "Little patch of yellow wall," and collapses, dead.

Dead forever? Who can say? Certainly, experiments in spiritualism offer us no more proof than the dogmas of religion that the soul survives death. All that we can say is that everything is arranged in this life as though we entered it carrying a burden of obligations contracted in a former life; there is no reason inherent in the conditions of life on this earth that can make us consider ourselves obliged to do good, to be kind and thoughtful, even to be polite, nor for an atheist artist to consider himself obliged to begin over again a score of time a piece of work the admiration aroused by which will matter little to his worm-eaten body, like the patch of yellow wall painted with so much skill and refinement by an artist destined to be forever unknown and barely identified under the name Vermeer. All these obligations, which have no sanction in our present life, seem to belong to a different world, a world based on kindness, scrupulousness, self-sacrifice, a world entirely different from this one and which we leave in order to be born on this earth, before perhaps returning there to live once again beneath the sway of those unknown laws which we obeyed because we bore their precepts in our hearts, not knowing whose hand had traced them there—those laws to which every profound work of the intellect brings us nearer and which are invisible only—if then!—to fools. (186)

The death that has imprinted its ineluctable advent upon the "masks" that hobnob and gossip in total obliviousness to their end in the Guermantes' salons only heightens the sense of urgency that surges over the narrator, who is now convinced of the necessity of his work.

As if to defy death, the work to be accomplished is embodied for an instant in the face of a young girl whose entire life lies before her, whose youth contrasts with the dramatic ageing of most of those around her: Mademoiselle de Saint-Loup, daughter of Gilberte and Robert de Saint-Loup, nephew of the Baron de Charlus and the Duchess of Guermantes, an officer who perished at the beginning of the war with whom the narrator had become friends dating back to his first sojourn at Balbec. This catalog of high society is of no interest except from the viewpoint that is henceforth the narrator's, by virtue of all that the young girl brings together, condenses, and mingles in herself for him, of time accumulated that she restores to him before he even notices.

Was she not—are not, indeed, the majority of human beings?— like one of those star-shaped cross-roads in a forest where roads converge that have come, in the forest as in our lives, from the most diverse quarters? Numerous for me were the roads that led to Mlle de Saint-Loup and which radiated around her. Firstly the two great "ways" themselves, where on my many walks I had dreamed so many dreams, both led to her: through her father Robert de Saint-Loup the Guermantes way; though Gilberte, her mother, the Méséglise way which was also "Swann's way." (1084–1085)

In her, the two faces of childhood meet, and with them the raw material of the book to come. She represents the master key. No sooner has he recognized in her his lost years, and the faint image of his youth than the narrator proclaims that he should construct his book like a church, perhaps even like a cathedral, an edifice that the excessive ambition of its architect threatens to leave unfinished, or "quite simply like a dress" (1090) pieced together—like the "paperies" that Françoise has helped him to assemble—from all the shreds of material his life and its worlds lay before him.

Already the narrator is speaking as though he has set himself to the task, and as though it were impossible to complete. Yet he could well add the words THE END without having brought it to an end. Just as, like the sleeper who "has in a circle round him the chain of the hours, the sequence of the years, the order of the heavenly host" (5), the narrator has put in place the arch that holds up his edifice; he may now people it with an infinity of scenes and characters, and die without ever having brought together its disparate threads.

What remains to be asked, and what we must attempt to answer, is this: what makes the edifice of the book, above and beyond its architectural and aesthetic success, a place of contemplation, an inexhaustible space for meditating upon life, friendship, and death? That architecture, meantime, will remain by and large invisible, emerging in all its delicacy only in the rereadings to which the work beckons us. Each theme, in fact, could well become the subject of an investigation that would follow it through all the narration's continuities and discontinuities, like a vein of gold that disappears only to reappear in the specific geophysical striations that contain it, and whose illustration in sound becomes Vinteuil's little phrase. One among these themes can claim particular importance, one that accompanies the recurrence of his music, and underlines its heart-rending melody: love.

Love and suffering, inextricably linked, are the powerful developer for the film upon which *Remembrance* has been captured. From mother and grandmother (two faces of the same love spread across two generations) to Albertine, by way of Odette, Gilberte, and the Duchess of Guermantes, the amorous object and the pain it causes are the two poles of the "electrical current," the alternating energy that powers the narrator. The work itself stands before us, at last, as the keeping *in extremis* of a long-broken promise implicitly made to the mother. It begins then with the scene of the motherly kiss, and to it we must now return. Her refusal to grant the kiss is unendurable; to fall asleep without her precious assent impossible; its expectation, criminal; the punishment that will chastise his audacity, terrible. The soirée has come to an end; Swann has departed. At the head of the stairs little Marcel awaits his mother, who upon seeing him falls mute with fury. Hearing the father climb the stairs, she implores him:

> "Off you go at once. Do you want your father to see you wait-ing there like an idiot?"
>
> But I implored her again: "Come and say good night to me," terrified as I saw the light from my father's candle already creep-ing up the wall, but also making use of his approach as a means of blackmail, in the hope that my mother, not wishing him to find me there, as find me he must if she continued to refuse me, would give in and say: "Go back to your room, I will come."
>
> Too late: my father was upon us. Instinctively I murmured, though no one heard me, "I'm done for." (38)

But this same father, who earlier in the evening and in full disregard for his undertakings and his principles had abruptly sent the little boy off to bed without allowing him to kiss his mother, now invoking the same arbitrary power drops all pretense of harshness at the sight of his son's distress and encourages his wife to spend the night with him.

> Many years have passed since that night. The wall of the staircase up which I had watched the light of his candle gradually climb was long ago demolished.... It is a long time, too, since my father has been able to say to Mamma: "Go along with the child." Never again will such moments be possible for me. But of late I have been increasingly able to catch, if I listen attentively, the sound of the sobs which I had the strength to control in my father's presence, and which broke out only when I found myself alone with Mamma. In reality their echo has never ceased; and it is only because life is now growing more and more quiet round about me that I hear them anew, like those convent bells which are so effectively drowned during the day by the noises of the street that

one would suppose them to have stopped, until they ring out again through the silent evening air. (39–40)

Even though the little boy had gained immeasurably more than he had ever dared hope, the exact opposite in fact, of all that he had feared, distress nevertheless sweeps over him:

> I ought to have been happy; I was not. It struck me that my mother had just made a first concession which must have been painful to her, that it was a first abdication on her part from the ideal she had formed for me, and that for the first time she who was so brave had to confess herself beaten. It struck me that if I had just won a victory it was over her.... (41)

Love has struck twice: the painful expectation it arouses in us also afflicts those who love us, and through their sadness, wounds us a second time.

That failure of nerve is reflected by another flaw of will that—we know—the young Marcel experiences early on with regard to his literary ambitions. Either he feels he has no talent for writing, or the careerist conception of the literary life shared by active individuals like Norpois has discouraged him even more deeply, touching him to the very quick of his aspirations (he knows nothing yet of literature, or the literary world). The emotional displeasure he has caused his parents is compounded by his rejection of literature. The rejection takes the form of his love affair with Albertine, of which Marcel's mother discreetly disapproves: the ease with which he falls in love is, in her eyes, a sign of the general deficiency that has disposed her son to seek tenderness and to spurn ambition. Love here stands (as it was for Swann) as an obstacle to creation. So much so that when the narrator informs his mother of his "final rupture" with Albertine, he feels impelled to "gratify [his] mother's wishes" (1150); and that, changing his mind the following day, he knows, when he announces his decision to marry her, how unhappy he will make her (1169).

Albertine, who has now come to live, a virtual prisoner, under the family roof, becomes the sacrilegious substitute for his mother—minus her constant demands. When his tender captive slips her tongue between his lips "like a portion of daily bread," her offering reminds him of the night on which his father had sent his mother to sleep with him (2). Conversely, coldness, remoteness on the part of his beloved revives in the little boy the suffering he had experienced at Combray at the absence of his mother's kiss. But if the loved one can call forth childhood suffering, she cannot put his mind to rest.

Maternal love, which is unconditional in spite of its educative severity, despite what psychoanalysis terms necessary castration, will always be simultaneously absent, omnipresent, and irreplaceable. Awakening primordial suffering as they do, love's subsequent passions reveal themselves as painfully creative, for their subject can never be attained. The narrator may well keep Albertine captive as long as he wishes, her essence will continue to elude him; he may well caress her, touch her, but he touches "no more than the sealed envelope of a person who inwardly reached into infinity." "How I suffered," he adds, "from that position to which we were reduced by the obliviousness of nature which, when instituting the division of bodies, never thought of making possible the interpenetration of souls!" (393). The wounds that reopen upon contact with the beloved lead into "that way out of one-self" that opens onto "the highway along which passes what we know only from the day when it has made us suffer: the life of other people" (394). "Love is space and time made perceptible to the heart" (392).

The succession of love and suffering in our lives teaches us the salutary truth that "our love does not belong to the person who inspires it" (933), and the very activity that consists in extracting "from our grief the generality that lies within it," like all acts of writing, "is for the writer a wholesome and necessary function the fulfillment of which makes him happy, doing for him what is done for men of a more physical nature by exercise, perspiration, baths" (939). The narrator himself may well rebel against enlisting passions in the service of art. But on closer reflection, art, in leading us from the particular to the general, extracts from those passions fragments of happiness through the understanding of them it grants us.

> Ideas come to us as the successors to griefs, and griefs, at the moment when they change into ideas, lose some part of their power to injure our heart; the transformation itself, even, for an instant, releases a little joy....
>
> These reflections enabled me to give a stronger and more precise meaning to the truth which I had often dimly perceived, particularly when Mme de Cambremer had expressed surprise that I could give up seeing a remarkable man like Elstir for the sake of Albertine.... A woman whom we need and who makes us suffer elicits from us a whole gamut of feelings far more profound and more vital than a man of genius who interests us.... As for happiness, that is really useful to us in one way only, by making unhappiness possible....

> The imagination, the reflective faculty may be admirable machines in themselves but they may also be inert. Suffering sets them in motion.... The happy years are the lost, the wasted years, one must wait for suffering before one can work.... And once one understands that suffering is the best thing that one can hope to encounter in life, one thinks without terror, and almost as of a deliverance, of death. (945–947)

Albertine ultimately inspires, after the fact, all that her presence seemed at first to impede. But she pays for it, after a fashion, with her life, for only through that most radical of all separations does the narrator find himself without the slightest escape in the face of suffering, in the face of the cruel, irreversible truth of solitude. We might even say that Albertine's death becomes necessary to the deliverance the narrator experiences upon his own death.

Love unrequited—as in a sense it always is—fertilizes thought; it is its finest fuel. But thought, in turn, delights in the truths it discovers and thus achieves inner joys that are stronger, longer-lasting than those that emanate from another person, in that they depend upon no one else. By the most tortuous and tormented pathways, Proust's thought dovetails with that of Plato and Spinoza. The great power that governs literary creation, the force that courses through *Remembrance*, is that of *absence*. Nowhere else does absence make itself so violently felt as in love, as in our inability ever to imprison its object, as the narrator so vainly attempts to do with Albertine. Nothing is ever quite so powerfully absent as the love object. The sole joy that subsists, one that is ours and ours alone, consists of understanding precisely what absence brings us: the joy of recapturing our life and our soul, rather than vainly wishing to lay hold of others'. Others may lend us their faces, but only we can give them the shape of our soul. In this way, from within, the writer attains the universal; in this way he can help each of us, whom he falsely addresses as "my reader," to become "the reader of his own self" (949).

Erotic knowledge, which we here discover as contemporaneous with, though more painful, than that of the *Symposium*, has validity only for such women and men as are, like Spinoza, convinced that *true life*, the life *we are at greatest risk of dying without ever having known, is life reflected upon.* Not simply a life devoted to reflection; not necessarily the scholar's life, but a life animated by the incessant desire to understand oneself and to plumb one's own depths. A life that, understood, gives us the strength to die in awareness of having lived, happy at having transformed dross into gold, at having transformed suffering into intelligence.

At the very end of *Remembrance*, just as the narrator has begun to regain a grip on his life, he hears "the peal—resilient, ferruginous, interminable, fresh and shrill—of the bell on the garden gate which [informs him] that at last he [Swann] had gone and that Mamma would presently come upstairs" (1105). The same peal of the bell that, earlier in the evening, had signaled the visitor's arrival, the narrator hears now within himself, where it has never ceased to sound, knowing now that it is there, within himself, that he must seek out its resonance, that he must go down to read his life, that he must descend to that depth in order to lay before him the years accumulated in his body from the first ring of the bell up to the present moment: his entire past, "no single second at which I had ceased or rested from existing, from thinking, from being conscious of," at the pinnacle of which he now perches, altogether less sagging at the knees than the Duke of Guermantes atop his eighty-three-year-old stilts of legs, yet still overcome by vertigo by the view from those heights, far below him, as below each of us, of Time. It is no coincidence that the vertiginous word that ends the book—Time—refers us back to its first word, its first sentence: "For a long time I used to go to bed early"—which, in a significant slip of the pen I could not bring myself to discard, I'd first written "happy"—a sentence that begins with the narrator recalling his body's various beds. It is as if the horizontal position of the sleeper at the beginning, lost in the semi-slumber of his worlds, is pointing us toward the vertical stance of the man awake at the end. Whoever reaches this end *experiences*, irresistibly, the necessity, the happiness of returning to the beginning. And then, rereading those first pages, which he discovers that he has never *read*, he knows that he has only begun to read. He begins his own book as the narrator sits down to write.

But because the narrator has written for us, the task of writing to which he summons us seems already complete—so complete that it can never be equaled. At the end of *Remembrance*, more than at the end of any other book, we are overpowered by the feeling that we have come too late into a world where, as La Bruyère puts it, "everything has been said." But that first impression, at first suffocating, begins to blur with rereading and finally disappears altogether in close proximity to the work. The feeling of being overwhelmed by its vastness gives way, once the floodtide has subsided, to the limitless fertility of the sediment that its river has deposited within us.

Like all great works of art, but perhaps more than any other, *Remembrance of Things Past* opens the door to all things possible. No time can claim it. Though its writing is classic, it breaks down all narrative linearity, all special arrangements, and stands Euclidean logic on its head. Proust, in the final analysis, is not telling a story; he is associating that which time and space, apparently walled up and hermetically sealed off from one another, appear to have irremediably separated. The unity of the ego possesses not a hint of substance; it is a meeting point for the being who thinks, who experiences; a turntable upon which all the egos of our life are contemporaneous, are one another's neighbors. The encounter of emotion and intelligence abolishes spatial and temporal barriers, returns the soul to its ubiquity, induces instantaneous shifts not unlike certain shamans claim to practice. So it is that each lesson from our experience, on condition that we make the effort to read it, enfolds virtually within it all the moments of our life. Our lives are nothing but bubbles swollen by all the instantaneous images of which it is replete and which, changing places with one another, are in a state of constant circulation within them. Each one may and can lead to all the others.

The narrative order no longer corresponds to any pre-established or explicative logic; the tale deploys itself, branches out along the shifting verities and correspondences that it encounters. The story itself emerges from the verities and the affinities that call one another forth. From this perspective, *Remembrance* is the prodigious novelistic realization of the celebrated poem by Baudelaire, and of its Rimbaudian response: *Correspondances* and *Voyelles*. Following in the footsteps of the poets who preceded him, Baudelaire, Rimbaud, and above all Mallarmé, Proust throws the narrative field open to all possible associations. Unlike the poets, he does so by laying before us an immense world that is entirely contained in the peal of a gate-bell, in the taste of a madeleine, or in a slight loss of footing between two paving stones. This infinitely tiny instant at which everything tips is an earthquake: breaking down time and space, it sets marching the epic of the spirit.

Between its lines, *Remembrance* throws wide the gates to the great works of the past. In it we can read Homer, Plato, Augustine, Dante, to mention only those few. And like the openings it creates in the singular universe of the narrator, and in each of our individual universes, it also abolishes the illusory distance that in our indolent segmentation of time divides up the great works by their "era." Just as Combray emerges whole from a cup of lime-blossom tea by virtue of a taste that it had encapsulated until that moment, so each work that crosses the boundaries of time has broken free from the era of its birth. Like those instants that have left their marks on our lives (be they visible or invisible), the great stories are all one another's contemporaries.

They belong to us, all of them, to the same degree. Unveiling as it does the secret of all creation, the great Proustian story, though historically anchored in a perfectly identifiable time and place (Parisian life at the turn of the twentieth century), itself belongs to all time, and stands, to a particularly powerful extent, as a contemporary to all the others.

Proust has invented nothing. He has made no attempt to write in a new way, in a new style. He has devised no literary theory. He restores to the obvious, to the apparent, what has always been theirs; he restores to literature, to art, and to poetry the place and the meaning that has always been theirs, and that fleeting fascinations and fashions cause us to forget. He strikes deep to the quick of the book lodged deep within each of us, shines light on its concealed mechanisms, bringing them to light by the magic of writing. Despite appearances, despite his lengthy sentences, Proust startles us with his simplicity. What he relates rests upon experiences that any one of us might have every day; thoughts, always connected to the merest nothings of life, succeed in prolonging the sensorial and emotional events upon which they are founded. Intelligence and sensibility are in a state of constant, free-flowing dialogue. Despite those few passages that may appear, taken in isolation, as demonstrative, as reasoned, *Remembrance* is anything but a demonstration, an intellectual display: in and of itself, by its abundance, by its liberty, by its suggestive power, it is living proof of that which the work of the artist can accomplish for all those interested in this work, for all those who desire to live *their* life, rather than the life convention imposes upon them. It testifies that the artist's work nurtures the most finely wrought, the most resistant, and the most veracious of joys. *Remembrance* summons each of us to take hold of his or her own life, in a way that only he or she can understand, and illuminate it with his or her spirit. An immense endowment that, far from bringing literature to an end—as an instant of discouragement might cause one to think after completing a book unlike any other, where the totality of human experience seems to have been spoken—opens it to the infinity of all possible readers, to all the readers the writer's work has nurtured, enchanted, and consoled in their ephemeral instability. To all of us, the authors of our selves.

BY THE SAME AUTHOR

Truth or Death: The Quest for Immortality in the Western Narrative Tradition (Vancouver: Talonbooks, 2004).

Imagining the Middle East (Montreal: Black Rose Books, 1992).